Communicating Rights

Communicating Rights

The Language of Arrest and Detention

Frances Rock
Cardiff University

First published 2007 by
PALGRAVE MACMILLAN
Houndmills, Basingstoke, Hampshire RG21 6XS and
175 Fifth Avenue, New York, N.Y. 10010
Companies and representatives throughout the world

PALGRAVE MACMILLAN is the global academic imprint of the Palgrave Macmillan division of St. Martin's Press, LLC and of Palgrave Macmillan Ltd. Macmillan® is a registered trademark in the United States, United Kingdom and other countries. Palgrave is a registered trademark in the European Union and other countries.

ISBN-13: 978–0–230–01331–5 hardback
ISBN-10: 0–230–01331–7 hardback

This book is printed on paper suitable for recycling and made from fully managed and sustained forest sources. Logging, pulping and manufacturing processes are expected to conform to the environmental regulations of the country of origin.

A catalogue record for this book is available from the British Library.

A catalog record for this book is available from the Library of Congress.

10   9   8   7   6   5   4   3   2   1
16   15   14   13   12   11   10   09   08   07

Transferred to Digital Printing 2008

In memory of my grandparents, Dorothy and Leslie Henley and Edna and Arthur Rock.

Understanding is something few people really understand. Most people do overstanding, which is thinking you know about something without taking the trouble to find out about it . . . . Understanding is provisional, because it takes time and, by the time you've understood something, it's probably changed.

Guy Browning, *The Guardian Newspaper*, 29 April 2006

Contents

List of Figures and Tables   x

Acknowledgements   xii

Terminology and Key to Transcription Conventions   xiv

Part I   Rights and Research: Orientation and Theory

1   **Introduction**   3
   1.1   Law, lay people and language   3
   1.2   The focus of this book   5
   1.3   Explaining rights: Using *legal language?*   8
   1.4   Outline of the book   12

2   **Beyond Language as Transmission**   14
   2.1   Introduction   14
   2.2   Senders, texts and receivers?   15
   2.3   A sociolinguistic approach to comprehension and comprehensibility   19
   2.4   Key concepts   22
   2.5   Is it possible to say the same thing twice?   24
   2.6   Why paraphrase? The functions of transformation   25
   2.7   Transformation and polyvocality   26
   2.8   Transformation and intertextual chains   28
   2.9   Transformation, organisations and power   29

Part II   Writing Rights

3   **Introducing Written Rights Communication**   33
   3.1   Introduction   33
   3.2   The *Notice*'s legal background   35
   3.3   The *Notice*'s textual background   36
   3.4   Multilingualism   39
   3.5   The revision texts   39
   3.6   Detainees   43
   3.7   Beginning revision   45

4 Working with Syntax and Lexis in Writing   **49**
   4.1   Introduction   49
   4.2   Evaluating syntactic revision   51
   4.3   Evaluating lexico-semantic revision   65
   4.4   Close   70

5 Working with Organisation in Writing   **72**
   5.1   Introduction   72
   5.2   Discourse organisation within the section   72
   5.3   Discourse organisation between sections   77
   5.4   Intertextuality   85

6 Working with Context: Rights Texts in Custody   **89**
   6.1   Introduction   89
   6.2   The Sergeant's aspirations   89
   6.3   Characterising the Sergeant's text: Orienting to
          detainees   92
   6.4   Was the Sergeant revision "objectively" successful?   96
   6.5   What happened to the Sergeant version in practice?   98
   6.6   Partial readers   100
   6.7   Close   107

7 Off the Page: Detainees' Reading Practices   **108**
   7.1   Introduction: Examining reading by
          examining readers   108
   7.2   Non-readers   108
   7.3   Reading   125
   7.4   Close   133

Part III Speaking Rights

8 Introducing Spoken Rights Communication   **137**
   8.1   Introduction   137
   8.2   The caution's legal background   139
   8.3   The caution's textual background   142
   8.4   Multilingualism   145
   8.5   Introducing data   147
   8.6   The label *caution*   150
   8.7   The official wording   154
   8.8   *The cautioning exchange*   158
   8.9   Assumptions underlying cautioning procedure   161
   8.10 Working with meaning   163

9	**Working with Lexis in Speech**	**166**
	9.1 Introduction	166
	9.2 Metonymy and polysemy in *court*	167
	9.3 Different situations, different cautions: *Questioned*	169
	9.4 Defining *something*	175
	9.5 Explaining negation	177
	9.6 Close	178
10	**Working with Organisation in Speech**	**180**
	10.1 Introduction	180
	10.2 Re-sequencing in principle	181
	10.3 Re-sequencing in practice	182
	10.4 Structural metalanguage	185
	10.5 The official paraphrase question	191
	10.6 Disparate practices within one force	200
11	**Checking Comprehension**	**205**
	11.1 Introduction	205
	11.2 The value of comprehension checking	206
	11.3 Mitigating comprehension checking	210
	11.4 Using comprehension checking	215
12	**Beyond Explanation: Using Cautioning**	**222**
	12.1 Introduction	222
	12.2 Scaffolding the performance of social activities	223
	12.3 Scaffolding human affiliation	230

Part IV   Righting Rights

13	**Description, Action and Uptake**	**245**
	13.1 Introduction	245
	13.2 Description	246
	13.3 Application?	249
	13.4 Uptake	252
14	**Epilogue**	**258**

Appendix	262
Notes	315
References	319
Index	335

List of Figures and Tables

Figures

1.1	A summary of texts and activities examined in Part II	6
1.2	A summary of texts and activities examined in Part III	7
2.1	A sample of the diverse methods for assessing comprehension	17
2.2	The paraphrase task used to measure comprehension of legal language	18
3.1	Police cell	33
3.2	Cell corridor	34
3.3	Rights communication within arrest procedure	36
3.4	Arrestees' experience of detention	44
3.5	The macro-sequence of the Parent *Notice*	45
4.1	Decreased use of *may*	57
4.2	Increased use of *can*	57
5.1	Overview of the right to legal advice as it is presented in the Parent *Notice* using notions of 'specific' and 'general'	73
5.2	The Sergeant's reworking of the section on legal advice	75
5.3	Back page of the Government revision	80
6.1	The Sergeant's three-tiered structure	90
6.2	The Sergeant's text	91
6.3	Detainees' reading practices	100
6.4	Reading in the corridor	103
6.5	The Parent *Notice*'s opening	105
7.1	Reading rights texts in a cell: Not such a common activity	111
7.2	Delivering rights at the custody desk	120
8.1	A place for making decisions	138
8.2	Speech acts and the caution's propositions	152
8.3	Fears about caution delivery	155
8.4	The caution's familiarity	157
8.5	The police interview room	161
8.6	Assumptions underlying cautioning	162
8.7	What does the caution mean to police officers?	164

 9.1 Examples of circumstantial elements following *when*
      questioned   171
 9.2 Post-positional information typically supplied with
      when questioned   172
10.1 Discourse sequence of officers' reformulations across all
      forces   183
10.2 Discourse sequence of officers' reformulations within
      forces   184
10.3 Repetitive reformulations in Force D   203

Tables

3.1 Additional information on *Notices* used by all police forces   38
3.2 The Sergeant's support networks   41
5.1 Summary of the Government revision   76
8.1 Cautioning exchange structure   159

Acknowledgements

This book is the result of several years of research in police stations around England and Wales. I am indebted to the detainees who allowed me to speak to them and observe their progress through the criminal justice process during this project. In all cases, my research made extra demands at an already demanding time.

This work would have been impossible without the support, interest and commitment of many police officers, civilian police staff and recorders from around the UK; I was privileged to receive unique insights into the legal process from them. Many I cannot thank by name as they, or the detainees with whom they put me in touch, were assured anonymity. However this does not decrease my gratitude. In this group, I thank all in the Custody Unit where I spent many months and all who were patiently verbally poked and prodded during interviews. I can thank by name, Inspector Mike Ledwidge, Acting Inspector Eric Eaton, DC Paul Brookes, Chief Constable Bob Wood, Sergeant Andy Hunter, Inspector Ian Flemming, West Midlands Police Shop Theft Team, PC Malcolm Taylor, and Sergeant Neil Malone, DC Alan Grainger. Thanks also to the staff at the Home Office, particularly John Woodcock, John Unwin and Diana Irani.

Those from the legal system who selflessly committed a great deal of time to helping me were Sergeant John Denton, Darren Dawson and Detective Inspector Bob Kearns, Patrick Thomas QC, William Andreae-Jones QC and Rex Tedd QC. For the help and friendship of Sergeant John Price and Constable Dave Cannon I am indebted. They both opened up fascinating new worlds to me. I am also extremely grateful to David Lewis, Fiona McGavin, Mark Stanton, Abi Searle-Jones and Emma Sadera from the Information Design team at Enterprise IG who so generously gave their time, preparing and commenting on texts and to Rob Waller. Thanks also to the police forces who agreed to their texts being used as examples in the appendices of this book.

I am grateful to the many academic colleagues and friends in linguistics and beyond who have made all sorts of contributions to this book. I am fortunate that these include staff and students in the English Department at The University of Birmingham, particularly those who formed its Forensic Linguistics Research Group from the late 1990s onwards. Professor Malcolm Coulthard's comments upon and enthusiasm for this work, and support of my steps into the world of forensic linguistics, are very much appreciated. Heartfelt thanks also to former colleagues on the Language and Linguistics Programme at Roehampton University, particularly Judith Broadbent, Eva Eppler and Jennifer Coates, and to current colleagues in the Centre for Language and Communication Research and School of English, Communication and Philosophy at Cardiff University particularly Chris Heffer. Their patience, support and shoulder-lending have kept me going. Students at both Roehampton and Cardiff have also provided inspiration and, though they did not know it, focus. Many thanks also to people who have made extremely interesting comments on this work, throughout its progress or made very direct contributions: Peter French, David Woolls, John Gibbons, Peter Tiersma, Larry Solan, Virpi Ylanne, Ben Rampton, Karin Tusting, David Barton, Martha Komter, John Sinclair, Deirdre Martin, Dave Walsh, Charles Owen, Sandra Harris, Diana Eades, Stephen Bax, Hannes Kniffka and Nik Coupland. Particular thanks to Alison Wray for meticulously reading an earlier draft and patiently providing invaluable comments.

Throughout this Sisyphean labour, I have benefited from the support of my friends and family. I am extremely grateful to them. So many have contributed directly, by reading chapters, and indirectly, through happy words and attentive ears. I could not have completed this work without their unfailing faith, reassurance and good humour which have meant more than they could know. Thanks also to Peter who may have missed me.

I simply cannot adequately thank my mother and father – always there, always optimistic!

I have recently enjoyed the help, experience and insight of the editorial team of Palgrave Jill Lake and Melanie Blair and at Integra, Geetha Naren.

Finally, I am grateful to the Arts and Humanities Research Board for funding this project through grant number BA98/3092.

Terminology and Key to Transcription Conventions

Terminology

Anglo-Welsh caution (the) – This book focuses on the rights information used in England and Wales, including the police caution. When discussing other jurisdictions it is, on occasions, necessary to refer back to the caution used in England and Wales. At these points, I refer to it as the Anglo-Welsh caution. When not differentiating from cautions used in any other jurisdiction, I call this form of words simply *the caution*. See also *Caution (the)*.

Appropriate adult – Appropriate adults are called to the police station to give "advice and assistance" to specific sub-categories of detainees (PACE Code C, 2006:para3.18). Of particular relevance to this study they might "help check documentation" for detainees (PACE Code C, 2006:para3.20). Juvenile detainees (under age 17) should be accompanied by an appropriate adult who is: their parent or guardian; a representative of the agency who cares for them (if they are in local authority care, for example) or a social worker. In the case of the "mentally disordered or mentally vulnerable" suitable appropriate adults include: family members; a guardian or someone "experienced in dealing with mentally disordered or ... vulnerable people". In either case the appropriate adult could also be a different "responsible adult" but should not be someone employed by the police (PACE Code C, 2006:para1.7).

Caution (the) – The caution runs: *You do not have to say anything. But it may harm your defence if you do not mention when questioned something which you later rely on in court. Anything you do say may be given in evidence.* See also *Anglo-Welsh caution (the)*.

Detainees – I follow Bucke and Brown who identify *suspects* as those who are "arrested under suspicion of committing a criminal offence". They present this group as a sub-set of *detainees* who also include "those in detention who are not under suspicion, including those arrested on a warrant for failing to appear at court or to pay a fine" (1997:2). I therefore use *detainees* to refer to all people in police custody or who might otherwise be informed of their rights. Unfortunately, I am therefore taking the label to include people attending the police station voluntarily, who may leave police custody "at will" (PACE Code C, 2006:para3.21). *Detainee* is not really a suitable label for these people who are, in no sense, detained. However, no short alternative term describes all people who might receive any rights information. This is therefore a label of convenience. This label is endorsed by the use of the form *detain-* in the label *Notice to **detained** persons* which names a text examined here which may be given to a range of people, whether strictly in detention or not.

Enterprise – Abbreviation used in this book to denote the company Enterprise IG: a document design company which redesigns documents for a wide variety of clients. This company employed the five information designers who individually provided data for this study by rewriting the Parent *Notice*. The label *Enterprise* is combined with a letter throughout this text (EnterpriseA, EnterpriseB, EnterpriseC, EnterpriseD and EnterpriseE) to label each of those five authors. Further detail of the Enterprise writers is provided in Section 3.5.3.

EnterpriseA to EnterpriseE – See *Enterprise*.

Force A to Force D and Force S – These are the police forces studied in Part III of this book. Each force provided data in the form of examples of police officers explaining the police caution in naturally occurring interviews. Further details of the police forces and the data they provided are given in Section 8.5.

Government revision – This is a text which was developed from the Sergeant text on the basis of the research described in this book. The Government revision is a rights notice which was introduced for use throughout England and Wales. Section 3.5.2 provides further detail.

Judges' rules – These rules formerly offered guidance on cautioning. They did not "carry the force of law, but failure to conform to them may have led answers and statements to be excluded from evidence in subsequent criminal proceedings" (Brandon and Davies, 1972:47).

Juvenile detainee – This category of detainees includes anyone who "appears to be under 17 ... in the absence of clear evidence that they are older" (Pace Code C, 2006:para1.5). In these data nearly one-fifth of detainees (19 per cent) were juveniles. See also *Appropriate adult*.

Legal advice/adviser – See *Solicitor*.

No comment – Giving a '*no comment* interview' or 'going *no comment*' means using the words *no comment* as a verbal 'equivalent' of silence. It offers a way of being silent, in not providing relevant responses to questions, but participating in interaction, in taking turns at talk.

Notice **(the)** – This abbreviation is used to refer to the main rights text used in detention, the *Notice to detained persons*. This is discussed in Chapters 3–7. References to the Parent *Notice* denote the official text which was in use from 1995 to 2004 and acted as a source or parent text for all of the revisions discussed in those chapters (see Section 3.3).

Notices **(the)** – This abbreviation is used to refer to both of the two written rights texts used in detention, the *Notice to detained persons* and the *Notice of Entitlements*. These are discussed in Chapters 3–7.

Novice – Detainees interviewed about the *Notice to detained persons* are classified according to their experience of detention. *Novices* are inexperienced having never been arrested before; *Occasionals* have some experience of detention and *Regulars* are frequently in custody. Each detainee interview is labelled according to level of experience of the detainee and assigned an arbitrary identification number. So, for example, the 13th inexperienced detainee to be interviewed is labelled "Novice 13". Section 3.6 provides further details.

Occasional – See *Novice*.

Parent *Notice* – See *Notice*.

pc – This abbreviation is used within references in the text to denote 'personal communication'. Thus, (Gibbons, 2003:pc) for example, indicates an informal communication between myself and John Gibbons which took place during 2003. Further details of these interactions are provided in the *References* Section.

PEC (the) – Plain English Campaign. A campaigning organisation which aims to promote and produce plain language.

Percentages – In this book numbers are sometimes given as percentages even if the total quantity of the set is less than a hundred. So, for example, half of a sample of 52 police officers might be referred to as "50 per cent of officers in this study". This convention is used for ease of reference for the reader. I imagine that, like me, you find such numbers easier to consider if they are translated into percentage format. This is not a quantitative study and many of the percentages are indicative so I hope the reader will not take this as an attempt to be duplicitous.

Regular – See *Novice*.

Solicitor – *Solicitor* is used with a specialist meaning in the *Notice*, and in detention. It includes accredited or probationary representatives of law firms not only solicitors with a current practicing certificate (*Code C*, 2006:para6.12). Lay readers might not expect its in-detention meaning and it is not explained in the *Notice* or elsewhere within detention procedure.

Sergeant text or **Sergeant revision** – This label denotes a version of the Parent *Notice* which, together with that Parent *Notice*, is the main focus of Part II of this book. The Sergeant version was produced by a working custody Sergeant and eventually formed the basis of a revised rights notice which is now used throughout England and Wales in police custody. The Sergeant text is introduced in Section 3.5.1.

Data excerpts

Coding

Data excerpts from authentic police interviews are labelled with the force initial used to anonymise police forces throughout this study (see section 8.5.1) and an identification number. For example, A12 is from Force A and arbitrarily assigned the identifier "12".

Data excerpts from research interviews in which I interviewed police officers are labelled similarly but with the addition of the letter "O" to indicate "officer". For example, AO12 is an officer interview from Force A and arbitrarily assigned the identifier "12".

Data excerpts from research interviews in which I interviewed detainees are labelled according to interviewees' levels of experience of detention. See *Novice* above.

Names and anonymisation

Consistent abbreviations are used throughout to label speakers in excerpts.

P	Police officer (if two officers speak within one excerpt the second officer will be labelled P2)
D	Detainee
S	Solicitor
AA	Appropriate adult
F	Frances (the researcher)

All names and other potentially identifying details have been anonymised. Pseudonyms have been inserted in place of personal names in some cases for ease of reference.

Key

<u>Underlining</u>	Indicates stress signalled by the speaker through a change in pitch and volume.
?	Rising intonation.
(.)	A micropause of 0.9 seconds or less.
(1.2)	A pause of 1.0 second or more, the duration appearing within the brackets. In this case, for example, the pause lasted for 1.2 seconds.
// //	Simultaneous or overlapping talk. Words within the double slashes on consecutive lines are simultaneous.
hhh	Audible out-breath.
.hhh	Audible in-breath.
=	Latching on.
-	Self-correction or speaker breaking off.
[ ]	Comments (for example [coughs]).
(( ))	Unclear speech (Double brackets either contain an attempt to decipher the unclear speech or, where that is not possible, an estimation of the number of inaudible syllables).
:	The preceding syllable was prolonged.
Bold face	Is used to highlight points of interest in data excerpts.
…	Indicates that words have been removed from an excerpt. Only fillers, false-starts and hedges have been removed. Their removal is intended to make the excerpts more readily intelligible for readers. Words have only been removed if they are not directly relevant to the point being made in analysis of, or commentary on, the excerpt.
… …	In Chapter 10, some excerpts have been abridged because their details are not relevant to the macro-focus there. This convention is used to indicate places where substantial sections have been removed.
*	Indicates invented examples.
ø	Indicates an 'empty set', an item which is absent or missing. This is used when an absence is marked or noteworthy.

Part I

Rights and Research: Orientation and Theory

1
Introduction

1.1 Law, lay people and language

This book examines the processes and practices of presenting and explaining rights in police custody. It asks why rights communication is important and shows how close observation of rights communication can positively influence arrest and detention and, in turn, contribute to a just society. The excerpt below is from the opening of an interview between a police officer and a person detained in police custody. Routine procedure dictates that, as interviews commence, detainees should be asked whether they require legal advice and if not, why not:

Excerpt 1

	1	P	do you wish to have a solicitor present or speak to one on the telephone?
→	2	D	I don't know [no?]
→	3	P	no? and I just have to ask you your reasons for waiving the right (.) why you don't want one?
	4	D	.hhh why I don't actually want a?
	5	P	yeah I just have to ask you why you don't want one?
	6	D	.hhh
	7	P	if it's because you just don't (.) you just don't?
	8	D	I just don't at the moment no
	9	P	OK right you can have one at any time though u::m if you can just confirm we haven't affected your decision in that at all?
	10	D	no you haven't no
	11	P	right that's good

Does the officer understand what the detainee says? Does the detainee understand what the officer says? What is the relationship between what is said and 'what is happening'?

At turn 2 the detainee's ambiguous *I don't know* creates considerable doubt about whether he does not want a solicitor or does not know whether he wants one. His intonation suggests incomprehension. Nonetheless, the officer recasts *I don't know* as an unambiguous right waiver and proceeds to probe its motivations (turn 3), formulating *a solicitor* of his first turn as *the right*. The detainee's subsequent two turns (4 and 6) suggest that he does not understand the officer's questions and possibly remains doubtful about whether he has declined a solicitor and whether they are even still discussing solicitors. The officer, who could be said to have created this confusion, does not address it. He does not reintroduce the word *solicitor* from turn 1, for example. Things are apparently resolved when the officer suggests a response to his own question (turn 7) which the detainee affirms. Finally, the officer closes with a loaded question leading to positive feedback (turns 9–11).

Excerpts like this invite bombastic statements, such as "it is vital that communication between legal specialists and lay people ensures mutual comprehension". Yet what does this mean in reality? What are exchanges like this really about? Who are they for? What do participants make of them? What is language's place here? These are the issues explored in this book.

This is a book about language and law – specifically, police officers' communication of law to lay people through language and the way that both law and language are transformed through that communication. Language is indispensable to both the enactment and enforcement of law (Mellinkoff, 1963; Tiersma, 1999a:1). Police officers, themselves, recognise this:

> when you're charging somebody with a Public Order offence and you read out the offence (.) the offence is so long winded and so complicated for them to understand that ... they'll like look at you as if "what?" (.) you know (.) they've maybe been fighting in the street and they've been charged with Section 4 Public Order and they're like "what's going on here I was just fighting in the street?" and then you have to obviously ex- so like you're used to explaining things in layman's terms

This officer describes using language at work. She highlights the potency of language in *transforming* texts and the centrality of *transformation* to her work. The research presented here considers aspects of police work in which police and lay people rely upon transformation to try to facilitate comprehension. This is something which may not have succeeded for the detainee in Excerpt 1.

1.2 The focus of this book

This book is divided into two investigative and analytic Parts (II and III) surrounded by an introduction (Part I) and conclusion (Part IV) which between them seek to explore the strengths and weaknesses of different ways of communicating rights in police custody in order to discover what successful rights communication might be and how it might be achieved.

Figure 1.1 summarises the texts examined in Part II (Chapters 3–7). The focus of that part is a written text, the *Notice to detained persons*, which is distributed to people who enter police custody to inform them of their rights. This text is not routinely rewritten by police officers. However, one officer, a sergeant employed in detention, decided to revise the text because he was concerned about its comprehensibility. His revision is examined here through comparison with the original *Notice* and using his comments on the revision task. His text shows what happens when someone who routinely engages with an institutional setting seeks to change the institution's expectations of that setting. His bottom-up exercise in philanthropic revision has successfully altered detention procedures. Five additional texts, produced by commercial information designers, are also examined to show how professional rewriters would perform the same task. Part II also explores the way that the Sergeant's revision was received in a working custody unit by both officers and detainees. These data, gathered through semi-structured interviews and close observation, provide a view of the Sergeant's text which would not be available through only textual analysis or comparison. The findings described in Part II ultimately prompted and influenced revision of the text which the Sergeant wrote and the resulting document is now used in police stations throughout England and Wales. Analysis of a working rights text in combination with scrutiny of its processes of production and contexts of use provides a very complete account of contemporary written rights communication.

Figure 1.2 summarises the texts examined in Part III (Chapters 8–12). The focus of Part III is the police caution, a predominantly spoken formulation although one which begins its intertextual journey in writing. The caution seeks to explain one of the rights which is also introduced

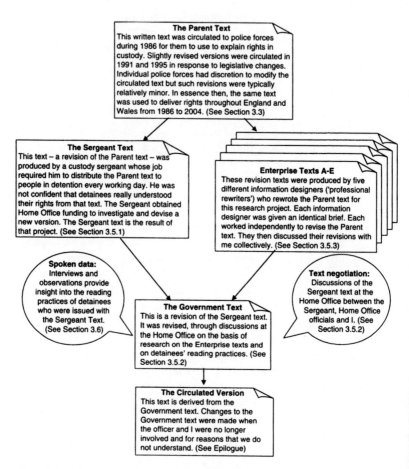

The Parent Text
This written text was circulated to police forces during 1986 for them to use to explain rights in custody. Slightly revised versions were circulated in 1991 and 1995 in response to legislative changes. Individual police forces had discretion to modify the circulated text but such revisions were typically relatively minor. In essence then, the same text was used to deliver rights throughout England and Wales from 1986 to 2004. (See Section 3.3)

The Sergeant Text
This text – a revision of the Parent text – was produced by a custody sergeant whose job required him to distribute the Parent text to people in detention every working day. He was not confident that detainees really understood their rights from that text. The Sergeant obtained Home Office funding to investigate and devise a new version. The Sergeant text is the result of that project. (See Section 3.5.1)

Enterprise Texts A–E
These revision texts were produced by five different information designers ('professional rewriters') who rewrote the Parent text for this research project. Each information designer was given an identical brief. Each worked independently to revise the Parent text. They then discussed their revisions with me collectively. (See Section 3.5.3)

Spoken data:
Interviews and observations provide insight into the reading practices of detainees who were issued with the Sergeant Text. (See Section 3.6)

Text negotiation:
Discussions of the Sergeant text at the Home Office between the Sergeant, Home Office officials and I. (See Section 3.5.2)

The Government Text
This is a revision of the Sergeant text. It was revised, through discussions at the Home Office on the basis of research on the Enterprise texts and on detainees' reading practices. (See Section 3.5.2)

The Circulated Version
This text is derived from the Government text. Changes to the Government text were made when the officer and I were no longer involved and for reasons that we do not understand. (See Epilogue)

Figure 1.1   A summary of texts and activities examined in Part II

in the *Notice to detained persons*: the right to silence. Police officers do not always transform the caution when they deliver it, but are institutionally invited to do so if necessary. Thus, individual police officers may explain this text frequently and with considerable freedom. Their explanations become the caution for many detainees in as much as they are usually delivered more slowly, with more words and in a more dialogic manner than the caution itself. Part III examines officers' explanations of the caution during their interviews with suspects. These naturally occurring data are complemented by interviews with officers about their views of their own cautioning practices and the activities of detainees and

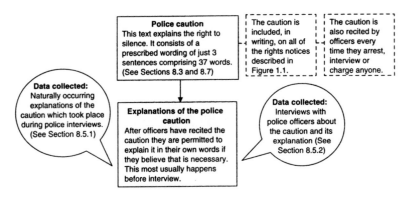

Figure 1.2 A summary of texts and activities examined in Part III

other officers during cautioning. Most previous studies of delivery of the right to silence have focussed on the caution's official wording as an invariant text. This study presents the diversity of cautioning practices to show that provision of an official wording does relatively little to regulate linguistic behaviour in an institutional setting. It illustrates how explanations are personalised, the extent to which they differ from their source and the resources which institutional actors draw on in explaining.

Parts II and III both examine legal *texts*, the written rights notice and spoken caution. They also examine these texts in *process* as police officers and others consider how to alter them and in *practice* as they become part of daily life in custody. This combined view of texts, processes and practices allows closer scrutiny of everyday reading and writing than is possible from one source alone (Barton, 1994:24; Heath, 1983; Potter and Wetherell, 1987:162; Street, 1984). It permits examination of legal texts and language "as forms of life" (White, 1990:xiv) by recognising that writing and speech are part of police officers' working lives and central to detainees' experience of criminal justice. Through this ecological approach I ask "how people take their life experiences to the text" (Fawns and Ivanič, 2001:82). Through a constructionist orientation I investigate how the everyday practices found "exhibit, indeed generate" social structures (Mehan, 1993:243) being "situated, concerted activities" (McDermott, 1988:47) which construct and reflect demands and restrictions which organise custody. Thus, examining texts, processes *and* practices offers a rich view of everyday language. It also provides insight into transformation as a theoretical construct and real-world achievement. The focus on transformation raises two sets of questions about variability and change around each of the two texts examined:

- First, along the theme of *syntagmatic relations* and *intertextual chains*: What changes between the 'original' and the transformed version? Is the transformed version 'like' the original in any recognisable way? Why or why not? How does it differ and what consequences might this have?
- Secondly, along the theme of *paradigmatic relations* or *polyvocality*: Are there any similarities among the transformed versions which are produced? Why or why not? How do transformations differ from one another and what consequences might this have?

As Silverstein and Urban observe: "not all texts are created equal. Some occupy special positions within a culture and become the focus of multiple realisations" (1996:12). This book examines two texts which are special because of their pervasiveness and potential to influence people's lives yet which change through multiple realisations.

1.3 Explaining rights: Using *legal language*?

Excerpt 1, at the beginning of this chapter, evidences features which could be said to characterise many interactions between police officers and lay people. It is reproduced below:

P do you wish to have a solicitor present or speak to one on the telephone?

D I don't know [no?]

P no? and I just have to ask you your reasons for waiving the right (.) why you don't want one?

D .hhh why I don't actually want a?

P yeah I just have to ask you why you don't want one?

D .hhh

P if it's because you just don't (.) you just don't?

D I just don't at the moment no

P OK right you can have one at any time though u::m if you can just confirm we haven't affected your decision in that at all?

D no you haven't no

P right that's good

Both speakers here experience *difficulty* in understanding and being understood. They ask questions which remain unanswered, for example. For both, the interaction is *multifunctional*. The police officer for instance uses the exchange to offer, elicit, suggest and even to protect himself through the request for confirmation that *we haven't affected your decision*. The excerpt features *performativity*; the officer's talk 'does' rights administration and the detainee's talk waives a right. For both speakers the exchange is deeply *political* in that it concerns giving and receiving socially significant help. The exchange concerns *literacies*, recalling a written rights text which the detainee may or may not have read. Finally, the exchange has the potential to have been *different*. The officer might have asked different questions or the detainee might have been more willing or able to speak. No doubt, if the two meet in interview again their talk will be different. Whilst the notion of a homogenous legal language is untenable, much language in legal settings shares some or all of these characteristics:

- a reputation as difficult;
- multifunctionality;
- performativity;
- political potential;
- a particular relationship with literacies;
- the capacity for difference.

Below, I briefly consider each characteristic in turn in order to sketch the sites examined in this book and the perspective I will take on them.

Language from legal specialists is perceived as *difficult*, particularly for those who enter legal domains infrequently. Police forces themselves imply this by offering, on their websites, glossaries of *police terms* (for example, Merseyside Police, 2006). Such sites are part of a widespread and powerful positioning of police language as foreign to lay people. Many lawyers believe, erroneously according to Charrow and Charrow, that difficulty in legal texts is not linguistic but that legal concepts themselves are simply too complex for many people to understand (1979:1318). Some writers attribute difficulty in legal language to "vagueness" (Endicott, 2000:1) or "ambiguity" (Walton, 1996:260). Unfortunately these notions, like difficulty, itself are slippery. Perhaps the root of the problem is that legal texts simultaneously address two audiences, one specialist and one lay. Researchers propose two solutions to this "two audience dilemma" (Gibbons, 2003:183–4).

First, "easification" (Bhatia, 1983:218) which involves "making legal language identical to ordinary English" (Tiersma, 1999a:200). Supporters of easification seek single, universally accessible versions of legal texts (Kimble, 1995:2). Others claim that easification erodes legal meaning especially for specialists (Bhatia, 1993:110; Jackson, 1995:123). These authors propose the "two document solution" (Jackson, 1995:133), which recognises "both legal and ordinary language" and encourages "translation" to the "monolingual" public (Tiersma, 1999a:200) creating "two different genres" (Bhatia, 1983:218). In the settings examined in this book, translation predominates. However the data indicate the existence of more than just two audiences. We will encounter police officers who question their own specialist status around rights information and 'expert' detainees who research legal concepts using legal texts intended for specialists. I will propose that rights delivery needs to move beyond two audiences to consider the diversity of people and practices in detention.

Language in legal settings is highly *multifunctional*. Studies of courtroom language for example propose that examination phases, particularly cross-examinations, do not simply display facts but do a wide range of other things, notably controlling *content* (for example, Matoesian, 2001) and *form* (for example, Conley and O'Barr, 1998) of witnesses' and defendants' contributions. Such multifunctionality occurs whenever "people appropriate texts for their own ends" (Barton and Hamilton, 2000:12). This is evident in rights administration where, I illustrate, much more takes place than simply presenting rights including facework, self-presentation and persuasion.

Performativity, the capacity to 'do' something, defines many legal texts. Performativity has imperceptibly been transferring to writing (Danet, 1997:19) such that the few remaining oral formulae typically require an exact official wording. In rights administration, performativity remains potent and providing the official wording (or a close approximation) through either speech or writing at the officially sanctioned time underpins that performativity. The data show that performativity is salient to police officers and greatly influences their rights delivery.

Legal language has a *political potential* in that it influences, and is influenced by, structures of power and equality. In Gee's terms "politics" refers to allocating "social goods" using "social interactions and relationships" (1999:2). Social goods are those things which provide socially recognised "power, status or worth" including control and knowledge (Gee, 1999:2). In this sense, the recontextualisations examined here are deeply political, influencing whether and how individuals are classified and empowered through language. Language which classifies and empowers *can* function to systematically reproduce inequality (Crowther and Tett, 2001:108) and create disadvantage. This is a matter of political concern. The data presented here reveal how some police officers accept legal language which appears dysfunctional (Danet, 1984a:1) while others strive for political change by exceeding institutional requirements and norms for explaining rights. I will also demonstrate how the political potential of rights communication extends throughout the legal system, particularly influencing courts.

Literacies are relevant because written legal texts have a special status, formalising relationships between law and society (Goody, 1986:142), bringing fixity (Barton, 1994:43) and receiving particular forms of attention. Rights administration is underpinned by written texts. Therefore this book examines literacy events, occasions where written texts are present or influential (Heath, 1983), and literacy practices, "common patterns in using reading and writing in a particular situation" (Barton, 1994:37). A defining feature of most written legal texts is that readers cannot ask questions of them (Goody, 1986:139); the texts are autonomous (Tiersma, 2001:433). Yet, in each setting examined here, police officers are sanctioned to 'speak for' each text. To illustrate, the caution is autonomous in that it is intended to be self-contained and possibly read long after it was written. Yet autonomy is scrambled by the institutional requirement that officers explain the caution. The data here show what happens when autonomous texts speak.

The officer in Excerpt 1 selected particular linguistic forms to deliver rights, for example interrogatives and repetition. He could have used other forms. His selections make this exchange *different* from others he and other officers might have. Analyses in this book show how officers' selections are influenced by technologisation (Scheuer, 2001:224), training, interactions with detainees or other officers, and indeed previous exposure to cautioning. These illustrate the realisations and ultimately the origins and consequences of both paradigmatic and syntagmatic difference.

This characterisation of legal language has identified features which are salient to the data examined here. Despite (or perhaps because of) the capacity for difficulty, multifunctionality, performativity, politics,

literacy and difference in Excerpt 1 the officer and detainee got something done. Through the excerpt, 'an understanding' was reached and
the detainee's words were recontextualised as institutionally meaningful. This book uses ethnography, and examination of naturally
occurring language and interviews to explore how police officers and
detainees accomplish rights administration and what they make of this
activity in this very distinctive language territory.

1.4   Outline of the book

This chapter has summarised the book's scope and perspective. The
next chapter introduces the book's rationale by presenting notions of
comprehension and comprehensibility which are usually used to assess
rights communication and measuring those notions against sociolinguistic criteria. Chapter 2 concludes that if we want to examine texts
which are used in social settings, we cannot consider only the texts but
must also examine those uses and settings.

Accordingly, Parts II and III both begin with chapters which introduce and describe the situations of use of the rights notice (Chapter 3)
and the caution (Chapter 8). Those introductory chapters also introduce the data and methods used in each part. Both parts then present
two chapters which examine what writers and speakers do when they
explain. The first chapters in each pair (Chapters 4 and 9) explore lexico-
syntax, characterising the reviser's task when working with writing
versus speech. The next two (Chapters 5 and 10) are also parallel,
both examining structural innovations and both revealing the pervasiveness of attempts to work with structure when revising either in
writing or speech. The chapters collectively critique and move away
from the notion that rights texts can be improved by simple revision. The final chapters in each part build on this idea by further
problematising restrictive notions of comprehension and comprehensibility. In Part II this involves reviewing whether and how detainees
read written rights texts and considering how text, context and wider
society influence the way rights are understood and used (Chapters 6
and 7). Part III's equivalent chapters offer a realist view of the whole
procedure of cautioning, demonstrating the full functionality of the
question *do you understand?* (Chapter 11) and the potential for rights
talk to be appropriated for purposes other than transferring information
(Chapter 12).

In Part IV, after summarising key points, the conclusion of Chapter 13
considers how sociolinguistic insights, collated throughout the earlier

chapters, might be converted into advice and recommendations to improve the lot of detainees in custody and police officers doing difficult work. It draws recommendations, and indicates how some have already been taken up. A short epilogue presents the challenges of transforming research into practice.

2
Beyond Language as Transmission

2.1 Introduction

The potential for texts to be understood (comprehensibility) and the degree to which they are understood (comprehension) might appear to be easily investigated. Comprehension and comprehensibility both apparently involve straightforward polar distinctions; texts are either comprehensible or not and people either comprehend or not. Studies of these topics have therefore tended to take a rather one-dimensional view of communication processes as resting on simply *transmitting* information or passing bundled knowledge from person to person. In this chapter I use literature and a little data to explore some shortcomings of transmission-based views of comprehension and comprehensibility and justify an enriched, sociolinguistically informed perspective. This examination sets parameters for the research reported in the rest of the book because it explains the perspective that will be taken on two sets of key questions. The first set concerns approaches to comprehension and comprehensibility: How should the notion of transmission figure in a sociolinguistic study of comprehension and comprehensibility? What can a sociolinguistic perspective bring to studies of comprehension and comprehensibility? How can sociolinguistic concepts such as recontextualisation, reformulation and transformation inform and structure work on understanding legal language? The second set of questions build on the introduction of the concepts of recontextualisation, reformulation and transformation to explore the nature of explanation and paraphrase by asking: How does the process of repetition influence the information which is repeated? What does repetition do to interactions and experiences? How do institutions and individuals shape the information which they explain and repeat? In answering this second set of questions I will illustrate how the issues raised will be addressed in this book.

2.2 Senders, texts and receivers?

2.2.1 Transmission

The transmission model of communication sees *senders* linked to *receivers* via *texts* which ideally transmit senders' intentions (Shannon and Weaver, 1949:34). In its most extreme formulation it views misunderstanding as "a strictly moral category", a malign influence which must be defeated if "smooth conduct" is to reign (Hinnenkamp, 2003:59). The transmission model underpins most attempts to measure texts' difficulty, to simplify and to assess readers' understanding. Yet the model's pervasive influence is matched only by the theoretical critique it has attracted.

The concept of a single, isolated *sender* has been unsettled by, for example: Goffman's delineation of principal, author and animator (1981); Cameron's description of speakers and stylistic agents (2000); Renkema's recognition of the "plural sender" (2001) and Bakhtin's delimiting of "the direct intention" of the speaking character from "the refracted intention" of the author (1981:324). Similarly the unitary *receiver* has been problematised (Bell, 1997:246–7; Fairclough, 1992:79–80; Heritage, 1985:101), as has their supposed passivity and unresponsiveness (Bakhtin, 1986:68). Even grouping and differentiating senders and receivers is not straightforward (Scollon, 1998:5). The notion that *texts* contain *a* message, waiting to be unpacked, has been discredited (Barthes, 1977:146; Fairclough, 1992:105) and the multiplicity of texts' forms and functions re-evaluated (Renkema, 2001:38). As well as disturbing these central constituents (senders, receivers and texts) theoretical advances have also undermined the credibility of the model's key processes: interference (Steiner, 1978:18), noise (Dixon and Bortolussi, 2001:22) and feedback (Gibbs, 2001). The model has certainly not been universally dismissed, however. It is useful if acknowledged as an abstraction of one aspect of communication (Bakhtin, 1986:68; Dixon and Bortolussi, 2001:21). Transmission is also a serviceable metaphor and shorthand; it can be hard to avoid when discussing communication (for example, Danet, 1984a:6; Gibbons, 1990:161–2).

Ultimately, the transmission model casts comprehension as a skill which, along with comprehensibility, can be measured and improved. This precipitates two areas of claims:

- Product claims – some text features are universally, inherently problematic. Examples include particular words;
- Process claims – some readers or hearers are troubled by texts. Such readers invariably misunderstand.

These claims and the underlying universalistic stance are as unresolved as they are pervasive. Questions remain about whether (and which of) the matrix of graphemic, phonological, lexical, syntactic, discoursal, pragmatic and extralinguistic features truly influence comprehension and in what circumstances, how and why. How does the transmission model fare when examining both texts and readers?

2.2.2   Product claims: Seeking comprehensibility

Looking first to texts, the plain language movement is thriving and internationally recognised. It is at the sharp end of a shift in public debate from blaming readers for their comprehension 'problems', to blaming writers and the organisations they represent for 'bad' texts (Solomon, 1996:283). Although its methods and boundaries remain somewhat ill-defined, the movement is underpinned by two laudable aims: First, propagating an English that considers readers rather than "legal, bureaucratic, or technological interests" (Steinberg, 1986:153); secondly, campaigning for "greater accountability in public institutions" (Danet, 1990:538). The movement attends to:

- Access and equity (misunderstanding restricts information);
- Safety (misunderstanding causes accidents);
- Economy ("misunderstanding … costs time and money").

(adapted from Solomon, 1996:281)

Early plain language activists, such as Charrow and Charrow (1979), worked directly on texts. The movement now also has a pedagogic agenda, offering technologies to assist writers (for example, Plain English Campaign, 1993:27–9), particularly guidelines which raise linguistic awareness (Solomon, 1996:289) and seek to instil confidence in would-be writers (Gunning, 1968:120). The movement's recommendations range from the researched and attested to the bizarre and ill-conceived (for example, Gunning, 1968:177–83).

There have been incredulous responses to the plain language movement stemming from popular perceptions of over-zealous prescriptivism and purism. More measured criticism claims that the movement disregards social context, prescribing as if documents "exist in a social vacuum" (Solomon, 1996:289) and all writing tasks (Schriver, 1989:244) and writers (Gunning 1968:163–4) are alike. The movement's recommendations ignore seminal linguistic theory (Solomon, 1996:295) such as Hymes's SPEAKING mnemonic (1974:54–64), and thus overlook the influence of rewriting on such aspects of texts as genre (Bhatia, 1993:207). In principle, sociolinguists could investigate which plain language recommendations might apply in which social contexts (Solomon, 1996:297; Walton, 1996:265). However, such attempts would probably prove futile due to the volume of linguistic, sociolinguistic and extralinguistic variables and their combinations (Jansen and Steehouder, 2001:29). So the transmission model lacks sophistication when applied to texts. How does it fare when investigating readers?

2.2.3   Process claims: Testing comprehension

Attempts to investigate readers or their comprehension have taken a number of forms (Figure 2.1).

Some of the methods summarised in Figure 2.1 have moved away from the transmission model. The method typically used to measure comprehensibility of rights information (summarised in Figure 2.2) has not.

Developed by Charrow and Charrow (1979), this paraphrase task has become a regular feature of studies of rights information in both the

- **Cloze procedure:** Readers fill textual blanks (Taylor, 1953). Texts are judged "appropriate" if readers "can guess about a third to half of the missing words" (Finn, 1995:241).
- **Protocol analysis:** Readers provide a commentary or "think-aloud" whilst reading. Used to investigate inference generation, "social meaning construction" and situated reading (Afflerbach, 2000:163–4).
- **Interviews:** Readers are verbally questioned (Clare and Gudjonsson, 1992).
- **Multiple-choice tasks:** Readers select from possible answers (Charrow and Charrow, 1979:1309n).
- **Focus groups:** Readers discuss texts in groups (Myers, 2004:47–66; Schriver, 1989).
- **The plus–minus method** (van Woerkum, 1982): Readers note "positive and negative reading experiences" in margins then discuss their allocations in interviews (de Jong and Schellens, 2001:64).
- **Performance-based measures** (Wright, 1999:95) and **Usability studies:** Readers' use of documents is examined (Danet, 1990:541; Diehl and Mikulecky, 1981:5; Gunning, 1968:136).

Figure 2.1   A sample of the diverse methods for assessing comprehension

Part 1 Initial presentation	• Entire test text read aloud to respondent slowly and clearly • Respondent asked whether they understand • Respondent asked to paraphrase whole wording (in writing or speech)
Part 2 Additional opportunity to understand	• Respondent given a written copy of the test text • Each sentence read in isolation • Respondent asked to paraphrase each sentence (in writing or speech)
Part 3 Analysis	Investigators decide which responses demonstrate comprehension, typically devising binary 'correct' or 'incorrect' criteria for each sentence (Fenner, Gudjonsson and Clare, 2002:88)

Figure 2.2 The paraphrase task used to measure comprehension of legal language (not all researchers use all components)

USA (Fulero and Everington, 1995; Grisso, 1981) and UK. Psychologists Isabel Clare and Gisli Gudjonsson have employed this method particularly thoroughly to investigate the Anglo-Welsh caution (for example, Fenner, Gudjonsson and Clare, 2002). The task provides "the maximum possible opportunity" for readers to demonstrate understanding (Clare, Gudjonsson and Harari, 1998:325). Advocates believe that subjects will not explain information which they do not understand or think important and will explain that which they do (Charrow and Charrow, 1979:1310). The task risks measuring skill at explaining (Owen, 1996:286), at explaining innovatively (Wright, 1999:94), remembering (Schriver, 1989:25) or orientation towards explanation (Clare and Gudjonsson, 1992:23) rather than measuring comprehension. It also relies on readers having read or heard test material verifiably, a situation which even Clare and Gudjonsson observe is far from replicating reality (1992:24). The method's shortcomings then centre on reliance on the transmission model which stems from an absence of sociolinguistic awareness.

People who use language in legal settings themselves point out that communication is more than linear transmission without context. (The data below, from interviews with police officers and detainees, are introduced in Section 1.2 and described in full in Sections 3.6

and 8.5.2). Police officers who I interviewed expressed sociolinguistically sophisticated ideas:

> it's not actually the words that [detainees] don't understand it's the meaning of the words and I don't just – I mean...the meaning of the words as in a sentence the possible repercussions of them failing to understand what they're being told at that time [Tony]

For Tony, whilst meaning revolves around words and their combinations, more importantly, understanding is about consequences – situated meaning for particular addressees. Detainees also presented meaning as much more than a simple transfer through language. Bob, who is regularly arrested, articulated this, describing his experience of written rights texts:

> I know the words on their own that's fine but when they are all together there I don't know (.) what they mean for me when everything's going on [Bob]

For him, understanding isolated lexical items was straightforward, but understanding their combinations and, crucially, implications (*what they mean for me*) in context (*when everything's going on*) presented problems. During my conversations with Bob, he paraphrased rights information convincingly yet described having had difficulties applying the information. Ultimately, the resulting frustration had the most negative possible consequences – Bob disregarded information on his rights.

2.3 A sociolinguistic approach to comprehension and comprehensibility

We have seen that sociolinguistic literature criticises the transmission model and that the model falls short when applied to real-world problems. Sociolinguistics offers alternatives to the model. Transmission-based perspectives saw meaning residing "in the text, the reader's task being to ferret it out" (Orasanu and Penney, 1986:2). Alternative perspectives recognise that readers create meaning using texts and their existing knowledge of texts. From this perspective there is no universal fit between a text and the meaning it generates. "Texts mean different things to different people and even to the same person on different occasions" (Short, 1994:171) including legal occasions (for example,

Shuy, 1993:16). If texts can be understood differently in different circumstances, or indeed if different readers have different needs, it becomes nonsensical to try to simplify once and for all. It also becomes possible to interrogate different readings as different rather than only problematising and disregarding them as wrong (meaning 'at odds with some intended meaning').

Rather than envisaging readers passively absorbing texts, an enriched perspective considers readers' characteristics (Meyer, Marsiske and Willis, 1993:235) and their activities with particular texts. This avoids hypothesising *the* "reader's experience" (Gunning, 1968:153–60), focusing on one hypothetical, ideal reader. Clark, for example, discourages assuming a shared mental lexicon (1996:580), urging that understanding varies along such dimensions as "nationality, residence, occupation, employment, hobby, religion, ethnicity, clubs, subculture, age, cohort and gender" (1996:581).

This expanded conception of texts, meaning and readers invites a redefinition of reading itself. The transmission-based perspective saw reading as applying a skill (Barton, 1994:65), plodding "word-by-word through a text" (Orasanu and Penney, 1986:3), using only a process in the head – cognition (Barton and Hamilton, 1998:20). The new view reinterprets literacy as multiple, flexible and interactional. In perhaps its most diluted formulation, "good readers [use] many strategies depending on their purpose, the nature and organisation of the material and their moment-to-moment success in understanding" (Orasanu and Penney, 1986:3). A stronger formulation has readers accessing not multiple strategies, but multiple literacies (Heath, 1983; Street, 1984). Here, readers are engaged communicative participants, "thinking and using language [as] an active matter of assembling the situated meanings... for action in the world" (Gee, 2000:199) and for "actively responsive understanding" (Bakhtin, 1986:69).

The difference between a transmission-based approach and a more sociolinguistic approach can be illustrated by comparing their perspectives on interviewing, a method used extensively here. As Section 2.2.3 showed, transmission-driven psychologists use interviews to collect data on comprehension by eliciting paraphrases and yes–no answers to tightly focussed questions. Interview data should not necessarily be seen as so straightforward. Any interview data are potentially influenced by interviewees' uncertainty about questions, their position as responders and their difficulty in contributing "in the fast give-and-take" of talk (House, 2003:21). Detainees I interviewed did not necessarily find the interview situation conducive to talking about written texts, for example:

> I do [know the answer] but I don't know how to put it into words if you know what I mean [Occasional arrestee]

> I know there's a difference I just can't say it if you know what I mean [Regular arrestee]

For the psychologist such comments might suggest the data are flawed. A sociolinguistic approach, on the other hand, explores the tensions and insights here, acknowledging the influence of the interview itself on the data gathered (Briggs, 1986:4; Rapley, 2001:317). Speakers who make such responses may do so to avoid appearing uninformed, for example. This reveals something about their orientation to texts or reading, not simply and straightforwardly about whether they understand. Taking a different example, research subjects in Clare and Gudjonsson's experiments on rights notices who recited from the written notices were judged as not having understood (1992:16). The analyses presented in this book do not take reciting to invariably indicate incomprehension because of the sociolinguistic notions that language is both multifunctional and a form of action. Indeed during interviews I used detainees' reciting and reading aloud from texts as a way into examining their navigation and reading practices, probing their attention to particular formulations. Sociolinguistically aware, semi-structured interviewing allows researchers to resist taking responses as disclosures of fact by using further dialogue during interview and reflexivity during analysis. Interview data do not simply expose the interviewee's world offering access to "the participant's internal state" (Potter and Wetherell, 1987:164). Rather interview data are mediated by 'selection' of a sample of interviewees, interviewees' selectivity in speaking during interview and 'filtering' inherent in the interview situation, the transcription process, analysis and reporting. The methods used in this book will not produce "the kind of broad empirical laws which are commonly the goal of social psychological research" – they can, however, "do justice to the subtlety and complexity of lay explanations" (Wetherell and Potter, 1988:182–3). In other words, these methods provide few insights into transmission but many into its materialisation in practice, providing opportunities to investigate not only 'what?' but also 'how?' and 'why?' (Holstein and Gubrium, 1995). The methods rely on dialogue with those investigated and with other researchers. They are therefore "unfinalisable", leading me to "reject a privileged claim to omniscience" (Scollon, 2000:142), a claim which the psychologist cannot reject.

This study does not rest on the transmission model at any stage. This is not only a theoretical or disciplinary imperative. The model generates and supports complaints about "communication problems" which tend to distract from real issues of socio-economic inequality (Penman, 1998). Furthermore simplified versions of legal texts for lay people do not alter the law's "ideological pretensions" (Jackson, 1995:134); a simplified message can be just as objectionable as a formal one. Thus any attempts to alter comprehension operate in their socio-political contexts "as vehicles for wider ideological and societal reproduction" (Clayman, 1990:80). In the settings examined in this book the meanings constructed moment-to-moment by individuals with particular social roles, operating in particular speech situations can change people's lives. Through these data, then, comprehension and understanding are powerful social phenomena, constantly created and recreated through language. The data show the need to recognise that understanding is something which one does rather than something which one has.

2.4   Key concepts

Having illustrated limitations of the transmission model, I now demonstrate an alternative theoretical orientation which takes textual change as its starting point. The activity of changing texts is explored under such headings as: *repetition* (Johnstone *et al.*, 1994); *formulation* (Atkinson and Drew, 1979; Garfinkel and Sacks, 1970; Heritage, 1985); *reformulation* (Merritt, 1994); *recontextualisation* (Linell, 1998; Sarangi, 1998a,b); *reanimation* (Fairclough, 1992); *representation* (Goodwin, 1994; Mehan, 1993); *transformation* (Eades, 1996; Gibbons, 2001a,b; Hodge and Kress, 1993; Walker, 1990); *multivoicing* (Barthes, 1977; Candlin and Maley, 1997; Mishler, 1984; Silverman and Torode, 1980); *recurrence* (Gault, 1994:150); *versioning* (Potter and Wetherell, 1987); *intertextuality* (Fairclough, 1992); *accounting* (Rapley, 2001); *decontextualisation* (Bernstein, 1990:60); *entextualisation* (Urban, 1996); *interdiscursivity* (Fairclough, 1992); *paraphrase* (Steiner, 1975); *repetition* (Cushing, 1994; Merritt, 1994; Tannen, 1989); *overlay* (Johnstone and Kirk, 1994:185); *replay* (Merritt, 1994:30); *polyvocality* (Linell, 1998:149) and *explanation* (Antaki, 1994; Sarangi, 1998b:243; White and Gunstone, 1992). These headings are not synonymous, but complementary. This catalogue illustrates that repetition is an established focus of discourse-level studies. Indeed repetition is fundamental to cognition and communication (Linell, 1998:154) and to the capacity for decontextualised thought (Denny, 1991:66). Its occurrence enables analysts to observe "the social reasoning that people go through in order to make sense of their worlds, and (perhaps) impose that sense on others" (Antaki, 1994:1).

In this book, I use terms from the array above when they are particularly pertinent. Three terms are eminently useful to this study and are used somewhat interchangeably. I employ these three extensively because each has particularly helpful and complementary connotations. However each invokes aspects of the other terms reviewed above and is therefore used in this book in the context of that extensive landscape of previous work on repetition-related phenomena. The first two, *reformulation* and *recontextualisation*, feature the evocative prefix *re-*, which alludes to 'doing again', "as in words like *recopy, reprint*" but also 'doing differently', changing, as in "*redefine, revise, rework*" (Linell, 1998:155, see also Sarangi, 1998a:304). Turning to specifics of these two *re-* terms, *reformulation*, through associations with *formulation* in second language learning, connotes pedagogy and in functional linguistics connotes system (Gledhill, 1995). The root *formulation* in Conversation Analysis denotes abstraction, "saying-in-so-many-words-what-we-are-doing" (Garfinkel and Sacks, 1970:351). Thus, reformulation concerns both form (in-so-many-words) and function (what-we-are-doing). *Recontextualisation* invokes transferring texts between contextual matrices and "dragging along some aspects of contexts" (Linell, 1998:148) or moving something of an earlier discourse to a later one (Urban, 1996:21). It does not mean textually importing context itself (Sarangi, 1998a:305). Coupland and Coupland suggest that recontextualisation may be too pervasive to be interesting as "all accounting and narrative discourses entail the recontextualising of experience" (1998:182). Bakhtin, in contrast, revels in ubiquity:

> Any speaker is himself a respondent to a greater or lesser degree. He is not, after all, the first speaker, the one who disturbs the external silence of the universe. And he presupposes ... the existence of preceding utterances – his own and others' – with which his given utterance enters into one kind of relation or another.
>
> (1986:69)

In *transformation*, *trans-* conveys "across, beyond, through" (*Chambers Dictionary*, 1994), highlighting that textual change can take many directions; *-form-* has instructive connotations both as a noun meaning "visible shape" or "configuration" and as a verb meaning "mould", "place in order" or "construct" (*OED*, 2006). *Transformation* has long been used as a general shorthand (Bernstein, 1990; Fairclough, 1992:79; Polanyi, 1981) but is developing as a linguistic term which implies shifts in register, mode, median and control along with filtering through the transforming person's "beliefs, comprehension, attention and know-ledge schemas" (Gibbons, 2001b:32). These concepts and connotations offer a more constructive point of departure than (only) the problem-atic notions of comprehension and comprehensibility. They facilitate consideration of the following important theoretical issues.

2.5   Is it possible to say the same thing twice?

Transformations, reformulations or recontextualisations which feature identity at any level could be seen as meaningless, simply saying again something already established. Yet the predominant sociolinguistic view is that any instance of discourse is unique and irreproducible, thus one cannot say the same thing twice. This view is supported by those who maintain that transformations involve shifts in:

- the contexts in which each version is embedded (Urban, 1996:21);
- meaning, realigning or even removing some semantic content (Linell, 1998:148);
- reciprocity and participation through the audience's reinterpretation (Tannen, 1989:52);
- the text's "position in relation to other texts, practices and positions" (Bernstein, 1990:60–1).

Even exact surface-level repetition influences and is influenced by its source, so it is inescapably different from that source (Jefferson, 1972:303; Kasper and Ross, 2003:86; Parker, 1988:188). Polanyi, who generally agrees that two texts simply cannot be identical, explains that a repetition will be influenced by:

- circumstances of telling;
- participants;
- participants' concerns in the form of recipient design;
- participants' relationships to events and circumstances represented;
- content;
- the text's place within the particular unfolding discourse structure;

- the text's situated relevance;
- the speaker's awareness of ongoing talk.

(summarised from Polanyi, 1981:315, 319)

Thus sociolinguistics rejects even the possibility of simple, exact repetition. However, the criminal justice system expects that 'the same' rights information can be delivered again and again. It falls to officers, detainees and ultimately courts to work with pretence. Recontextualisation holds many tensions for these participants. First it involves selectivity as participants potentially compete "over the correct, appropriate, or preferred way of representing objects, events or people" (Mehan, 1993:241; see also Bernstein, 1990:184; Linell, 1998:151; Sarangi, 1998a:307). Secondly it involves reification which potentially "obscures the dissonances and disjunctures among many different voices and texts" that precede a repetition (Ravotas and Berkenkotter, 1998:233).

Having noted the "theoretical principle that, when something is repeated, its meaning changes", analysts must "say what the different meaning is" by examining the minutiae of changes between versions (Johnstone, 1994:12). In this book examination of such details in reformulations produced by police officers and lay people exposes the tensions inherent in reformulation.

2.6 Why paraphrase? The functions of transformation

By examining transformation in legal settings we can investigate what the linguistic options and, ultimately, selections made in those settings do. In order to understand how rights information and explanation is used and received it is important to consider the interactional, experiential and pedagogic functions of transformation in custody. Transformation serves wide-ranging *interactional functions*. Of particular relevance here are: creating cohesion (Halliday and Hasan, 1976; Johnstone, 1994:8); creating coherence (Tannen, 1989); maintaining, refocusing or augmenting meaning; pointing; summarising; dividing and correcting (Kasper and Ross, 2003:86; Norrick, 1987:254–63). Transformation also serves *experiential functions*. Relevant examples include: controlling (Fairclough, 2001:113–14); agreeing (Heritage and Watson, 1979:123); persuading; disagreeing; collaborating; acknowledging; reminding; exploring; reassuring (Johnstone, 1994:6–11); shaping roles and behaviours (Candlin and Maley, 1997:202; Goodwin, 1994:606) and representing (Fang 2001; Fowler, 1991; Hall, 1997;

Hodge and Kress, 1993; Winston, 1986). A substantial body of research centres on the functionality of transformation in *learning, teaching and socialisation* (Bean and Patthey-Chavez, 1994:207; Ravotas and Berkenkotter, 1998:218; Swales, 1990:220). Whilst issuing rights is not instructional *per se*, it shares with instructional settings the fact that "the novice's goal is to accomplish the task at hand,...the expert's goal is to approach an optimal point of information transfer...so that the novice can make use of it" (Bean and Patthey-Chavez, 1994:207).

Perhaps most importantly for this study, recontextualisation is multifunctional (Mertz, 1996:232; Section 1.3). We will see how police officers and detainees exploit this multifunctionality, but will observe Johnstone's caveat that "function is in principle indeterminate, at the moment of occurrence...function is always a hypothesis" (1994:10). This is particularly relevant in these legal contexts where transformations are simultaneously part of local interactional and global institutional agendas.

2.7   Transformation and polyvocality

Representation creates order out of chaos, or at least, foregrounds one privileged order from a chaos of possible orders. A major resource in examining this has been the identification of voices (Silverman and Torode, 1980). Mishler distinguishes a "voice of the lifeworld" associated with lay people from a professional voice. He examines the interface between the two and notes the prioritisation of the professional (1984). Mehan pursues this, asking how representation produces clear "social facts" such as criminality "from the ambiguity of everyday life" (1993:242). This shift from 'everyday' to specialist often coincides with a move from speech to writing (Iedema and Wodak, 1999:13) as, for example, individuals' decisions and understandings achieved in informal, personal meetings become depersonal, formal written reports (Scheuer, 2001:237). Police interviews have already been identified as serving this ordering function (Aronsson, 1991:217), forcing "disambiguating distinctions onto matters which may have been vague in the lay world" (Linell, 1998:149). I consider similar shifts in the way that informal drafting and debate become formal written rights texts.

The legal world features not only shifts from lay to legal, from lifeworld to professional – the explanation of rights exemplifies shifts in the opposite direction too. We shall see how the depersonalised, formalised, written caution is re-peopled in the police interview. This shift is well illustrated through analogies. In classrooms, learners are "mastering" information but also working on "ways of looking at, thinking about, and reacting to it" (Bean and Patthey-Chavez, 1994:215). I will show how some detainees not only 'master' rights but also gain perspective on them as usable artefacts. In job interviews, "applicants personalise accounts by drawing on informal language practices such as...telling jokes...varying speech style is tantamount to personalising the interaction" (Scheuer, 2001:238). In rights-giving too participants find little space for the individual unless they exploit institutional turns.

Voices are not necessarily heard predictably. On occasions institutional actors appropriate a lifeworld voice whilst lay people employ a professional voice (Silverman, 1987). This may be manipulated deliberately as part of *technologisation*, a process which "import[s] communicative features" across social positions (Scheuer, 2001:224), creating discoursal "resources or toolkits" for institutional actors, like police officers, which change their communicative styles (Fairclough, 1992:215). These discourse technologies "have particular effects on publics...who are not trained in them" (Fairclough, 1992:216) and are therefore potent in lay–legal interactions. Increasingly, technologisation blurs boundaries between technical and vernacular talk so professional voices become powerful through their apparent, increasing informality (Fairclough, 1992:204–5; Fowler, 1991:128). While institutional interactions are still characterised by formality and depersonalisation (Scheuer, 2001:238) they are no longer invariably impersonal (Iedema and Wodak, 1999).

Rights communication is being technologised through spoken, informal explanation and written plain English. In both speech and writing the institution has created a space for technologised forms (informal explanations and a new rights text respectively) but has not specified what should fill that space. This allows change from "below" (Fairclough, 1992:239). The data here show how officers not only take on technologised models offered in training or uncovered by their own research but also use these alongside their own ideas.

Institutionally integrating written rights texts into custody can be seen as a move towards providing "information-and-publicity" – an instance of the colonisation of institutions by advertising. Such integration operates alongside commodification, which appears to make lay people more powerful than institutional figures. The crucial question of whether this power-shift is "substantive or cosmetic" (Fairclough, 1992:117) is pursued here by asking whether the move towards routinely distributing rights texts and the move towards explaining the caution empowers detainees or only *appears* to do so.

The distinction between lifeworld and professional voices has not been universally accepted. A number of scholars identify a greater plurality of voices than only two (Linell, 1998:149). Candlin and Maley, for example, describe mediators drawing on a rich tapestry of professional discursive practices (1997:209–11). Amongst other critics of the lifeworld concept, Coupland and Coupland argue that distinguishing two voices hardly begins to cover the interactional complexity of talk (1998:182). This raises "doubts as to whether the professional and the personal should be seen as distinct modes of social life" (Scheuer, 2001:238). This book contributes to this debate by showing not only voices in interaction but also interactants' comments on those voices and the relationship between voices and function.

2.8   Transformation and intertextual chains

Fairclough develops the notion of intertextual chains or series of texts related through "regular and predictable" transformation (1992:130; see also Linell, 1998:149). Ravotas and Berkenkotter illustrate that psychotherapists' written patient records are intertextual because they work on immediate talk; fit with broader talking and writing "cycles" and enter the agency's "network of texts" (1998:212). Multiple layers of intertextuality underpin the sites examined here too. Officers' texts join existing intertextual chains and precipitate others. Bernstein's depiction of agencies which produce or recontextualise texts in the pedagogic setting offers, by analogy, an overview of manifestations of recontextualisation examined in this book. He identifies:

- *The primary context*: Ideas and associated discourses are produced and modified. This is a context of production. In the settings examined here, this describes contexts where legal 'facts' are agreed and laws debated and encoded.
- Moving from production to reproduction, *the secondary context*: Selective reproduction takes place through classification and framing of the ideas and discourses produced in the primary context. This is key in the data examined here: it is where officers transform rights texts.
- Around and mediating between these contexts, Bernstein distinguishes the *recontextualising context*: Rights-related sites described by this label include (i) police training and policy units; (ii) individual officers and teams discussing rights formally or informally;

(iii) groups surrounding the police force such as interest groups representing suspects or those in a regulatory role including Home Office
departments.

(1990:60)

Extended intertextual chains (cf. Solin, 2001) present a challenge, for
example, to officers who, at the end of long intertextual chains, "must
accommodate their expertise, knowledge and messages to meet the
needs and expectations of people with other interests and backgrounds"
(Linell, 1998:151).

2.9 Transformation, organisations and power

Recontextualisation is essential to organisational talk (Atkinson and
Drew, 1979; Heritage, 1985:101; Linell, 1998:143), even at its heart
(Iedema and Wodak, 1999:5). Yet who benefits from this influential
phenomenon? Does the transformation process give power to those who
compose texts for transformation, or to those who make, regulate or
receive transformations?

Many scholars are convinced that speakers are powerful in bringing
meanings to the texts which they transform because transformation is
constitutive. From this perspective organisations are "created and recreated in the acts of communication between organisational members"
(Iedema and Wodak, 1999:7) and "exist only in so far as their members
create them through discourse" (Mumby and Clair, 1997:181). However,
Fairclough counters that this creativity or productivity is not available
to all, being "socially limited and [itself] constrained upon relations of
power" (1992:102–3). Urban observes that while copiers might appear
to have the power to shape transformed texts others, including the
originator, have a stake in copiers' talk for example in settings where
copies are produced "for public inspection, appreciation or approval"
(1996:41). For him the question is "how far the copier can go in effecting
changes. When will the editorial work draw criticism for its modific-
ations?" (1996:41). This book will examine in detail the constraints
and freedoms on copiers who rearticulate rights and the way that these
constraints and freedoms constitute detention.

We can only fully understand individuals' influence in institutional
processes through "deeper understanding of situated demands" (Merritt,
1994:24–5). I scrutinise very localised aspects of police work, searching
for patterns in the practice of transforming text in its lived diversity.
Scollon's view of texts as mediational means clarifies this possibility,

because it sees texts as "the tools by which people undertake mediated action". This offers a significantly enriched perspective on what transformation does:

> It is possible, on the one hand, to focus our attention to just those aspects of texts which are of relevance to the actions taken by participants in any particular situation. At the same time, it is possible to focus our attention not on the texts themselves, but on the actions being taken and to see how the texts become the means by which sociocultural practice is interpolated into human action.
>
> (1998:14–15)

The study of transformation offers the opportunity to study this interpolation as if in slow motion. In rights communication, as we will see, the text and the action it achieves have very special relationships.

Part II
Writing Rights

3
Introducing Written Rights Communication

3.1 Introduction

How should the police communicate with those they detain? The experiences of two people in custody, both arrested for the first time, illustrate the unique discomfort of the unfamiliar, unnerving detention setting (Figure 3.1 and Figure 3.2).

Police–lay communication in this setting is fraught but very important. Alongside matters like deaths in or following custody

I've never seen the inside of a cell before and I sat there and I thought "I'm only going to be here a few minutes and then I'll be told off and that" you know and hours later I was still in there and I thought "good grief" and then the lights went on and I thought "we're going to be here all night" [Novice 35]

Figure 3.1　Police cell

I've heard people in the cells while I've been here this weekend and they've played up here at the front desk played up blind shouting and swearing and kicking and then [police officers] have stuck them in the cells to try and calm them down and [detainees] have demanded this and they've demanded that [Novice 34]

Figure 3.2   Cell corridor

(England and Wales saw 28 in 2005–2006) (Teers and Menin, 2006:6), communicating about rights in custody may appear trivial. Nonetheless a moral society should expect that the state acting on its behalf tells detainees clearly about relevant rights. Attention to rights communication has three positive consequences: First, to position treatment of detainees as socially important with positive knock-on effects for detention practice; secondly, to help to prevent miscarriages of justice which involve unjust denial of rights (Gudjonsson, 2002); finally, to halt the development of a discourse which marginalises conscientious rights communication by representing it as the concern only of pedants and busybodies.

Between 1986 and 2004, two written texts (hereafter the *Notices*) were the communicative channel of choice to explain detainees' rights and entitlements and, implicitly, officers' obligations. The texts were offered to each person arrested in England and Wales, usually at the beginning of their detention.[1] The more important of these two texts, the *Notice to detained persons* will be discussed at length in this book and, for convenience, referred to as the *Notice*. It is included in Appendix 1. The accompanying *Notice of entitlements* which is less important only in that it describes entitlements rather than rights is included in

Appendix 2. These *Notices* were intended, along with some complementary verbal explanation, to enable detainees to make vital decisions about whether, when and how to invoke rights and entitlements. Nonetheless, concerns were raised about the documents' adequacy. In May 2004, new documents were introduced. In Part II, after sketching the background of written rights communication, I explore how these new texts were produced by a working police sergeant, and what they aimed to achieve. This illustrates how one individual used language and metalanguage to take action to alter the institutional world which he was within. I also examine his new *Notice* in detail, comparing it to its predecessor and to other equivalent texts. This illustrates the strengths and weaknesses of the new text and the ways that sociolinguistic research can examine institutional textual change. Finally, I consider how the new *Notice*'s first draft was received by detainees in custody and how it was revised using some of the research described in this book. This illustrates the value of ethnographic research and the potential for such research to inform textual and institutional processes.

3.2   The *Notice*'s legal background

Until 1986, those arrested faced considerable indeterminacy in custody. They were not necessarily told about their rights or even given access to a solicitor, under the guidance of the *Administrative directions to the police* (Home Office, 1978) and the quasi-legal *Judges' Rules*, created in 1912 (last revised, 1964). However the Police and Criminal Evidence Act (1984) (PACE), born of the Royal Commission on Criminal Procedure (1981), sought to "codify and rationalise" police procedures (Home Office, 1985:2) through *Codes of practice*. Whilst the *Codes* themselves are not statutory, they were intended to have teeth; officers were made well aware that their breach could result in disciplinary action and the exclusion of evidence. PACE and its *Codes* sought to provide "the powers the police need[ed] to enforce the law" while "clarifying the safeguards for the rights of citizens" (Home Office, 1985:2). An important part of this related to changes in custody. PACE stipulated that the *Notice to detained persons* would be a central component of rights administration. Paragraph 3.2 of Code C of the *Codes* introduced the first *Notice* which came into force on 1 January 1986. The current version of that paragraph (2006) states that the custody officer must give detainees a written notice telling them of:

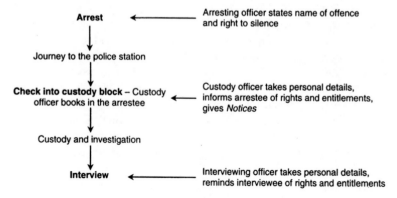

Figure 3.3 Rights communication within arrest procedure

- "the right to consult these *Codes of practice*";
- "the right to have someone informed of their arrest";
- "the rights to consult privately with a solicitor" (the *Notice* should also clarify that that advice will be "free" and "independent" and it should explain "the arrangements for obtaining legal advice");
- "the right to a copy of the *Custody record*";
- the right to silence (discussed in Chapters 8–12).

The other mainstay of the new regime was a dedicated police officer, the custody officer, to oversee detention. That officer should use spoken language to support the written text, telling detainees "clearly" about the first three rights outlined above (Code C, 2006:para3.1). PACE specifies that communicating rights is one of the custody officer's "most important tasks" (Brown, 1997:76). Figure 3.3 shows how rights notices fit into detention procedure.

3.3 The *Notice*'s textual background

Previous studies use the definite article to critique and discuss **the** *Notice*, a single text. However the text varies across time and place. Recognising this variation is important to characterising the text.

Looking firstly at variation across time the *Notice*, circulated nation-wide by 1986, sits within a temporal intertextual chain. As well as the influence from its predecessor, the *Notice to prisoners*, its original template was *National form 7*, prepared by the Association of Chief Police Officers (Home Office, 1985:9). Before the 2004 revision by a police sergeant described in this book, there were two major revisions to the 1986 *Notice*. First, in 1991, along with updates to the *Codes of practice* (Home Office, 1991:3); secondly, in 1995, to accommodate changes arising from the Criminal Justice and Public Order Act 1994. Thus, the *Notice* has evolved repeatedly. Criticism of the *Notice's* comprehensibility has surrounded this evolution, focusing initially on the 1986 *Notice* (Gudjonsson, 1990). Improving comprehensibility of that document was not a stated aim of the 1991 revision (Home Office, 1991); nonetheless the 1991 text added metalanguage and made lexical replacements suggesting that comprehensibility may have been considered informally (for example, *the person you **nominate*** (1986 version) → *the person you **name*** (1991 version)). The 1991 and 1995 texts, in turn, attracted critical claims that some sections had become more difficult than their 1986 equivalents (Clare and Gudjonsson, 1992:7).

On the spatial dimension, police forces have discretion to adopt, adapt or replace the *Notice*. When offering the 1991 *Notice*, for example, the Home Office provided camera-ready copy for "forces wishing to take advantage of this" (Home Office, 1991:3–4). Cotterill asserts that the *Notice*, whilst "standardised in content, ... may vary in layout and typeface" between police authorities (2000:4–5). In fact, rather surprisingly, presentation varies and also content. Some of this variation is due to a perception amongst forces that the *Notices* distributed to them were poorly formulated (see Section 3.7). Three police forces were so dissatisfied with the *Notice* supplied in 1995 that they implemented substantial changes. Leicestershire Constabulary, Durham Constabulary and Essex Police added information; West Midlands Police adopted a completely novel layout with significant alterations to content and form; whilst Greater Manchester Police commissioned the Plain English Campaign (PEC) to devise a new version of the text, although the resulting document was apparently never used (all five texts are included in Appendix 3). Other forces made more *ad hoc* changes: the version used by one southern English police force included handwritten additions. Every police force made some changes to the source text, most commonly adding a reference number for internal use, a date of revision or their own crest or logo. Strangely, 70 per cent of police forces added information for people not under arrest but attending the police station voluntarily (illustrated in Appendix 3, the *Notice* from West Yorkshire Police). This is an odd extension of a *Notice to **detained** persons*. Information added to rights notices may be salient to officers (for example, procedure around the Road Traffic Act 1988), to management (for example, data protection information) or to external organisations

Table 3.1 Additional information on *Notices* used by all police forces

Additional material supplied	Number of forces supplying this material, Total forces = 43 (100%)
Information to specify and identify the document	
Reference number	38 (88%)
Revision date	30 (70%)
Information for voluntarily attenders	30 (70%)
Force branding	
Force name	29 (67%)
Force crest or logo	10 (23%)
Force motto	1 (2%)
Information about procedure	
DNA Profiling	1 (2%)
Fingerprints/Photograph	1 (2%)
Video and audio recording in the custody area	1 (2%)
The lay visiting scheme	1 (2%)
Drink-drive procedures	1 (2%)
The Road Traffic Act	1 (2%)
The administration of "Personal/Medical matters"	1 (2%)
Text organisation	
Additional titles or revised titles	4 (9%)
Page numbers	3 (7%)
Miscellaneous	
Information about drugs, alcohol or other substances	4 (9%)
Information about the Data Protection Act 1998	1 (2%)
Information about the paper (sourced from sustainable forests)	1 (2%)
Chart monitoring ethnicity	1 (2%)
Information about copyright and printing	1 (2%)
Crimestoppers telephone number	1 (2%)

(for example, information about drugs referral schemes). Table 3.1 summarises the additional information provided across police forces.

Despite both temporal and spatial variability it is practical to discuss one 'source' *Notice* in this book. This is a fairly standard version of the 1995 text which was in use between 1995 and 2004 in Force E and which was used as the source text for all of the revisions discussed here (Appendix 1). I will refer to this version of the *Notice* as the *Parent* text from now on because it was the parent or source text for all of the revisions which are examined in this book. Whilst the label Parent *Notice* describes the text in terms of its relationship to these revisions, as I have explained, the text denoted by that label here is a working legal text which had been in use in one form or another for almost 20 years.

3.4 Multilingualism

The *Notices* raise two questions in relation to multilingualism. First, within the Anglo-Welsh jurisdiction, are the *Notices* available in languages other than English or Welsh? Secondly, how do the *Notices* compare to equivalent documentation provided in other countries? Taking England and Wales first, migration has increased "cultural, educational and linguistic" diversity here (Solomon, 1996:282). The original *Notices* were distributed by the Home Office in seven languages. By the late 1990s, 29 languages were available although non-English versions were not always readily accessible, particularly in police stations where they were needed infrequently. Provision of multilingual versions is improving rapidly. The 2004 text was initially circulated in 38 languages with audio-recorded spoken versions available to police forces (Home Office, 2004). The text is now available in 44 languages and a website provides both written and spoken versions (Home Office: 2006a).

The availability of multilingual versions of the *Notices* challenges officers to judge when a detainee needs a translated version, whilst the still low number of languages provided challenges detainees who are not catered for. Whilst the current provision might reduce disadvantage for some, simply offering translations is a token response to the diverse knowledge, resources and experiences of detainees from different linguistic backgrounds. Efforts to improve and standardise translation services are currently underway (Home Office, 2006b) and may, in time, more tangibly improve multilingual rights communication.

Rights information is not distributed in other parts of the world as freely as in England and Wales. The understated system in the Netherlands, for example, provides leaflets detailing rights yet does not proceduralise their distribution. There, officers are unsure whether written information is available in languages other than Dutch and English (Komter, 2002:pc). In Scotland, similarly, detainees must be asked whether they wish to have a solicitor present and to have someone informed of their detention. No written documentation supports that verbal procedure (Malone, 2003).

3.5 The revision texts

I now introduce additional data for Part II by presenting information about each of the texts which have sought to improve on the Parent *Notice* and about the writing practices around those texts. By examining rewriters' practices we can see how their social, cognitive and psychological worlds influence their writing and "what they make of what they do and how it constructs them as social subjects" (Clark and Ivanič, 1997:90). Each revision text is included in Appendices 4–6; I recommend you review them along with the Parent text in order to become a little familiar with their layout, structure and content before reading on.

3.5.1   The Sergeant revision

The Sergeant revision was produced by a Custody Sergeant who had used the Parent *Notices* daily for several years. After attending a training session about detainees with learning difficulties, he became sceptical about those *Notices* and investigated them using readability tests, particularly the Flesch index (1948). He explained how this led him to action:

> I thought "mm terrible and we're handing all these out?" and I spoke to a couple of solicitors and they said "yeah they're bloody awful aren't they I've always thought that" (.) "nothing's been done about it?" (.) "well no" (.) so I made some enquiries and no (.) nothing had been done about it and (.) I hear then about the Home Office research grants so I applied

Following the award of a Home Office grant, the Sergeant began researching and revising in 1999. By the time I began working with him, he saw his version as largely finalised. I initially examined his text and his talk about the text.

The Sergeant's revision practices were driven by the belief that, on one hand, complex language is needed to express law and, on the other, simple language is needed for lay readers. He explained *that's been the interaction if you like ... keep it legal (.) keep it understandable*. This legal-understandable balancing act informed his writing and shaped his writing process and he achieved the balancing act by ingeniously employing help from those around him. Writing scholars recommend making colleagues and readers "integral" to rewriting "not just a final 'stamp of approval'" (Hartley, 1981:26; Wright, 1999:92). Some suggest casting the net more widely for sources to help with rewriting – like Schriver, who advocates combining expert judgement–focussed methods (calling on individuals who know about "the text, its audience or writing itself"); text-focussed methods (such as readability formulae and writing guides); and reader-focussed methods (evaluating readers' comprehension) (1989:244–5). Along with text-focussed readability scores the Sergeant unilaterally incorporated expert judgement–focussed strategies, actively seeking relevant 'authorities' to help with his writing, in particular combining authorities on law (to *keep it legal*) and on language (to *keep it understandable*, or as he disparagingly glosses it here, to *dumb down*):

> if the Plain Language Commission[2] say "yes you've made that simpler" but the Home Office say "you're still legal with it" I've meshed it together nicely (.) I haven't dumbed it down as far as it could go because you have to stay legal

The Sergeant created a sophisticated support network of these authorities from which he sought:

- Sanction – sources to provide 'official' approval as authorities on the matter in question;
- Check – sources to proof or problematise.

Marks in Table 3.2 show how the Sergeant used each authority (if authorities provided both sanction and check, their predominant role receives two marks).

Table 3.2 The Sergeant's support networks

Language authorities	Sanction	Check	Discounted
• Flesch readings	✓		
• The Plain Language Commission	✓✓	✓	
• The PEC			✓
• A Teacher and ex-Head of a school for children with learning difficulties. She, in turn, provided a secondary source – a young man she has been working with as a probation volunteer	✓	✓✓	
Legal authorities			
• The Home Office	✓✓	✓	
• The Legal Aid Board	✓		
• The Law Society	✓		
• The Crown Prosecution Service	✓		
• The Local Law Society	✓		
• Force Solicitor	✓	✓✓	
• Chief Constable		✓	
Authorities on law who also commented on the text – *Legal–simple* intermediaries			
• Solicitors		✓	
• Colleagues in custody suite		✓	

The Sergeant evaluated and rejected other authorities, for example Clare and Gudjonsson's research on comprehension of rights *Notices* (1992), despite their potential to bridge the *legal–simple* dichotomy. He also initially rejected reader-focussed methods, not having time or inclination to canvas detainees' opinions on his text. This illustrates how the "social and material resources" available to drafters influence their texts (Ormerond and Ivanič, 2000:99–100).

3.5.2 The Government revision

A revised version of the Sergeant's text is now used in police stations throughout England and Wales. This version was revised using the research described here and during discussion of that research between the Sergeant (who wrote the text), policy-makers at the Home Office (who specified the text) and me (who had investigated the text and its use in custody). Those discussions used data which I collected in police stations to contest the Sergeant's global and local decisions and the Home Office source material. Labov and Harris note that asking policy-makers about legal texts uncovers inconsistencies and misunderstandings even amongst those people (1994:268). In this case contestation led the Sergeant to reanimate the text, legitimising decisions in sometimes unexpected ways or recognising that his drafting had not functioned as he anticipated. The process also illuminated Home Office proscriptions. For example, our meetings explored the possibility of exploiting the written medium in presenting the caution more visually. Ultimately, this was abandoned as Home Office officials viewed even potentially positive changes to the wording or punctuation of the caution in this text as risky. Bhatia reports an extremely similar encounter (1993:217). There are clear relationships between "the characteristics of the collaborative writing process and...the text features appearing in the documents that result from that process" (Janssen and Maat, 2001:172). Whilst "bad writing" may be caused by writers having to "deal with language mandated by the government and with the difficulty of writing documents by committee" (Williams, 1986:166), we sought to avoid allowing the text to become a means to group consensus (Janssen and Maat, 2001:208). Nonetheless, this text is from a "plural sender" (Renkema, 2001:38) so it can only be a compromise. I refer to the version which we submitted to the Home Office as the "Government revision". The version which the Home Office circulated underwent further revision subsequent to the involvement of the Sergeant or me (see Epilogue).

3.5.3   The Information Design revisions

Information Design (also called Document Design) involves "defining, planning, and shaping of the contents of a message and the environments it is presented in" to respond to users' needs (International Institute for Information Design, 2006). Information Design has a broader remit than the plain English movement, in terms of both its methods and aims (Pettersson, 2002). Information designers typically have an academic background in a language- or design-related discipline (Wright, 1979, 1981).

Five information designers from a design company Enterprise IG rewrote the *Notice* for this study. My brief to them presented writing objectives which mirrored those of the Sergeant (replicating his task) and the brief asked the information designers to write as they normally would (replicating their normal work as far as possible). Their texts were produced independently so each is quite different from the others. My discussion of their revisions and rewriting practices indicate how 'expert writers' respond to the *Notice*. I will refer to the five Enterprise IG writers as EnterpriseA to EnterpriseE.

Davison and Kantor used rewriters' texts to recreate the reasoning and motivation behind revision decisions (1982:191). In my study, as well as providing texts for analysis, the five information designers subsequently discussed their writing with me. This gives direct access to their accounts of the intentions and ideas which shaped their revisions.

3.6   Detainees

In addition to the data introduced above, Part II also examines data which provide a different perspective on the Sergeant text, showing how it was received by detainees in custody. These data were gathered during observation in a busy custody suite and clarified during semi-structured interviews with detainees. The sample of detainees interviewed is small (52) because the detainees were interviewed in depth. The sample is broadly representative of the national average of those taken into police custody across both age and sex (Appendix 7 illustrates). Whilst the interview data could have been categorised along such traditional dimensions as age and sex, for the purposes of analysis a different characteristic is more salient – detainees' prior experience of detention. Not all detainees are naïve. Indeed as in many institutional settings there is no simple, predictable "dichotomy between professionals' possession of professional/technical knowledge and clients'...possession of lay knowledge" (Drew and Sorjonen, 1997:100). Sarangi suggests that the defining factor separating professionals from lay people is the relative uniqueness of the professional–lay interaction to each. This notion of a continuum of lay participants (1998a:303) is usefully transferred to this study:

- Sixteen interviewees had never been arrested before ("Novices");
- Fourteen had been arrested before but not within the preceding 12 months ("Occasionals");
- Twenty-two had been arrested frequently and within the preceding 12 months ("Regulars").

Novice detainees are important to this study because of their likely unfamiliarity with rights information: They offer the uninitiated view of the Sergeant text. At the opposite extreme *regular* detainees, arrested in some cases within the preceding 2 to 14 days, are important because of their familiarity with, and thus particular perspective on, detention which may influence their reading of the Sergeant text. Between these extremes *occasional* arrestees, some of whom could only remember last having been arrested between 10 and 29 years ago, oriented predominantly as newcomers. The proportions of these three types of detainee within the sample are shown in Figure 3.4.

Degree of experience of detention has been found to correlate to the likelihood that detainees will assert their rights (Leo, 1998b:211) although not, universally, with knowledge of detention (Fenner, Gudjonsson and Clare, 2002:90). We will see that in these data relative experience has an expansive influence.

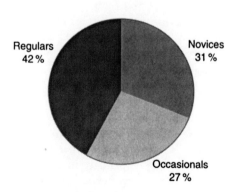

Figure 3.4 Arrestees' experience of detention

3.7   Beginning revision

In Section 3.3 I explained that when the Parent *Notice* was circulated, individual police forces modified it. One aspect which they altered enthusiastically was its macro-sequence. I will end this chapter by considering this macro-sequence (summarised in Figure 3.5). This will introduce the *Notice*, the revisers' work, the place of detainees in revision and the challenge of presenting revisions to decision-makers.

The Parent *Notice* began by summarising the three main detention rights followed by the caution and the words *More information is given below:* (Figure 3.5). This sequence suggests that readers should expect *more information* about the caution particularly in the absence of a prepositional phrase suggesting otherwise. What follows, however, is an explanation of four rights, the three introduced in the initial summary and an additional right not mentioned there (marked with arrows in Figure 3.5). The caution is not elaborated. Thus, the anaphoric *more information* is intended to leapfrog backwards over the caution to the initial rights summary and to connect text selectively.

Summaries potentially improve comprehension (Abrahamsen and Shelton 1989, in Kempson and Moore, 1994:48) yet this summary, due to the uncomfortable cohesive relations just described, might disorient

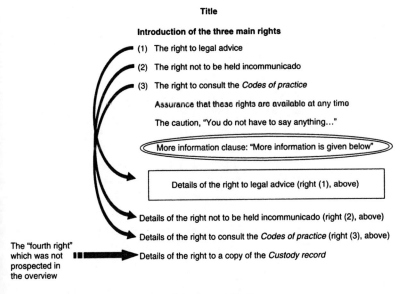

Figure 3.5 The macro-sequence of the Parent *Notice*

more than help. Nonetheless 65 per cent of police forces simply adopted this sequence. Others innovated, placing the caution before the rights summary so that the summary and full version linked directly through the *More information* clause (exemplified in Appendix 3 [Derbyshire Police]). This innovation, by over 25 per cent of police forces, suggests disquiet about the Parent text arrangement. Indeed, West Midlands Police removed the *more information* clause altogether, although without inserting any alternative orientation device (Appendix 3). Possibly these 25 per cent of police forces were somehow issued with a different version of the source text so this re-sequencing is chance. However, the Enterprise rewriters' activities suggest that summary–body relations are important to drafters, because they all worked on cohesive relations between the overview and subsequent sections. They did more than just resequencing, making changes which were:

- *Visual* – using page-layout, lines and tints (EnterpriseE);
- *Textual* – using explicit, detailed cross-references (EnterpriseC);
- *Structural* – summarising each right immediately before introducing it rather than in a separate, initial summary (EnterpriseD).

As well as sequence, rewriters responded to the inclusion of 'the fourth right' which had been absent from the summary but appeared in the body text (Figure 3.5). Apart from its disorienting unheralded appearance, this inclusion is odd because statutorily detainees cannot invoke this right whilst in custody. Logically too, one cannot expect a record of detention while detention is ongoing.

EnterpriseB responded most imaginatively to the fourth right, relocating it to visually distinguish it and indicating its relevance to detainees by noting their capacity to validate or condemn the record by providing or withholding signature. The Sergeant's redraft, in contrast, had not addressed this conundrum. His first-page summary detailed three rights, which he numbered 1–3, whilst the main body of his text explained four rights, numbered 1–4. This incongruity troubled detainees. Some believed that they could see or have the record whilst in detention by analogy with the adjacent rights. Few apparently realised that they could have a copy long after release. Detainees' comments suggested this needed to be addressed. A response which would have been, in some ways, ideal would have removed this 'fourth right' from this text. This is, however, precluded by the *Codes'* dictates. Therefore, Home Office writers proposed an addition to the text:

NB. Your right to a copy of the *Custody record* cannot be exercised while you are in police detention.

Whilst this wording addressed detainees' comments by flagging the difference between this right and the others, it did not really tackle the problem of three rights becoming four and, in order to be successful at all, required close, thorough reading and some inferencing from detainees. They would need to work out the relevance of this negative sentence which carries "special types of presupposition which...work intertextually, incorporating other texts only in order to contest or reject them" (Fairclough, 2001). In this case the negative sentence rejects its cotext as well as rejecting the *Custody record* text.

Having discounted removing the fourth right from the Sergeant's *Notice* and encountered the shortcomings of textually marking it, another response would remove numbering throughout. Numbering helpfully separates each item but potentially misleadingly links them, implying:

- sequential relationships, suggesting stages to traverse in turn;
- dependency relationships, suggesting '2' depends, in some way, on having invoked or declined '1' and so on;
- significance relationships, suggesting that right '1' is more important than '2' and so on.

As a by-product of removing numbering, the proposed new *Notice* would have avoided such connotations. However, without numbers, rights became less distinct (Goldman and Rakestraw, 2000:319; Hartley, 1981:20; Jackson, 1995:128; Tiersma, 1999a:209). Furthermore, removing numbering would merely conceal three rights becoming four which might increase, rather than reduce, confusion. The Government revision adopts a different approach. Each right is numbered in the rights overview and the corresponding rights are numbered identically in the document's main body, giving cohesion. The fourth right, when finally introduced (page three), is not numbered; is separated from the other rights and is presented in a different format. This visually and conceptually separates that right from its fellows, reflecting its difference from them. Unfortunately, the version which the Home Office circulated removed this space cramming this right immediately below its fellows and disrupting the pagination of all subsequent pages (see Epilogue).

These few, relatively superficial aspects of the *Notice* have begun to indicate the complexity of revising even a short text like this. The remainder of Part II considers rewriting and reception in more detail to show revision in action. Chapter 4 analyses micro-syntactic, lexical and semantic features and Chapter 5 intra- and intertextuality. These analyses compare the texts introduced above and consider their relative merits. That comparison permits recommendations about how to improve the texts. However the chapters show how operating only at the level of the text does not allow the analyst to understand the reality of comprehension and comprehensibility in context and can be misleading. Therefore, Chapters 6 and 7 examine the Sergeant's texts in use in order to consider how and indeed whether they are read. These chapters also move beyond the texts to consider their wider contexts of administration and reception because this illustrates how written information functions in this institutional setting which indicates the shortcomings of communicating rights through writing. This combination of scrutinising texts in detail and in context avoids an "atomistic approach" which simply 'measures' sentences in isolation but allows examination of "what elements of the text are causing difficulties" and why (Owen, 1996:292–4).

4
Working with Syntax and Lexis in Writing

4.1 Introduction

Some readers persevere with written texts which they find difficult, re-reading slowly and repeatedly until they understand (Jansen and Steehouder, 2001:18). Writers who do not demand such sterling efforts do so by not creating 'difficult' texts. Researchers trying to establish what causes difficulty point to particular troublesome features at the levels of lexis, syntax, discourse, prosody and beyond (for example, linguistic philosophers Gillon, 1990; Walton, 1996:260–3). These difficult features are, not coincidentally, also said to characterise legal language (Danet, 1990:359; Mellinkoff, 1963). Attention to levels of language has come to typify both critiques and revisions of legal texts. Critiques with this focus have made some spectacular claims; for example, identifying legal notices which were "so inadequate...as to be unconstitutional" (Levi, 1994:7–9) and jury instructions which influenced jurors' decisions (Horowitz, Foster-Lee and Brolly, 1996:757). Revisions too have caused such phenomena as reductions in erroneous insurance claims (Danet, 1990:541) and increases in valid welfare entitlement appeals (Labov and Harris, 1994:277).

Some revision measures are superficial, obvious and easily evaluated in context. Signposting is one such innovation. It was used extensively by the information designers (introduced in Section 3.5.3, included in Appendix 5) who rewrote the rights *Notice* (introduced in Sections 3.1 and 3.3, included in Appendix 1). The information designers' signposting potentially oriented readers by indicating relationships between:

- parts of the text (in the example below parts arising from paper's physical properties):

  Please turn the sheet over

- sections (here guiding reading):

  Please read this panel before the rest of the sheet

- documents (here flagging intertextuality):

  Now please read the sheet called 'About how you will be treated...'

  [All examples from EnterpriseC]

Whilst such metalanguage is a sticking plaster in some texts (Labov, 1988:162; Labov and Harris, 1994:279), the value of textual signposts "in all but the most elementary writing" is widely acknowledged (Garner, 2001:75). However neither the Parent *Notice*, nor the Sergeant's revision (introduced in Section 3.5.1, included in Appendix 4) provided explicit logical or textual orientation. Detainees negatively evaluated the Sergeant's lack of metalanguage, because it caused them to overlook some sections:

> F was it clear there was information **on the back** of that page?
> D oh no I didn't look at that
> F ah [both laugh]
> D no you should have a "please turn over" there because I mean when everything's going on (.) I probably would have [turned the page] when I got home
>
> [Novice 26]

In response to such comments, the Government revision added *Please turn over* to each front-facing sheet. This difficulty in the Sergeant's text was immediately apparent to the detainee. The revision is also uncontroversial. Its benefits are likely to outweigh its costs. Other revisions which I will discuss in the rest of this chapter are less easily assessed and their value in the fast, tense flux of detention is less clear.

Appendix 8 contains an annotated section of the Parent *Notice*. This crudely summarises some of the text's most obvious potentially difficult features at various levels as plain language activists would see them. This chapter focusses on just two levels, syntax and lexis, exploring five syntactic features (grammatical metaphor, particularly nominalisation; passivisation; modality; noun phrases and clause relations) and two lexical matters (jargon and register). Each section of the chapter examines recommendations on these features which have been made by writing guidelines and academic authors. Each section then considers each feature's presence in the Parent *Notice* and its revisions. The chapter views revisers' complex, sophisticated treatment of these features as moves in revision practice (cf. Davison and Kantor, 1982; Duffy, Curran and Sass, 1983; Faigley and Witte, 1981) and examines readers' responses to those moves. The chapter uses a sociolinguistic approach to raise critical questions about whether the presence or absence of particular linguistic features truly indexes difficulty. The analysis shows that syntactic and lexical revisions are difficult, if not impossible, to evaluate meaningfully in use.

4.2 Evaluating syntactic revision

4.2.1 Grammatical metaphor

Halliday's notion of grammatical metaphor (2004:592, 626) proposes that when ideas are first introduced, they are generally congruent: "things appear as nouns, processes as verbs, attributes as adjectives... and so on" (Gibbons, 2003:19). I might congruently say that I have *delivered* information. Yet, in writing, congruence is often lost, skewing underlying semantic relationships (Gibbons, 2003:19). I might non-congruently say I have achieved information *delivery*, converting the verb *deliver* into a noun. Nominalisations which are said to be "vague because they share the weak characteristics of both nouns and verbs" are a form of grammatical metaphor which attract particular criticism (Onrust, Verhagen and Doeve, 1993, in Jansen, 2001:133). Plain language organisations consistently recommend their removal (for example, PEC, 1993:31–2) because verbs rather than nominalised forms are claimed to be:

- "more direct and effective" (Tiersma, 1999a:206);
- more intuitive (Halliday, 2004:636);
- "preferred and read more quickly" (Wright, 1985, in Kempson and Moore, 1994:42);
- more informative (Charrow and Charrow, 1979:1321);
- less abstract (McCawley, 1968, in Charrow and Charrow, 1979);
- capable of marking syntactic relationships (Halliday, 2004:636);
- more likely to have an unambiguous referent and overtly expressed agent (Jansen, 2001:133).

The exact mechanism by which grammatical metaphor brings difficulty is somewhat unclear. Jansen, who neatly reviews empirical work which aims to clarify this, explains that initially analysts believed that readers would find nominalisations difficult because tracing the nominalised form back to its 'source' verb costs "processing time" and "cognitive energy" (2001:132). However, lay people might not realise that a particular usage is non-congruent as usages like *investment* and *reduction* may become sufficiently normalised that they appear more 'normal' than their congruent counterparts. Similarly, there is no guarantee that in all cases where a noun and verb exist the verb was used first and the nominalised form is a derivation or that that chronology causes difficulty in itself. Accordingly Walton, who calls nominalisation "inflective ambiguity", is more critical of shifts between grammatical categories within a text than shifts to a non-congruent category *per se* (1996:261).

Solomon demonstrates that, despite their proscriptions, even advocates of plain English include nominalisations in their texts. Grammatical metaphor potentially improves comprehensibility, by permitting syntactically flatter sentences (Gibbons, 2003). It allows the bundling of concepts which have been explained or accumulated already (Gibbons, 2003:21), reduces words and allows writers to "progress" (Solomon, 1996:295). It is accordingly "a linguistic resource for making specific types of meaning" (Solomon, 1996:296). Although nominalisations offer pros and cons for both writers and readers, these are unlikely to be universal. Even second-language learners and novice readers do not universally benefit from denominalised writing, for example (Spyridakis and Isakson, 1998, in Jansen, 2001:134). The Parent *Notice* contains much grammatical metaphor:

In the text...	Congruent → incongruent
suspected offence	[verb *suspect* → adjective, verb *offend* → noun]
access to legal advice	[verbs *access* and *advise* → nouns]
exceptional circumstances	[preposition *except* → noun *exception* → adjective *exceptional*]
provision of breath	[verb *provide* → noun]
investigative and administrative action	[verbs *investigate* and *administer* → adjectives, verb *act* → noun]
procedures	[verb *proceed* → noun]
record of your detention	[verbs *record* and *detain* → nouns]

a copy of the *Custody record*	[verbs *copy* and *record* → nouns]
this entitlement	[verb *entitle* → noun]
your release	[verb *release* → noun]
on request	[verb *request* → noun]

Revisers tended to replace these forms. For example, all replaced the pervasive combination of nominalisation and ellipted possessive determiner *on request* with a complete clause, either declarative *you can ask* or directive *please ask*. Similarly:

Parent formulation	Became	Writer
your/police detention	→ you have been arrested	[EnterpriseA]
the custody officer has discretion	→ up to the custody officer	[EnterpriseA, EnterpriseC, EnterpriseE]

While the revisers removed nominalisations fastidiously the effects of their efforts on comprehension in context cannot be measured with any certainty.

4.2.2 Passivisation

Gunning warns against passive constructions, explaining that "strong-flavoured, active verbs give writing bounce and hold a reader's attention". He describes writing in the passive as excusable from "a scholar out of touch with life" but unacceptable from "men of action" (1968:107–8). Others are less florid but similarly stoic in their criticisms of passivisation (for example, Hartley, 1981). Yet, for some, "whether passives cause comprehension problems is a bit less clear [than whether nominalisations do]" (Tiersma, 1999a:206) with "no evidence that passive constructions are necessarily more difficult than active equivalents" (Wright, 1969, in Jansen, 2001:135). The PEC too are cautious, permitting passivisation in three circumstances: first, if an active construction would move the topic to the end of the sentence; second, if the agent is obvious (although they do not explain how authors might determine what readers will find obvious) and third, "when an active verb would sound too hostile" (1993:31). Charrow and Charrow provide caveats too, claiming passives in subordinate clauses are the only really tricky form (1979:1337; see also Jackson, 1995:119). Others suggest that passive constructions may only trouble some, such as deaf people (agentless passives only) (LoMaglio, 1985) and adolescents with learning difficulties (Abrahamsen and Shelton, 1989, both in Kempson and Moore, 1994:48). Jansen concludes that, as with nominalisations, difficulties around processing passives centre not on the construction itself, but on the agent deletion which both constructions allow to hinder or prevent inference-drawing (Jansen, 2001:136). The Parent *Notice* contains extensive passivisation:

> **A record**...will **be kept** by the custody officer
> The section in capital letters **is to be read** by the custody officer

And agentless passivisation:

> You **have been arrested**
> Whilst you **are detained**
> More information **is given**
> Access...can only **be delayed**
> If the person...**cannot be contacted**
> the information **has been conveyed**
> **will be made available**
> When you...**are taken**
> You...**will be supplied**

As with nominalisations, the revisers tended to replace passives, for example:

If the person you name cannot be contacted →	
If the police cannot contact...	[EnterpriseC, EnterpriseD, Sergeant]
If the police cannot get in touch...	[EnterpriseB]
If they too cannot be contacted →	
If they cannot contact these people	[EnterpriseC]
If the police cannot get in touch with them	[EnterpriseB]

Some passive constructions were universally reformulated, like the string *The Codes of practice will be made available*.

As with nominalisations, passives are not universally criticised. Some agent deletion is desirable (Gibbons, 2003:166) because a focus on a verb's object may aid comprehension (Tiersma, 1999a:206) and a constantly active voice can adversely affect experiential meaning and thematic progression (Solomon, 1996:299). Some authors included passives deliberately. EnterpriseB inserted a passive into his section on the right to see the *Codes*:

> The rules about [the] way that the police deal with people who have been arrested **are set out** in a legal document – 'The Codes of practice for the Detention, Treatment and Questioning of Persons by Police Officers', also called the PACE Code.

This passive is strategic; it allows the author to avoid either: specifying who wrote the *Codes*, which would be irrelevant by any measure; or placing the long noun phrase, beginning *a legal document*, sentence initially. Davison and Kantor present such practices positively, observing "adaptors are often able to foresee the effects of changes and compensate for them", calling this the "Domino Effect" (1982:196). As with nominalisation, however, it was impossible to measure the results of such specific changes on detention.

4.2.3 Modality

There is some agreement amongst language guidelines that modal auxiliaries are a necessary evil. Specific modals attract conflicting advice, however. Tiersma castigates *shall* with its "archaic and legalistic feel", advocating replacement with *must* in language for the public (1999a:207). Conversely, others favour *shall* – Kerr, for example, urges "use *shall* not *must*" (1991, in Solomon, 1996:288). The Parent *Notice* featured only one occurrence of *shall*, in explaining that a copy of the *Custody record shall be supplied*. All of the rewriters replaced this auxiliary. Modal verbs in the *Notice* and in some of the revised texts brought more specific ambiguities.

May is both prevalent and important in the Parent *Notice*. Most typologies of modal meaning recognise two possible meanings for *may*, one concerned with 'possibility' (epistemic or extrinsic modality) and one with 'permission' (deontic or intrinsic modality) (Coates, 1983; Perkins 1983; Quirk *et al.*, 1985). Two sentences from the caution illustrate this duality clearly:

> It **may** harm your defence if you do not mention when questioned something which you later rely on in court. Anything you do say **may** be given in evidence.

The first occurrence is epistemic: 'it is possible that mentioning may harm your defence – only time will tell'. The subsequent occurrence, in contrast, seems predominantly deontic: 'it is permissible to give your words in evidence – the law states this', yet there is certainly a possibility here too. If, following this caution, a detainee is not charged, their words will not be used in evidence so this second *may* also mean 'it is possible that we will use your words in evidence – in appropriate conditions'. Such duality is rife in the *Notice* where *may* occurs a further six times:

Section where *may* occurs	Realisation
Rights summary	You **may** do any of these things now (1)
	If you do not [do any of these things now], you **may** still do so at any other time (2)
The right to a solicitor	the solicitor **may** come to see you (3)
	the police **may** question you without a solicitor (4)
The right to outside contact	You **may** on request have one person…informed…of your whereabouts (5)
	you **may** choose up to two alternatives (6)

Unambiguous modal verbs are the exception (Hodge and Kress, 1993:122), yet sometimes ambiguity is quite acceptable. Clauses 1, 2 and 6 seem to convey both 'you are permitted' and 'you can choose' to do these things. The difference seems fairly inconsequential in these instances. Indeed readers might best take both meanings. However, ambiguity is problematic elsewhere. PACE suggests that clauses 3, 4 and 5 are intended to convey permission ('a solicitor is permitted to come to see you' (3); 'the police are permitted to interview you alone' (4) and 'you are permitted to have someone informed' (5)). Unfortunately, detainees who instead take them to convey possibility may be unnerved. For example, an epistemic reading of (4), 'the police might choose to interview you alone', suggests that the police have unregulated power. Thus, *may* creates "systematic ambiguity about the nature of authority" (Hodge and Kress, 1993:122). How did the rewriters respond to modal auxiliaries? Each Enterprise version used fewer *may*s than the Parent text (Figure 4.1).

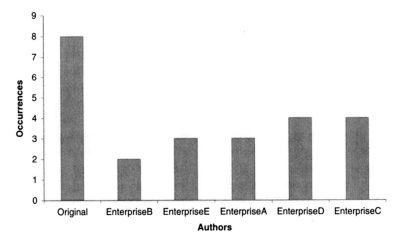

Figure 4.1 Decreased use of *may*

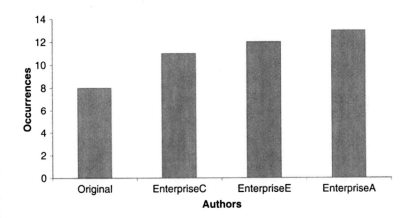

Figure 4.2 Increased use of *can*

The Enterprise information designers specified that they rejected *may* to avoid ambiguity. Frequently, they replaced *may* with *can*. For example, all who reformulated occurrences (1) and (2) did this. Three of the information designers particularly valued *can*, using it more than the Parent text did (Figure 4.2).

The Sergeant who rewrote the notices took this further than any other redrafter, incorporating only 4 *may*s to 17 *can*s. However, *can*, like *may*, is deontic–epistemic ambiguous. Indeed things become particularly muddling when the Parent *Notice* juxtaposes *can* and *may*, for example:

> You **can** speak to a solicitor...at any time. You **can** talk to the solicitor in private on the telephone and the solicitor **may** come to see you at the police station.

Both auxiliaries are deontic–epistemic ambiguous; why have they been combined? The text's situation of use reveals that detainees would more likely speak to solicitors by telephone (conveyed by *can*) than in person[1] (*may*). Therefore, *can* perhaps intends to connote greater certainty than *may*. This notion that writers may employ modal verbs systematically is more than an intriguing possibility. It emerged, during discussions with the Sergeant, that his decisions in assigning modal verbs were far from arbitrary or isolated. Consider how he revised the text just discussed:

(i)   You **must** be allowed to talk to a solicitor at any time

(ii)   You **can** talk to a solicitor on the telephone

(iii)   A solicitor **may** come to see you

The Sergeant explained that he envisaged a modality scheme (underlining indicates his emphasis):

> PACE says (.) that you <u>must</u> (.) be allowed to talk to a solicitor (.) at any time...so you've <u>got to be allowed</u> to talk to him [*sic*] (.) you <u>can</u> talk to him on the 'phone (.) and he <u>might</u> come and see you at the police station (.) because in some cases they just give 'phone advice (.) so it was a sort of <u>must</u> (.) <u>can</u> (.) <u>might</u> (.) you know...as in careful choice of words

The Sergeant's system addressed clauses of the Parent text which he felt expressed deontic modality ambiguously. Through the system he hoped to convey permission, possibility and relative likelihood transparently. However, understanding his system would require readers to recognise and accept that system. This is impossible. In revising the Sergeant's text we built on his attention to modal verbs but removed dependence on impossible insider knowledge. Example (i), above, had replaced the epistemic–deontic confusion of *can* with an epistemic–deontic–alethic ambiguity through *must*.[2] Whilst alethic or epistemic readings would be somewhat far-fetched, some readers might invoke them because the intended deontic meaning is obscured by the absence of a party who is obliged through *must*. By specifying that party, through an active structure, the deontic reading becomes more apparent:

The police must let you talk to a solicitor at any time.

In examples (ii) and (iii), the Sergeant hoped to convey through *can* 'permission' – solicitors are normally permitted to visit detainees; and through *may* 'decision' – solicitors choose whether to visit. Detainee interviews revealed that they had missed this subtlety. As a result one detainee, whose solicitor had simply decided against a personal visit, believed his right had been withheld. A possible revision removes the modal but fails to introduce solicitors' autonomy:

A solicitor is allowed to come to see you...

The Government *Notice* therefore adopted:

A solicitor can also decide to come to see you...

Tiersma condemns such circumlocutions, preferring "ordinary modal verbs" although without explaining why (1999a:207). Of course, circumlocution brings what plain language advocates see as additional syntactic problems, typically increasing complexity within verb groups. Here, however, *can* conveys possibility, permission or both whilst *decide* presents the solicitor's autonomy. *Also* was inserted to reinforce cohesive links with (ii).

As with nominalisations and passives, these changes are so subtle yet so pervasive that it is difficult to evaluate their effects. Experimental studies might evaluate the texts' theoretical effectiveness but what would their results mean for detainees in custody?

4.2.4 Noun phrases

Noun phrases incorporating strings of qualifiers are said to produce difficulty (Wright, 1979, in Kempson and Moore, 1994:42). The rewriters problematised and altered many such phrases in the Parent *Notice*. This became a particular focus in revising the section reproduced below which contains extensive third-person reference (bold and numbered):

Parent text

Sentence 1   You may on request have **(1) one person known to you, or who is likely to take an interest in your welfare,** informed at public expense as soon as is practicable of your whereabouts.

Sentence 2   If **(2) the person you name** cannot be contacted you may choose **(3) up to two alternatives.**

Sentence 3   If **(4) they** too cannot be contacted **(5) the custody officer** has discretion to allow further attempts **(6)** ϕ [to contact **other people**] until the information has been conveyed.

These personal references presented three problems:

- long noun phrases in two cases involving rank-shifting and anaphora (1) (2) and (3);
- pronouns with unclear antecedents (4);
- elision (6).

Some of these noun phrases attracted fairly straightforward rewording, although not necessarily shortening, from the information designers and Sergeant, for example:

the person you name [Parent text (2)] →	
the person	[EnterpriseD]
the person you choose	[EnterpriseA]
the person you have told them about	[EnterpriseB]
your first choice of person	[EnterpriseC]

up to two alternatives [Parent text (3)] →	
two others	[EnterpriseD]
2 other people	[EnterpriseA]
the names of two more people to try to contact	[EnterpriseB]
2 more	[Sergeant]

The Parent text's longest noun phrase (occurrence (1)), however, contained semantic oddities and attracted more detailed revision. In that phrase *known* connotes relative unfamiliarity: a public figure may be *known* to me, but I may not *know* them. The *who-* prefaced relative clause incorporates rank-shifting and the coordinator *or* suggests a very odd choice between someone known to me and someone interested in me. Whilst the Parent *Notice* suggests that detainees might contact anyone with a general interest in them, the Sergeant's version specifies that contact depends on *need*. The Sergeant drew on his participant knowledge to condense occurrence (1) to become *someone who needs to know*. He explained his choice:

> when you get down to kids (.) if you say "who do you want to know?" (.) they don't want their mum and dad to know (.) but their mum and dad do need to know and we have a need to tell them... it's not down to what they want

This achieves precision for children but *need* is also appropriate for adult readers who may themselves need to contact someone. Elsewhere he added *want* to indicate that necessity (*need*) is not a condition of this right.

The Sergeant simplified third-person reference here in other ways too, reducing the complexity of the network of contacts introduced. Where the Parent text introduced three layers of contacts:

- the person you name
- up to two alternatives
- further attempts

The Sergeant condensed the second and third levels into *at least two more*:

> If the police cannot contact the first person..., they will try at least two more until someone knows. [Sergeant]

This reduced the risk of detainees incorrectly tracing anaphoric ties from pronouns by providing fewer potential antecedents. The Sergeant additionally replaced the notion that custody officers can please themselves about whether to continue attempting contact with the certainty that they *will* keep trying *until* successful. This alters the sense of the original. The Home Office quietly removed this paragraph before circulating the *Notice* to police forces (see Epilogue). Like nominalisations, passives and modal auxiliaries, the effects of changes to noun phrases are difficult to assess. These changes, in particular, had numerous syntactic, lexical and semantic knock-on effects so, even if detainees were asked tightly focussed questions about their understanding of particular sections, the analyst could not be sure which of the revisions had influenced their comprehension.

4.2.5 Clause relations

Some researchers suggest that conjunctions influence comprehension; for example, that particular people struggle with conjunctions (Irwin, 1980, in Davison and Kantor, 1982:206) or that particular conjunctions influence readability (Wright, 1979, in Kempson and Moore, 1994:46). Certainly, this aspect of a text's surface structure guides readers on how to connect concepts (Goldman and Rakestraw, 2000:313). All of the rewriters made surface-structure changes to paragraph 3 of the Parent *Notice'*s section on the right to legal advice (mapped below, numbering clauses and coordinators):

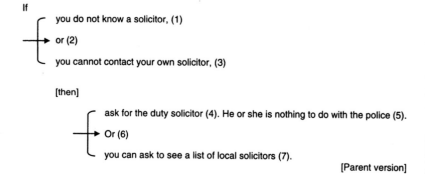

If
- you do not know a solicitor, (1)
- or (2)
- you cannot contact your own solicitor, (3)

[then]

- ask for the duty solicitor (4). He or she is nothing to do with the police (5).
- Or (6)
- you can ask to see a list of local solicitors (7).

[Parent version]

This paragraph rests on potentially unfamiliar concepts. It assumes that readers will know what a *duty solicitor* is and who to ask should they wish to speak to one. It introduces a list which can be requested but does not mention how that list might be used. All of this is compounded, however, by the paragraph's chaotic coordination. Clause 4 apparently resolves the previous two conjoined clauses yet, after an intervening clause, comes an *or* conjunction (6), which asks readers to temporarily disregard clauses 4 and 5 in order to coordinate the coming clause (7) to the opening units (1–3). In other words, resolution of (6) and (7) involves cataphoric reference to (1–3), whilst (4) and (5) interpose in a parenthesis relation (Beekman, Callow and Kopesec, 1981). As a result, *nothing to do with the police* implies that list solicitors are less impartial than duty solicitors. All of the rewriters responded to this structure and the resulting implicature. Most of the information designers re-sequenced, introducing the list before independence. This generated some problems itself. Authors who moved clause 5 to a final position found that its original subject, *he or she*, no longer tied cataphoric-ally to its original antecedent, *duty solicitor*, closely enough to ensure cohesion. EnterpriseA, EnterpriseC and EnterpriseE therefore reinserted *duty solicitor* into their relocated clause 5. Unfortunately that suggested, perhaps even more forcefully than the Parent text, that duty soli-citors are independent from police whereas list solicitors are not. For example:

> You can ask for the duty solicitor or ask to see a list of local solicitors. The duty solicitor is nothing to do with the police.   [EnterpriseA]

For these writers, attention to one potential difficulty (lengthy anaphora) maintained, or intensified, another potential difficulty (vagueness about independence), illustrating, once more, Davison and Kantor's Domino Effect (1982:196). Only EnterpriseB specified that inde-pendence characterises all solicitors, but he had to dedicate a sentence to this:

> Both the duty solicitor, and the solicitors on the list are completely independent of the police.

The Sergeant's knowledge of detention informed his reformulation, enabling him to sidestep these matters:

> If you do not know a solicitor **in the area** or you cannot get in touch with your own solicitor, there is a person called the duty solicitor. **The police will help you contact him or her.** He or she is nothing to do with the police.

His experience is that officers rarely offer an extensive solicitor list to detainees; therefore, he deleted all reference to lists. His contextual knowledge also enabled him to augment the paragraph with the items highlighted in bold above.

The second sentence of the section which presents the right to a copy of the *Custody record* also contains extensive subordination and coordination. Its passive main clause (bold below) is accompanied by an array of other components, resulting in a complex, almost periodic sentence:

When you leave police detention
or   —— **When** one can ask for copy?
are taken before a court,

- -

you
or
your legal representative   ____ **Who** can ask for copy?
or
the appropriate adult

- -

shall be supplied
on request
with a copy of the Custody record ____ **What** can be copy?
as soon as practicable.

= **when x, you shall get y.**

The when-who-what sequence indicated above is quite disorientating. Commentators advocate presenting 'what' first (Owen, 1996:290). Additionally, the sentence introduces two temporal referents and three people, requiring readers to hold much in mind. Most redrafters signalled dissatisfaction with all this by using multiple sentences or reducing the number of coordinated noun phrases which introduce people. The Sergeant, for example, unpacked the subordination which occurs towards the end of the original sentence, creating one sentence outlining the detainee's right and a separate sentence explaining officers' obligations:

Detainee's right	When you leave the police station, you, your solicitor or your appropriate adult can ask for a copy of the Custody record.
Officer's obligation	The police have to give you a copy of the Custody record as soon as they can.

The Sergeant's solution here attends to the different roles of detainee and officer.

Within the sentence too, syntactic issues in the Parent text bring potential problems:

- **Active–passive combinations** – Active *When you leave police detention* is coordinated to passive *are taken before a court*. This changes voice and agent mid-sentence. We might expect two active clauses with detainee as agent (*when you leave custody or go to court*) or two passives with police as agent (*when you are released from custody or are taken before a court*). Rewriters responded here. EnterpriseA used passive + passive. The Sergeant, on the other hand, removed this active–passive combination by removing all reference to court, consequently removing some detail of the right's flexibility but positing that this information was unnecessary in context.

- **Inconsistent use of determiners** – The detainee's legal representative is specified using possessive *your* while the appropriate adult is denoted using the definite article. This suggests that the solicitor is exclusive to the detainee and the appropriate adult is not. The Sergeant attended to this, using the possessive in both cases.

This sub-section has illustrated that subordination and coordination raise ambiguity throughout the Parent *Notice* in combination with other features. The rewriters responded to these matters in ways that might help readers, although not necessarily in ways which writing guidelines could even cover. The Sergeant's revisions are very obviously motivated by his knowledge and perceptions and by an orientation towards detainees' concerns.

4.3 Evaluating lexico-semantic revision

4.3.1 Jargon

Jargon expressions "have a special trade or professional meaning" which is unfamiliar to non-specialist readers. Jargon might be used 'accidentally', without considering readers, or 'maliciously', intending to "impress, confuse or humiliate" readers (PEC, 1993:26). The section of the Parent *Notice* which offers the *Codes of practice* begins:

The right to consult the Codes of practice
The Codes of practice will be made available to you on request. These Codes govern police procedures.

Sentence 1 uses the jargon *Codes of practice*, yet that jargon is only explained in sentence 2; an illogical discourse sequence. Owen problematises this sequence, explaining, "people who know what something is are more likely to know whether they want to look at it" (1996:290). He also recommends that jargon like this should be accompanied by more detailed glosses (1996:292). This short gloss neglects the *Codes'* function, content and relevance to detention.[3] We might expect rewriters to replace jargon (Davison and Kantor, 1982:205). However, the rewriters here maintained the term *Codes of practice*, to avoid presenting police officers with two tiers of terminology. They therefore also maintained a gloss for lay readers. Most addressed the issues of both sequence and superficiality, placing a fuller gloss in an initial position, as the Sergeant revision demonstrates:

> The Codes of practice is a book that tells you what the police can and cannot do while you are at the police station. [→ **Gloss**]
> The police will let you read the Codes of practice... [→ **Offer**]

The gloss assumes no prior knowledge from detainees by explaining from the start that the *Codes* is a book (cf. Clare and Gudjonsson, 1992:42). It also focusses on the *Codes'* relevance to detainees in regulating police activity *while you are at the police station*, rather than foregrounding (Danet, 1984a:5) its institutional relevance in governing *police procedure*. Three of the Enterprise rewriters similarly adopted a detainee-centred perspective.

Turning to a different term *Custody record*, the Parent *Notice* glosses before offering the relevant right:

> A record of your detention will be kept by the custody officer. [→ **Gloss**]
> When you leave police detention...you...shall be supplied on request with a copy of the Custody record.... [→ **Offer**]

Whilst in this case the initial sentence potentially clarifies the jargon term, that sentence is not presented as a gloss (for example, using *The Custody record is...*) so detainees must infer its explanatory function. Surprisingly, several rewriters were unconcerned about this term. EnterpriseA removed the gloss and EnterpriseC reduced its prominence and detail. In contrast, the Sergeant glossed *Custody record* more fully and explicitly linked the gloss to the headword, if rather clumsily:

> Everything that happens to you while you are at the police station is... called the Custody record.

Despite the glosses of both *Codes of practice* and *Custody record* being revised and resequenced in the Sergeant revision, some detainees who received that revision in detention remained confused. Patterns of misunderstanding emerged during my interviews with detainees about the Sergeant text (these interviews were introduced in Section 3.6). First, detainees misassigned labels, offering the following definitions of these jargon terms:

- *Codes of practice* means:

  all the records that you're allowed to see...where they fill out what time you have a cup of tea and what time you have exercise and all that   [Regular 20]

  This detainee has instead glossed *Custody record*, fairly accurately.

- or it means:

  they were quite clear I'm on record now for 5 years caution   [Novice 18]

  This detainee has instead glossed the *Criminal record*, an institutional database of individuals' offences which is not even mentioned in the *Notice*.

- *Custody record* means:

  all the things you've done like illegal things   [Regular 43]
  all your files on record...who you are what you've done   [Occasional 37]

  These detainees too have glossed *Criminal record*.

These misassignments may stem from the graphological and phonological coincidence of the initial 'c' /k/ shared by *Codes of practice*, *Custody record* and *Criminal record*. Other detainees who similarly appeared confident that they understood these terms also glossed them incorrectly by misappropriating other artefacts of the legal process, claiming:

- The *Codes* specifies offences:

  say I get done for 'A B H section 18 with intent' then that's what it will be in there...it will tell you in there everything about it   [Regular 50]
  it would be a good book to get like and all the different laws and the different situations they can charge you with   [Regular 28]

- The *Custody record* is a time-limit, perhaps through analogy with some sporting *records* measured in time:

  F   and do you know what the *Custody record* is?
  D   no- 24 hours is it?   [Novice 18]

The Sergeant revision glossed technical terms using a discourse sequence which is recommended in relevant research literature and incorporated a range of formulations and orientations which appear well-motivated and carefully considered. Nonetheless, readers remained confused. It is difficult to know how rewriters should respond or how the texts, alone, might be further modified to address the particular misunderstandings expressed. These data show that even revisions which 'improve comprehensibility' do not necessarily 'improve comprehension'. They suggest that, in this text at least, if detainees are to understand, then providing only a revised text is not the whole answer.

4.3.2   Register

Despite calls for legal drafters to use short words (Gunning, 1968:302–15; PEC, 1993:80–1), the Parent *Notice* is peppered with words which have shorter near-synonyms. Accordingly, systematic lexical replacement occurred throughout the revision texts, rewriters replacing words which "readability formulas would predict are more difficult" (Davison and Kantor, 1982:204):

Parent version	Occurrences		Becomes
request	(3)	→	ask
to consult the *Codes*	(3)	→	to see the *Codes*
[Metaphorical]			to read the book
			to look at the *Codes*
informed	(2)	→	told
as soon as	(2)	→	as soon as...
practicable			...possible
			...they can
			...it's available
govern	(1)	→	cover
			covering
			set out
			tell
spoken to	(1)	→	talk to
independent	(1)	→	nothing to do with
telephone	(2)	→	'phone
which require	(1)	→	which means that you must

Although these revisions 'simplify', they might also be characterised as performing register shift, thus changing the *Notice*'s character, its affect

(Hayes, 1996) or experiential meaning (Nevile, 1990). As far back as the 1940s, when Flesch devised his readability formula (1948), he also developed a complementary measure of 'Human Interest' to investigate writers' "tone" (Wright, 1999:91) because he saw simplification and affect as inextricably linked. More recently, Jackson has summarised that 'long words' are valued in legal texts as part of a "familiar style" which "is sensed as 'the' right and appropriate one" by the legal in-group, but as an alienating "ploy" by lay people (1995:132–3). Thus difficult language "carries a social message concerning the power and authority" of its user (Gibbons, 1999:160). The potential for legal language to instil fear or obedience through its affective force is not lost on police and lawyers, who may resist alternative forms (Gibbons, 1999:160) which "might compromise the 'majesty' of law" (Jackson, 1995:117). There are parallels in the medical domain where practitioners may exploit knowledge asymmetries, controlling patients and interactions through vocabulary choices (Roter and Hall, 1992). Nonetheless, much legal language revision and research ignores the experiential potential of either formality or simplification, assuming that "only propositional information is communicated by, for example, police cautions" (Gibbons, 1999:160).

Rewriters studied here, on the other hand, considered potential experiential consequences of their revisions (cf. Dixon and Bortolussi, 2001:18–19). The Enterprise rewriters aimed to produce a relatively "gentle", more "reassuring" and "less intimidating" text than the original.[4] The Sergeant initially contemplated abandoning a conventional written format in favour of cartoon presentation, a format which has been found valuable elsewhere, "especially [for] less able readers" (Hartley, 1981:23). Indeed, cartoon versions of the *Notice* already existed (Cotterill, 1999:pc). However, the Sergeant explained that an advisor whom he had appointed, the Head-Teacher of a school for children with learning difficulties, problematised drastic simplification:

> if you...say "OK how simple can you get?" (.) "do it as a cartoon"...you're going to say "here's a cartoon" they're actually going to feel quite insulted and they won't read it because it's too dumb for them

Thus, the Sergeant rejected what he felt was a potentially patronising format. Throughout his writing process he considered the affective potential of his text, hoping to engage readers by 'pitching' at an appropriate 'level'.

Research literature problematises register shift, warning that a *Notice* simplified for disadvantaged subjects might become more difficult for able readers (Owen, 1996). Furthermore, simplification can create "friendly" texts "as if this kind of relationship can be assumed" (Solomon, 1996:289). Detainees in this study commented on the register of the Sergeant's text. Some felt that informality was present but necessary:

F   was [anything] being repeated too much or being too simple or
D   I didn't think so because some people are simple and they need
     it explaining to them

[Occasional 03]

Others felt, like Solomon, that simplification can be overdone:

it comes across as being **"we're here to help"** you know what I mean that's I mean you've only got to read a few lines of it and **it's more like being in a hotel** really isn't it

[Novice 25]

Some concluded that the document and associated custody practices were ultimately too informal:

these guys shouldn't be friendly to me they should be scowling at me and saying "you're a naughty boy aren't you"

[Novice 25]

Here we rather surprisingly see detainees' responses to the Sergeant's register shift but their responses are equivocal. Some detainees valued simplification but others felt patronised. Possibly, a more formal text would have attracted different but similarly equivocal comments.

4.4 Close

At the lowest level, this chapter has reiterated that writing guidelines are not all in agreement with one another and, indeed, that some of their recommendations are in direct conflict. Furthermore, the chapter has illustrated that even though the revisers were not necessarily following writing guidelines their revisions tended to concur with the recommendations of those guidelines. This implies that guidelines' recommendations have an intuitive value. The Sergeant, in particular, intended to use short words and sentences but had not specifically considered nominal-isations, passives, modality and so on and would probably be the first to admit that such details were beyond his sphere of expertise. His uncom-plicated strategy for simplification and his instinctive decisions about features which would present difficulty created a text which appeared plain Englished. His text had also had some attention from a plain English organisation (see Section 3.5.1).

At a higher level, the chapter does not tell us what effect the changes described here have on readers in context. Whilst detailed psycholin-guistic study could examine the effect of such changes in controlled circumstances working on tiny quantities of text, there is no valid, reli-able way to test the influence of a range of linguistic forms in a text which is the length of a rights notice. Some features such as partic-ular lexical innovations can be evaluated to an extent by asking readers whether they have 'understood' particular terms. However, in the deten-tion context the notion of 'understanding' begins to unravel. What of the detainees here who confidently explained terms like *Custody record* incorrectly? What of the detainees who experienced rights texts as offering friendly help? In real-world settings information is not considered in bite-sized chunks and is not used in ways that its senders can control. These are the central matters of interest for the sociolinguist. Accordingly, the next chapter examines higher levels of text structure and the final two chapters in this part (Part II) consider the text as more than strings of words on paper.

5
Working with Organisation in Writing

5.1 Introduction

Moving now to text organisation, this chapter concerns higher-level features – organisation within and between sections and intertextuality with other texts. It illustrates the way the rewriters strived towards logical sequencing, connecting related propositions and providing useful referring devices.

5.2 Discourse organisation within the section

The excerpt below sees a detainee asked to explain his rights waiver by an officer as his police interview is about to begin:

> P   do you want to have a solicitor present at this interview?
> D   [carefully] I don't <u>think</u> I require a solicitor
> P   you have continued to decline legal advice and we'll now have to ask the question what were your reasons for this it's just (.) to clarify
> →   D   u:::m (5.6) ur I'm not clear how a solicitor would help me=
>   P   =yep understand that's absolutely fine I'm going to caution you again sir

> [B16]

This detainee, who would have been offered the Parent *Notice* (included in Appendix 1), appears to have passed through the entire detention process without having developed any understanding of the solicitor's role. When he finally voices this uncertainty it is dismissed as *absolutely fine* and his expression of doubt apparently taken as a rights waiver. Some jurisdictions see such "ambiguous statements" or "uncertainty about what to do" as not constituting rights waivers, preferring "direct and unqualified assertions" about rights (Shuy, 1997:192, see also Ainsworth, 1998:283; Eades, 2003:210; Leo, 2001:1020). If incomprehension is to be taken as rights waiver then incomprehension must be eradicated.

The right to legal advice is perhaps the most important right in contemporary Anglo-Welsh detention because its exercise potentially provides practical, one-to-one help in all matters. However, the section which presents it in the Parent *Notice* combines lexical, syntactic and micro-structural oddities with disorganisation on every level. Looking first to internal organisation of that section, Figure 5.1 overviews the section's trajectory:

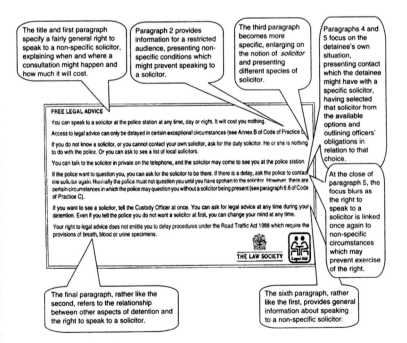

Figure 5.1 Overview of the right to legal advice as it is presented in the Parent *Notice* using notions of 'specific' and 'general'

There is little topical coherence between paragraphs. For example, paragraph 1, which outlines the right, and paragraph 3, which explains its invocation, are separated by paragraph 2, which describes restrictions to the right (see Section 5.3.1). Through initial negation paragraph 3 indeed implies some dialogicity with something which is not readily apparent, perhaps intending to recall paragraph 1. Paragraphs 3 and 6 which both explain how to obtain a solicitor are separated by paragraph 5, which covers several unrelated topics. Discourse organisation like this is particularly detrimental to comprehension (Levi, 1994:16–18) and may distract readers (Charrow and Charrow, 1979:1327). This section also dispenses information non-chronologically with no apparent alternative motivation. For example, paragraph 6, which explains how to request a solicitor, might more sensibly precede paragraph 3, which details selection of a particular solicitor following that initial request. This is unhelpful according to Zwaan and Radvansky, who propose that congruence between text structure and the structure of the related situation aids comprehension (1998, in Goldman and Rakestraw, 2000:318).

I examined all authors' changes, removals and additions by dividing the Parent text into semantic units and tabulating each author's response to each unit. Although each response is very different, their treatments have some themes. For example, all authors maintained something of what was originally paragraph 1, which summarised somewhat. Additionally, each has maintained this paragraph's position, early in their document, although the Sergeant incorporates it later than any other writer. Most indicated that the original first paragraph was incomplete by moving various later propositions into it. They felt the need to inform detainees, early on, that they can:

- invoke this right even having initially   [EnterpriseC, EnterpriseA]
  declined it
- speak to a solicitor either by tele-   [EnterpriseD, EnterpriseB]
  phone or in person and in private
- ask, to invoke this right   [Sergeant]

Both between and within paragraphs most redrafters re-sequenced, they claimed, more appropriately. EnterpriseD offers the most radical example, cleaving the section into two parts: one concerned with the right's application before interview, the other with its application during interview. One detainee described reading the text during interview to make a snap decision about legal advice. This structure might have helped him had it been used in the version he read.

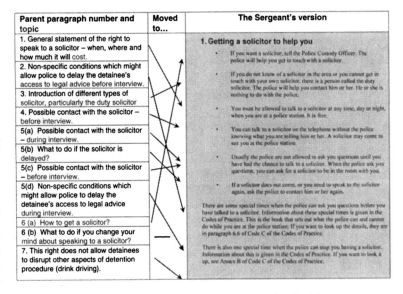

Parent paragraph number and topic	Moved to...	The Sergeant's version
1. General statement of the right to speak to a solicitor – when, where and how much it will cost.		**1. Getting a solicitor to help you**
2. Non-specific conditions which might allow police to delay the detainee's access to legal advice before interview.		• If you want a solicitor, tell the Police Custody Officer. The police will help you get in touch with a solicitor.
3. Introduction of different types of solicitor, particularly the duty solicitor		• If you do not know of a solicitor in the area or you cannot get in touch with your own solicitor, there is a person called the duty solicitor. The police will help you contact him or her. He or she is nothing to do with the police.
4. Possible contact with the solicitor – before interview.		• You must be allowed to talk to a solicitor at any time, day or night, when you are at a police station. It is free.
5(a) Possible contact with the solicitor – during interview.		• You can talk to a solicitor on the telephone without the police knowing what you are telling him or her. A solicitor may come to see you at the police station.
5(b) What to do if the solicitor is delayed?		• Usually the police are not allowed to ask you questions until you have had the chance to talk to a solicitor. When the police ask you questions, you can ask for a solicitor to be in the room with you.
5(c) Possible contact with the solicitor – before interview.		• If a solicitor does not come, or you need to speak to the solicitor again, ask the police to contact him or her again.
5(d) Non-specific conditions which might allow police to delay the detainee's access to legal advice during interview.		There are some special times when the police can ask you questions before you have talked to a solicitor. Information about these special times is given in the Codes of Practice. This is the book that sets out what the police can and cannot do while you are at the police station. If you want to look up the details, they are in paragraph 6.6 of Code C of the Codes of Practice.
6 (a) How to get a solicitor? 6 (b) What to do if you change your mind about speaking to a solicitor?		There is also one special time when the police can stop you having a solicitor. Information about this is given in the Codes of Practice. If you want to look it up, see Annex B of Code C of the Codes of Practice.
7. This right does not allow detainees to disrupt other aspects of detention procedure (drink driving).		

Figure 5.2   The Sergeant's reworking of the section on legal advice

The Sergeant re-sequenced and removed some propositions. He divided the remaining text into more paragraphs than any other rewriter using paragraphing to separate functionally different parts (Figure 5.2).

The Government revision developed this sequence using analyses of each author's revisions and detainees' comments. It re-inserted some propositions from the Parent *Notice* which the Sergeant had unintentionally omitted but also augmented the Parent text's content. It grouped paragraphs according to topics (Table 5.1) which attempt to anticipate potential readers' potential questions and to address actual questions identified in detainee interviews (Hoey, 1988:57; see Section 6.6.1).

Aside from these structural problems, the Parent *Notice* also fails to specify how or, indeed, whether a solicitor might help: an omission from *Miranda* warnings too (Shuy, 1997:186). The section's title *legal advice* hints at this, but only late in the section does paragraph 5 even allude to solicitors' likely activities, and even then explaining only that they can attend interviews. This omission may have affected the detainee cited at the beginning of this chapter. Detainees do not all imagine that an authority figure like a solicitor, with apparent connections to the police, would greatly assist them.[1] Those I interviewed expressed unease around invoking legal advice. This had various causes, including cynicism and

Table 5.1 Summary of the Government revision (Appendix 6 shows the text in full)

Paragraph	Summary of content	Macro-sequence
1	What a solicitor will do	Introduction
2	What to do if you want a solicitor – summary	Making initial contact with a solicitor
3	When you can talk to a solicitor – how much it costs	
4	What to do if you want a solicitor – detail – introducing duty solicitor	
5	Telephone and in-person consultations	What a solicitor will do during extended contact
6	Solicitor's role during interviews	
7	Implications of speaking to a solicitor	
8	What to do if the solicitor does not appear or further contact is needed	Re-initiating contact
9	What to do if one has not requested a solicitor but changes one's mind	

a desire to resolve their own situation. Similarly, Barton and Hamilton have found people "ambivalent about professional experts, deferring to them though lack of confidence, but privately sceptical" (1998:244). For all these reasons it is important to tell detainees what rights invocation might provide. The rewriters identified this need. One added information about solicitors' role and allegiances:

> Solicitors help to protect the legal rights of people in custody, and also give them legal advice. [EnterpriseB]

The Sergeant, too, introduced the solicitor, in his summary section, as someone *to help you while you are at the police station.* The Government version built on this, adding later: *A solicitor can help and advise you about the law.* The Sergeant buttressed his representation of the legal adviser's positive presence and alignment with the detainee using the positive semantic prosody of *chance* (Louw, 1993:157ff.; Section 9.3) to formulate speaking to a solicitor as having *had the chance to talk to a solicitor.*

The Sergeant felt that this right was the most important for detainees, so he sought to prioritise it through visual cues (affording it a whole, dedicated page; more space than any other right) and sequential cues (placing it first). Some detainees suggested this had been successful:

- Visual cues:

    makes it look more important because there's only a little section on everything else but there's a whole front page on [that]   [Regular 50]

- Sequential cues:

    I would have thought if you wanted a solicitor that would probably be your first thing it says that...having the *Custody record* the *Codes of practice* I think those probably come at the right end   [Occasional 45]

Some indeed felt that the *Notice* was somewhat persuasive. Regular 12, for example, noted that it implied a directive: "*look (.) get a solicitor*". Regular 45 agreed that those *in doubt* might particularly feel this. It seems, from detainees' comments, that the Sergeant's revision achieved his aim of highlighting this right. Whether these revisions to sequence and content, alone, would reduce interactions like the one at the beginning of the chapter is unclear.

5.3   Discourse organisation between sections

5.3.1   Restrictions on rights and prohibitions from their exercise

Some of the problems of sequence discussed above also afflicted other sections. These sequential problems had the potential to generate misunderstandings which would prevent detainees from invoking their rights. These problems centred on failing to present "the general before the specific and the overall statement or rule before any...exceptions" (Tiersma, 1999a:208–9). The text presents relatively unusual restrictions (to specific detainees' rights) and prohibitions (which apply in specific situations) before outlining the rights' normal operation.

The Parent *Notice*'s presentation of the right to a solicitor illustrates the problem. This section's second paragraph indicates that the whole right might be withheld in *certain exceptional circumstances*. The section limits the right before even outlining it thus implying that limitation is quite likely (Shuy, 1990:293–6). Early sentences like these are "given more weight [by readers] as measured by longer reading times and more frequent reinspections" than later ones (Goldman and Rakestraw, 2000:317). Yet, these circumstances apply to few detainees. After several unrelated paragraphs, the section reiterates the existence of *certain* restrictive *circumstances* part-way through its fifth paragraph. Repetition reinforces the impression that restrictions are likely. The text returns to restrictions again in a completely different section of the *Notice*. Thus, information about restrictions is scattered through the *Notice*, twice within the section on the right to legal advice:

> Access to legal advice can only be delayed in certain exceptional circumstances. [Paragraph 2]

> ... there are certain circumstances in which the police may question you without a solicitor... [Paragraph 5]

Once within the section on the right to external contact:

> The right can only be delayed in exceptional circumstances.

These propositions are very different from their cotext in three main ways. First, and perhaps most obviously, they are topically distinctive – withholding rather than providing rights. Secondly, they have a very different audience from their cotext, consisting of the relatively few detainees they affect, fewer than one in just under every 4000 according to Bucke and Brown (1997:viii). They deliver information which is not for all readers before and amongst that which is (cf. Dumas, 1990:349). Finally, these propositions have relative unexpectedness. Detainees in these data were surprised to learn of possible rights restrictions – writers must consider this.

Just as these restrictions are distinguished from their cotext by these three factors, they are correlatively connected to one another by the same factors: topic-focus, a relatively small audience and unexpectedness. Nonetheless, they are not connected to one another in the Parent text, except through some lexical coincidences. Their prominence and repetition unduly foreground possible ineligibility for rights. This may particularly confuse the 6 per cent of detainees who Bucke and Brown found did not receive their requested legal advice, for reasons other than those covered by these restrictions (1997:viii).

All rewriters attended to these scattered restrictions. Two of the information designers were sufficiently convinced that these clauses were irrelevant to most readers that they removed some or all of them, either incorporating them in a separate document (EnterpriseB) or asking officers to explain, only when necessary (EnterpriseD). Others grouped restrictions and moved them to the end of the section in which they originally occurred (EnterpriseA, EnterpriseC, the Sergeant).

These restrictions were not the only anomalous propositions in the Parent *Notice*. It also contained equally different and unexpected propositions which circumscribe detainees' conduct: prohibitions. These, too, were distributed throughout, contributing to a muddled patchwork of giving and withholding rights, offering and forbidding. One occurred in the section on the right to legal advice:

> Your right ... does not entitle you to delay procedures under the Road Traffic Act. [Paragraph 7]

And two in the section on the right to see the *Codes*. In that section, which is ostensibly concerned with offering the *Codes*, prohibitions dominated. Almost three-quarters of its words deal with prohibiting rather than providing (highlighted in bold):

> The Codes of practice will be made available to you on request. **The right to consult the Codes of practice does not allow you to delay unreasonably any necessary investigative and administrative action neither does it allow procedures under the Road Traffic Act 1988 to be delayed.**

These prohibitive clauses may appear to the analyst or writer somewhat superfluous like the restrictions discussed above. Those which concern *procedures under the Road Traffic Act* relate to situations which will be relatively unambiguous and in all cases the officers who wish to prevent detainees from delaying will be on hand, by definition, to explain their actions because the procedures in question involve obtaining bodily samples from detainees. Accordingly, some of the writers responded, as they had to the restrictions, by removing some or all of these propositions (EnterpriseA, EnterpriseC). However, interviews with custody officers revealed that these prohibitions were, for them, an important part of the *Notice* because they apply to the frequent activity of demanding samples from unwilling detainees. Officers described using these sections as a written authority in potentially confrontational situations, holding up the paper to validate their position. The Sergeant had accordingly moved the prohibition relating to the right to a solicitor to its own page at the back of his text, and indeed officers described finding this detached prohibition easier to invoke within their verbal explanations than when it had been buried within running text. Thus, whilst restrictions and prohibitions appeared to demand the same treatment as one another their place for participants is very different, text about restrictions being a rarely used distraction and that about prohibitions an important tool for Sergeants. The Sergeant reviser's text thus reflected his experience, relocating useful text to make it more useful (at the end of the document) and relocating largely irrelevant text for minimal interference (at the end of each section). The Government revision built on the Sergeant's scheme by moving all text which noted restrictions and prohibitions out of the main body of the text to its back page (Appendix 6 and Figure 5.3).

These relocations are perhaps the most important development made when we transformed the Sergeant's text into the Government version because they separate sections which give rights (the main body) from those which withhold or modify them (the back page), thus separating sections for relatively few readers from those for all, and unexpected

---

Special Times

Getting a solicitor to help you
There are some special times when the police might ask you questions before you have talked to a solicitor. Information about these special times is given in the *Codes of practice*. This is the book that that sets out what the police can and cannot do while you are at the police station. If you want to look up the details, they are in paragraph 6.6 of *Code C* of the *Codes of practice*.

There is one special time when the police will not let you speak to the solicitor that you have chosen. When this happens the police must let you talk to another solicitor. If you want to look it up, it is in Annex B of *Code C* of the *Codes of practice*.
— Restrictions

Telling someone that you are at the police station
There are some special times when the police will not allow you to contact anyone. Information about these special times is given in the *Codes of practice*. If you want to look it up, it is in Annex B of *Code C* of the *Codes of practice*.

Breath tests
If you are under arrest because of a drink drive offence, you have the right to speak to a solicitor. That right does not mean you can refuse to give the police samples of breath, blood or urine, even if you have not yet spoken to a solicitor.
— Prohibitions

Figure 5.3   Back page of the Government revision

from more predictable material. This arrangement also avoids the implication, stemming from repetition, that rights are likely to be withheld or detainees constrained and allows the rights-giving sections to be organised more cohesively. Understanding a text "includes understanding the connections between the points being made" (Hoey, 1988:57). The visual separation of restrictions and prohibitions intends to make connections explicit, thus saving readers from the task of untangling them. We organised the back page around titles which correspond to those in the body of the *Notice* to indicate the relationship between restrictions and the sections which they govern. As rewriters' changes at different levels of language interact with one another (Davison and Kantor, 1982:205), this restructuring had knock-on effects on lower-level features. It reduced internal contradictions and pronominal and lexical ambiguity.

5.3.2 Knock-on effects from improving discourse sequence

Turning first to internal contradictions, the restrictions, which deny rights to some individuals, and the prohibitions, which deny rights in some situations, directly contradict reassurances which also permeate the Parent *Notice*. The text opened by summarising all rights and then assuring detainees:

(1) YOU MAY DO ANY OF THESE THINGS NOW, BUT IF YOU DO NOT, YOU MAY STILL DO SO AT ANY OTHER TIME WHILST DETAINED AT THE POLICE STATION

Within the *Notice*'s body too, the prepositional phrase *at any time* stresses flexibility about invoking the right to legal advice:

(2) You can speak to a solicitor at the police station **at any time**, day or night. [Paragraph 1]
(3) You can ask for legal advice **at any time** during your detention. [Paragraph 6]
(4) Even if you tell the police you do not want a solicitor at first, you can change your mind **at any time**. [Paragraph 6]

Cotext indicates that the phrase *at any time* is used polysemously, describing flexibility within:

- **the 24-hour clock** – in occurrence 2, the recast *day and night* suggests rights pertain even if it is 4AM or lunch time, for example;

- **the ongoing detention period** – in occurrences 1 and 3, the prepositional phrase *during your detention* suggests even if you are being interviewed, for example;
- **an unspecified time-frame** – in occurrence 4, cotext does not delimit.

The Parent *Notice* thus suggests both that rights can be exercised at any time (through these reassurances), and that they cannot (through the restrictions and prohibitions just discussed), yet its disorganisation conceals this contradiction. The assertion that rights can be invoked at any time is also somewhat contradicted by a directive asserting that detainees seeking legal advice should do so *at once* (paragraph 6, the right to a solicitor). Most rewriters noted this, finding *at once* unnecessary, particularly as a directive. This contradiction was easily resolved. Conversely, the contradiction between the *at any time* phrases and the restrictions and prohibitions is somewhat unavoidable. Logically, this could be resolved by stating that detainees can *normally* invoke their rights at any time. However incorporating *normally* would allow propositions which apply infrequently to dilute those which apply frequently. The Government text's relocation of restrictions and prohibitions resolves this. The repositioning avoids concealing the contradiction, by asserting that the rights are not time-restrained in the main body and only describing time-restrictions where they apply.

In addition, the relocation illustrated in Appendix 6 addressed confusion caused by 'simplification' around pronouns. The Parent *Notice* asserted *There are certain circumstances in which the police may question you without a solicitor*. This sentence should address only some readers. However, all readers might feel personally addressed through these second-person forms. This was intensified in the Sergeant's proposed new *Notice*, which increased the incidence of second-person pronouns, a common ploy in revising impersonal texts (Davison and Kantor, 1982:202).

> ...the police can ask you questions before you have talked to a solicitor...the police can stop you having a solicitor...the police will not allow you to contact anyone...

Some detainees correctly understood that these restrictions related to particular people detained in relation to particular crimes, suggesting they applied *in situations around arms* or *if you're a terrorist* (Regulars 35; 50). Others believed that the restrictions applied to them (Regular 12).

One detainee even erroneously believed that the restrictions had been invoked in his case (Novice 11). As Ng has observed, second-person address can be a great motivator (1990). Moving the restrictions and prohibitions out of the main text made it clear that those items only addressed a sub-set of readers.

Ambiguity caused by the discoursal positioning of restrictions and prohibitions in the Parent *Notice* is compounded by lexical challenges within those restrictions and prohibitions. The three clauses which limit rights feature the head *circumstances* modified by *exceptional* and, in one instance, *certain*. These lexical items are vague, having "no clear cut-off points or borderlines" (Walton, 1996:2–3). They appear to be precise but are not (cf. Labov and Harris, 1994:266–76). Specifically:

- pluralisation on *circumstances* makes it unclear whether legal advice is only restricted if several different circumstances coincide or whether one of several possible circumstances might apply;
- *certain* does not detail how numerous these circumstances are;
- *exceptional* might seem to specify *certain* but invites questions itself: Exceptional, in terms of what? By whose definition? Detainees may be unable to answer such questions and to thus distinguish an *exceptional* circumstance from any other;
- the whole string, as a description of frequency, may be understood by readers in unexpected ways, as are other frequency terms such as *seldom* and *regularly* (Wright, 1999:87–8).

Clare and Gudjonsson report that experimental subjects who read the original *Notice* were indeed "unsure of the meaning of *exceptional circumstances*" (1992:8). We might expect the rewriters to respond to such ambiguous vocabulary (Davison and Kantor, 1982:205), and four did. EnterpriseA was the most inventive, seeking to clarify by exemplifying *circumstances*. Others removed one or both words (EnterpriseE, EnterpriseA) or replaced *exceptional* with *a few* (EnterpriseC) or *some* (EnterpriseE) – possibly more familiar, but still vague, words. The Sergeant replaced *exceptional circumstances* with *special times*. This formulation was also used by Clare and Gudjonsson who produced a research-driven version of the *Notice* which was never introduced (1992). Unfortunately, for detainees *special times* introduced unintended and apparently distracting connotations. First, *times* convinced some detainees that there are particular *times* of day when rights might be denied (for example late at night) or particular *times* during an individual's detention (for example early in detention). Secondly, *special* had positive connotations connected to 'special treat' for some detainees. Most importantly, the formulation is no more informative than *exceptional circumstances*, both offering, what Owen calls, a "bureaucratic escape hatch", a flexibility which will "tend to favour the rule-makers over the governed" (1996:293). Oddly, there is no reason for such vagueness here. The *circumstances* referred to in this part of the text are tightly defined and clearly delineated so it is not necessary for rights notices to focus on their vague aspects; their infrequency (*exceptional*) or importance (*special*). This should be addressed in future rewrites but the Home Office did not wish to specify it in the 2004 revision.

The Sergeant was firm on not only using the formulation *Special times* within his text but also as the title of his back page (see Figure 5.3) due to its capacity to replace more formal wordings. As a title, the formulation does not serve well because it does not prospect the text which it is intended to label or directly address its limited audience. Something like *Have the police stopped you from having your rights?*, *Why might the police limit your rights?* or *Reasons that some people are not allowed all of their rights* might be more informative.

The prohibitions also contain vague lexis in noting that whilst exercising the right to read the *Codes* detainees are forbidden from delaying *unreasonably any necessary investigative and administrative action*. Detainees are unlikely to know which police actions are *necessary* and by whose definition (Investigators? Custody staff? Rules?) or what would constitute an *unreasonable* as opposed to a reasonable delay. If, for example, officers wanted to transport a detainee between police stations and the detainee wanted to delay, until having read the *Codes* to discover whether this was a *necessary action*, would the detainee be delaying *unreasonably*? As with *exceptional circumstances*, redrafters removed or replaced these words thereby also removing grammatical metaphor (EnterpriseB, EnterpriseD, EnterpriseC):

to delay ... investigative and administrative action →

to delay
  anything that the police need to do [EnterpriseC]
  police work   [EnterpriseD]
  the police   [EnterpriseB]

This whole sub-section illustrates the power of discourse sequence. If these *restrictions and prohibitions* had not been moved to the back of the document they would have remained problematic. Once on the back page, it becomes clear that each restriction is *special* because it is part of a general set of *special times*; second-person pronouns address only a sub-set of readers directly so contradictions have nothing to contradict. The back page placement therefore offers a way to avoid either omitting or foregrounding restrictions and prohibitions.

5.4 Intertextuality

The *Notice* sits at the end of an intertextual chain (Fairclough, 1992:130) which runs predominantly from the Police and Criminal Evidence Act (1984) (PACE). Although the *Notice* does not mention PACE explicitly, it is manifestly intertextual with the intervening link, the *Codes of practice*, through a series of cross-references to *Annex B of Code of practice C* and *paragraph 6.6 of Code of practice C*. Bhatia sees cross-references as "textual-mapping devices" which reduce information load (in Jackson, 1995:195). Jackson however cautions that cross-referencing can involve "complex intellectual operations" (1995:129). Sure enough, readers who move through the *Notice* linearly will encounter three cross-references to the *Codes* before the term itself is glossed. Indeed, if they do not read the document fully they may never meet the gloss. These unexplained references assume that:

- detainees will know what the *Codes* are and how to obtain them when reading the early cross-references, in which case the later gloss is redundant; or
- readers will hold the cross-references in mind until they reach the gloss and then remember the references sufficiently to follow-up or discard. This makes expectations about detainees' literacy and memory.

Recognising this, the Sergeant glossed the *Codes* alongside his text's first cross-reference:

> This is the book that sets out what the police can and cannot do while you are at the police station.

He also expanded the referential formulations. The Parent text had simply provided the directives *see Annex B...* and *see paragraph 6.6...* which assume that detainees will understand how the referenced text relates to the *Notice*. In contrast, the Sergeant combined a conditional (*If you want to look up the details*) and declarative (*they are in paragraph...*) which enunciates the relationship between the referring and referenced texts and explains the process of following a reference. Several of the information designers used this combination too, however it was not entirely successful. Some detainees expected this kind of organisation (Regulars, 16 and 50) and used it comfortably (Novice 34).Others understood what the references were but remained uncomfortable with using them:

> I could have a book that's got the *Codes of practice* in it...but what [reads aloud] "paragraph 6.6 of *Code C* of the *Codes of practice*" is I don't know   [Novice 10]

Readers who understand the concept of a cross-reference might still be stumped by the text-organisation conventions within these particular references: annexes; paragraphs and sub-paragraphs. EnterpriseC attended to this by removing all specifics, replacing them with a directive about talk: *Please ask to see the relevant part of the Codes*, unperturbed by the reduction in detail. She optimistically proposed that, as a useful by-product, resulting interactions might encourage detainees to ask officers other questions.

We can help readers by identifying aspects of texts and text organisation which might be familiar to them which they might "hook predictions onto" as readers will predict "on the basis of what is already familiar" (Baynham, 1995:189). In the case of the *Codes* detainees did indeed describe searching for the familiar. Those who had not engaged with the detail of cross-references in the Sergeant's *Notice* navigated or would have navigated the *Codes* using other reading practices. One suggested that detainees would read the book from start to finish as *it's not that big* (Regular 36). Others used analogies with the organisation of other specific texts. One explained that he expected the *Codes* to be alphabetic through reference to dictionary conventions (Novice 26). A larger number invoked generic expectations about the organisation of informative books, proposing that, unconvinced by the references, they would have sought an index. The Sergeant anticipated this and capitalised on it. He proposed to insert a summary index into the back of each copy of the *Codes*, pointing only to items of particular relevance to detainees. He introduced this index at the beginning of his *Notice of entitlements*:

> To find out more, ask to see the book called the Codes of practice. Inside its back cover you will find a list of where to find all these things.

Unfortunately, few detainees apparently spotted this pointer; only two even alluded to it. Nonetheless, prevalence of mention of an index, even amongst those detainees who were only hypothesising about how they might have looked up information, suggests that they might use a summary index even if they only find it by chance. Thus providing a dedicated index offers one way to draw on detainees' existing literacy practices.

Some previous research on rights texts implied that readers' practices were irrelevant. Gudjonsson, for example, expresses interest only in people's abilities "to read and comprehend the content of the document irrespective of their knowledge of the law" (1990:27). Yet personal interests can influence reading practices, precipitating "the active pursuit of experiences, knowledge and skills associated with those interests" (Alexander and Jetton, 2000:298) and enabling readers to "become expert" in particular parts of domains like health and law (Barton and Hamilton, 1998:232–3). Reading and writing are part of this, enabling people "to make changes in their lives" (Barton, 1994:50). If, in studying reading, we ignore readers, we risk making odd or tantalising claims like Gudjonsson's that "a person with an IQ below 100 is unlikely to understand all the sentences in the document, although he or she may be familiar with his or her legal rights" (1990:27). Using cross-references in the *Notices* is not simply about tracing links and identifying glosses. Some detainees described being simply too nervous to even contemplate the *Codes*:

> I was going to ask what the *Codes of practice* were but I thought well I'm in a whole new world of trouble as it is [Novice 25]

For others, however, the references had an affective function, suggesting that the *Codes* and implicitly the *Notice* are not 'for' detainees in two ways. First, their level of detail connoted, for some, a specialist audience. Secondly, all of the *Notice's* references direct readers towards parts of the *Codes* which restrict or deny rights not parts which offer them. This is unfortunate because cross-referencing "authorises only those connections which are explicitly made; others...are implicitly excluded" (Jackson, 1995:129). Detainees' comments revealed that the resulting representation of the *Codes* suggests that it is concerned only with exception and irregularity. Even some who had read the *Codes* proposed that they related to *very serious crime...terrorism...bank robberies* (Occasional 45). As one detainee who claimed to have closely read the *Codes* observed:

there was sort of only probably one or two paragraphs that really involved me anyway um the rest was all sort of anti-terrorism and all this kind of thing   [Novice 34]

Perhaps as a result of this apparent preoccupation relatively few detainees expressed any interest in reading the *Codes*.

When working on a common text different writers in different writing situations produce revisions which overlap in some ways but differ markedly in others.

Chapters 4 and 5 have explored and illustrated how text features function and combine to have various effects one on another and on readers. However these final paragraphs, about readers' claims to expertise through engagement or claims to indifference through lack of engagement, place readers firmly in the picture by indicating that texts are only as comprehensible as their readers allow them to be. This theme is taken up in the final two chapters of Part II.

6
Working with Context: Rights Texts in Custody

6.1 Introduction

In seeking to improve comprehensibility, exclusively text-focussed revision is insufficient (Dumas, 2000:56) and can even produce texts which are "worse" than their originals (Schriver, 1989:244). Likewise, in examining revision, a focus only on text risks objectifying misunderstanding "as something to be grasped as exterior to the participants who are involved" (Hinnenkamp, 2003:60). This focus could lead both revisers and analysts to ignore the influence of "features of everyday language" like indirectness, reader's role and prior knowledge (Clark, 1996). Therefore the final two chapters in this part consider how the Sergeant revision, the main focus here, was received by detainees in custody. This makes it possible to "ascertain [the text's] value in real life" (Clare and Gudjonsson, 1992:1) and explore "whether [it] is in fact understood by typical subjects" (Owen, 1996:285). To explore reformulation in context one must observe both how texts are used and how "different participants construct what is going on for themselves and others" (Baynham, 1995:187). I will therefore begin by illustrating the Sergeant's intentions, showing how he sought to make his text work for detainees. Where possible, detainees' comments were used to refine the Sergeant's text before it was circulated to police forces and some of those revisions are also described in this chapter.

6.2 The Sergeant's aspirations

Early in his writing process, the Sergeant identified two main aims for his rewrite. He realised the first aim, balancing *simple* and *legal*, described in 3.5.1, through lexical replacement and syntactic change. However this rendered his second aim, creating a one-page document, problematic. In the Sergeant's words *every complex word that you take and explain (.) it takes four, five, ten sometimes*; 'simplifying' lengthened the document. This led him to unpick his second aim and ultimately pursue the underlying motivation he uncovered – brevity. He achieved brevity by building his text on a *three-tiered* structure (Figure 6.1).

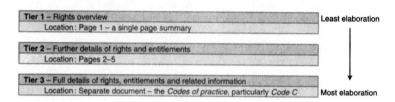

Figure 6.1   The Sergeant's three-tiered structure

The Sergeant described tier 1, the initial overview, achieving a modified version of his brevity aim. Whilst he had not produced a one-page rights document, he had achieved a one-page rights summary supported by two more detailed tiers. The Parent *Notice* used a summary too, but the Sergeant proposed that its lexis, layout and position made it *intimidating*. In contrast his isolated, large overview was intended to make reading the summary and recognising it as summary almost unavoidable. The Sergeant anticipated that detainees who were unable or unwilling to read the whole *Notice* could hardly avoid seeing the first-page overview, his first tier, which relays what he called *the key parts*.[1] This summary page is analogous to a proposal by Clare and Gudjonsson for a card for detainees summarising key rights information (1992).

The Sergeant saw increasing elaboration through the three tiers as crucial to his document. He explained that readers would take up this structure differently, depending on their:

- **Reading ability** – some would only view page 1, whilst *somebody who can read a bit better* might read pages 2–5 and very *able* readers would request the *Codes*;
- **Desire for detail** – the first tier supplies minimal readers but *if they wanted any more they delve in a bit further*, reading pages 2–5 and could use the *Codes* to find out *even more*.

The Sergeant anticipated that the structure would further function to give readers autonomy, enabling them to be *self-selective as to how far they... go through.* Figure 6.2 shows how his document, containing his first two tiers, materialised.

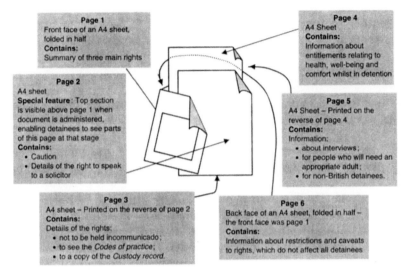

Page 1
Front face of an A4 sheet,
folded in half
Contains:
Summary of three main rights

Page 2
A4 sheet
Special feature: Top section
is visible above page 1 when
document is administered,
enabling detainees to see parts
of this page at that stage
Contains:
• Caution
• Details of the right to speak
  to a solicitor

Page 3
A4 sheet – Printed on the reverse of page 2
Contains:
Details of the rights:
• not to be held incommunicado;
• to see the *Codes of practice*;
• to a copy of the *Custody record*.

Page 4
A4 Sheet
Contains:
Information about
entitlements relating to
health, well-being and
comfort whilst in detention

Page 5
A4 Sheet – Printed on the
reverse of page 4
Contains:
Information:
• about interviews;
• for people who will need an
  appropriate adult;
• for non-British detainees.

Page 6
Back face of an A4 sheet, folded in half –
the front face was page 1
Contains:
Information about restrictions and caveats
to rights, which do not affect all detainees

Figure 6.2 The Sergeant's text (see Appendix 4)

Particular lexicalisations were intended to reinforce this structure's potential to engage readers. For example, the Sergeant explained the sub-heading *Getting a solicitor to help you*, and its location – on page 2 but visible above page 1 when the document was closed – saying:

> it feeds you in to (.) opening it if you like it's "oh how <u>do</u> you get a solicitor to help you?"... if they've just got that [unfolded A4 pages] ...they go (.) you know "is it something frightening that's inside the first page?"

As well as its positioning, the formulation of this sub-heading expects that detainees will, having opened the document, be wondering how to invoke a right which they already recognise from cotext (the first page rights summary) and from context (custody desk talk). The Sergeant began all sub-headings with *-ing* participle verbs, foregrounding actions in each case (for example, *Looking at the Codes...*; *Having the Custody record*). Thus, each right was presented as given which reinforced intra-textual ties to the tier 1 summary and extratextual ties to earlier interactions.

Some detainees appeared aware of, and comfortable with, the Sergeant's structure:

> the way I saw it you read this [indicates page 1, the first tier] and it tells you what you can do and then you know if you're not sure about any of it see you can read this [indicates pages 2–5, the second tier] ... it was self-explanatory really "here's your rights you know (.) you don't understand it? read the next page" [Novice 25]

Other detainees addressed the third tier, noting that the *Codes* would add detail:

> they tell you everything in the *Codes of practice* this [indicates the *Notices*] just tells you basic   [Regular 50]

Others were oblivious to this, overlooking the difference between parts of the *Notice*. Occasional 7, for example, saw the document as *one handout really* rather than *further-details* attached to an overview. Regular 12 could imagine no difference between the *Notices* and the *Codes*. Readers who had not identified the tripartite structure encountered an odd, repetitive text floating in textual space.

In the light of these observations, when the Sergeant's *Notice* was revised to become the Government revision we sought to highlight inter- and intra-textual relationships more fully. We used lexical changes and added a metalinguistic sweetener on the summary page: *You will find more details about these rights inside.* The Sergeant had deliberately omitted such metalanguage, believing that encouragement to read should be contextual rather than cotextual and should emanate particularly from the custody sergeant. As well as locating his document in a textual world, through this tripartite structure, then, the Sergeant was also concerned that his text should be located in interactions between detainees and officers.

6.3 Characterising the Sergeant's text: Orienting to detainees

Concern for detainees, manifest in attempts to present information from the detainee's perspective, was a central feature of the Sergeant's text. Reformulation potentially realigns the social world because it involves "processes of categorisation and selection" through which "participants attempt to impose their own modes of interpretation on others" (Lee, 1992:21). In these revisions, rather than imposing their own sense on detainees, the revisers tried to take the detainee's perspective, inventively drawing the reader into the text. This is exemplified through their treatment of the Parent *Notice*'s string *Road Traffic Act*. This label contains "high frequency" or at least "short" words which writing guidelines would deceptively identify as "easy" yet which combine into a label which might mystify detainees unfamiliar with legislation (Owen, 1996:292). Both the Sergeant and EnterpriseB accordingly replaced reference to the *Act* with reference to *offences*. Whilst subject to the *Act*, detainees will be accused of *offences* so both reasoned that *offences* would be more salient to detainees. The Sergeant also refers not to *road traffic* but *drink driving offences*. This increases specificity and accuracy, and responds to Owen's observation that collocational familiarity of terms like *drink driving* might assist detainees (1996:294).

The Parent *Notice*'s formulation *independent solicitor* presents the solicitor through their relationship to police, not detainees, yet does not acknowledge this perspective which makes *independent* ambiguous. The Sergeant revision transforms this noun phrase, not by simply substituting a more 'familiar' word for *independent*, but by representing solicitors' independence from the police in terms of its implications for detainees:

An independent solicitor	→	a solicitor to help you while you are at the police station
[Parent version]	→	[Sergeant]

In a related sentence, the Parent text presented the detainee's consultation with the solicitor in terms of its appearance to officers:

You can talk to the solicitor in private [Parent version]

The Sergeant replaced *private* which at best implies the involvement of at least two people by zooming in on the detainee, enlarging on privacy in terms of its implications for detainees:

You can talk to a solicitor... **without the police knowing what you are telling him or her** [Sergeant]

In some instances the Sergeant's familiarity with custody helped him to write with detainees in mind where the other authors could not. The Parent *Notice* states:

> If the police want to question you, you can ask for the solicitor to be there. **If there is a delay, ask the police to contact the solicitor again.** Normally the police must not question you until you have spoken to the solicitor.

The highlighted sentence neither states who or what might be delayed, nor who or what by, rendering it ambiguous. The cotext included above suggests two possible readings:

> *if there is a delay . . . :*
> '. . . in beginning questioning' (assumes anaphora with preceding sentence);
> '. . . in the solicitor's arrival' (assumes cataphora with subsequent sentence).

The Enterprise rewriters took *delay* to refer to delay in solicitors' arrival but doubted its relevance, suspecting that police would chase-up absent solicitors routinely. Accordingly, two of them removed the whole sentence. In contrast, the Sergeant's experience was that this proposition could encourage detainees who erroneously believed they had requested a solicitor to seek clarification. His familiarity with anxious detainees led him to maintain reference to delay and insert an extra proposition which addressed another common concern:

If there is a delay,	→	If a solicitor does not come,
ø		or you need to speak to the solicitor again,
ask the police to contact the solicitor again.	→	ask the police to contact him or her again.
[Parent text]	→	[Sergeant text]

The Sergeant consistently oriented his text to detainees through his knowledge of both detention and detainees' responses to detention. This led him to alter levels of specificity as in the following two, separate excerpts:

ask for the solicitor to be **there with you**	→	ask for the solicitor to be **in the** room
A record . . . **will be kept** by the custody officer [Parent text]	→	ø [Sergeant text]

In the first example the *Notice*'s anaphoric *there* which could imply that the solicitor might be at the police station but not in the interview itself is replaced by the Sergeant's more detailed formulation. The second example sees the Sergeant removing detail about who maintains the *Custody record*, believing officers' tasks are irrelevant to detainees.

In some sections, the Sergeant orients to detainees subtly but consistently. For example, his revision of the section on the right to a copy of the *Custody record*, which, atypically for him, contains more words than its source, shifts from the abstract formulations of the Parent text to more concrete representations:

(i)	the record **will be kept**	→	everything that happens **is put on paper**
(ii)	this [right] **lasts for 12 months**	→	you can **ask** for up to twelve months
(iii)	when you leave police detention	→	when you leave **the police station**

In (i), the Sergeant moves from prospection into certainty by removing auxiliary *will*. He also replaces *kept* by specifying how the record will be kept, *on paper*, objectifying the record by presenting it as a real, written text. When referring to time, in (ii), he replaces the tricky abstract entity, an entitlement lasting for a duration, with the more concrete idea of making a request within a time-limit. Excerpt (iii) sees the notion of leaving an abstract state (*police detention*) replaced with that of leaving a physical place (*the police station*).

Of course, the Sergeant may not be best placed to evaluate readers' needs as he has different "conventions of meaning" from them (Orasanu and Penney, 1986:2) and does not share their naivety (cf. Davison and Kantor, 1982:207). However, he had, at least, thought carefully in orienting to readers. This care was evident at all levels of his text. He explained how he had assigned structure:

when they're sat in their cell…what are they going to be saying (.) they're not going to say "I wonder what's for lunch" I mean the regular criminals do…but I mean if you've been arrested for the first time and thrown in a cell (.) the thoughts that are going through your head are "who can help me" [reads from his text] "tell the police if you want a solicitor" [mimics] "um I was due to see my mom and dad this afternoon" [reads] (.) "tell the police if you want somebody told" (.) and then we do have to say- they're not going to say the *Codes of practice* but if they do (.) [mimics] "ooh what's happening what's going on what's the process"

The Sergeant recursively asks "what would the reader do next?", projecting likely psychological processes (Wright, 1981:12) and using his conception of the situated meanings that will accompany his text to envisage readers' experiences and needs.

However, detainees did not respond as one might anticipate. The Parent *Notice*'s section on the right to contact someone outside detention presents the cost of invoking that right from an institutional point of view (*at public expense*) rather than from that of the detainee (*free to you*). We can only speculate unfavourably on possible motivations for adopting the institution's perspective. Despite the Sergeant transforming this to *it is free*, one detainee indicated that the very concept of public expense discouraged those who wished to minimise imposition, or to be seen to minimise imposition, from invoking rights. The Sergeant's move towards the detainee's perspective did not realign the social world for this detainee. Whilst presenting information with the detainee in mind is certainly preferable to ignoring the detainee, in this instance at least, the texts' underlying meaning was distracting, however it was expressed.

6.4   Was the Sergeant revision 'objectively' successful?

Detainees who read the Sergeant text positively evaluated its appearance, unprompted, praising, for example, its use of bullets and space (*it's better…not on one piece of paper all squashed up*, Regular 29) and layout (*it's pretty well set out*, Regular 13). Looking to more substantive matters, some detainees demonstrated that the Sergeant's *Notice* enabled them to locate information easily in order to check details (Novice 10). Others had read so carefully that they noticed such features as a lack of parallelism between sections:

F   is there any time of day that you couldn't make a
    'phone call?
D   um I never read that in there that there wasn't at any
    time of day I did read that a solicitor was there for day
    and night I don't know about the 'phone call it didn't
    mention 'phone calls day and night   [Occasional 45]

Detailed reading had led this detainee towards inferences concluding "from the absence of information that certain possibilities do not exist" (Labov and Harris, 1994:275). Certainly then, some detainees considered the Sergeant's revision carefully, some even made positive general comments on comprehensibility (*it's more easier to read*, Regular 28), but was the text successful? Did detainees who received it in custody show signs of rights comprehension? Did detainees understand more than they might have from the Parent *Notice*? Superficially detainees answered questions in a way which suggested so. Crudely summarising their comments on each right in turn, almost all were able to explain how they would get a solicitor if they wished to with only two exceptions (Occasional 40; Novice 21). Similarly, most knew that they could speak to a solicitor at any time during detention and at any time of the day or night. Four were unsure of this (Occasionals, 40, 41; Novices 15, 24). One, for example, thought detainees only became eligible to receive legal advice after 6 hours of detention. Additionally, only one detainee thought that he needed to know a solicitor in order to call one; all others seemed comfortable with the concept of a duty solicitor.

All apparently knew about their right to send a telephone message (explained within the *Notice*) and entitlement to make a telephone call (explained within the *Notice of entitlements*), some in considerable detail, despite a tendency to conflate these two forms of contact (cf. Brown, 1997:80). Information about the *Codes* seemed more troublesome, which Brown would attribute to lack of understanding of what the *Codes* are or why they might be useful (1997:80). Indeed 42 per cent of detainees initially claimed uncertainty about what they were. However further talk revealed that many knew that they had something to do with police procedure. Many ultimately commented on the *Codes*:

- Format:
a booklet	[Occasional 03]
a little tiny booklet thing	[Regular 36]

- Content:
where you stand	[Occasional 32]
the rules that they've [the police] got to abide by	[Regular 07]
what you're allowed and what you're not allowed	[Regular 50]

- Or both format and content:

a flimsy book it's only got them in it like what you can and can't do   [Occasional 32]

a booklet of the law what the police have to abide by   [Occasional 08]

Clare and Gudjonsson attribute some apparent incomprehension in interviews about their simplified *Notice* to their interviewees' reluctance to provide answers which seemed obvious. They point particularly to the section of their text which asserts *The Codes of practice is a book* (1992:23). Unwillingness to state the obvious seemed to be a factor in detainees' comments on the Sergeant's text too, illustrating just one reason not to rely only on quantitative interview data to investigate understanding (see Section 2.3).

Detainees were able to say less about the right to a copy of the *Custody record*. Many were confused about what the *Custody record* might be, what right they had in connection with it and when and why they might invoke that right. Ninety-three per cent of novices, 71 per cent of occasionals and 36 per cent of regulars appeared to have no idea what the *record* was. Experience of detention seemed more significant than reading. Crucially, many detainees did not even remember having encountered the term *Custody record*. The major finding of questions about the *Custody record* was, then, that very few detainees read this far into the Sergeant text. In fact it was clear from the interviews that detainees did not necessarily read the *Notices* at all yet many did know a good deal about their rights. This clearly requires more investigation.

6.5   What happened to the Sergeant version in practice?

Brown reports that many studies have shown that "90% or more" of detainees receive and sign for written rights notices, yet that even their signatures do not guarantee that the texts were really administered (1997:76). Clare and Gudjonsson too report anecdotally that the *Notice* is read by "only a minority" of detainees (1992:21). It is meaningless to assess any rights text without considering whether ostensible readers have in fact read it. My study revealed a chasm between having been offered a written rights notice and accepting it, and between accepting and reading it. Many officers were sceptical about detainees' take-up of the *Notices*, observing, *they never seem to read them or take them to the cells to read them* (Officer A1) and *it's all some kind of bravado thing not to accept it* (Officer A18). Some detainees shared their doubts:

[detainees] want to get out there's enough stress and that really (.) normally [the *Notices*] just get chucked around   [Regular 36]

everybody thinks they know their rights...I suppose it's a shame for those people that have just come in...but do they read them? [Regular 16]

The data gathered here answer this detainee's question, confirming that the Sergeant text was often discarded by detainees before they had even left the custody desk. In these data:

61%   took the papers from the desk (32)
35%   did not take them (18)[2]

Those who kept a copy did not necessarily read it. Across all detainees:

23%   read both of the Sergeant's *Notices* (12)
21%   read some parts of the papers (11)
56%   did not read the papers at all (29)

Thus, in these data,[3] over half of detainees did not read the available rights text and a third did not even keep a copy.[4] We might expect this from those who are regularly detained, yet Figure 6.3 shows how reading was distributed across regular, occasional and novice detainees (see Section 3.6).

The black columns reveal that less than a third of regular detainees read the rights texts entirely whilst only around a fifth of occasionals and novices did. These figures, although only indicative due to sample size (52 detainees, introduced in Section 3.6), suggest that novices – those who may most need to read the whole text – do not all do so, and indeed do so less than those potentially most familiar with their content – regulars. This low take-up of the whole text by novices is set against the dark grey column on the right, which shows that half of novices read the text in part, more than read it entirely or not at all. Interestingly, as the absence of a dark grey column on the left indicates, no regulars admitted reading only part of the text, they either claimed to have read it all or ignored it. In summary, more detainees disregarded the Sergeant's text than did anything else with it. This indifference could be a defensive response to information overload (cf. Postman, 1995). Some detainees admitted that they simply *couldn't be bothered* to read despite professing no idea what the text contained (Regulars 02, 33).

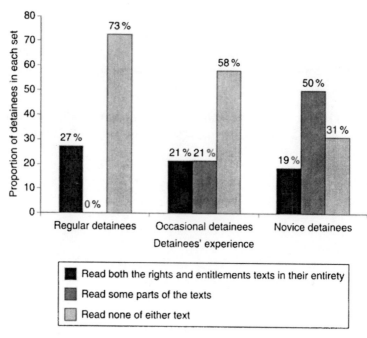

Figure 6.3   Detainees' reading practices

Those who did read presented diverse, often unpredictable reasons for doing so such as boredom (Novice 21; Occasional 27) or a desire to pass the time (Regular 50).

What are we to make of this? If detainees do not read rights texts, an investigation of rights communication which only examines those texts is distracting and pointless. The remainder of Part II therefore systematically investigates interviews with detainees and officers about reading practices in custody and presents these data alongside ethnographic data collected in police custody suites.

I will begin by discussing the reading practices of the rather intriguing set of detainees who read the *Notices* in part.

6.6   Partial readers

All sorts of texts are often read incompletely including forms (Frohlich, 1986), technical texts, which are mostly "used in a consultative fashion" (Diehl and Mikulecky, 1981:5), and functional texts like rights notices whose readers "jump from section to section, sampling content as their question changes" (Wright, 1999:89). Even for people who claim to have read a text, 'reading' may mean very different things. Readers might "visually examine" parts of the text, might skim read or might focus closely on individual words (Morris *et al.*, 1998:88). Partial readers of the Sergeant's revision fell into one of two categories, those who claimed to have:

- dipped into several sections of the *Notice*;
- read only isolated sections, particularly the first-page summary.

Examining the activities involved in both kinds of partial reading illuminates readers' practices. This offers a fresh perspective on the Sergeant's text and a source of further recommendations for that text.

6.6.1 Dipping in

Looking first to readers who dipped into several sections, it is clear that some chose this reading pattern quite deliberately. Occasional 03, for example, read the Sergeant's texts in part, getting a gist of the whole and focusing in according to what he called *need*. Some read to inform specific decisions, like one detainee, Occasional 47, who found her own solicitor was unavailable. She described being *quite interested* in the Sergeant's texts, using them to decide whether she *was going to bother with the duty solicitor*. This phenomenon of having a purpose or question is potent, influencing "willingness and ability" to read and shaping readers' strategies (Diehl and Mikulecky, 1981:5; Hoey, 1988:52). The diverse purposes which readers might bring (Duffy, Curran and Sass, 1983:157), even to a text which seems as mono-dimensional as this, make one definitive rewrite impossible. Asking questions, as Occasional 47 did, is common in reading functional texts. Unfortunately, potential readers without a question might not read unless the text alerts them to "information that they did not realise they needed" (Wright, 1999:89). For readers with or without questions, legal–lay texts are usefully "drafted from the perspective of the actions to be carried out by citizens"; not just providing information but helping readers to respond (Jansen and Steehouder, 2001:21–2). Such texts can use familiar question-based structures which anticipate readers' problems ("my family will be wondering where I am") or goals ("I want to speak to my daughter"), for example (cf. Hoey, 1988:65–9). Some revisions of the *Notice* incorporate questions explicitly. For example, the PEC's version, commissioned by Greater Manchester Police,[5] introduced each section with an interrogative which might echo detainees' concerns:

> Can the police delay my rights?
> What must the police allow me to do?
> How can I get legal advice?

Interrogative sub-headings which potentially engage readers may be more helpful than declarative ones (Hartley, 1981:18). Yet questions risk alienating those for whom they do not resonate. The Sergeant considered detainees' possible questions but transformed these questions into directives in formulating the text using *tell the police if you want...* (see Section 6.3). Directives leave readers in no doubt of the action they need to take to invoke rights.

Different partial readers, without specific questions, skimmed selectively for anything they might need to know. Occasional 06, for example, browsed the Sergeant's *Notices* without reading completely, instead navigating using sub-titles, particularly in the *Notice of entitlements*. Headings and sub-headings supposedly help readers to scan, select, retrieve and comprehend (Goldman and Rakestraw, 2000:315; Hartley, 1981:18). This aspect of the Sergeant's text apparently worked well. One exception was the heading *Having the Custody record* which appeared ineffective perhaps because it included the term *Custody record*, which a number of readers misassigned (see Section 4.3.1). Given that readers described deciding whether to read particular sections using subheadings, the inclusion of this poorly understood technical term here is unhelpful. This was therefore replaced in the Government revision with *Getting details of your time at the police station*. The technical term *Custody record* was then only introduced later, following a gloss (see Section 4.3.1).

The Sergeant's attention to cursory readers was not confined to sub-headings. This is illustrated through his revision of this prosodic sentence from the Parent *Notice*:

> You may on request have one person known to you, or who is likely to take an interest in your welfare, informed at public expense as soon as is practicable of your whereabouts.

As we saw in Section 4.2.4, the Sergeant restructured around a *to*+infinitive declarative. He incorporated the original rank-shifted elements and prepositional phrases into either a single noun phrase, beginning *someone,* or one of two subsequent sentences:

Sergeant

S	V	O
You	can ask	the police

	V	O
	to contact	someone who needs to know that you are at the police station. It is free. They will contact someone for you as soon as they can.

Detainees who only skim the Sergeant's text might disentangle the main proposition more easily than from the original and will get the gist from reading only the first eight words.

6.6.2 Reading opening sections

The other kind of partial readers perused only *bits* of the initial over-view (Occasional 27). Sometimes detainees have no choice but to read incompletely. Novice 26, for example, described only having *a few*

Figure 6.4 Reading in the corridor

minutes to myself in a corridor (Figure 6.4). Appropriate adults (typically a parent, guardian or social worker) are called to give "advice and assistance" (Code C, 2006:para3.18) to juveniles (aged under 17) and detainees who are "mentally disordered or mentally vulnerable" (Code C, 2006:para7.1). By definition they cannot fulfil their role without having read and discussed rights texts with the detainee. Appropriate adults were particularly likely to call on rights information without having had time to read that information fully.

Ideally, detainees and their aides would receive "ample time to study" rights notices (Gudjonsson, 1990:27). My data suggest that in reality readers may only get as far as the opening words so it is crucial that those words convey accessible gist. Unfortunately the opening of the Parent *Notice* potentially discourages would-be readers. The Parent *Notice*'s title, introduction and overview therefore deserve further scrutiny.

Titles are "serious stuff"; we use them when deciding whether to read (Bazerman, 1985; in Swales, 1990:222–4). The Parent *Notice*'s nebulous title *Notice to detained persons* offers orientation without abstract in Labov and Waletzky's terms (1967). It does not prospect content, form or pragmatic intent. In a text which warns, advises and informs, this is risky (Dumas, 1990). Possibly *Notice* intends to convey that the text pragmatically 'notifies'. However, the nominal form appears ineffective, having perhaps undergone semantic bleaching. The text redundantly introduces itself through reference to its already captive audience. It uses the regular but formal pluralisation *persons* to speak to represented rather than interactive participants (Kress and van Leeuwen, 1996:119), institutionally classifying potential readers within an in-detention mass and through *persons* rather than *people* signalling distance between writers and readers (PEC, 1993:34). Enterprise revisers criticised this title. Their titles prospect content and pragmatic intent, incorporate the irregular plural *people* and use second-person reference to personalise. In the original *Notice*'s favour, its title is instantly recognisable to a range of public servants from legislative drafters to custody officers. EnterpriseC identified the dilemma of a label which is salient to insiders but opaque to outsiders. She resolved this by maintaining the original title, reducing its size and preceding it with what she felt was a more useful title for detainees: *About your arrest and your rights*.

The Sergeant was so unimpressed with the original title that he claimed to have removed it from his text. On his second page, visible from the front of the document (Figure 6.5), is a sub-heading which adapts that title but works very differently:

Like the Enterprise writers he criticised the original's institutional orientation, explaining *no one is going to see themselves as a "detained person"*. By renaming the document he removed nominalisation (*Notice*), specified the agent of detention (*police*) and incorporated *people*. Through *information*, he foregrounded one of the text's functions and through *further* created cohesion with the rights summary on his first page. As this title is visible when the folded document is administered the Sergeant also intended *further information* to link exophorically to the custody sergeant's verbal rights explanation at the custody desk.

Once the Parent *Notice* gets underway it immediately suggests that it is not directed at those *detained persons* of its title after all, as Figure 6.5, from the Parent *Notice's* opening, shows.

Looking first to the initial instruction, third-person reference ensures that detainees are not directly addressed. Propositional content too concerns custody officers' responsibilities, not detainees' rights. For detainees who have heard the capitalised sections before reading, the sentence is redundant. For those who have not heard those sections, reading about a procedural oversight does not rectify that oversight. Locally the sentence transforms the subsequent capitalised text into a script through which the organisation acts on the detainee, rather than a pedagogic text to inform the detainee. The

---

The section in capital letters is to be read to the detained person by the custody officer before giving the notice to the detained person.

YOU HAVE THE RIGHT TO:

1 SPEAK TO AN INDEPENDENT SOLICITOR FREE OF CHARGE
2 HAVE SOMEONE TOLD THAT YOU HAVE BEEN ARRESTED
3 CONSULT THE CODES OF PRACTICE COVERING POLICE POWERS
  AND PROCEDURES

YOU MAY DO ANY OF THESE THINGS NOW, BUT IF YOU DO NOT, YOU MAY STILL DO SO AT ANY OTHER TIME WHILST DETAINED AT THE POLICE STATION.

Figure 6.5 The Parent *Notice's* opening

sentence appears to address custody officers, yet they should need no reminding of their core responsibilities so, for them too, the words lack ideational and interpersonal function (Halliday, 2004). Two of the rewriters removed the sentence. The others addressed readers using second-person forms and placed the custody sergeant in the subject position (for example, *your custody officer must read these rights to you*... (EnterpriseC)). The Sergeant's text replaced the instructions to custody sergeants with the formulation *remember your rights*. Whilst this implicitly recalls the custody sergeant's obligation to read rights, it presents given-ness of the upcoming rights overview from the detainee's perspective. Where readers of the Parent *Notice* might have been dissuaded from reading by the prospect of repetition, the Sergeant sought to encourage his readers by the prospect of a reminder. As he explained:

> the custody sergeant has already said (.) "you've got these rights"... and that's why I'm saying here – it is "remember your rights" (.) so it's reinforcing what the custody sergeant is saying

Turning now to the rights overview itself, the Parent *Notice's* overview addresses detainees using the capitalised sections of Figure 6.5 (above). Summaries like this potentially prospect content, orient readers and help memory and comprehension (Hartley, 1981:17). However, in this particular summary, in order to understand each numbered point as a rights-stating declarative, readers must realise that each takes the form of an infinitival clause following from and sharing *to*; each effectively begins *You have the right to*. Readers who do not understand this will read the points as imperatives, and may therefore take them for instructions or givens, not rights to be invoked. EnterpriseB and EnterpriseD both removed this structure, instead introducing each right uniformly. The Sergeant too repeated, using the construction [imperative] + *if* + [present simple conditional], so each point stands alone:

Remember your rights:

1. Tell the police if you want a solicitor to help you while you are at the police station. It is free.
2. Tell the police if you want someone to be told that you are at the police station. It is free.
3. Tell the police if you want to look at the book called the Codes of practice...

For the Sergeant, the imperative was an appropriate mood to convey proactively offering rights. It leaves partial readers who view only opening sections in no doubt about rights invocation.

6.7 Close

This chapter has shifted the terms of debate, illustrating that rights texts cannot be viewed as straightforwardly communicating rights, and that providing such texts demonstrates only that they have been provided. This has driven more detailed investigation of reading practices. Having asked why detainees read incompletely, in Chapter 7 I will ask why some do not read at all and, at the other extreme, why others read in full. This makes it possible to consider how detainees might be encouraged to read, but also whether they should be encouraged or whether, in fact, written rights notices have limited utility. Data presented in Chapter 7 prompt both more esoteric and more far-reaching conclusions than have been generated so far.

7
Off the Page: Detainees' Reading Practices

7.1 Introduction: Examining reading by examining readers

As good writing depends on discovering "what readers seek from texts" (Hoey, 1988:51), good writers might investigate readers' purposes, by considering "three distinct types of reading task" (Diehl and Mikulecky, 1981:6). These were apparent in my data. The first, *reading-to-assess*, skim reading to evaluate relevance, was perhaps the most common way of reading the Sergeant's text; second, *reading-to-do*, using texts for reference often whilst doing, was apparent even during police interviews when one detainee described re-reading his rights notice to decide whether to request legal advice; finally, *reading-to-learn*, often away from a task, describes some detainees who read within their cells or even read before detention (adapted from Diehl and Mikulecky, 1981:7–8). It is a great challenge to institutional texts to respond to such different purposes, to respond to readers without a purpose and to respond to those who cannot read at all.

7.2 Non-readers

7.2.1 Those who cannot read

Quite possibly, some detainees who did not read the *Notices*, even some who claimed that they did, could not read. Few detainees who I interviewed mentioned reading difficulties, claiming that normally they could read as much as their daily lives required.[1] Nonetheless, more generally many detainees will find texts difficult or impossible to read. Surveys suggest that 56 per cent of young offenders are dyslexic compared to 10 per cent of the general population (BDA and BYOT, 2004:5) and that 57 per cent of adults in prisons have reading and writing skill levels below those of a competent 11-year-old (Davis *et al.*, 2004:2). Young people in prisons themselves identify a need for learning and education in their lives (Lyon, Dennison and Wilson, 2000:102). Whilst detainees are not necessarily destined to join the prison population, these figures are portentous. Detainees in my data spoke of the importance of considering and somehow assessing reading ability at the custody desk. Occasional 47, for example, proposed asking detainees to read a little of the *Notice* aloud, a test which some custody officers regularly use, although one which almost certainly inadequately measures likely comprehension and has unintended negative effects. Identifying detainees who may need help with reading is certainly a challenge for officers (Fenner, Gudjonsson and Clare, 2002:87), as one described:

> when you bring people into custody … you will go through the rights at the time and they'll say "yes no yes no" and you'll say "right just sign there for your rights" … and they'll just put a squiggle there then you'll go into the interview room and you'll discover they can't read or write and they've done it because of the embarrassment and they've done it because they don't want to be discovered that they can't read or write and if they've never been in custody before we're obviously not aware of this [AO10]

Reading in detention is particularly difficult because it necessitates reading alone. Outside detention, detainees may be "parts of larger systems, often composed of other people and other sorts of language, symbols and tools, across which 'cognition' is distributed" (Gee, 2000:198). Such social networks are important to using and understanding texts (Mace, 1992:51–2; Wilson, 2000:65). In networks, people with reading and writing 'problems' are neither isolated from all domains where reading and writing figure nor dependent on others but are interdependent, offering their own skills in return for help (Barton, 1994:201–2). Detention dismantles networks. This is unfortunate because personal networks are particularly important "when people confront … official worlds" (Barton and Hamilton, 1998:254), specifically, helping poor readers to move from simply "finding and understanding" information to making decisions or planning actions (Wright, 1999:92).

Whilst detention dismantles networks it potentially offers an alternative form of support for detainees who ask for help or are identified as needing it: the appropriate adult (see Section 6.6.2). If provided, an appropriate adult simulates what Barton and Hamilton would see as a "public, formal official and structured" network rather than offering a "private and informal everyday" network (1998:16). Detainees may not know their appropriate adult. This provision attempts to balance the needs of the institution – which quite correctly wants to investigate crimes without involving suspects' friends and relatives unnecessarily – with the needs of detainees – who may be disadvantaged if they receive inadequate help with reading, understanding and using written texts.

PACE Code C "does not require an appropriate adult to be called solely to assist [those who cannot read] in checking...documentation" (2006: para 3.20). It is clearly totally unacceptable for detainees who cannot read to have to get along alone in custody. Officers in this study claimed to obtain an appropriate adult for anyone who they discovered could not read. Indeed they sometimes erred on the side of caution, allocating appropriate adults to detainees who claim not to need one if in doubt, or on the basis of past allocations. Whilst this may be wise, one officer described how it frustrates detainees who are attempting to establish autonomy and fend for themselves in custody. Reading and writing practices were important currency for officers and detainees.

7.2.2 Why ignore rights notices?

Besides detainees who *could* not read in detention, others *did* not read. Observations and interviews with officers suggested two themes to account for incuriosity in the *Notices*: one relates to novices, proposing that their emotional responses to detention prevent them from reading; the other to regulars, proposing that they resist reading because they see themselves as detention-savvy and wish others to share that view. Detainees' own comments support these themes and add a third – the importance of expectations in decisions about whether to read (Figure 7.1). The remainder of Section 7.2.2 investigates these general themes which were raised repeatedly to account for not reading. The rest of Chapter 7 develops this scrutiny by examining talk from and talk about those who choose not to read or are unable to do so before turning to those who do read in custody.

7.2.2.1 *Novice detainees*

We might expect some detainees to read more attentively than normal in detention as "a certain degree of pressure or stress can improve powers of concentration" (Owen, 1996:287) and "high levels of affect induce deeper processing of information" (Martins, 1982:141). Indeed pressure has been found to propel readers "up to two grade levels above their supposed reading ability" in some settings (Sacher and Duffy (1979)

Figure 7.1 Reading rights texts in a cell: Not such a common activity

in Diehl and Mikulecky, 1981:5). However, the stress of detention also has obvious potential to unnerve (Russell, 2000:36) and
this was how many novices explained their indifference to the
Sergeant's rights texts, presenting their capacity to read in relation
to their detention experience. Even a novice who eventually read
both the Sergeant's texts and the *Codes* closely described initially
relying on talk in preference to those written texts because of his
disquiet (34). Several detainees similarly noted that reading was difficult:

> I just wanted to get out of here my dear and forget about it ... I read
> it and I was just concerned what was going to happen you know I
> mean your mind is at the time on other things
>
> [Novice 18]

This detainee went on to explain that, despite distractions, reading was
worthwhile as the text conveyed information which became important
to him. For other novice detainees, detention was simply too much.
For example one, who wanted to *get home*, explained that although
he had intended to read the papers he was *just too overawed by what
was going on* (48). Detainees who did not engage with the Sergeant's
text because of their response to detention were aware that the texts
were 'for' them. One, for example, noted the irony of his inability to
focus:

> I was all of a panic and didn't know what was happening ... whereas
> I suppose somebody who's been in 2 or 3 times they know it anyway
> [Novice 10]

These detainees were not necessarily uninterested in the *Notice*'s content but found that their discomfort with the detainee role (Goffman, 1959) rendered its written format unhelpful.

7.2.2.2   *Experienced detainees*

For detainees who represented themselves as very familiar with detention, not reading rights texts was a very different activity. Within social contexts "the very act of reading or writing takes on a social meaning: it can be an act of defiance or an act of solidarity, an act of conforming or a symbol of change. We assert our identity through literacy" (Barton, 1994:48). Some experienced detainees positioned themselves as too 'expert' for rights notices and performed this expert status through indifference to those texts. They explained, implied or demonstrated that, for them, there was little point even taking the papers from the custody desk, commenting, for example: *I know what it's all about* (Regular 30). Detainees who took the papers from the desk but did not read them expressed similar indifference. Regulars were predictably vocal here, claiming confidently: *I know the procedure* (14); *I know my rights anyway* (16). Some relatively experienced occasionals too indifferently proposed that they would find the *Notices'* content familiar: *I pretty well know the law through being in trouble in the past* (05). Even a novice detainee adopted this discourse, observing that he *had a rough idea what [the text] was going to be about* (19).

Those who presented themselves as 'expert' non-readers did not all unambiguously denigrate the Sergeant's text however. One regular (52) claimed that he saw the text as *rubbish* but qualified that it would be useful to detention newcomers. Others shared this position:

> to someone who hasn't been arrested before "yeah" but ... I've been
> in institutions like 26 years so I know the ins and outs   [Regular 07]

The possibility that the *Notices* were redundant for 'expert' detainees was noted by novices too:

> these are very good for me I think you're wasting a lot of time and
> effort on people who do it all the time because I bet you anything
> they just bin these   [Novice 26]

Detainees who see themselves as having sufficient rights expertise, that any information offered in custody is redundant present quite a challenge to a legal system which genuinely wants to communicate with them. This becomes particularly important when detention procedure changes. Several detainees suggested that they had indeed read the Sergeant's texts simply because they looked different from the usual rights notices and might therefore contain something novel, indicating the power of difference. Other detainees were quite clear that they read rights texts specifically to update themselves, to *check out what's going on* (Regular 35). One occasional arrestee intended to read the *Notices* retrospectively as revision, saying he would keep them *just to have a browse through later to see what um new things they'd done* (Occasional 38). Such comments suggest that should any rights information change, confident detainees, who are likely to routinely ignore rights texts, can be alerted to the changes through presentation and that they should be alerted very directly.

Experienced detainees did not necessarily reject all legal texts. Consider the following detainee's comments on navigating the *Codes of practice* (the Sergeant's third tier):

F   did you find it easy to find your way round it because it's =

D   =

       oh I found it a bit... [like] the Archbold similar sort of set

       out   [Regular 35]

By naming *Archbold*, a text which is aimed at lawyers preparing criminal cases for trial (Richardson, 2007), this detainee constructed himself as cognisant in legal matters, a presentation which he maintained throughout interview. Other regular detainees also connected the *Codes* to learning about law and their rights from books:

F   do you know why somebody might want to read those *Codes of practice*?

D   um they might want to study law my brother like he's- 120 pounds my brother paid for his book he doesn't study law or owt [≈ anything] he's just like studying his rights   [Regular 50]

For these detainees, self-presenting as expert readers or as part of expert reader communities was as important as performing expertise by not reading. Of course, detainees should not be expected to keep their libraries up to date, reinforcing the importance of rights communication to the detention dab hand.

7.2.2.3 Expectations

Detainees' expectations about the *Notices* were the final major influence on their reading decisions. Their expectations were organised around factors which have been found to influence reading elsewhere: genre familiarity (Drew and Sorjonen, 1997:103–4; Gibbons, 2003; Goldman and Rakestraw, 2000:313); text structure (Wilson and Anderson, 1986:40) and an understanding of purpose (Brown, Armbruster and Baker, 1986:58).

Detainees were discouraged if they lacked generic expectations about the texts and did not find cues in the texts or their administration, suggesting how they should be read or used. One novice commented, for example, *I didn't know what I was meant to be reading* (26), whilst five detainees reported no knowledge of the *Notices'* purpose or likely content, and several others suggested that they only found out about these when they began reading. Expectations about genre, content and function influenced those who did decide to read the Sergeant's notices. The text's potential to help motivated them particularly:

> anything like that that could constructively help in what you're about to face then it's applyable for anybody to read them really [Novice 34]

> I don't know anything about police stations and arrests and everything so just [read them] to help me   [Novice 26]

There is consensus that learning from text results from a combination of "skill, will and thrill" (Alexander and Jetton, 2000:296), from engagement through expectations about texts and goals, from values and beliefs about texts (Guthrie and Wigfield, 2000:404). Detainees' expectations about rights notices might influence them to read or ignore, whether those expectations are correct or erroneous.

We have seen that non-readers in detention are isolated from support networks by institutional rules. We have also seen that detainees who can read may not read completely or at all in detention because they are preoccupied by the novelty of their situation, because they see themselves as veteran or because they are simply mystified by rights texts. Yet detainees in all of these groups were able to answer questions about their rights in detention (Section 6.4). Therefore the next sections of this book ask how detainees who are unwilling or unable to read rights notices find out about their rights. Brown *et al.* found that "well over 90%" of detainees understood that they had rights and understood some specifics of those rights, yet Brown's team do not attribute this to rights notices because only around a third of their interviewees apparently referred to the texts (1992, in Brown 1997:79). Even Clare and Gudjonsson acknowledge that "in real life, factors other than the complexity of the language in which the [rights notice] is written might influence comprehension" (1992:4). Whilst these authors leave this unexplored, I ask where detainees get rights information, if not from the texts which purport to give that information?

7.2.3 Alternatives to rights notices

Any "text is embedded in a matrix of contexts made up from an array of different contextual resources" including assumptions, prior discourse and background knowledge (Linell, 1998:144). Detainees draw on such resources extensively in custody. When asked about the meaning of *Custody record*, for example, one detainee commented:

> I never read that bit really I must admit (.) but I presume it's … so that they know who's here and who isn't   [Novice 10]

This novice made an 'educated guess' about rights, having ignored parts of the Sergeant's text. Guessing, which also occurs around other comparable information texts (Labov and Harris, 1994:271), was not the only alternative to written rights texts. Seemingly, detainees also call on talk, previous experience and reason.

The detainee(s) seem(s) to be relying on:	This source is suggested by:	Excerpts (suggestive features highlighted in bold)
Talk, rather than written information	Reported speech marking	**they said** I could use the 'phone if I needed to [Novice 18]
Experience of detention	Perfective aspect and time adverb	**I've never** had a limit on that **I've never** been told that I couldn't 'phone somebody else [Regular 31]
Reason	Speech and thought representations	D you can use the 'phone … depends who it is **I suppose** isn't it

(Continued)

The detainee(s) seem(s) to be relying on:	This source is suggested by:	Excerpts (suggestive features highlighted in bold)
Reason	Speech and thought representations	F ...are there only certain people you can get in touch with? D um **I'd say** other people that are involved [Occasional 50] --- F was it clear how many people you could speak to? D well **I assumed** it was just the one [Occasional 47]

In addition detainees also draw on resources which are completely external to detention.

7.2.3.1 *Alternatives outside custody*

Detainees' use of resources from outside custody in making sense of rights is significant because those resources are beyond the legal institution's control. Detainees used the outside world in drawing analogies to make sense of rights. One, for example, explained the lawyer–client relationship by likening it to more familiar encounters with professionals, describing it as *like your doctor...something you don't tell nobody* (Novice 18). In fact consultation with a lawyer is private, not necessarily confidential. Another presented the audit function of the *Codes* through analogy with his work in a restaurant regulated by health and safety guidelines (Occasional 49).

Even novices potentially enter police stations with considerable rights information from television. For example, one reported preconceptions about his rights' limitations:

> it's through **watching TV** and saftness[2] like that ... you know pretty much it's one 'phone call so it's pointless sort of taking the Mickey   [Novice 34]

Whilst another described gaps in her knowledge due to partial television coverage:

F   did you know anything about the things that the police have to give to people when they're arrested?

D   no because you don't really see that **on telly** do you [Novice 26]

The phenomenon is mirrored in the USA where experimental subjects incompletely understood *Miranda* warnings due to incomplete media portrayals (Dumas, 1990:329). Yet television, film and radio have positive potential to inform the public about law (Jackson, 1995:139). Widely discussed in my study was the popular London-based police drama-soap *The Bill* which is currently broadcast on British television screens year-round, having been a regular fixture since 1984. Programmes like this, though ostensibly delivering only entertainment, apparently also have a public information role in educating viewers about police procedure (cf. Leo, 2001:1012). Detainees' many references to television suggest that programmes' accuracy is important.

Taking *The Bill* as a case study, systematic observation of the programme reveals that the caution, for example, is recited in full if it has dramatic importance (illustrated in a scene where a sobbing mother hears her son arrested beyond a closed door, having contributed to the arrest). In other cases however it is often recited as background to other action (fights, people getting into police cars and so on) or partially before a cut to a different scene. Very occasionally it is tokenised through replacement with, for example, "you're nicked" (based on observations between 1998 and 2002). A *Bill* story researcher confirmed "if the caution is sometimes not shown in full, it would be for dramatic reasons where it is more interesting to cut to a different part of the action or another scene". Decisions about this are "entirely left to the writer and their script editor" (Carter, 2003:pc). One of the show's writers independently added that any unrealistic procedure "has at least been thought about" (Lindsey, 2003:pc). Both sources stressed the programme's quest for realism. Carter reported that the programme is "extremely proud of its adherence to police procedure" and aims to be "topical and truthful" in that adherence. To that end, the programme employs two full time ex-Metropolitan police officer advisers, issues writers' guidelines which include caution wordings (Carter, 2003:pc) and sends all new writers on "a day out in a real police car" (Lindsey, 2003:pc). Conversely, a *Bill* designer commented "we tend to leave out the procedural stuff because it's too slow ... it doesn't bring anything to the drama" (2003:pc). Viewers are apparently sensitive to the programme's portrayal of procedure. One wrote to the programme's producers asking "we often see an officer...enter the custody office and check an aspect of the law in a book...Can you tell me what this book is called?" (The Bill, 2006). This question, which addresses the *Codes*, illustrates that realism is a responsibility. The pedagogic function of programmes like this cannot be overestimated.

There may be many reasons for detainees' focus on television. Principally, however, television fills a void in communicating rights to lay people outside detention. Detainees did not mention encountering information through institutions such as schools, yet educational settings are perfect for introducing such practices as form-filling (Fawns and Ivanič, 2001:80) and reading expository texts (Goldman and Rakestraw, 2000:323–4). If this study was replicated 10 years from now detainees might identify school as having provided information on rights because the Citizenship component of the National Curriculum in England now specifies that young teenagers should learn about "the legal and human rights and responsibilities underpinning society" and "basic aspects of the criminal justice system" (National Curriculum, 2006). Many schools choose to illustrate these through "teaching about what happens when someone is arrested...and exploring rights and responsibilities in this situation" (Craft, 2005:pc). Introducing rights information into public discourses may directly influence comprehension because "familiar items require less processing time" (Merritt, 1994:33) as readers' prior knowledge is "a principal determiner" of comprehension (Wilson and Anderson, 1986:32).

The Internet increasingly offers free, convenient information (Jackson, 1995:139). A *Google* web search for the string "if you are arrested" yields almost 100,000 sites (as at 24 December 2006). Such information can be part of a "striking counterpoint" to official documentation (Barton and Hamilton, 1998:232) although not one mentioned by detainees in these data. The Home Office itself now provides rights texts, *Codes* and legislation along with a staggering array of other institutional texts via its website (Home Office, 2006d). Whilst these might not be an alternative to information in custody for the many novice detainees who are surprised to be there, more seasoned detainees like those who described preparing for custody (see Section 7.2.2.2) might increasingly use such sources as the Internet becomes more affordable.

7.2.3.2   Alternatives inside custody: Custody desk talk

Inside detention the only alternative to delivering rights on paper at present is to use talk. Are detainees likely to prefer talk to writing? In other institutional settings, at one end of a continuum, Biber notes a preference for writing above speech in education, business and politics (1988:6–7). At the other extreme, Sticht's army personnel would rather ask colleagues for information than use a written manual (1972). Between these poles, Diehl and Mikulecky find written material is seen as just one of many workplace resources (1981:6). To complicate matters affect means that this continuum is not linear. Fawns and Ivanič find writing emanating from institutions is stigmatised due to its potential to inherently unnerve (2001:80). The low take-up of the Sergeant's *Notice* illustrates the importance of verbally explaining rights in custody.

Writing and speech both have pros and cons. Custody officers are required to summarise detainees' three main rights once they reach custody (PACE Code C, 2006:para3.1) (see Figure 6.5). This typically happens at the custody desk as detainess are checked-in (see Figure 7.2). Clare and Gudjonsson applaud this provision, recommending that it be extended and the written *Notice* drastically reduced or abandoned (1992:21, 26, 29). Despite the Sergeant's enthusiasm for his written rights text, even he tellingly observed:

> I think the more important thing is how the Sergeant approaches it (.) how he does his pitch

Other officers too flagged the importance of the custody sergeant's words, reporting their impression that detainees *tend to rely on the Sergeant telling them rather than them actually reading it* [AO01]. Even detainees who had read the Sergeant's text took up this theme, prioritising custody desk talk above the text time and again. This regular arrestee who had read the *Notice* and was looking over a copy with me at this point, nonetheless answered my question about text by describing talk:

> F   if you wanted to speak to a solicitor is it clear from that [indicates page 2] how you'd arrange it?
>
> D   yeah well they ask you straight away on the desk it's one of the first questions they ask you "do you want a solicitor?"
>
> [Regular 07]

Using talk to deliver rights information has two risks. First, officers may fail to administer the information for one reason or another. In the years soon after PACE was introduced as many as 15 per cent of suspects missed out on verbal information at the custody desk (Sanders *et al.*,

Figure 7.2 Delivering rights at the custody desk

1989). Yet, by the late 1990s, spoken rights administration was rarely omitted except in accordance with PACE (Brown, 1997) which suggest that this provision may have settled over time. If rights are delivered, the second risk is that delivery may be ineffective. Brown cites extensive evidence that, whilst rights are mostly explained by custody sergeants "clearly", a minority of explanations are unconvincing, perhaps due to time pressures and the volume of information to convey (1997:76). In Part III of this book, we will see the difficulty which interviewing officers experience when explaining just one right (the right to silence) in a comparatively controlled environment.

On the other hand, spoken rights administration offers some advantages over writing. Talk might allow miscommunication to be identified and resolved because talk "comprises repair as an inbuilt design feature" (House, Kasper and Ross, 2003:2). However, if that mechanism is to work it must enable speakers to evaluate their formulations and hearers to check their comprehension (Goffman, 1981:12). This may be unlikely to happen in custody where interpersonal power asymmetry may render detainees unable to "negotiate their comprehension problems" (Gibbons, 2003).

The Sergeant sought to bolster rights talk at the custody desk, by devising a script for custody officers (Appendix 9). The script, which he called PR1, delivered rights and requested information from detainees about their health and welfare. This procedure was already in place when the Sergeant wrote PR1 but he intended his script to formalise and improve it. The long-term adaptation of PR1 by custody officers would need to be monitored, particularly given the need to accommodate to different detainees (see Sections 10.5.2, 10.5.3) and the tendency for officers to innovate on standard wordings (see Section 10.5.1). Detainees' reception of rights administration through speech would also need to be monitored.

7.2.3.3   Other alternatives inside custody

Good rights communication involves responding to comprehension problems at any stage of detention, not just at the custody desk. Clarification exchanges could be proceduralised throughout detention. They already happen informally during journeys to police stations, when they might be particularly influential. Clarification also comes within custody through informative interactions beyond the first encounter at the custody desk:

> I had somebody come in the next morning ... just after breakfast and again he went through "remember your rights" and said to me "are you sure you don't want a solicitor?"
>
> [Novice 34]

Additional explanations of rights were apparently valuable to detainees. Such informal encounters constitute this text in use, illustrating "what kind of information" people receive while "trying to understand" the written text (Labov and Harris, 1994:267).

In addition to rights notices and custody desk talk, rights are currently administered in other ways too. Posters are required in each custody unit, "advertising the right to legal advice" (Code C, 2006:para6.3) in multiple languages (Home Office, 1991:4). Detainees also write as part of rights administration. They must sign the *Custody record* in order to authorise their decisions about whether to invoke two of their rights (Code C, 2006:10, para3.5), using the powerful "assertion of truth or consent" offered by a signature (Goody, 1986:152).

The Sergeant recommended increasing the diversity of modes of rights administration further. For detainees who cannot read, he devised electronic versions of his text using static images and speech. These replaced the linear form of the Parent text with non-linear text, which "guides or prompts readers to re-access or extend the main text" (Alexander and Jetton, 2000:290). Jackson presents hypertext as a possible solution to the difficulty of legal texts through its ability to add depth to the printed page and to allow audiences to see interrelationships (1995:134).

This might be particularly useful to this text with its intertextuality (see Sections 5.3, 6.2). The Sergeant also suggested providing rights information on a video-loop in custody waiting areas. Video- or audio-recordings could incorporate findings such as those reported by Fox Tree (1999:50), that overhearers typically remember more of dialogues than monologues, perhaps due to the increased discourse markers or multiperspectivity of dialogues. As Fox Tree notes, some aspects of dialogue might inhibit communicative effectiveness but these could be controlled by a script. Radical thinking about how to convey rights information may be essential to reaching non-reading, uninterested detainees. There are lessons to learn from other kinds of professional–lay communication. In involving patients in decisions about medical care, research teams are developing an impressive array of patient "decision support technologies". For example, those considering whether to undergo particular treatments might watch videos in which actors animate narratives from real patients who have already received treatment (Evans *et al.*, 2007). Narratives describing real detainees' experiences of receiving or foregoing legal advice or invoking or waiving the right to silence might be equally instructive to those in custody. These could be generated from interviews with detainees like those interviews described here. It is becoming increasingly practically and economically viable to provide computers or DVD players in custody suites. Such animated narratives could also be made available online.

7.2.4   Encouraging reading

7.2.4.1   *Repetition and rights*

Administering information repeatedly via any mode creates opportunities to arrive at "clearer", "altered" or "deeper" understandings (Spolsky, 1994:141–2). It may facilitate speedier reading (Raney, Therriault and Minkoff, 2000:76–9) and increase (Merritt, 1994:33) or focus (Johnstone *et al.*, 1994:3) attention. Providing repeated, multimodal information enables detainees, rather than officers, to decide when, where and how rights information is transferred. Yet "too much repetition can have negative effects" (Merritt, 1994:32). Even if different formulations are used, readers may be "totally confused by ... unnecessary redundancy" (Charrow and Charrow, 1979:1327). Specifically, detainees have been found to ignore the *Notices* because their content has already been related orally, even if oral delivery was poor (Brown, 1997:76). Detainees I interviewed recognised the multimodality of rights administration, noting particularly the interrelationship of custody desk talk and the *Notice* (highlighted in bold):

> **he said** I could have a book to read if I wanted and it's the Code of-
> it just breaks the law down and everything **which is what it says**
> **there**   [Novice 26]

Some detainees claimed to have benefited from the written–spoken intertextuality:

> everything he told me up the front...it was all sort of like in there
> what he'd already told me but it's sort of like it gives you time to
> read it because there's so much going on and so many people around
> [Novice 26]

Custody officers might usefully exploit the potential for rights talk to orient readers to rights texts. Numerous studies suggest that instruction on unfamiliar texts' structures can benefit readers (Goldman and Rakestraw, 2000:323).

7.2.4.2 *The influence of rights talk on reading decisions*

The data gathered here have shown that spoken interactions have a *communicative function*, replacing rights notices for the many detainees who are unwilling or unable to read. I will now turn to their *affective function*, influencing detainees' decisions about whether to read. By considering what persuades detainees to read we might devise ways to improve the take-up of rights texts.

USA officers attempt to downplay rights information, presenting it such that detainees will not recognise it as crucial to their future but will dismiss it as "equivalent to other standard bureaucratic forms that one signs without reading or giving much thought" (Leo, 2001:1019). The Sergeant reviser had been concerned about this, so he devised a wording to be used when handing over the *Notice* at the custody desk. He included this in his script PR1 (see Appendix 9). He intended the wording to prevent officers from delivering the text using a police-centred utterance such as *the police have to give out this Notice* which might discourage engagement. Deixis was apparently crucial:

> they should be <u>hand</u>ing not making it available (.) not saying "over
> there (.) somewhere if you want to help yourself" (.) "here" (.) and
> actually get the person to take hold of it

The formulation he devised for PR1 was intended to introduce the text's tiers (Section 6.2), explicitly:

> Here is a sheet that tells you the main things I have said. [Tier 1, the fold-over cover]
> There is some more information attached to it.　[Tier 2, pages 2–5]

He hoped that explicitly connecting custody desk talk to the written texts would reduce perceptions that the written texts were redundant. Comments from the detainees above suggested some success here. Custody desk talk convinced some detainees to keep the Sergeant text:

> I haven't really read them I just kept them because they ((asked me to)) keep it 　　　　　　　　　　　　　　　　　　　　[Regular 44]

Talk even persuaded others to read:

> the Sergeant told me to read it so I thought I might as well read it
> 　　　　　　　　　　　　　　　　　　　　　　　[Occasional 06]
> it was put in front of me and the guy said "have a read" so I did
> 　　　　　　　　　　　　　　　　　　　　　　　[Novice 25]

This last detainee added that he eventually felt too distracted by circumstances to continue reading, underlining the importance of the custody sergeant in potentially fulfilling both the communicative and affective functions mentioned above. This deference to officers recalls Gumperz's work on contextualisation cues, which points out that in institutional settings "[w]hile downgrading their own status, lay persons ... depict the official as being all-powerful and in control, thus able to assist in finding a solution" (1992:245). With this power comes the officer's responsibility to hand over the text conscientiously.

Generally detainees shared the Sergeant's concern about the influence of the mode of administration of rights notices, particularly their handing (Scollon, 2001). Regular 46 problematised handing at the custody desk because the texts were easily left there, being *the last thing on your mind*. He suggested putting rights notices into cells instead, although the Sergeant had already discounted this as impractical. The practice of handing the notices at all compares favourably with other jurisdictions, like the Netherlands, where leaflets containing rights information are kept in the custody area but there is "no policy for distributing" them (Komter, 2002:pc). Current handing procedure also improves on the previous system in England and Wales. One occasional detainee, who recognised being offered the text during custody desk talk, did not recall a similar speech event when he was last arrested some years before:

> there was nothing printed up anywhere or if there was it was little leaflets in a corner like "there" or something   [Occasional 49]

However, uninterested administration of the *Notices* still happens:

> the way I saw it when I was given it it was like "OK everybody gets these bits of paper read it and then just sit tight and wait for the bullet" like you know so no I didn't think of getting a solicitor when I read this   [Novice 25]

His comments suggest PR1 was ineffective, failing to present the rights notices as relevant to detention (cf. Leo, 2001:1016). Quite possibly these very different responses to handing of the texts from Occasional 49 and Novice 25 were the result of custody officers' idiosyncratic ways of taking on PR1, or indeed their rejection of it. The Sergeant reviser himself pointed out that one custody officer within this study who continued to deliver rights information *the old fashioned way* had a *significantly lower take-up* of rights texts than other officers. This simultaneously suggests the success of the script in encouraging detainees to take the *Notice* from the custody desk, but also its failure in easily being ignored by officers.

Although custody desk talk and orientation might encourage reading, it would be naïve to hope that they would guarantee reading any more than administering the written texts does itself.

7.3 Reading

Even if detainees have read the rights texts and claim to understand them, it is not the end of the matter. Readers do not passively absorb "whatever the writer sees fit to communicate" (Hoey, 1988:51), rather they act on the information presented to them, asking:

- Where is this text coming from?
- What is it trying to do to me?
- Am I going to accept this and work with it?
- Am I going to reject it?
- Am I going to try to work with it on a modified basis?

(Baynham, 1995:206)

Detainees are, by this definition, critical readers (Crowther and Tett, 2001:109) and must be investigated as such.

7.3.1 Trust the text?

Chapter 6 showed that many detainees easily answered questions about rights, apparently exhibiting good understanding. However, this was not the full story. For example some, who 'understood' their right to a solicitor, had not apparently appreciated how it would materialise in practice, a problem identified by Shuy (1997:186–7) in the USA setting. My data connect this problem to a lack of an 'in-detention' content schema (Schank and Abelson, 1977) or limited prior experience (White and Gunstone, 1992:12). One detainee, for example, described at length frustration at apparently being denied this right. In fact it emerged that it was never denied, rather his solicitor had taken some time to arrive and he had not expected or integrated this delay which is not explicitly specified in the Sergeant's text. Here then, a detainee without access to the appropriate schema to complete inferential gaps between text and context either activated or constructed an erroneous reading. In Enkvist's terms the *Notice* was not "interpretable" to him because he could not "build around [it] a scenario in which it [made] sense" (1990:169). In contrast, another detainee who also initially assumed that a solicitor might be available on-site modified his assumptions when custody staff explained:

> they said they would just 'phone [a solicitor] up and deal with the arrangements that was pretty clear I [previously] thought they might have one dangling about the building somewhere   [Novice 25]

A related communicative mismatch is illustrated by a detainee who showed reluctance to work with what he had read in the *Notices* about when a solicitor can be consulted:

1	D	it says "day or night" there I don't know
2	F	so it should be any time?
3	D	yeah
4	F	great and do you know if there's any time that you wouldn't be allowed to speak to one?
→ 5	D	(.) I would say night time would be a bit of a problem (.) mm I would say night time

[Novice 11]

This detainee successfully identified the relevant part of the *Notice* to state when a solicitor can be consulted, even locating the significant string *day or night* (turn 1). This could have been taken to indicate comprehension. However, despite my leading question (turn 2), by turn 5 he appears unconvinced either that he has understood, that he has identified the appropriate words or even that the text was correct. He therefore supplements his original correct answer from the text with a 'common sense' answer which is incorrect. Idioms like *day or night* can be ambiguous. For example, some readers who encounter the word *mealtimes* within patient information take it to mean "at the times of day when people typically eat meals" others "when you are eating" (Wright, 1999:91). However, it is difficult to see how *day or night* could be similarly ambiguous, particularly as it is preceded by *any time*. Therefore this detainee does not appear to believe his eyes.

Detainees also looked outside the Sergeant's text when considering the boundaries of rights, suggesting that rights had caveats not mentioned in the text. They proposed, for example, that the right to external contact only allowed calls to family members. Occasional 31, a 20-year-old, believed that he could only telephone his parents. Similarly the Sergeant revision declares of legal advice, *it is free*. Nonetheless one detainee was totally unsure whether legal advice was free (Novice 19) and three more were rather doubtful. This too did not necessarily stem from the *Notice* itself:

F do you have to pay to speak to a solicitor?
D according to this [the Sergeant revision] no   [Occasional 45]

This detainee distinguishes having to pay from what the *Notice* says about it. Other detainees further suggested criteria governing eligibility for free legal advice:

you get free legal aid if you're not working   [Regular 14]
[you have to pay] if you've got a job   [Occasional 38]
the first time I think it's free   [Regular 28]

In other parts of the legal system advice is indeed only available to people who have limited means. However, everyone in custody who selects an approved adviser will receive free advice, therefore none of these detainees' criteria apply. Rights information apparently fares poorly when competing with expectations. In response to detainees' comments, the Government revision added *The duty solicitor is free*. This addition repeats the claim that legal advice is free and specifies alongside the more general assertion. As a by-product, the formulation avoids ambiguous *it*.

We have seen that not only do detainees dip into, supplement and ignore rights texts, but they do not necessarily 'believe' the texts even if they have read them.[3] Comprehension in context is apparently about how readers:

- relate the text to the situation which confronts them;
- perceive the reliability of the text's content;
- perceive the likelihood that they will understand.

Background expectations potentially hijack reading, leading to misunderstandings (Alexander and Kulikowich, 1994).

This phenomenon of lacking faith in an informative text is not unlike *non compliance* with medical texts which occurs when readers "correctly interpret what they read but nevertheless decide that they can behave in a way that does not fully accord with this understanding" (Wright, 1999:91). This may stem from readers' emotional responses to the message – a feeling that they know better, for example (Wright, 1999:88–9). Anyone who proposes that the language of rights information is "too complicated" must "demonstrate what sort of language would be better understood" (Owen, 1996:287). Comments from detainees who demonstrably read and navigate rights information yet do not seem to take on that information indeed make it difficult to know how to respond. Like non-compliance, not believing a text is not unambiguously driven by "any actual characteristics of the senders or sources" (Pettersson, 2002:106). Yet it can have serious consequences, as Leo has observed, suspects who doubt that *Miranda* "should be taken at face value" "may feel that they have no choice but to comply with their interrogators" (2001:1013).

7.3.2 Beyond rights communication

"As much effort needs to be put into getting people to exercise their rights as to know them" (Owen, 1996:294). Accordingly, I now move from discussing rights communication *per se* to discussing rights themselves. I present empirical evidence on a question that is difficult to answer and has accordingly been somewhat neglected: Why do detainees reject and waive rights? It has been suggested that rights' delivery and explanation influences their take-up (Cotterill, 2000:7–8 summarises). However Brown exhibits reservations about this (1997:79), which the detainees in these data suggest are well founded. Not only were detainees' decisions about whether to engage with rights *information* complex, but their *responses* to the texts were not simply about arrest, detention, linguistic features and the institution but also detainees' views and representations of themselves as detainees and the presentation of a particular relationship with the text and detention.

Writers are encouraged to use second-person pronouns because they engage readers (Jackson, 1995:124) and improve comprehension (Tiersma, 1999a:205). However, there is an "inseparable constitutive relationship between the linguistic devices for person reference and managing institutional activities" (Drew and Sorjonen, 1997:99). A general shift towards second-person pronouns and resulting informal tenor have been taken to indicate how "the private sphere increasingly colonizes the public", reducing social distance without allowing informality to "infringe the claimed authority" of institutional actors (Candlin and Maley, 1997:206–7). *You* creates a vacant subject space which lay people who use government paperwork might accept or contest (Fawns and Ivanič, 2001:88). Some non-readers rejected the Sergeant's text through discomfort with the subject positions it offers. Novice 09, for example, was aware of the *Notice*'s likely content and its potential to help him, yet claimed to have ignored the text because he had *nothing to hide*. For this detainee, any engagement with the rights texts was highly interpretable, signifying a call for help and, implicitly, admitting guilt.

Detainees attached considerable significance to invoking rights and were apparently discouraged from doing so by matters other than comprehension of, or even perception of, rights. Some declined legal advice because, they claimed, they were innocent:

> I didn't get a solicitor because I haven't done anything wrong
> [Novice 51]

This explanation erroneously presupposes that only the guilty need legal advice. Others agreed:

> 1   D   if you think you've done something you've got to speak to a solicitor haven't you if you think you haven't you won't necessarily need to
> 2   F   but there are cases when you might?
> 3   D   well yes there is yeah...he just give me my rights and said "get a solicitor because the charges I've brought you under are quite serious charges" but I still declined the solicitor because I knew I ain't done nothing wrong
> [Novice 09]

My question to Novice 09 (turn 2) addressed his assertion that innocent people would not *necessarily* need a solicitor. I expected he would respond by clarifying that even the innocent might need advice. However, for him, even when confronted by contrary advice from a police officer, innocence mitigated the need. This connection between rights waivers and innocence claims is rather startling because it is not confined to legally inconsequential research interviews but also appears in detainees' responses during police interviews. The examples below are from preambles to police interviews, during which officers request explanation of any rights waiver 'on record' (as in the very first excerpt in this book):

> P   you've continued to decline legal advice er I'm therefore obliged
>   to ask you what your reasons are for declining it?
> D   because I ain't done anything   [B102]

Protestations of innocence were a frequent response to requests to explain rights waivers across different interviews:

> [I don't need advice] because I believe I am in the clear and I have
> nothing to worry about   [B108]
>
> I don't see why I need a solicitor when I haven't done nothing [B103]
>
> I don't need one I'm innocent   [B105]

Other detainees introduced honesty, rather than innocence:

> P   do you want to have a solicitor present in this interview?
> D   no...
> P   OK any particular reason for that?
> D   I've got nothing to hide   [B101]

These explanations could be seen to suggest that naïve detainees, unsure of a solicitor's role, might deny themselves their most valuable right because they believe its exercise sends out the wrong signals. Indeed the two Force E detainees above who cited innocence as their reason for declining legal advice were both novices. In case detainees hold this misunderstanding strongly enough to prejudice themselves, the Government revision explains that requesting a solicitor does not indicate guilt. This addresses detainees who read the *Notice* and are genuinely unsure of the implications of invoking rights. However, detainees who take this line at the beginning of an investigative interview may not simply misunderstand. A social constructionist view of these claims of innocence or honesty sees the claims prospecting detainees' upcoming talk, framing it as that of an innocent or honest person. The institutional agenda at this point of the interview preamble focusses on eliciting confirmation that nobody has coerced detainees into waiving rights. Whilst in the excerpts above detainees did not subvert this agenda, they used the floor it offered to construct themselves as sufficiently convinced of their innocence or honesty to reject the help of a person who they represent as only appropriate for those less convinced. Here then we see pre-interview rights talk being appropriated to accomplish innocent self-presentation before the officially sanctioned verbal investigation of guilt or innocence has even begun.

Presentation of an innocent or honest self was not the only unexpected positioning during police interviews. Some detainees gave apparently oddly benevolent explanations for rights waivers:

[I] don't want to get someone out of bed for nothing   [B93]

I ain't done anything wrong so I don't see why I should waste anyone else's time   [B107]

These detainees thus present themselves as reasonable and considerate, as well as innocent. Rights talk provides a space where detainees can begin to establish the position which they anticipate developing throughout interview. This position is not necessarily fixed, as one detainee suggests when declining advice before interview:

well at the moment...I don't think I've done anything well I know I haven't done anything so (.) I'll wait until I hear anything   [B109]

He is prepared to reconsider his innocent self-presentation if his innocent status should be shifted by external (re)categorisations of his actions. As Gergen puts it, "interpretations may be suggested, fastened upon and abandoned as social relationships unfold" (1985:6).

Other detainees cited not innocence but guilt as a reason for declining legal advice:

I just- I'm just- I know what I done wrong   [B71]

just owning up for what I've done   [B82]

This seems distinctly odd. We have just seen how these speakers could have used this turn-at-talk to make an on-record claim of innocence yet they voluntarily confess before their interviews proper have even begun. Although these responses position the speakers differently from the earlier examples they nonetheless serve "important social functions" (Potter and Wetherell, 1987:108), facilitating detainees' "situational accomplishment of social identity" (Drew and Sorjonen, 1997:95) in orienting to the subsequent interview. Through these responses detainees acknowledge guilt and implicitly delimit their crime, denying other crimes. They also self-present as accountable, facing the consequences of their actions willingly. Finally, they appear, like those with *nothing to hide*, as honest, here honest enough to confess.

Detainees who had read the Sergeant revision also adopted this 'guilty but honest' position. The novice below, for example, is ostensibly explaining having declined legal advice (points of interest are numbered):

I decided not to speak to a solicitor because

(1) what I'd done I know I'd done wrong um and
(2) I was caught for it
(3) I mean it's not a terrible offence or anything like that
(4) but it is bad enough
(5) so I couldn't see the point in wasting tax-payers money on a solicitor who's just going to sit there
(6) and basically say the same as I am that I'm very sorry I shouldn't have done it and all this kind of thing   [Novice 34]

In (1), he demonstrates awareness of his guilt and, though *wrong*, morally evaluates that guilt. He then moves to the outcome of his wrong-doing, stating that he was caught, without evaluation or commentary, drawing on what we might call an 'it's a fair cop' discourse which surfaced frequently in my interviews. The emerging picture is of a reasonable, repentant individual who recognises cause and effect. He then turns to his crime in (3). Here he does evaluate, minimising and legitimising through comparison with other crimes. His shift to the legal register, presenting an *offence* not a *wrong*, adds gravitas to his evaluation. Having established that his offence was minor, he appears to contradict that in (4) but he does not go as far as to say his offence is *bad*, simply *bad enough*. Thus he reinserts a moral self to whom all crimes are *bad*. In (5) he commodifies solicitors as an expensive luxury funded by public money which might be better spent elsewhere. Thus he introduces a responsible self with altruistic ideals despite his fall from grace. Finally, in (6) he orients to his crime, taking a regretful, apologetic stance and authorising that stance and by presenting it as one which would have been validated by the imagined solicitor. In explaining his rights waiver, this detainee interactionally produces a positive self.

Barton describes a form for jobseekers which asked: *If you are offered a job can you start right away?* and provided the possible responses *yes* or *no*. He points out that the form has been "plain Englished" such that the question and possible answers are composed of "common and well known" words and the syntax is "straightforward". He notes, however, that claimants need to know the intentions behind the question; they must answer *yes* if they are to claim benefit. Thus a difference emerges not between those who can and cannot recognise and read the words on the page but between experienced and novice claimants (1994:61). This emerged in detention too. One detainee was sufficiently familiar with the entitlement procedure to subvert it:

> I have to lie to the police and tell them that- (.) my Mom and Dad said they didn't want to speak to me (.) so I lied and said I was ringing someone else   [Regular 33]

This detainee pretended that his parents had been unavailable, to avoid having used his telephone entitlement on what he saw as a null call. Amongst detainees we see something more than Barton's jobseekers. They recognise the institutional framework and superimpose their own framework over it, appropriating the institutionally provided turn-at-talk for their own ends (see Section 12.3.4).

7.4 Close

The Sergeant's revisions:

- 'improved' the text by attending to:
  - occasional local features (such as the *more information* clause);
  - recurrent local features (such as the overuse of nominalisations);
  - global features (such as discourse sequence).
- made the text 'for' the detainee, by:
  - considering their lifeworld (Schutz and Luckman, 1973);

- ○ considering their ways of reading;
- ○ encouraging them to read.

- located the text within:

  - ○ an intertextual chain of written texts;
  - ○ an extratextual world of speech, where its content is not novel.

His text was successful in that many detainees appeared able to reproduce its content but what that really means in context is difficult to ascertain. Detainees are apparently influenced by texts, their own questions and others' talk about the text (Alexander and Jetton, 2000:291) but ultimately the text might not meet their needs, no matter how it is formulated and delivered. Hertfordshire Constabulary attempted to address detainees' real concerns at the behest of one of their officers, introducing a "cell welcome pack". This answered routine practical questions about detention, like where and when detainees can smoke, and general information, for example, explaining drugs and alcohol referral schemes (BBC News Online, 2003). Yet even the Hertfordshire document is driven by what the institution and its actors want to convey. Detainees' own concerns are likely to be disparate and ultimately impossible to address. As one officer explained:

> sometimes we are asked questions that we do not have the answer for um rightly or wrongly varying degrees of people coming in with obviously varying degrees of intelligence and you'll find that the more of- an intelligent person...can be very inquisitive and will scrutinise what we are saying to them and then will ask us questions based on what we've told them...and sometimes we cannot give then an answer because procedure doesn't dictate us to give them the answer they've been looking for ...a lot of them are "when am I going to be interviewed" "when will the solicitor be here" "how long am I going to be here" and we can't answer those questions when they're brought in because we don't know all we can say is well we can keep you here for 24 hours if need be but hopefully you won't be here that long   [AO10]

Whilst endeavours to represent rights fairly, honestly and fully are laudable, rights communication is different every time it takes place and perhaps the most useful tool for officers is one which provides them with resources to respond to this diversity.

Part III
Speaking Rights

8
Introducing Spoken Rights Communication

8.1 Introduction

Everyone detained by the police in England or Wales is verbally cautioned at three stages of their detention: at arrest, interview and, if applicable, charge. Detainees may also read the caution in the *Notice to detained persons*. The caution is intended to inform detainees about their right to silence and the implications of invoking that right. It states:

> You do not have to say anything. But it may harm your defence if you do not mention when questioned something which you later rely on in court. Anything you do say will be given in evidence.[1]

The caution, conveyed through language, also has a metalinguistic dimension, giving information about silence. Silence is powerful (Goody, 1986:151; Jaworski, 1993; Tiersma, 1999b). Yet in detention detainees' silence is disempowering because it can be ascribed negative significance (Graffam-Walker, 1985:55–6). Detention skews the immediate interactional function which silence might otherwise have. The caution must communicate this unusual context and signification.

"To be of any use, the language of the law ... must not only express but convey thought" (Mellinkoff, 1963:vii). The question of whether the caution does so is vexed. Relevant research has had, until recently, two main foci: First, formulation of the official wording (Cotterill, 2000; Kurzon, 1995, 1996); secondly, reception of that wording, usually in experimental settings (Clare, Gudjonsson and Harari, 1998; Fenner, Gudjonsson and Clare, 2002). Whilst the caution's formulation and

reception are important they are not all that is necessary to investigate cautioning because officers are permitted both to deviate from the
official wording (Code C, 2006:para10.7) and moreover to explain in
their own words (Code C, 2006:note10D). This appropriation and transformation by individuals ultimately determines the caution's influence
on detainees. Even experimental psychologists advocate studying the
caution "as it would be in real life" (Fenner, Gudjonsson and Clare,
2002:89). A new focus has accordingly emerged recently: examining
cautions in use (Greenwood, 2002; Hall, 2004; Russell, 2000). The
chapters in Part III of the book contribute to this emergent area by
examining a large quantity of naturally occurring data from police interviews in which officers explain the caution. This is complemented by
scrutiny of interviews with both officers and detainees about cautioning
alongside observations in police stations.

Some police officers view the caution as *immaterial* to detainees
(AO44), a *waste of time* (AO17) and *part and parcel of the detention procedure*
(AO39). One officer described it as:

> the least useful thing that [detainees] get ... it can't possibly be
> digested and acted on by them ... I don't think it has any use at all
> for the suspect   [AO44]

Nonetheless, detainees use notions contained in the caution in making
decisions from the moment of arrest (Figure 8.1).

when I was picked on
camera ... he arrested
me there and said "do I
want to say anything"
and I thought oh
"oops" so I didn't
say anything then I
thought "no I'll wait
and see you know how
much trouble I'm in"
and then sort of say
"help" you know and
that was it [Novice 25]

Figure 8.1 A place for making decisions

8.2 The caution's legal background

The right to silence, a protection against self-incrimination, is long established in adversarial systems, originating in the seventeenth century (Morgan and Stephenson, 1994:2) from *ius commune* law applied throughout Europe (Alschuler, 1996:156), long before any formal police force (Clare, 2003:27). It follows from the principle that those accused of crimes need do nothing to prove their innocence, the onus being on the prosecution to prove guilt. The right was formalised in England and Wales by the Police and Criminal Evidence Act (PACE) (1984)[2] but by the late 1980s the Government noted concerns that it was being abused by defendants who presented evidence too late for prosecution investigation, the 'ambush defence'. A Home Office Working Group investigated the matter (Home Office, 1989). The eventual response, section 34 (s34) of the Criminal Justice and Public Order Act (CJPOA) (1994), permits courts to draw "such inferences ... as appear proper" from "failure or refusal" to answer questions at interview or charge in relation to evidence which is relied on in court (CJPOA, 1994: s34). Thus s34 modified the right to silence. It did not outlaw the ambush defence but altered its significance.[3] Section 34 was communicated, from April 1995, through the revised caution (included at the beginning of Section 8.1, above). Previously, police cautions had advised detainees only of their right to silence (maintained in the caution's first sentence above) and the recording of evidence (the final sentence). This new formulation added a long medial sentence, which presented the possibility of adverse inferences. The Government intended s34 and its caution to beleaguer "professional criminals, hardened criminals and terrorists" (Howard, 1994). However, prior to, during and since their introduction both measures faced extensive criticism from academics (Kurzon 1996; Morgan and Stephenson, 1994), media commentators (Bennetto, 1994), civil rights groups (Carol, 1994:1) and legal practitioners (Lindsay, 2006:4) amidst fears that they would erode, even effectively remove, the right to silence.[4] Two Royal Commissions even condemned inference-drawing (Royal Commission on Criminal Procedure, 1981:para4.53; Royal Commission on Criminal Justice 1993:para22–5).

Subsequently, the Human Rights Act (1998) has influenced discourses around s34, although without halting inference-drawing as some had suspected it might. A body of case law and appellate opinion in Britain and Europe has restricted s34 (exemplified in Appendix 10), the most significant of which illustrates that appeals around s34 have considered circumstances of particular cases, possible inferences and weight attached to inferences. R *v*. Argent [1996], in particular, led the Court of Appeal to specify six conditions which must be met before a jury can draw adverse inferences from silence in interview. These include a requirement that the accused only needs to have mentioned facts which are to be *relied* on in a defence and that the accused only needs to mention facts which could reasonably have been expected during questioning or charging. The six required elements following from Argent are presented as key to police officers in investigative interview training (Grainger, 2006b). Appeals have further clarified that:

- a case cannot rest solely on the accused's silence or failure to answer questions and that judges must elucidate this to juries (Dennis, 2002:28);
- a detainee only needs to mention facts if the prosecution's case unambiguously requires a response (JSB, 2001:38);
- a detainee only needs to mention facts if questioning has provided an "opportunity" to do so (Bucke, Street and Brown, 2000:x).

Appeals using s34, particularly on human rights grounds, have caused consternation amongst police officers. One groaned:

> don't tell me they're going to change it and bring a new [caution] in (.) I'll stop locking up (.) I can see it being extended now to include this will be a breach of your rights and all this sort of- this is not a breach of your human rights
>
> [AO22]

Cautioning procedure has indeed changed in response to one European Court of Human Rights judgement (Murray *v*. UK), enacted through the Youth Justice and Criminal Evidence Act (YJCEA) (1999) (section 58). That legislation forbids drawing inferences from silence, in cases where detainees have not been allowed legal advice. This is communicated to detainees through an alternative caution along with a lengthy prescribed explanation (PACE, Code C. 2006:Annex C). This ever-increasing variability in the caution's wording, explanation and application increases demands on both detainees and officers.

Changes to the right to silence arising from legislation or case law are influential only if they alter the behaviour of juries and magistrates in deciding cases, or defendants in selecting courses of action. Juries are assisted by judge's directions, typically compiled using the Crown Court Bench Book which contains specimen directions on silence in interview (s38) (JSB, 2001). However, jurors may misunderstand directions (Heffer, 2005). Indeed Birch blames s34's complexity, for judges and jurors, for the limited impact of s34 (1999:796). Jurors may furthermore ignore the directions, considering or disregarding silence at will. Indeed CPS employees believed that juries drew adverse inferences from silence even before s34 permitted them to do so (Bucke, Street and Brown, 2000:xii, 62). Defendants' decisions about whether to testify appear to have been unaffected by the revisions to the right to silence and statistics indicate no increase in conviction rates following s34 (Bucke, Street and Brown, 2000:65–7).

The message which most police officers take from all this is that s34 and its caution are ineffectual, *legislation rushed through* (AO14), which thus failed to influence:

- verdicts (*I don't know of an instance where they've actually looked grimly on the fact that someone hasn't mentioned something*, AO14);
- or sentences (*I don't think the court takes one bit of notice about whether they've lied or said nothing in an interview they don't get any more or any less at court*, AO06).

Although officers were largely unconvinced of the caution's effectiveness in court, some described how it nonetheless altered the interview room environment dramatically, recasting interrogation aims. As one officer explained, *it used to be you've got to get a cough*[5] *it's more what they don't say that's important now* (AO04). This is also reflected in solicitors' behaviour. Solicitors now often encourage detainees to provide a written statement during interview, rather than simply advising silence.

Despite the influence of s34 on officers' working environment the changes described above, precipitated by the YJCEA (1999), can be seen as part of an "increasing trend to restrict the operation of section 34", reducing it to the status of an "extraordinarily technical rule of corroboration" (Dennis, 2002:37; see also Birch, 1999:769; Appendix 10). Given such systematic reduction in the potency of s34, it seems odd that its restrictions on the right to silence are so foregrounded within police procedure by prioritisation and repetition of the caution at key stages of detention. This repetition, combined with the quagmire of law and its representation in the media, leads some detainees to suggest that they have no right to silence. After passing through detention, interview and change, this detainee observed:

isn't there a new law out saying that your right to silence is finished?
[Occasional 41]

Cautioning must overcome such misapprehensions early in detention, to avoid penalising those who were not the target of this legislation. Spoken language is crucial to achieving this.

8.3   The caution's textual background

8.3.1   The history and production of the official wording

Under Judges' Rules, before the 1980s, three cautions operated, used in different circumstances. The short form read:

> You are not obliged to say anything unless you wish to do so, but what you say may be put into writing and given in evidence.
>
> (Police Mutual Assurance Society, 1976:2)

In 1964, the *Police Review* observed that the detainee who chose to speak in interview was "probably more of a fool than a knave" (in Brandon and Davies, 1972:47–9). This pre-empts contemporary criticism of the current caution as potentially penalising only naïve detainees illustrating how "stable and enduring features of our everyday world" are assembled, partly, through "historical processes" (Mehan, 1993:243). The wording changed slightly in January 1986, under the governance of PACE (1984), removing *obliged* and reference to writing, reflecting the introduction of audio-recording:

> You do not have to say anything unless you wish to do so, but what you do say may be given in evidence.
>
> (Clare, 2003:63)

Shortly before the provision of the current caution, which introduced inference-drawing, a longer wording was proposed to do the same job:[6]

> You do not have to say anything. But if you do not mention now something which you later use in your defence, the court may decide that your failure to mention it now strengthens the case against you. A record will be made of anything you say and it may be given in evidence, if you are brought to trial.
>
> (Bennetto, 1994)

This formulation was seen as superior to the official wording shown at the beginning of this chapter by some, who accordingly used it as explanation (Wolverhampton City Council, 2004). Clare, Gudjonsson and Harari's experimental work found no advantage to the shorter official wording as it simply condensed information (1998:327). Nonetheless, that wording was placed before the House of Lords with the following endorsement:

> We believe that [these words] strike the right balance between legal accuracy and brevity. We believe that the caution will be easy for the police to remember and easy for suspects to understand.
>
> (Baroness Blatch, 1995)

Police officers recognise the demands of caution drafting, identifying similar priorities:

> I suspect it was quite a challenge to write that in a manner that was easily learnt easy to deliver not too long (.) but yet conveyed the meaning as clearly as possible
>
> [AO45]

Unfortunately, whatever challenges drafters faced, controversy has surrounded the wording. Shepherd, Mortimer and Mobasheri propose that it was drafted to "fulfil legal criteria" not to ensure comprehension (1995:65). The wording apparently underwent no field-testing prior to its introduction (cf. Dumas, 1990:349). Indeed apocryphal tales suggest that it was barely finalised before being hastily despatched to officers for immediate introduction.

Although miscomprehension of the caution or its explanations has not generated case law (Prince, 2003:pc), linguists and psychologists frequently provide opinion or testimony on the likelihood that particular individuals have misunderstood their rights (Carlin, 2003:pc; Cotterill, 2003:pc). Specific aspects of the caution can be said to cause comprehension difficulties. Very generally, the caution is a written formulation which is spoken in use. This raises problems of translating between modes, which are not exclusive to the caution. A designer from *The Bill* noted that the main reason scripts were modified during filming was because "words look fine on paper but just don't work when you say them" (2003).

8.3.2 Recontextualising the official wording

Section 10 (s10) of Code C requires officers to explain the caution "in their own words" "if it appears a person does not understand"

(2006:Note10D). Thus officers' reformulations are obligatory, "required ... by regulation or convention" yet spontaneous, arising from "judgement of a prevailing situation" (Cushing, 1994:55). Officers should allow spontaneity to govern obligation. However, s10 does not help them in making spontaneous decisions by specifying, for example, how to recognise detainees who "appear" not to understand. It also lacks an adverbial, clarifying why they should assess understanding. Should explanations seek comprehension or are they for explanation's sake?

Cautioning is organised around a distinctive "production format" of animator, author and principal roles (Goffman, 1981:144, 167, 229; see also Heydon, 2002:76). Officers *animate* the words, producing or uttering the caution's sound sequence. Government drafters have taken the *author* role, having prepared the text. Other government actors, particularly in the Home Office, acted as the *principal*, devising the caution's meaning on the basis of their commitments or beliefs. When delivering the official wording this role distribution creates difficulties for officers because in animating a pre-prepared script they cannot "take the local environment and the local hearership into consideration" (Goffman, 1981:255). When explaining the caution, however, the officer is able to consider local interactional factors by becoming the *author* of the reformulation and, to some extent, of the procedure around it. As cautioning is interactive, it cannot be examined without connecting "recontextualisation as a discursive resource" to these configurations of participants' roles (Sarangi, 1998a:306).

The requirement to explain the caution exemplifies "political changes changing the demands on people" and on "the way they communicate" (Barton, 1994:52). When PACE and its *Codes* were introduced, the Home Secretary reportedly recognised that learning the new procedures "created a major task for the police" (Home Office, 1985:2). The current caution, in turn, compounded these demands, attracting predictions that its semantic and illocutionary complexity would deter officers from reformulating through fear of misconduct allegations and appeals (Shepherd, Mortimer and Mobasheri, 1995:66). Whilst some officers in these data indeed described avoiding reformulation, for others the opportunity to explain was crucial to communicating meaning:

> I have to say it that way [the official wording] (.) what I have to get across to people is the fact that I have to get across this caution (.) once I've said the caution I can then get across the fact what it means
> [AO39]

Some officers even saw explanation as integral to, and inseparable from, the caution:

F   do you think it's well written...?
P   I don't know that it particularly ... [recites sentences 1 and 2] well I don't know because again when I do it ... I just split it into sections you know

[AO40]

For officers like AO40 there was little sense in evaluating a rarely isolated wording in isolation. Part III examines cautioning in context.

8.4   Multilingualism

Like the written rights notices discussed in Part II, spoken rights texts raise two questions around multilingualism. First, what provision is made for the many detainees who do not understand the language of administration sufficiently for rights communication to even begin? Secondly, how do the caution and associated procedures measure up to equivalent rights presentation in other countries? Examining multilingualism within England and Wales first, detainees should not be interviewed without an interpreter if "they have difficulty understanding English"; the interviewer does not speak their language or they want an interpreter to be present (PACE Code C, 2006:Para13.2). The question of how the caution is best explained changes dramatically with the involvement of an interpreter. Berk-Seligson finds that "problems can emerge" around explanations of spoken rights information even if the interpreter is a "highly competent professional". Her review of appellate court decisions throughout the USA shows that all too frequently interpreters are neither competent nor professional (2000:232). Russell too, working in Britain, finds the entire interview preamble characterised by "disfluency, inaccuracy and uncertainty" from interpreters which is most pronounced when explaining the caution (2000:45). Cautioning raises many difficulties for interpreters. Stone (2002:pc) and Graham (2003:pc), who both provide British Sign Language interpreting in police stations, independently described officers' tendency to call on them to evaluate detainees' comprehension and thus to move right outside their area of responsibility and expertise. Both actively resisted this.

The caution is available via the *Notice to detained persons* in 44 languages (see Section 3.4). Spoken versions are available in police stations and online (Home Office, 2006a). However, Russell recommends additionally introducing a standard translation of the caution and its reformulation specifically for interpreters (2000). A standard explanation translation should be tested for appropriate register and comprehensibility (Kempson and Moore, 1994:44) and produced in sufficient languages and detail (Hulst and Lentz, 2001:92–7). Whilst such translations would doubtless improve the lot of interpreters and detainees, inter-ethnic communication is not simply about this potentially token provision (Gumperz, 1992:245). Rather, training in multilingual interaction is important for people who provide services which "may critically affect an individual's opportunities, rights or well-being" or which offer "an opportunity for developing some form of communicative relationship however limited" (Roberts, Davies and Jupp, 1992:386). Both of these circumstances apply to police officers cautioning with an interpreter. Interpreters informally report that officers often struggle to incorporate them into interviews and to appreciate the detail of their role (Graham, 2003:pc; Stone, 2002:pc), suggesting the need for training.

Cautioning is not exclusive to England and Wales, although the wording and procedure here are fairly unique. Consideration of other systems illustrates, not least, how novel the caution may be to detainees from overseas, particularly from Roman Law systems, complicating the translator's task. Looking first to the form of international cautions, the Police Service of Northern Ireland uses a scripted caution, as do police forces in Australia (Gibbons, 2001a) and the USA (Berk-Seligson, 2000; Shuy, 1997:177). However, scripting is relatively rare. In Scotland, for example, there is no fixed wording according to Cooke and Philip (1998), although they imply that officers rely fairly heavily on formulations disseminated in training. Indeed, convergence towards cautioning norms is so widespread that some Scottish officers suggest that there is a standard wording (Malone, 2003). Cautions are not scripted in Israel (Kurzon, 2000:245), France (Russell, 2000:43) or the Netherlands – where they are nonetheless somewhat normalised (Komter, 2002:pc) as in Scotland. Scripted cautions are reportedly misunderstood across jurisdictions (Berk-Seligson, 2000; Dumas, 1990:329; Gibbons, 2001a, 2003; Shuy; 1997), although the same can be said for their non-scripted counterparts (Cooke and Philip, 1998). Turning now to cautions' meaning, few detainees from beyond England and Wales will have encountered the combination of a right to silence with the possibility that negative inferences will follow from that silence. Investigative procedures are sufficiently different in Roman law countries that the whole system will be unfamiliar, while USA citizens enjoy constitutional privilege against self-incrimination (Constitutional Amendment V, 1789) which renders the US right to silence more resilient to restriction than the caution has proven, for now (Kamisar; 1990:2679). The administration of the right also varies between jurisdictions. Israeli law, for example, explains "a version of the right of silence" only before interrogation not at arrest (Kurzon, 2000:245) and the Anglo-Welsh caution is not unusual in being administered both in speech and writing, rather than speech only.

Different jurisdictions' systems present subtly different challenges to detainees. In the USA, for example, Shuy notes a "strange everyday discourse illogicality" in *Miranda*, which offers the right to silence and only then offers the lawyer who might help in its exercise (1997:178). In the Anglo-Welsh system this plays out differently because the right to silence and the right to a solicitor are introduced at different times from one another and typically in different places: at arrest and on entering custody respectively.

Rights function differently in the Anglo-Welsh system and its USA counterpart. Under *Miranda*, questioning should stop if detainees invoke either their right to silence or to legal advice (Shuy, 1997:177; cf. Ainsworth, 1998:284; Leo, 2001:1013). In England, Wales and Northern Ireland officers can put questions irrespective of whether detainees have exhibited any inclination to answer (cf. Cotterill, 2000:17). In England and Wales then detainees must perform, rather than request, their right to silence.

8.5 Introducing data

8.5.1 Authentic interview-room data

The exchanges examined here in Part III, in which officers explain the caution to detainees, occurred during genuine police interviews. Participants were unaware in advance that their cautioning exchanges would be studied. In this respect there is a "complete absence of researcher influence on the data" (Potter and Wetherell, 1987:162). These data, totalling 41,849 words, illuminate officer practice in four police forces:

Force label	Location	Number of cautions
Force A	Northern England	49
Force B	Southern England ⎱ adjacent forces	36
Force C	Southern England ⎰	6
Force D	Wales	32
'Supplementary data'	Various locations, see below	21
Total		**151**

Forces A–D are geographically spread so their data provide a snap-shot of cautioning practice around England and Wales. Cautions from these forces were administered in 2000, when the current wording had been in use for around 5 years so had bedded down somewhat. Interviews in the Supplementary (S) group took place in various police forces soon after the caution was introduced. They therefore evidence an embryonic stage of emergent cautioning practice. Due to its heterogeneity, the Supplementary group is not considered in any statistical overviews; similarly Force C is excluded from statistics, being a particularly small sample. The interview room data show the reality of cautioning.

8.5.2   Officer interviews

I interviewed 48 police officers about cautioning and reformulating. All were from Force A. The semi-structured interviews yielded 157,024 words or over 17 hours of audio-recorded talk. The officers were diverse along several dimensions, providing a spectrum of cautioning experience. They were spread across two territorial divisions and based in five police stations: two suburban; one city-centre; one rural and one in a market town. They had wide-ranging roles and experience, from 'rookies', still training, to experienced officers nearing retirement. Relevant demographic information is summarised below:

Sex[7]	39 male officers
	9 female officers
Length of service	Longest = 29 years, 10 months
	Shortest = 5 months
	Average = 15 years (arithmetic mean)
Rank	37 Police Constables
	2 Detective Constables
	6 Police Sergeants
	2 Detective Sergeants
	1 Inspector

Officers who fulfil 19 different police roles were interviewed, including intelligence officers, incident-handlers and file-preparation officers. The most prevalent groups in these data administer the caution particularly frequently:

- **Uniformed patrol or 'beat' officers and uniformed response officers** – patrol on foot or by car and answer routine calls. They frequently make arrests and, in this Force, sometimes interview (19);

- **Uniformed interview or investigating officers** – are dedicated to interviewing (7);
- **CID officers** – investigate serious criminal offences, they arrest and interview (4).

These interviews were augmented by comment from five police trainers from different forces on their role in, and the significance of, cautioning training.

Police officers are somewhat unusual in that most are audio- or even video-recorded at work, some routinely. All interviewees therefore appeared comfortable talking at length, on tape. The interviews were conducted in officers' own police stations, usually away from their immediate working environment.

Not all officers showed insightful introspection in describing their aims and methods in reformulating. Asking speakers to try such a task stretches their metalinguistic capabilities. Some officers resorted to simulating interview preamble. Their talk illustrates an extreme observer's paradox, being purely illustrative (cf. Cotterill (2000) and Clare, Gudjonsson and Harari (1998) which both analyse officers' simulations). However, in most of the interviews it was possible to get beyond simulation to access officers' metalinguistic knowledge (Davies, 1997) about cautioning and reformulating. The interviews reveal a great deal about what explaining is in relation to this text and context. Officers who expressed doubt about the usefulness of their interview contributions, paradoxically, made comments which suggest that they critically reflect on:

- institutionally prescribed written and spoken texts;
- the quality of their cautioning practices;
- the task of reformulating and its institutional and interpersonal place and ends;
- reformulations as artefacts;
- the resources available to them in cautioning.

Whether one condemns or condones the requirement for officers to explain the caution these interviews suggest that many officers are neither cavalier nor ingenuous about explaining; indeed some were keen to find out more:

I would be interested to see the result you'll publish it? ... some of those questions that you ask suddenly make you step out of yourself and think from their point of view and I think that's interesting

[AO38]

Some aspects of the caution are invariant. First, the label *caution* itself and, secondly, the prescribed, official wording. Sections 8.6 and 8.7 consider the adequacy of these permanent fixtures by combining relevant research literature, police interview data and officers' comments. This makes it possible to conclude the chapter in Sections 8.8 to 8.10 by turning to the aspect of cautioning which varies enormously and which is the main focus of Part III; the explanation of the caution and its place within the macro-structure of cautioning.

8.6   The label *caution*

8.6.1   *Caution* and pragmatic intent

Some misunderstandings of the caution begin with the label *caution* itself (Rock, 2000; Russell, 2000:41), which many officers use within cautioning exchanges:

	1	P	you're under caution [states official wording] that's the caution and quite an important part of this interview can you explain to me in your own words what that caution means?
→	2	D	(3.7)
	3	P	what does that caution mean name?
→	4	D	the caution?
→	5	P	yeh the thing I just read out to you
	6	D	oh yeh u::::m that you're not (.) obliged to say anything... [B34]

This detainee's hesitation (turn 2) and question (turn 4) and the success of the officer's clarification (turn 5) suggest that the detainee did not link *caution* with the wording he had heard. Yet the officer began with *you're under caution* and reinforced the link between *caution* and the wording through the cataphoric summary *that's the caution* and deictic *that caution* towards the end of turn 1. Cautioning in interview is part of interview preamble, which also includes introductions of participants 'for the tape' and the reiteration that free legal advice is available.

Cautioning exchanges can be lengthy, and sometimes indistinct from preamble co-text even if explicitly distinguished with the word *caution*:

> P   so that I'm happy that you understand the caution can you just
>   explain it as you understand it tell me what it means to you
> D   that I need if I need a solicitor I can have my solicitor here [A19]

Empirical evidence recommends using "conventional warning labels" when presenting warnings (Dumas, 1990:348) as these officers do. Yet 17 per cent of officers in these data did not use *caution* at all when delivering the wording. This is quite legitimate as the official formulation does not include the word. Certainly, the detainees in the excerpts above did not benefit from its inclusion.

Along with the question of whether officers should label the caution when reciting it, we might also ask whether *caution* is the right label in any case. Most common law countries call cautions by that name, the USA Miranda *warnings* being a notable exception (Gibbons, 2003:187). For one officer, at least, *caution* is perfect:

> the actual word *caution* is quite good because it is saying to them (.)
> "stop and think (.) I'm cautioning you (.) just be wary now from this
> point onwards this is official listen to everything that's going on" ...
> so I think it's advice and information it is a warning I think its all
> those things the word *caution* I think in itself sums it up for me
> [AO42]

Yet, authors problematise both *caution* and *warning*, proposing that neither are appropriate because the caution's "intended meaning" concerns, instead, advice-giving (Cotterill, 2000:12). Potentially the caution might also be evaluated, in speech act terms, as promising, ordering or reassuring. According to lay people it is pressurising or threatening (Shepherd, Mortimer and Mobasheri, 1995:64–6). The caution's various propositions might be best evaluated separately as shown in Figure 8.2.

Some officers recognised this diversity, specifying the speech act function of individual parts of the caution, typically the medial sentence as warning (cf. Cotterill, 2000:14).

Whatever label is used it should reduce ambiguity, as "one needs to know the speech act ... before one can understand it" (Barton, 1994:65). However, the speech act ambiguity of the wording and its parts is further complicated by the respective roles of detainees, officers and the institution. Officers may not be truly in a position to issue all of

Sentence from the official wording	Predominantly concerned with:	Also potentially concerned with:
1. You do not have to say anything.	*Informing (I hereby inform you that you do not have to...)*	Reassuring, advising
2. But it may harm your defence	*Warning (If you do a then b)*	Threatening, advising, ordering
3. Anything you do say may be given in evidence.	*Warning (If you do c then d)*	Threatening, advising, informing

Figure 8.2 Speech acts and the caution's propositions

the speech acts within cautioning to detainees whom they are about to interview. In cautioning and recontextualising the caution, animating officers (Goffman, 1981:167) shift footing (Goffman, 1981:128), moving from aligning as investigator to teacher (Berk-Seligson, 2000) or translator (Cotterill, 2000; Tiersma, 1999a). The legal institution, as author and principal of the caution (Goffman, 1981:167), also shifts from exercising its power, to fulfilling its responsibility. If these shifts are not accomplished successfully or detainees do not recognise them the caution's pragmatic intent will be clouded, the wording becoming "ineffective" (Cushing, 1994:55) either in terms of illocution or perlocution. In view of this interpersonal context the caution can be seen as telling about a warning rather than straightforwardly warning.

8.6.2 Misaligning the label *caution*

In police detention the label *caution* is a homonym. *Caution* denotes not only the official statement of the right to silence but also has a completely unrelated referent, the "indefinite article caution" (Cotterill, 2000:4) or 'reprimand caution', issued to adults who admit a minor or first offence (Home Office, 2006c). To successfully issue a reprimand caution officers must gain informed consent to receiving a caution and must convey the reprimand caution's deterrent intent. The reprimand caution is different in almost every way from the warning caution, examined here, yet detainees confuse them. The detainees below are speaking at the beginning of their police interviews, having heard the warning caution introduced with the label *caution*. They have been asked to demonstrate comprehension, through explanation:

it just means that you're telling me off ... what is it the same caution
as last time I've had   [A24]

it means (.) you get a caution (.) and you just get it on the criminal
record   [A40]

Both describe the wrong caution. This illustrates a serious shortcoming
of *caution*'s homonymy and suggests that *caution* is a biased homonym
(having one dominant meaning). The COBUILD Corpus reveals that
police caution denotes the reprimand caution much more frequently than
the warning caution, at a 17:1 ratio in newspapers; the detainees above
may simply be evoking background knowledge from beyond detention.
These misunderstandings are not unpredictable. In reading, biased homo-
graphs trouble readers, receiving longer gaze durations than unambiguous
control words (Rayner, Pacht and Duffy, 1994). It is vital that detainees
recognise the warning caution as such because it defines, substantiates
and explains the interview which it prospects. Detainees who have misid-
entified the caution are not participating in the same speech event as
other detainees nor in the kind of speech event that the criminal justice
system intends or will subsequently take them as having participated in.
Moreover, detainees are disadvantaged if they believe that their detention
has reached its outcome – reprimand – when, in fact, they are about to be
interviewed to determine outcome. Such misappropriation may even elicit
confessions because in order to receive a reprimand caution an offender
must admit his or her offence (Home Office, 2005). The officers who
heard the two reformulations above responded very differently from one
another. Those who heard the first example simply offered a reformulation
without flagging the existence of two different *caution* referents:

P   do you want do you want us to explain
P2   I'll go through it shall I?
D   alright then   [A24]

In contrast, the officers who heard the second example drew attention
to the source of the detainee's confusion, saying:

P   nah that's a different type of caution
P2   ((you're thinking- thinking of))
P   [laughing] yeah (.) I'll go through it   [A40]

The problems caused by using the same label for two different but significant parts of the criminal justice process, both of which are well known to lay people and both of which occur at the police station, appear real. Police officers' responses to such confusion are crucial.

8.7   The official wording

8.7.1   Critiquing the formulation

Police officers discussing the caution's official wording in these data more often voiced condemnation than praise. However, they also moved beyond the general to discuss subtleties. A content–form distinction was particularly salient to many assessments:

> I don't know how they could improve it you know (.) not in a literal (.) wordy sense [= form] whether it should have more safeguards in for the prisoner I don't know [= content]   [AO01]

At the content level, the dominant view, as AO18 succinctly put it, is that *the law itself is unwieldy*. Turning to form, whilst officers applauded a short official wording they felt that brevity prevented the caution from giving *the full picture* (AO24). Therefore they exhibited realism about the caution's function which they saw as not necessarily about conveying information:

> how can you get the amount of information over to somebody in just a line or a few words? because when you give the caution to actually explain it involves a lot more   [AO09]

Many were resigned to a somewhat token caution:

> there's no way you can get a full explanation well you could do but we'd end up like America carrying a big card about   [AO05]

Officers proposed that the caution presents particular difficulty for some audiences (AO21, AO05), especially juveniles and novices (AO22). Some admitted finding the text baffling themselves (AO38). Others felt that arrest and interview contributed to – even caused – difficulty by inducing stress (*I'm not so sure it's that understandable considering somebody is under pressure*, AO48) or distraction (*their mind's closed all they're thinking about is going in a cell*, AO22). Accordingly, some sought to *improve* the official wording through delivery (AO18). AO03 prioritised pace and gaze, explaining that, when possible (in interview), officers recite the caution *slowly* whilst *looking at* detainees. AO10 agreed that when cautioning during interview preamble *you can actually pause when you're supposed to pause*. AO48, a custody sergeant, attended to wider aspects of intonation, giving short shrift to officers who deliver the caution hastily and do not *say it with meaning* or *put any emphasis on it or any particular words*. He described hearing the official wording delivered so speedily that it became inaudible:

> I've actually said "look just say that again but say it like I could hear you as well as him there" and they've sort of laughed and embarrassed about it- but they've said it again

Such informal styling (Cameron, 2000:331) is prevalent in these data (see Section 12.3.1). Concern about idiosyncratic delivery of the caution was expressed, even from its introduction, by the *Police Review* (1997:25), a widely distributed magazine for officers (Figure 8.3).

Figure 8.3 Fears about caution delivery

8.7.2 Formulaicity

The use of an official wording generates frozen register (Danet, 1984a:4; Joos, 1967). Such formulaicity or pre-patterning can be a "resource for creativity" (Tannen, 1989:37), imbuing recurring items with "meaning or symbolic value" (Merritt, 1994:33) and, in legal settings, can afford verbal formulae a "special strength" (Goody, 1986:151) creating "the myth" that they have "special, quasi-magical powers" through a strong "ritual element" (PEC, 1993:46). In cautioning, legal language does have special powers because cautioning is a felicity condition for arrest and detention. "Rituals of authority" also bring "an aura of stability and regularity" (Bazerman, 1997:44). This is another important function of cautioning. Formulaicity can make warnings conspicuous (Dumas, 1990:348). However, it might conversely cause contamination through poetisation (Danet, 1984b:143) or over-familiarity, a criticism also levelled at courtroom oaths (Jackson, 1995:122) and *Miranda* with its "familiar numbing ring" (Leo, 2001:1012). Ritualisation can lead to "statements and situations losing their cognitive impact and participants falling into patterns of simply going through the motions" (Cushing, 1994:63). The caution is indeed so recognisable that it is played on in cheeky – or unsavoury – seaside humour (Figure 8.4).

At the root of formulaicity is repetition. The caution is globally (Johnstone *et al.*, 1994:4) or diachronically repetitive (Tannen, 1989:2) for officers, echoing other cautions that they have read, heard or said, and for detainees, recalling previous arrests or media representations (see Section 7.2.3.1). Slightly more locally, the caution, delivered in interview or at charge, echoes earlier instantiations within the current detention for both speaker and hearer. At the most local level (Johnstone *et al.*, 1994:5), synchronic repetition (Tannen, 1989:2) of the caution occurs within a given interview or explanation. Such extensive repetition risks undermining "the overall success" of interactions (Cushing, 1994:57). Ironically, cautioning repeatedly might make cautioning impotent because so much detention procedure is repetitive that "repetition eventually becomes the less foregrounded option and suddenly *not* repeating is foregrounded" (Johnstone *et al.*, 1994:19).

The caution's scripted familiarity produces "hyperfluent" recitations from officers (Goffman, 1981:189). Some recited it in as little as 6.5 seconds in these data. Such haste, also noted by Leo in USA *Miranda* recitations, potentially conveys that rights warnings are "little more than a bureaucratic triviality" (1998a:67), which "do not merit the suspect's

Figure 8.4 The caution's familiarity (Billboard, South Promenade, Blackpool, 2002) [8]

concern" (1998b:216). Many officers described the way the official wording becomes for them *almost second nature* (AO03), regurgitated *parrot fashion* (AO39), like a *metronome* (AO48) or *like changing gear on a car* (AO16). The diversity of metaphors through which officers described assimilating the caution was striking, suggesting hyperfluency's pervasiveness. Some officers felt internalisation of the wording negatively affected their delivery and their conception of it, making them oblivious to its:

- Meaning
  - you don't even think about it really   [AO15]

- Significance to detainees
  - I don't think the police officers are reminded ... you're doing this there's a reason   [AO48]

- Potential difficulty
  - sometimes when you look at it yourself you think "oh God it is a bit unwieldy isn't it"   [AO01]

Officers perceived a high risk of forgetting a wording which had become so automatic, and attached great significance to this risk (AO45), even giving temporary forgetfulness a name, *keyboard lock* (AO12). Officers narrativised this aspect of their cautioning experience, providing colourful anecdotes about cautioning gaffes, which suggested three factors as particularly likely to hinder recall:

1. Residual memory of previous cautions – which caused some officers to need *two or three goes before it was right* (AO26);
2. Cautioning in disorienting circumstances – particularly when *suddenly ... thrust into interview* (AO16) or in court (AO22) *when the solicitor tries to put you on your back foot by just straight away saying "well what's the caution?"* (AO06);
3. Cautioning only occasionally – which is *worse now that the caution is longer* (AO27).

To complicate matters, some detainees hear the caution more regularly than officers. AO09 described accidentally delivering the 1986 caution long after the introduction of its successor and being corrected by the detainee. While this might appear to exemplify a careless police officer, he, like others who made cautioning errors, did not take it lightly. Their accounts evidence the unique test presented by a standard wording.

Having considered the label *caution* and the official wording which are both relatively fixed, this chapter closes by introducing the less fixed aspects of the caution; its explanation by individual officers and their remarks on that explanation. This offers orientation for the rest of Part III which considers explanation in detail.

8.8   *The cautioning exchange*

This book's focus on recontextualisation or explanation precipitates, to some extent, a focus on cautioning at interview as officers are most likely to explain at interview. A relatively predictable exchange structure (Sinclair and Coulthard, 1975:64) has emerged around cautioning at interview (Table 8.1).

Cautioning thus has a canonical form, minimally consisting of one obligatory slot (marked with asterisks, in Table 8.1), typically consisting

Table 8.1   Cautioning exchange structure

Speaker	Activity	Sample realisation	Interactional category
Officer	Introduces official wording	first of all I must caution you (.) you do not have to say anything... [A38] the interview will be conducted under caution which is that you... [A2]	/
=*Officer=*	=*States official wording=*	...	/
=+Officer=+	=+Checks understanding (yes-/no-inviting question)=+	d'you understand all that? [A4] you understand what I mean by that caution? [A6]	Initiation
=Detainee=	=Responds (Yes/no/variant)=	yes	Response
Officer	Requests a detainee reformulation	can you just explain to me what you believe that means? [A4] could you just tell us in your own words what you think it means? [A8]	Initiation/ Feedback?
Detainee	Responds	whatever I say can use it against me in a court of law [A1] (.) means (2.1) erm that I (.) I don't know [A44]	Response/ Initiation
Officer	Reformulates	right yep basically it means that but also ... [A37] I'll just explain it to you anyway ... [A7] basically the first bit means (.) don't say anything if you don't want ... [A48]	Response/ Feedback?
+Officer+	+Checks understanding+	now do you understand that? [A3] is that OK? [A14]	Initiation
Detainee	Responds (Yes/no/variant)	yes	Response
Officer	checks understanding with a third party	[to appropriate adult] are you happy with that too? [A45] [to solicitor] are you quite happy he understands? [A25]	Initiation
Third party	Responds (Yes/no/variant)	yes	Response

of at least three slots (marked with = signs) and maximally consisting of this much longer series of moves (Goffman, 1981:24).[9] Within this structure officers ostensibly assess detainees' comprehension twice, in the slots marked with + signs. Some moves connect in "predictable ways" (cf. Cody and McLaughlin, 1988:116). For example, the response to *do you understand* is almost invariably *yes* (Chapter 11). Relationships between other constituents are less predictable. For example, an incomplete reformulation from a detainee does not always precipitate a 'corrective' reformulation from an officer (Chapter 11). Additionally, each constituent might be performed very differently by different speakers (Chapters 9–11). For example, some officers respond to detainees' reformulations with explicit evaluation (exemplified by the excerpt from A37, in Table 8.1), others by prospecting their own reformulations (A7, Table 8.1) and yet others by simply beginning a reformulation of their own (A48, in the table).

Cautioning exchanges potentially mystify detainees. For example, officers state the caution without advising detainees that they might imminently be asked to explain. Furthermore, detainees rarely initiate "*negotiated* misunderstandings" cued, for example, by metadiscursive admission of misunderstanding (Blum-Kulka and Weizman, 2003:110). Of the 151 cautioning exchanges examined here, only one sees a detainee request a reformulation and that request is only prompted by cautioning procedure itself:

P   can you just tell us what you think [the caution] means
D   er well I don't- you'll have to explain it to me
P   right   [A32]

Whilst detainees may benefit from an explanation, their apparent lack of interest in receiving one suggests that explaining concerns more than detainees' needs. Ultimately, not only detainees are addressed through cautioning exchanges as Figure 8.5 indicates.

Figure 8.5, showing the detainee's perspective on a police interview room, illustrates that the absent, overhearing courtroom audience who may later hear or see a recording or transcript of the interview has, to some extent, a presence in the interview room through the cassette recorder or video camera which, in this case, dominate (cf. Heritage, 1985). Gibbons describes the courts as the "first" audience of statutory wordings like the caution (2003:186). Indeed both officers and detainees orient to the presence of these potential overhearers throughout cautioning exchanges (Chapter 12).

Figure 8.5 The police interview room

An additional challenge to officers is to know when comprehension checking is complete. At present, the cautioning exchange structure is so established that once the structure in Table 8.1 has been completed, cautioning is almost inevitably completed too. The procedure is governed by institutional rather than interpersonal criteria. In other settings, repetition and redrafting continue until "the final product of the exchange, the solution, is achieved" (Bean and Patthey-Chavez, 1994:210). However, at the beginning of the cautioning exchange the detainee's affirmative response to comprehension checking is taken to indicate incomprehension, whereas at the end of the exchange it indicates the opposite. Expecting officers to judge that they have assured comprehension is rather unrealistic. For example, interactants might calibrate comprehension differently according to "the person who is doing the understanding" (White and Gunstone, 1992:7); it is difficult to be objective about comprehension. Additionally, police procedure gives no guidance on what to do if reformulating fails. On the rare occasions when detainees repeatedly clam incomprehension, officers' only recourse is to re-explain.

8.9   Assumptions underlying cautioning procedure

If the law genuinely intends a standardised caution wording to inform all individuals about their rights in custody, it assumes communication is linear and that the caution is a conduit (Reddy, 1979). However, if the law then offers a more spontaneous rendering and asks officers and detainees to discuss meaning, it problematises these assumptions. Cautioning procedure then rests on conflicting assumptions about the nature of communication, outlined in Figure 8.6. Ultimately, it asks officers and detainees to buy into a commodification of comprehension as assessable and countable.

Providing an official wording assumes that:
- the transmission model of communication holds (see Section 2.2);
- AND there is one optimal formulation for delivering any given proposition(s) to all people, across settings and situations;
- OR, if there is not one optimal formulation, there are other motivations for using one official formulation which override that. These motivations might include achieving performativity through an official formulation and practical considerations like assisting officers' memory.

Conversely, allowing officers to reformulate assumes that:
- there is not one optimal formulation for delivering particular proposition(s) to all people, across settings and situations;
- speakers have an innate ability to explain propositions effectively;
- OR speakers can be taught to explain propositions in a maximally effective way;
- speakers can successfully tailor explanations to their interlocutors after minimal interaction.

Repeating an official wording at different stages of arrest and detention assumes that:
- addressees will recognise identical wordings as being 'the same' across different situations, settings and contexts;
- YET, addressees will recognise that identical wordings have different meanings across different situations, settings and contexts (recognising that although the same wording is used at arrest and interview, it is not intended to mean the same thing on each occasion);
- addressees will understand propositions more deeply if they are exposed to them repeatedly.

Figure 8.6 Assumptions underlying cautioning

Checking comprehension using a yes-/no-inviting question assumes that:

- language users can make sense of a binary 'understanding vs. not understanding' distinction and that such an opposition is useful;
- language users share common notions of 'understanding';
- addressees can assess their own comprehension, irrespective of whether they understand;
- addressees will assess their own comprehension honestly, in detention.

Requesting a reformulation in order to check comprehension assumes that:

- ability to articulate indicates comprehension;
- inability to articulate indicates incomprehension;
- ability to articulate indicates ability to apply information.

Both comprehension checks assume that:

- officers can make sense of and assess detainees' words and can respond accordingly;
- the caution is likely to be understood (cf. Heydon, 2002:187).

Cautioning immediately before interviews assumes that:

- addressees can act on information as soon as they receive it.

Figure 8.6 (Continued)

8.10 Working with meaning

An important legal and linguistic question is "what does the caution mean?" Officers explaining to detainees had evidently thought long and hard about this. Figure 8.7 amalgamates information introduced across all reformulations: the caution's meaning as officers present it (individual officers did not present all points).

Chapters 9–12 examine how the semantic possibilities of Figure 8.7 are incorporated into officers' work and detainees' lives.

As well as examining officers' explanations of the caution, Chapters 9–12 use officers' introspections to examine their representations of explanation. As Chapter 2 indicated, "recontextualisation is never a pure transfer of a fixed meaning" (Linell, 1998:144) and because officers orient to institutionality differently (Drew and Sorjonen, 1997:99) they

Official wording	Meaning	
You do not have to say anything	You have a right to total silence	
	You have a right to partial silence (silence in response to some questions)	
But it may harm your defence	Some linguistic (in)activity during the investigation may be detrimental to your case causing the court to draw negative inferences	
	Linguistic (in)activity may not be detrimental to your case because, although the court may draw negative inferences from that (in)activity, it may nonetheless disregard those inferences or their outcomes	
	Linguistic (in)activity may not be detrimental to your case as the court may not draw negative inferences on the basis of that (in)activity	
	Linguistic (in)activity may not be detrimental to your case as the court may draw positive inferences from it	
	The courts can draw particular inferences, specifically that the detainee • is guilty • has something to hide • has "guilty knowledge"	
If you do not mention ... something which you later rely on in court	The court can draw negative inferences if detainees "come up with a story" when they reach court having been silent during interview	The court can *only* draw negative inferences if the detainee answers specific questions in court which are identical to those not answered in interview
		The court can draw negative inferences if *any* defence evidence (verbal or otherwise) uses anything which the detainee might reasonably have been expected to answer or raise during interview, but did not
	The court can draw negative inferences if detainees "change their story" when they reach court having given a different story during interview. (This is now deemed beyond the caution's meaning (R v. Shulka, 2006; Rock, forthcoming)	The court can *only* draw negative inferences if the detainee answers specific questions in court which are identical to questions asked during interview with responses which differ from those they provided during interview
		The court can draw negative inferences if *any* defence evidence (verbal or otherwise) uses anything which the detainee said during interview, but about which they said something different during interview
When questioned	The caution only applies to your answers to my questions	
	The caution only applies to your comments during "questioning" (interview)	
	The caution applies to anything you say whilst at the police station	
	The caution applies to anything you say whilst under arrest	
Anything you do say may be given in evidence	Words exchanged during interview can be presented as evidence [The method of presentation might be exemplified]	
	All officers words can also be given in evidence	

Figure 8.7   What does the caution mean to police officers?

explain differently. As well as working on meaning (illustrated in Figure 8.7) officers' explanations work on the caution's affective value, representing the social world (Fairclough, 2001:93).

A few officers were acutely aware of cautioning's potential, accordingly identifying a need to avoid *blurring* distinctions between explaining (officers' responsibility) and advising (solicitors' responsibility) (AO45). These officers claimed to be *careful* in order to avoid giving *the impression that they're influencing the suspect* (AO26). One sergeant indeed described encouraging colleagues to leave reformulation to solicitors wherever possible because *that way I'm not going to mislead them* (AO18). Other managerial officers conversely encouraged officers to reformulate *'to be on the safe side' as you're never going to get criticised for that* (AO28) (cf. Cameron, 2000:326). Officers who overlooked the potency of explanation had an overly simplistic understanding of their explanation task:

> every officer probably explains it differently but the meaning is always the same ... we all look at one word and read it in a certain manner we'd all read a book and summarise that book in a different way but also at the end of the day the core meaning of it is the same
> [AO19]

For him, the meaning of a reformulation inevitably duplicates that of its source, making biased reformulations inconceivable. AO23 agreed, explaining *I don't think you could ever misconstrue [the caution] to make it to the police advantage ... it's for their benefit that it's being explained.* He suggests that audience needs determine meaning. This diversity in understanding the very nature of explanation drives the coming chapters.

Chapters 9 and 10 explore officers' explanations of the official wording. Chapter 9 examines sequence and responses to sequence. Chapter 10 examines officers' explanations of particular words and potential affective consequences of their choices. Chapter 11 moves from officers' explanations to their methods for evaluating comprehension and their use of detainees' talk to that end. All of the chapters in Part III consider more than only the referential function of cautioning. The final chapter in this part (Chapter 12) moves away from the referential function completely to examine how both officers and detainees appropriate cautioning for interpersonal and interactional ends.

9
Working with Lexis in Speech

9.1 Introduction

By inviting officers to explain the caution the institution gives detainees *the opportunity to say "well talk to me in English"* (AO42). Officers' responses vary enormously. It is extremely profitable to ask why (cf. Polanyi, 1981). This chapter does so by exploring the four lexical items highlighted in the official wording below. The data themselves recommended these items for scrutiny in that these were words explained in reformulations (cf. Cotterill, 2000):

> You do not have to say anything. But it may harm your defence if you do **not** mention when **questioned something** which you later rely on in **court**. Anything you do say will be given in evidence.

Each of these words is packed with meaning in the caution. We will see that, in explaining them, officers unpack this meaning by bringing the caution to life or, as Linell puts it, by "relating that which is to be interpreted and understood to something, a set of contextual properties, which is already known or partially understood" (1998:144). This is important because, as one officer proposed, detainees see the caution having no significance in the lifeworld and local decisions:

> F   do you think people [in police interviews] have any sense of why you're saying all the stuff you do at the beginning of the interview?
>
> P   yeh well no a lot of people will say "ur well yeh but it doesn't affect me it doesn't affect me"   [AO39]

Officers, like many other institutional actors, must contextualise institutionally sanctioned information in ways which make it personally relevant (Adelswärd and Sachs, 1998:194, 207) if they are to help detainees to make decisions (Sarangi, 1998a:312). In some cases they add detail which simply brings specificity. In other cases their additions bring new meaning or even affective change.

Officers had strong views on what made a good reformulation. For some, comprehensible language was a relative concept requiring *different words with different people* and a fit to *particular circumstances* (AO47). For other officers, *simple* language equated with *normal English* which was unitary and comprehensible to *the public ... whether juveniles or pensioners* (AO29). For some, simplicity related to text length. AO48, for example, praised long reformulations which explore and *embellish*, whilst AO47 associated lengthy recontextualisation with excessive detail. Explaining particular lexical items and register shifting are likely to be important to caution explanations as detainees misunderstand some of the caution's words through "interference from their real-world lexicon" (Cotterill, 2000:15) because the caution, like other legal texts, uses "everyday words in a specialised sense" (Gibbons, 1999:158), "common words with uncommon meanings" (Jackson, 1995:113). This phenomenon can afflict some quite unlikely words and phrases (Kempson and Moore, 1994:43) such as those examined in this chapter, *not*, *questioned*, *something* and *court*. These do not appear technical "at first sight", so lay readers might not realise that they need "special attention" (Jansen and Steehouder, 2001:18) or might have difficulty distinguishing when legal versus non-legal senses apply (Jackson, 1995:113). Thus one task of the reformulating police officer involves identifying which words have a legal sense and explaining that sense.

9.2 Metonymy and polysemy in *court*

The first example here, *court*, attracted officers' attention because they suspected that detainees might simply miss its full legal sense. AO27, for example, identified a need to *explain the process ... how the courts work*. Twenty-six per cent of officers who explained the sentence which contains *court* addressed its metonymy in denoting a place and particularly people. They called attention to all its possible human referents:

the court and it's magistrate or judge and jury	[S4]
the magistrates or the judge or the jury	[C1]

Others were less exhaustive, identifying just one potential referent and in some cases combining that with catch-all pronouns:

the magistrates	[D15]
the magistrates or whatever	[B21]
the judge	[S21]
the judge whoever	[S16]

Such illustrations additionally attend to *court*'s polysemy. British courts presently try offences either by magistrates or a judge and jury. Many offences are automatically allocated to one of these trial modes, with some triable 'either way'. Officers who glossed *court* as either denoting *magistrates* or *judges* were possibly prospecting the likely mode of trial if their addressees attended court. Anglo-Welsh courtrooms also feature clear role-allocation: some participants decide guilt or innocence; others oversee cases and pass sentence. Officers attended to polysemy along this dimension too, exemplifying potential court participants by role either mentioning overseers:

whoever the judge or magistrates	[A13]

or decision-makers:

the jury or: the magistrate whatever[1]	[D19]

Other officers provided more detail: They presented judges and juries working together and in so doing described a small aspect of trial procedure:

the judge may direct a jury	[S11]
it would be open for a judge to direct a jury	[S20]

Two officers avoided naming particular decision-makers; instead simply pointing out that metonymic *court* denotes people and not a location:

the court people in the courts	[A33]
people	[C6]

Whilst illustrating *court*, the final four examples above could be negatively evaluated. In summarising procedure S11 and S20 introduce the 'specialist' sense of the 'everyday' word *direct* and by using *people* A33 and C6 risk implying that all people in court decide cases. These officers all explain by providing detail, fleshing out the word to be defined. Nonetheless all simply explain, they do not evaluate the court or suggest an orientation to court for the detainee. The other examples in this chapter are rather different.

9.3 Different situations, different cautions: *Questioned*

The short, vague, subordinated adverbial clause *when questioned* features in the caution at arrest and in interview.[2] At arrest, officers can only ask detainees limited questions so, then, *when questioned* prospects interview, a distant interaction. Yet in interview, the same words prospect imminent talk. Effectively the meaning of *when questioned* in the caution depends on the situation in which it is said. Officers identified problems around this variable meaning:

> I think it's often about timing with prisoners when they're in custody (.) they're not sure at which point ... they should say things and they shouldn't say things   [AO05]

Officers appreciated institutional justifications for including *when questioned* at arrest but were nonetheless uncomfortable about its implicature, through the maxim of relation (Grice, 1975), that *questioned* might denote something imminent (Levenson, Fairweather and Cape, 1996:218):

> at the point of arrest it's not wholly appropriate to start talking about when they're going to be questioned because ... it doesn't mean anything to them at that point ... they're not sure whether in our terms they're being questioned at the moment [of arrest]   [AO05]

AO40 noted that, institutionally, any talk from detainees about the investigation at arrest is evidentially dubious, explaining *I would rather I didn't get anything at that stage because ... this is where you're open to accusations like the old days* although, as AO02 acknowledged *that's a time ... when they're more likely to say something.* The Law Society shares these concerns and accordingly recommends that when the caution is recited at arrest its second sentence (*But it may harm your defence ...*) should be removed completely (2002:7). Officers too suggested a solution – relexicalisation, replacing *questioned* with *interviewed*, which was felt to be less ambiguous (AO05). For the moment, however, officers must work with this ambiguity. At arrest they accordingly caution tactically to silence detainees, telling them *don't talk about it now ... we need to talk about it but it has to be later and it'll be on tape* (AO07) and even *you've been given the caution my advice would be part of that caution is you do not have to say anything and I think it would probably be in your best interests if you keep quiet* (AO01). This happens on arrest and during journeys to the police station:

> a lot of them will still try and talk to you about the offence while you're travelling in the car and you have to explain to them "look this is not the place to talk"   [AO11]

At interview, officers add different circumstantial elements (Halliday, 2004:176) and do not necessarily intend to silence detainees as they did at arrest. The typical example below is divided and formatted for reference:

	S	V	iO	dO
1	now (.) **myself and Jim** here's going to **ask** you some **questions**			
2	**about why** we came to see you (.) you know what we was on about this morning **why** we came to see you			
3	and **we'll be inviting** you to make replies to those questions			

                                                                           [A12]

- In (1), the officer's active construction thematises two questioners and specifies a questionee. He converts *questioned* into the verb + direct object *ask ... some questions*, prospecting upcoming activities exactly;
- In (2), he provides, recasts and repeats a questioning topic;
- Finally, in (3), he prospects the detainee's involvement.

This officer therefore translates *when questioned* into a detailed description of its entailment in context. The officer below packages detail differently, but still specifies the identity of a questionee (*you*), questioner (*me*) and questioning time (*now*):

> when questioned you're only going to get questioned by me once and that's now OK?   [D6]

The caution does not provide circumstantial elements so officers add them *ad hoc*. To omit such details from the official wording is rather anomalous alongside other 'everyday' texts such as newspapers. Providing a simple comparison, occurrences of *when questioned* in the news sections of the COBUILD Corpus are typically followed immediately by specification of the items shown in Figure 9.1.

Indeed, throughout the speech and news sections of the Corpus, 97 per cent of the string's occurrences collocate with a circumstantial element, most commonly a topic (see Figure 9.2). The three most common words to follow *questioned* in those section of the corpus (by *t*-score), *by*, *about* and *whether*, each introduce such clarification (cf. Fox, 1993:184).

Circumstantial detail varies across cautioning situations so cannot, of course, be incorporated into a single official wording. Nonetheless, officers could usefully receive guidelines indicating what details they might specify, perhaps illustrated with naturally occurring examples. By providing context-specific details, officers transitorily make the caution relevant.

As well as specifying *when questioned*, the excerpts above also alter affect. Officers were quite clear that their reformulations at arrest were

Circumstantial Element	Examples – *when questioned* ...
Topic	***about*** *his intentions* ***as to*** *why he made the calls* ***on*** *their ambitions*
Temporal referent	***after*** *the study was completed* ***during*** *the ... press conference* ***in*** *the 1970s*
Location	***at*** *the airport* ***in*** *London*

Identity of questioner	Using a name
	
	   • ***by*** *O'Donnell*
	
	Using a social/political/professional role
	
	   • ***by*** *defence lawyers,*
	   • ***by*** *the pollsters*

Figure 9.1 Examples of circumstantial elements following *when questioned*

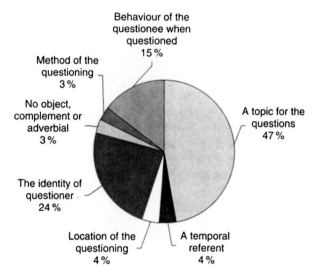

Figure 9.2   Post-positional information typically supplied with *when questioned*

intended to bring silence whereas at interview silence was not necessarily desirable. Officer D6 above used the time adverb *once* to highlight the interview's uniqueness and perhaps encourage talk. Other officers state uniqueness on-record too:

> this is your opportunity to explain the circumstances of what I'm going to ask   [B28]

This officer, like the others in this section, is explaining *when questioned*. This is less obvious than in the previous excerpts because, rather than including a lexical item with a clear semantic connection to 'questioned', his reformulation is based around the more evaluative *opportunity*. He thereby re-presents questioning not only by specifying circumstantial elements (the questioner *I* and topic *circumstances*, for example), but also through words which have been "metaphorically transferred" from elsewhere (Fairclough, 2001:94–5). His representation is not inaccurate, the interview is an *opportunity* to present a defence, and detainees who miss that opportunity might indeed regret their reticence eventually. However, the interview is also an opportunity for detainees to remain silent; through silence they might avoid court altogether, and this may be obscured if officers represent 'questioning' as an *opportunity* to speak. This example is not anomalous – over a quarter (28 per cent) of all officers who explained the caution in interview referred to the interview as an *opportunity* or *chance*, invariably to speak, never to remain silent. Officer interviews revealed that this kind of presentation might be strategic, using cautioning *to our advantage as best we can* (AO23). Leo notes similar "attempts to convince the suspect" when explaining USA *Miranda* rights by urging detainees to tell "[their] side of the story" while they can (1998b:216–17), as this might ensure that officers will put in a good word for detainees (Leo and White, 1999;421). In Britain, the appropriation of the caution to support investigative endeavours continues throughout interview as one officer explained:

> it's really towards the end of an interview when you're reminding somebody that "this is your chance to give your version of accounts alright and there's no point going to court and saying something else which you're not going to say here"   [AO04]

This narrativisation of the reconstituting of *questioning* sheds light on what officers' reformulations 'are' – interpersonally (to detainees and between officer and detainee), textually (whether they are 'explanations') and pragmatically (whether they do whatever the original did). Semantic prosodies (Louw, 1993) and connotations (Fang, 2001:591, 604; Fowler, 1991:80–109) of *opportunity* are positive, so officers who use this reword (Fairclough, 2001) add potentially persuasive meaning which may cause detainees to reinterpret 'questioning' as including a "discriminatory aspect" (Linell, 1998:151). There was variability in the persuasiveness of co-text used with *opportunity*:

I just want to give you	the opportunity now for you	to answer	our questions	[B21]
this is	your opportunity	to explain	the circumstances	[B28]
it's	an opportunity for you now	to like explain	the situation	[D10]
this is	your opportunity	to tell me	what happened	[S10]

Some precede *opportunity* with a definite article (≈ this *opportunity* to explain is unique [B21]); conversely others use an indefinite article (≈ this *opportunity* is one of many [D10]); others use possessive pronouns ($\approx$ this *opportunity* is all yours [B28, S10]) – each presenting rather different opportunities. Their predicates are more uniform, each presenting interview as a time to do something relatively unremarkable, to *answer*, *explain* or *tell*. Not all officers complete the verb group with an expectation of such impartiality from detainees, however:

> it gives you   an opportunity (.)   to give   an account   [A45]

A45's 'indefinite article + *account*' suggests that he does not anticipate hearing **the** *account*, or even that only one account exists. Therefore this officer could be said to be constructing a different opportunity here, one which encourages the detainee to do something tactical. This emerges even more clearly elsewhere:

> this is   your opportunity   to give   your version of events [D1]
> now is   your opportunity   to tell me   your side of the story [A19]

These officers present the interview as a slot in which detainees can provide their story of choice. Thus officers position detainees as strategic players.

The officers below also present questioning as an opportunity but incorporate this differently:

> the magistrates or judge or whatever are going to say "well hang on you had the **opportunity** here to answer these questions"   [D12]

> the court may (.) think "why didn't you say it when you had the **opportunity** during the interview?"   [A38]

The earlier officers incorporated *opportunity* without suggesting who might view interview as opportunity other than, perhaps, the speaker. These officers incorporate interview-as-opportunity into the hypothesised worldview of the court which may eventually assess the detainee. Detainees who heard those earlier reformulations could either accept or reject their truth-claims, possibly deciding that, in their view, the interview was not an *opportunity*. Detainees who reject these later presentations would need to convince themselves that the court would not behave as predicted by a police officer. Officers are sensitive to different perlocutionary potentials of the caution at arrest and at interview. Their presentations of *when questioned* can be seen to encourage silence at arrest and, in some cases, talk at interview.

9.4 Defining *something*

Something implies that detainees should mention some particular thing because *some* is "specific though unspecified" (Quirk *et al.*, 1985:391) unlike "*any*thing" and "*every*thing". *Something* is positioned in the caution in a negative polarity environment and conditional clause, an uncomfortable environment for it (Leech, Conrad, Cruickshank and Ivanič, 2001:482; Quirk *et al.*, 1985:782). Some explanations removed *something*. Throughout the 134 reformulations of the medial sentence examined here, although *something* remained dominant (131 occurrences), an alternative pronoun *anything* appeared 53 times. The officer below, for example, replaces *something* with *anything*:

anything that you later m- (.) mention (.) could go against you [A9]

A different pronoun can "effectively alter listeners' interpretation of a situation and their probable course of action" (Labov, 1988:168; Labov and Harris, 1994:285–6); *anything* suggests greater inclusiveness than *something*. Officers also specified what kind of evidence *something* might denote (bold, underlined or italicised below):

say this goes to court and you mention something during the trial like *a defence* or **an alibi** something along...that sort of line   [B34]

the court can...say..."why didn't you tell the police that at the time" you know for example **if you wanted to say "well it was so and so that did it"**   [D23]

if it goes to court you come up with this (.) <u>reasons for your actions like your involvement</u>   [C5]

if you go to court and you're going to (.) tell the jury (.) ah either thum- you know the <u>reason why you did something</u> or **you're going to say "it wasn't me because (.) of (.) <u>this</u>"**   [S24]

The first two officers present their examples as illustrative by introducing them with *like* or *for example*. The other two imply that their explanations are exhaustive. This may influence detainees. Furthermore we may wonder – why has each officer selected their particular examples? Do the officers see them as archetypal? Are they the first potential referents which came to mind? Are they particularly relevant? The explanations present *something* as denoting evidence which:

- acknowledges guilt and legitimises or mitigates guilty actions (underlined above);
- asserts or seeks to demonstrate innocence (**bold above**)
- are somewhat ambiguous about whether concerned with guilt or innocence (*italicised above*)

Detainees thus hear different representations of evidence, from different officers, some exemplifying only guilt (C5) or innocence (D23), others more 'balanced', having multiple referents (B34, S24).

Officer interviews suggest that examples are not habitual or chance, but that their selection may be:

- **Intertextually motivated** – Before interview, detainees sometimes indicate their intentions. For example, they may intimate whether they plan to *go no comment* (AO15) or conversely to *throw themselves on the knife and cough the whole lot* (AO45).[3] Examples of *something* may address such prior talk. For example, interviewees who have voluntarily entered custody to mitigate guilt do not need to hear that *something* means "evidence of innocence", since in context innocence is irrelevant;
- **Contextually motivated** – Even if officers are unaware of detainees' plans for interview, they may invoke contextual information about the alleged crime, interviewee (experience, disposition and so on) and available evidence in order to decide how to exemplify *something*.

Conversely, officers may ignore such 'facts'. Their examples may be:

- **Discursively motivated** – Officer C5 (above) presents interview and court as offering opportunities to express and explain guilt. This could be said to render his reformulations persuasive.

A final set of officers provided examples of *something* which were not at all 'neutral':

if you wait until the court to decide (.) you know what **your excuse** was (.) for example   [A15]

say this goes to court and you come up with (.) **a fantastic story**
which you didn't mention to me   [A46]

Such representations potentially cast detainees as predisposed towards
dishonesty (cf. Levinson, 1983:97f) or imply that silence in interview
might suggest dishonesty.

9.5   Explaining negation

There are two occurrences of *not* in the caution and officers respond
differently to each. The first occurrence is in the verb group of the
caution's first sentence, *you do not have to say anything*. Many officers'
explanations here centred on:

1   Simple contraction:
    you **don't** have to say anything   [A21]

2   Altering the main verb (*say* becomes *answer*) and
    accordingly, the direct object:
    you don't have to **answer** my questions   [B17]

3   Moving negation from the verb group as a hidden
    negative or negative pronoun:
    you have the right t- to remain **silent**   [D11]
    every English man and woman is entitled to (.) say **nothing**   [S8]

These syntactic and lexical changes are fairly minimal. Some officers
added clauses which stressed that the silence-talk choice is the
detainee's:

it's up to you if you want to answer them or not you don't have to
(.) you can answer some of them all of them or none of them (.) and
that's up to you   [A26]

Finally, as we will see in Section 12.2.2, some officers even seemed to
encourage silence when reformulating the first occurrence by illustrating
how detainees might be silent. Officers' presentations of the right to
silence as it occurs in the caution's medial sentence (*it may harm your
defence if you do not mention when questioned...*) were very different.
Popular opinion has it that the medial sentence encodes silence using
fail (*if you fail to mention*). This would be fairly inappropriate, implying
that invoking rights constitutes failure. Nonetheless, some officers reformulate using *fail*:

if you answer a question now or **fail** to answer a question now [A16]

if you **fail** to give an account   [S6]

This word is not confined to officers' reformulations: some use *fail* when reciting the official wording, creating the impression that the legal institution itself sees silence as undesirable. Other officers used a different loaded word:

if you **refuse** to answer questions   [A27]

if you do answer a question now or if you **refuse** to   [C1]

These officers present silence as even more calculated. Failing to speak connotes inadequacy, but refusal connotes deliberate obstruction. Obviously, detainees who choose silence during interview may indeed do so obstructively. *Refuse* might excellently capture that. However, whether it is an appropriate word to use when offering and explaining the right to silence is a different matter, because "the choice of a particular way of representing events gives them a particular meaning" (Mehan, 1993:241). Viewed critically, these officers disincentivise, even de-legitimate, silence. Some go even further:

if you **fail** or **refuse** to answer any questions   [B19]

if you **fail** or **refuse** to answer questions put to you now   [B23]

Whilst these formulations have the potentially manipulative perlocutionary effect of discouraging silence, their source may be innocuous. The police *Codes of practice* collocates the string *fail or refuse* repeatedly with notions of silence, so these officers may simply have borrowed the formulation from there (for example, PACE Code C:para10.11). Thus, far from evidencing attempts to goad detainees into unguarded talk, widespread appropriation of this string might rather evidence intertextuality: Officers very obviously appropriating official discourses.[4] Nonetheless, *fail or refuse* casts silent detainees extremely negatively. Therefore, its use in written institutional texts is problematic if that use dissipates into explanations of the right to silence.

9.6   Close

Sarangi finds that within investigations of child abuse, professionals "may attribute different evidential status to the same piece of information" and may classify information differently at different stages of an investigation (1998b:247–8). Police officers attribute different signification to the caution, depending on when they deliver it, and to whom. This is potent as "the most effective use of power occurs when those with power are able to get those who have less power to interpret the world from the former's point of view, [then power is] exercised not coercively, but subtly and routinely" (Mumby and Clair, 1997:184). The exercise of power is perhaps incidental not deliberate as "much of the time people in their lay explanations will not be strategically planning, or self-consciously adjusting their discourse in a Machiavellian fashion, but just 'doing what comes naturally' or 'saying what seems right' for the situation" (Wetherell and Potter, 1988:171).

I have not speculated on the impact of officers' reformulations on comprehension, but on perlocution. The detainee may find extrapolation helpful because it demystifies or distracting because it provides excessive detail. The caution densely packs meaning into certain words. Officers unpack and represent this information, expanding on the wording through reference to context, sometimes simply 'explaining', sometimes apparently or actually seeking to achieve something more through explanation. In explaining, some officers preserve the caution's ambiguity and vagueness, simply relexifying; others disambiguate, fastening meaning at a particular point within the potential semantic territory. Explanation also creates a tension between maintaining, mitigating and amplifying pragmatic force in a variety of ways, such as foregrounding the limits of the caution's applicability. The caution cannot avoid being vague as it is a universal formulation which must apply in all situations. However, officers often reduce this vagueness by specifying. They might usefully receive guidance on creating fixity in context.

10
Working with Organisation in Speech

10.1 Introduction

The caution has a fixed structure (division into discrete units) and sequence (ordering of those units). Russell has noted that its structure consists of three "ideational sections" which correspond to its three sentences (2000:33). Police training divides the caution and its explanation this way (Grainger, 2006b; National Crime Faculty, 1998:173) as do officers themselves. Officers are not all confident in the sequence of these units (shown in Section 8.1). As one explained:

> whilst [detainees] are trying to understand the first bit the second bit's thrown at them and then they're ((laid)) with the third bit "what was that again?"
>
> [AO22]

Academics too have criticised the arrangement (Cotterill, 2000; Russell, 2000; cf. Shuy, 1997:178). In this chapter, I therefore examine the sequences which officers use for their explanations and the implications of their choices. Specifically, I illustrate how officers draw attention to sequence when they explain and ask why they do this. Next, I show how the institution can influence the sequence of officers' explanations when it provides an official paraphrase for them to read aloud instead of asking them to explain in their own words. I consider officers' uptake of such guidance and their views on it. Finally, I exemplify both explanations of the caution which neglect to present some parts of the caution's structure and other explanations which present some parts several times. I begin by considering two alternatives to the current sequence in general terms before relating them to naturally occurring data.

10.2 Re-sequencing in principle

Perhaps the most obvious reordering of the caution's sentences moves the medial sentence, apart from the coordinator *but*, to a final position (below, and throughout this chapter, numbers in square brackets indicate the original sequential position of subsequent text):

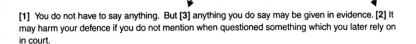

[1] You do not have to say anything. But [3] anything you do say may be given in evidence. [2] It may harm your defence if you do not mention when questioned something which you later rely on in court.

This '1-3-2 sequence' makes sense. It preserves the right to silence, historically the caution's main focus, in the initial position and it places the caution's two relatively certain propositions first and its relatively vague middle sentence last. It also allows the now final sentence to have a shallower syntactic structure than in the original, without *but* coordination. Finally, it prevents detainees from taking *it* of sentence 2 as anaphorically invoking the previous sentence through analogy with unattended demonstrative *this* (Finn, 1995:242) (*You do not have to say anything. But it may harm your defence if you do/do not*).

The new position of *but* is also influential. It links the two now adjacent *anythings* directly, foregrounding their identity. More importantly, it realigns adversative relationships (Halliday and Hasan, 1976; Russell, 2000:35) and interactive implications (Hoey, 1988:62–3). Generally, *but* indicates unexpectedness or contrast (Winter, 1976, in Hoey, 1988:61). Therefore offering a right followed by *but* implies that that right has a sting in its tail. This plays out differently in each sequence. Sentence 2 concerns silence so the initial two sentences of the official formulation connote 'you do not have to speak but if you are **silent** you might regret it', whereas sentence 3 concerns speech so the initial two sentences in the 1-3-2 sequence convey 'you do not have to speak but if you **speak** we will record you'. Thus, the formulation in use somewhat invites speech whereas the 1-3-2 sequence somewhat invites silence.

An alternative 2-1-3 sequence moves the right to silence from its initial position presenting silence's consequences before presenting silence:

[2] It may harm your defence if you do not mention when questioned something which you later rely on in court. But [1] you do not have to say anything. [3] Anything you do say may be given in evidence.

This too alters the caution's underlying meaning. The official wording's 1-2 arrangement implies '... so you might as well say whatever you can now'. Whereas, the 2-1 sequence above implies '... so you might as well keep quiet because you can'.

Thus, the sentence-sequence of the official wording tends to encourage speech more obviously than either of these other possibilities. In Shuy's terms it is coercive (1997:178). Nonetheless, these alternative sequences contain all three original sentences so, some might argue, maintain the original cumulative force, rendering the preceding discussion relevant only to moment-by-moment comprehension. Such pragmatists might further note that the official wording's sequence is fixed and, in practice, officers are likely to maintain its sequence when reformulating in order to track 'where they are' in their ongoing reformulation and create a copy which is like the original in a way which will be obvious to their interlocutor and to any subsequent overhearers. As one Force A officer explained:

> [the official wording] tells them in that order so it sounds logical to explain it in that order
>
> [AO01]

However, Russell has found that officers do re-sequence. Examining 13 authentic caution reformulations, she showed that 7 presented the caution in its original order but 6, apparently inexplicably, re-sequenced, reversing the second and third sentences (2000:33). Russell's re-sequencing officers are not anomalous; indeed the larger data set used here reveals the extent and complexity of officers' re-sequencing.

10.3   Re-sequencing in practice

Figure 10.1 overviews the sequences adopted by each of the 144 officers in my data who reformulated.

Across all forces, well under half of the 144 officers used the original discourse sequence (42 per cent, 60). Remarkably, a quarter of all officers re-sequenced, predominantly selecting a 1-3-2 sequence (25 per cent, 36). Only one officer who reformulated completely and linearly began with anything other than the right to silence. He adopted a 2-1-3 sequence.[1] The two sequences explored in the opening sub-section of this chapter are, therefore, the two alternatives which officers employ. Yet this only accounts for 67 per cent of officers; what of the others?

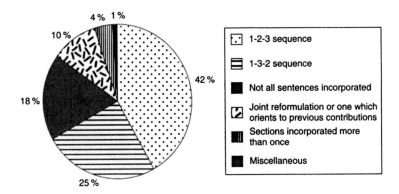

Figure 10.1   Discourse sequence of officers' reformulations across all forces

Figure 10.1 reveals that almost one-fifth of officers removed the propositional content of some sentences from their reformulations altogether (18 per cent, 26). On the other hand, 10 per cent represented particular propositional content repeatedly (14). Thus, at the macro level, officer reformulations in these data are not 'the same' as one another; some are differently sequenced, others incomplete.

Cushing conceptualises repetition using a series of oppositions. These can be used to illustrate what officer revisions should, presumably, be:

The officer paraphrase should be:	It should not be:
genuine (actual and intended replication)	**virtual** (resembling a previous utterance significantly but not intentionally)
conceptual (replicating meaning)	**literal** (only replicating words)
correct (substantially replicating relevant features)	**incorrect** (failing to 'replicate some key feature')
full (an entire replication)	**partial** (replicating only part of a previous utterance)

Adapted from Cushing (1994:55)

Cushing's vision highlights what makes explanation demanding. For example, a literal repetition which simply regurgitated the official wording would not constitute explanation here. However, in Russell's data, some officers did simply repeat parts of the official wording when ostensibly reformulating (2000:40). This might seem indicative of impoverished explanation. However, in my data too, literal repetition was present, typically divided into sections interspersed between the main conceptual repetitions, thus structuring reformulations and potentially providing "catch-up" time for detainees "whose attention may have lapsed" (Merritt, 1994:28). This may be very helpful when there is noise, and for emphasis, "especially when people have to communicate through very controlled language" (Johnstone *et al.*, 1994:9).

The picture becomes more intriguing still. We might expect that if 42 per cent of officers reformulate using the original sentential sequence, these 42 per cent would be spread fairly evenly across each force in the data set. However this was not the case (Figure 10.2).[2]

Figure 10.2 reveals that detainees are most likely to hear:

- A predictable 1-2-3 sequence in Force A (53 per cent of officers).
- A 1-3-2 sequence in Force B (47 per cent of officers).
- An incomplete or repetitive reformulation (the three striped sections of Figure 10.2) in Force D (45 per cent of officers).

This overview is a catalyst for qualitative analysis. Accordingly, this chapter examines sequence in reformulations delivered in all forces. It uses that examination to consider how institutional policy and interpersonal networks influence explanations.

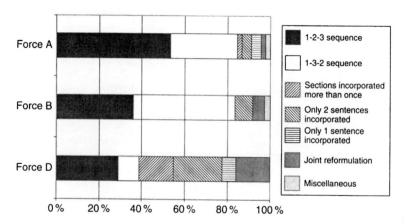

Figure 10.2 Discourse sequence of officers' reformulations within forces

10.4 Structural metalanguage

10.4.1 Metalanguage in cautioning

In the reformulation below, the cautioning officer leaps from explaining sentence 1 to sentence 3 without marking the division between them and without noting that his reformulation is differently sequenced from the official wording which he had just delivered:

```
1   P    [1] I'm going to ask you some questions (.) it's up to you
         whether you answer some or all of them [3] the ones that you
         do answer are recorded on this tape machine and may be
         used in a court of law if required to do so =
2   D                                           = that's fine =
3   P                                                  = [2] if
         I asked you a question tonight (.) and you declined to give
         me the answer (.) but the question is asked in court and you
         provide an answer to the same question (.) inferences will be
         drawn from the court as to why you didn't tell me
                                                        [A3]
```

Such re-sequencing offers a novel view of the caution's semantico-pragmatic territory but potentially bewilders detainees. Indeed, this detainee's latched evaluative acceptance (turn 2) may suggest that he believes the reformulation has concluded long before it has. Many officers potentially avoid such confusion using metadiscourse (Davies, 1997; Hyland, 1999) or metalanguage (Maschler, 1994) to mark their reformulations' structure. As AO33 explained, the caution is *not difficult when you break it down*. Such metalanguage was first noted by Russell who cites an officer prefacing his reformulation with the words *there are three parts to the caution* and identifying particular parts with, for example, *the first part is* ... (2000:34). The following three excerpts illustrate this practice and its diversity in more detail. In the first, the officer identifies and delineates *parts*:

it's split into **three parts the first part is** you're- when I'm asking the questions now or in this interview you don't have to say anything OK hhh **the second part is** (.) if you don't mention something now when I'm asking you questions and if it g- goes to court it goes to court and you bring something new up that you haven't mentioned at the interview the magistrates or judge or whatever are going to say well hang on you had the opportunity here to answer these questions or give your side and you haven't mentioned it there why are you bringing it up now OK? and **the third part is** anything you do say here in this interview can be used if it goes to court OK

[D12]

His *three parts* correspond to the caution's three sentences and he introduces each through explicit reference to the sequential position of its source in the original, orienting his interlocutor to the relationship between the original and the reformulation throughout. This may have some positive effects; it increases intertextuality with the source text. Also, as in written texts, such enumeration devices may help readers to monitor their own ongoing comprehension (Goldman and Rakestraw, 2000:315). A side effect of this 'tripartite metadiscourse' appears to be that the reformulation follows the original sequence. However, other reformulations did not show this effect, using orienting metadiscourse in a potentially disorienting way:

1   P   [it's] **split into three parts** (.) **the first bit** you don't have to say anything (.) you don't have to answer any question I put to you alright? you can remain silent throughout [coughs] anything you do say may be given in evidence **the last bit** (.) anything that's said (.) here (.) is on tape and it can be played to a court if need be (.) alright
2   D   yes
3   P   **the middle part** (.) it may harm your defence if you do not mention when questioned something which you later rely on in court (.) that means (.) if I ask you a question now in the interview (.) and you refuse to answer it (.) and then at a later date in court actually give an answer for the same question (.) the court can think to itself well why didn't you answer the question in the first place alright? ......

[A2]

Here, the adjectives *first, last* and *middle* indicate the sequence of the official wording but not of the reformulation. This could confuse this officer's interlocutor who might, quite reasonably, expect *the last bit* to signal the reformulation's conclusion. By re-sequencing, and using metadiscourse, this officer introduces and foregrounds a complication which he does not explain (cf. Russell, 2000:34). Other officers abandoned tripartite reference towards the end of their reformulations and some only dipped into it despite reformulating all three parts. Contrast that lack of orientation with the metadiscourse here:

1 P I'll break it down into three parts **first part** is **straightforward and simple** you don't have to say anything don't have to answer my questions do you understand that

2 D mm hm

3 P the **last part- third part** is **also straightforward and simple** it says whatever you do say may be given in evidence hhh the interview's being tape recorded at the end of the day =

4 D   = take it to court or owt [≈ anything]

5 P yeh they can take the the tape to court and play it if needed right?

6 D mm =

7 P   = the **middle bit** says but it may harm your defence if you don't mention when questioned something you later rely on in court what that mean is that if you decide not to answer my questions that's fine that's your right (.) but if the matter went to court anyway and at (.) court on a later date you decided to give some explanation as uh to what went on last night......

[A49]

Like the officer in the previous excerpt, this officer alters sequence but flags tripartite structure throughout. Unlike the previous speaker, he additionally uses evaluative metalanguage which links *the first part* and *the last part* by echoing the phrase *straightforward and simple*. Whilst this lexical and evaluative echoing does not explain his re-ordering explicitly, it indicates its motivation; uniting parts which he sees as similar. This provides for his interlocutor to orient to each part on the basis of the difficulty presented.

Whilst officer reformulations are spoken they have some writing-like characteristics (Clark and Ivanič, 1997:94; Stubbs, 1980) because, as Section 12.3.1 will show, they are pre-prepared at least to some extent. Writing gives additional planning time which allows "increased explicitness" in texts' logical structure. This is manifest in signposting through numbers, headings and text-internal links, which produce "less of 'next' but more of 'first, second, third'" (Gibbons, 2003:162–99). These features are highly reminiscent of these officers' revisions. Indeed officers A2 and A49 above show considerable sophistication in using metadiscourse to delimit their reformulations in two ways:

- First, by introducing the reformulation as consisting of *three parts*. This avoids keeping addressees guessing about just how many components might be on the way;
- Secondly, by not simply using ordinal numbers which describe sequence in isolation from one another (*first, second, third*) and instead limiting and structuring even more explicitly using *first, last* and *middle* which position each part in relation to the others. Other officers used *beginning, middle* and *end* similarly.

Most officers who referred explicitly to tripartite structure employed one or both of these delimiting strategies, marking the bounds of the three-part structure either at its outset or within.[3] This impressive practice echoes Charrow and Charrow's advice to organise and highlight text structure by "numbering each of the ideas, and informing the listener beforehand on the number of ideas that will be covered" (1979:1327). It also addresses Shepherd, Mortimer and Mobasheri's empirical observation that delivering the caution whole is "inherently meaningless" and should be replaced with delivery sentence-by-sentence (1995:66; see also Clare, Gudjonsson and Harari, 1998:327).

10.4.2   The extent of tripartite metalanguage

During reformulations, 52 per cent of officers used tripartite metalanguage. Officers also used reference to three parts elsewhere within cautioning exchanges. In some cases this was when checking comprehension either within their reformulations, asking, for example, *do you understand that?* after delivering each part (A49) or at the end of their reformulations (*do you understand all those three bits?* (A46)). This practice is now being encouraged by police training in some forces which recommends both delivering the caution explanation in three separate units and checking comprehension of each unit in turn (Grainger, 2006b; Knight, 2006:pc). Some officers use the tripartite structure innovatively in responding to detainees' reformulations. The detainee below, asked to demonstrate comprehension by explaining the caution, presents only the medial sentence:

D (.) um that I have to- that I should (.) if I rely on something
   in court (.) that I haven't mentioned when questioned here
   it throws the the the issue into doubt
P basically **that's the middle** of the caution **but of course it
   starts off at the beginning** and says that you don't have to
   say anything
D right yes
P so you could if you wanted just stare out the window and
   also ends there anything you do say may be given in
   evidence

                                                              [D30]

The officer's assessment of the detainee's talk introduces the notion of
three parts and builds the detainee's contribution into his emergent
three-part presentation. The notion of parts may help the officer to
process the detainee's reformulation quickly through a swift analysis of
inclusions and exclusions. It may also focus the detainee's attention on
the propositions he had omitted more effectively than simply adding
the missing information without structural orientation.

Officers additionally used tripartite reference to incorporate lower-
level structures into their reformulations. In reformulating *the first bit*,
Officer A2 delivers the first sentence's propositional content three times
(indicated using letters below):

> **the first bit** [A] you don't have to say anything (.) [B] you don't have
> to answer any question I put to you alright? [C] you can remain silent
> throughout

By marking all of this repetition as *the first bit* and providing prosodic
cues, the officer indicates that he is iteratively encoding one sentence,
not offering three unrelated propositions. A11 does this rather less eleg-
antly, embedding *three options* within *three parts*:

> **I'll break it down into three parts the first part means exactly
> what it says** (.) you don't have to say anything you can sit there
> and sort of say not a word if you like but it basically gives you **three
> options** and those options are to answer **some** of the questions but
> not others (.) to answer **none** of the questions or **all** of the questions
> it's entirely up to you (.) if uhr (.) you choose not to answer one or
> more of the questions (.) it would be helpful if you'd just say either
> no comment or I don't want to answer that (.) OK? (.) that (.) just uhr

(.) stops me and you staring at each other when I've asked a question and you don't want to give an answer I know we can carry on straight to the next thing then (.) **the middle part** is a tricky bit (.) that's where it says it may harm your defence if you do not mention when questioned something which you later rely on in court ...

[A11]

Thus officers use tripartite metalanguage in organising, delimiting and signposting their reformulations. The data cannot show directly whether this helps detainees by highlighting comprehension-building structure or distracts them with unnecessary detail. However detainees themselves oriented to the tripartite structure too:

	1	P	do you completely understand that?
	2	D	yeah sort of
	3	P	sort of? OK I need to be sure that you've got it there in your head exactly what it means are you able to explain it to me in your own words?
→	4	D	yeah **which bit do you want me to explain to you?**
→	5	P	**the caution bit**
→	6	D	um hhh **the don't have to say anything bit is** I don't have to say anything (.) if I don't I can go no comment or just not say anything at all
	7	P	yep
→	8	D	**what was the next bit the next bit's** =
	9	P	= that it may harm your defence if you fail to mention when questioned something which you later rely on in court
	10	D	in other words if I'm charged with (.) the offence I've been arrested for and it goes to court and I don't (.) mention something which could go against me or help me (.) it it could go against me <u>not</u> mentioning it
→	11	P	yeah great? **then the last bit** anything you say may be used ......

[C4]

This detainee's response to the explanation request is not simply to begin raggedly attempting to reformulate the whole caution but to seek clarification about exactly which part of the caution the officer expects (turn 4). The officer, presumably accustomed to something less sophisticated at this point, not surprisingly misinterprets the detainee as seeking clarification about which part of the whole interview preamble she should explain, specifying only *the caution bit*. The detainee, undeterred by this lack of clarification, begins with *the don't have to say anything bit*. Although she uses no numerical or delimiting labels to mark *bits*, she is clearly using the tripartite division. The officer acknowledges her reformulation of the first sentence and, in turn 8, the detainee begins to grope for the second sentence. The officer has now apparently tuned-in to the detainee's structuring and offers the wording of the second sentence (turn 9) which the detainee duly presents *in other words* (turn 10), finally adding *the last bit* (turn 11). It is the detainee who initiates this structure, either appropriating an officer style following previous arrests or identifying the structure for herself.

Metadiscourse about tripartite structure was particularly significant in Force A. It was used there by a staggering 93 per cent of officers. To contextualise this figure, in all other forces, tripartite reference was used by 32 per cent of officers +/– 4. Could this reformulation practice affect reformulations' content? Figure 10.2 revealed that 86 per cent of Force A reformulations were complete in comparison with only 55 per cent in Force D. There is therefore a small-scale correlation between reformulations structured around tripartite metadiscourse and reformulations which are complete. Metadiscourse may encourage completeness. This has implications for officer training, particularly in forces prone to incompleteness. Figure 10.2 also revealed that Force A officers used the 1-2-3 sequence more frequently than officers in any other force. Therefore a second, related possibility is that officers who use this metadiscourse are more likely to present the caution's parts in their original order.

10.5 The official paraphrase question

10.5.1 Understanding sequence

A 1-3-2 sequence was prevalent in Force B, adopted there by almost half of officers (47 per cent). Force D again offers some context: only 9 per cent of officers there used this sequence (Figure 10.2). Why have so many Force B officers re-sequenced in a way used so sparingly elsewhere? A likely cause demonstrates the impact of force policies on officer practices. Force B provides an official paraphrase in every interview room which adopts a 1-3-2 sequence:

---

[1] You have a right not to say anything if you do not want to.

[3] Anything you do say can be given in evidence. This means if you go to court, the court can be told what you have said.

[2] If there is something you do not tell us now, when we ask you questions and later you decide to tell the court, then the court may be less willing to believe you.

As well as its re-sequencing, this paraphrase intriguingly repeats the source text of the relocated sentence 3 before paraphrasing which contrasts with officer practice. Officers most commonly repeat sentence 2 within reformulations.

Providing an official paraphrase evidences standardisation, "making and enforcing rules for language-use with the intention of reducing optional variation in performance" (Milroy and Milroy, 1998, in Cameron, 2000:324). It places "new linguistic demands on workers [which] may in practice entail new (or at least, newly intensified) forms of *control* over their linguistic behaviour, and thus a diminution of their agency as language-users" (Cameron, 2000:323; also Cameron 1995:76). The introduction of a standard paraphrase of the caution has been strongly recommended (Cotterill, 2000:21; Russell, 2000:45). However, these data suggest that providing a standard paraphrase is not straightforward, not a panacea and would undermine some officers' practices.

Force B officers used their official paraphrase in one of five ways. A first set of officers simply read it aloud, the response one might expect. These have not been included in this chapter's statistics which are concerned with officers' own reformulations. However, they were fairly numerous and show the tendency identified by Heydon (2002:83–5, 185, 187) to resort to institutional formulations readily. A second set of officers almost used the paraphrase, but augmented it minimally, as in the example below, where additions are highlighted in bold:

I'll just explain to you what the caution means (.) you have a right not to say anything if you don't want to (.) anything you do say can be given in evidence (.) this means if you go to court (.) the court can be told what you said **here today** if there is something you do not

tell us now when we ask you [reads from card] less willing to believe
you **do you understand that?**

[B11]

The officer adds initial orientation and appends a final comprehension
check. He also inserts *here today*, addressing an omission from the official reformulation by clarifying which words can become evidence (see
Section 9.3). Other Force B officers too identified this gap, inserting
the prepositional phrase *in interview*, for example. Thirdly, at the other
extreme of responses to the paraphrase were officers who apparently
disregarded it entirely – providing an official paraphrase is no guarantee
of its uptake.

Between these extremes of total or near-total adoption and total rejection of the paraphrase, a fourth group of officers used its leitmotiv
but improvised relatively extensively. Improvisations typically incorporated evaluation (Thompson and Hunston, 2000), rewording (Fairclough,
2001:94) or repetition particularly altering pronouns (cf. Cameron,
2000:324). The fifth response incorporated short, specific elements of
the official paraphrase into officers' own reformulations. Some borrowed
a string here and there, whilst others appropriated clause-structure. Most
notably, officers borrowed one particular predicate, *may be less willing to
believe you*. Seven of the ten officers who borrowed only part of the official paraphrase borrowed this part. Many officers interviewed reported
finding reformulating the caution's medial sentence tricky, particularly the concept of inference-drawing. The tendency to borrow only
this predicate indicates how gladly officers accepted help here (Rock,
forthcoming).

This use of the official paraphrase in Force B suggests three upshots.
First, that official paraphrases are filtered through practice. Accordingly
any paraphrase must be assembled with its likely appropriation in mind,
and will only be as 'good' as the reformulations it spawns. Secondly,
institutionally advocating an official paraphrase, by placing it in interview rooms for example, will dictate its uptake. Force A officers were
also offered a 1-3-2 official paraphrase but much more informally – it
was distributed to officers yet few remembered encountering it (AO29)
and its influence was not discernible. Finally, individual officers will use
a paraphrase in very different ways.

10.5.2 Attitudes to official paraphrases

Force A officers who were interviewed about cautioning were unanimous
that the current caution requires explanation. Despite having autonomy

to reformulate on a case-by-case basis, some reformulate identically every time, using their *pat* (AO01) or *spiel* (AO25) to consistently adopt *the same role* during interviews (AO12) and, they believe, avoid repetitive or circuitous reformulations (AO30). This speaks for a standard paraphrase; if officers simply regurgitate their own 'standard', they might as well regurgitate an institutionally assessed and accredited one. Some officers indeed advocated a standard paraphrase, identifying particular problems with autonomy as AO18 summarised:

some police officers either
(1) **haven't got the nowse [≈ wits]** to be able to explain it properly or
(2) **don't understand it themselves** and I don't know what it is but I've sat in on some interviews where some people have tried to explain it... and
(3) they've spent **five minutes rambling** with him so a short explanation- and
(4) it would also get over that problem... where I **might put a slant on it** wrong

Other officers who also championed an official paraphrase proposed that it *would be less confusing* to regular detainees, who currently encounter different reformulations on successive arrests (AO25)[4] (cf. Cameron, 2000:331); would *make things easier* (AO26) for officers and *would be an accepted text which would rule out any argument* from solicitors (AO26). Officers who took this position represented the extended cautioning exchange as fulfilling institutional needs (demonstrating comprehensibility and unassailability) rather than psycholinguistic needs (genuinely creating comprehension) or interpersonal needs (contributing to an emergent officer–detainee dynamic). Some officers who agreed that cautioning primarily addresses institutional overhearers were nonetheless opposed to a standard paraphrase. They felt that a standard wording would perform attention to comprehension less persuasively than a spontaneous explanation. AO22 explained:

if there was [a standard paraphrase] it would purely be down to us trying to prove to the courts and those lovely people in the jury that we've bent over backwards trying to make sure that everything is understood

Overall, continued use of own-word reformulations scored more highly with more officers than scripting. Some cited practical motivations, claiming that it might be impossible to devise a standard formulation which would be beyond criticism, would not interfere with officers' internalisation of the official wording (AO42) and would be easier to remember than an extemporised explanation (AO16). Others could not envisage what a standard explanation of the caution would 'be' – how it would fit into the model of the cautioning exchange, suggesting *if it becomes rigid then somebody will ... say ... that might as well be the new caution* (AO38):

> you can't have ... another set of words as a standard set of words to explain the first set of words otherwise you'd have another set of words to explain the standard set of words you'd be going on *ad infinitum* wouldn't you?
>
> [AO41]

Officers feared having to *explain the explanation* (AO07) through blurring cautioning components. At the extreme, an effective standard paraphrase was completely implausible to some, like AO19, who proposed that it would rely on *some microchip in our head that tells us automatically*.

Most pervasively, officers who opposed a standard paraphrase were simply concerned about the potential for scripted explanations to fail through loss of *that personal touch* (AO10). AO41 summarised distinguishing the caution, *the form of words*, from its explanation, *your own personal relationship with the person you're talking to* (AO41). For him reformulation is not essentially something one does to words but something one does to, and as a result of, detainees. Three themes emerged from officers' comments on the value of free, unscripted reformulation:

- Detainees have different *levels* of comprehension (AO05);
  - there's such a variety of people and their understanding is different for each one (AO11)
- Officers must evaluate detainees' comprehension in context;
  - I would put it down to each individual to assess the situation [which may be] volatile or stressful (AO28)
- Cautioning exchanges must accordingly fit particular detainees.
  - what is a suitable explanation to one might not be to somebody else (AO35)

Many officers described tailoring their reformulations to particular detainees, claiming, for example, *I vary it ... to however I think they're going to understand it best* (AO05). Some did this routinely, like AO45 who used a tripartite structure but selected words for that structure *according to the audience* and AO24 who *moderated* his reformulation to be *in the other person's language*. AO48 forcefully advocated allowing officers to respond to diversity through tailored reformulations even if, as a result, some detainees only get *the basic understanding*.

A few officers stated that they *always* reformulate due to the evidential significance of interviews (AO34). On the other hand a few do so very rarely (AO22). The dominant set of officers however decide whether and how to recontextualise case-by-case. Some officers draw on their perceptions of detainees' comprehension. They attend, for example, to extra-linguistic cues, reformulating *if it would appear...that [detainees] don't understand* (AO02) *by the look on their face* (AO17). Chapter 11 will show that when some officers ask detainees to explain in order to check comprehension they attend to detainees' words extremely carefully. A greater number supplement or even replace information gathered during cautioning exchanges themselves by using a variety of measures to evaluate detainees' likely comprehension before interview has even begun. These measures range along a continuum from the impressionistic to those based on objective, observable criteria. This practice recalls Adelswärd and Sachs' description of the work of a nurse, communicating risk to patients, who "modified the meaning and risk of test results according to her assessment of each patient" (1998:197).

Looking first to "objective" measures, many officers described considering detainees' ages when deciding:

- whether to recontextualise (*if it's a juvenile I automatically go through* (AO02)) and
- how to recontextualise (*if it's a youngster ...you might take a bit more time* (AO03) or avoid *certain words which they may not understand* (AO02) *adapting attitude, demeanour and language* (AO09)).[5]

As AO09 explained, he responded to youth when modifying his explanation through lifeworld experience (*I'm a father I know the way you have to speak to children to get it over*) and through a humanitarian attitude to youngsters (*just because they've been out stealing or whatever it doesn't make them not a child*). Detainees' experience of detention also influenced explanations. Whilst a few officers give *a short explanation* (AO19) even to 'regular' arrestees, generally the less familiar one is with detention the more likely one is to hear a recontextualisation. Thus most officers said that they would never recontextualise for regulars, *the hardcore* (AO14), because there was *no point* (AO15). Such detainees were *pretty clued up* (AO11) and *probably knew it better than* officers (AO47). Likewise, others suggested that they would only explain to novices (AO25) who were likely to receive *some depth* (AO19) and recontextualisations which were *slower* and *more clear* (AO03). Officers also claimed to consider *intelligence* (AO10), noting whether detainees had a *mental health background*[6] (AO31) or degree (AO48).

These factors are 'objective' in that officers can know them with some certainty. However, many officers call on (inter)personal evaluation of detainees when taking recontextualisation decisions too; for example, in the case of *intelligence* seeking to *get an impression* (AO24). Amongst these more 'impressionistic' criteria for recontextualisation decisions, officers drew on perceptions of what we might call socio-economic class. AO11, for example, varied his explanations to *suit* his interlocutor, whether someone *living in a big posh house somewhere in a nice area* or *Joe Bloggs on some of these council estates*. This kind of interactional work can share features with crossing as officers converged towards "an absent reference group" (people in posh houses) rather than "the immediate addressee" (Cameron, 2000:325; Rampton, 2005). Alternatively, it can be driven by close interpersonal observation; AO31 explained to novice detainees who exhibited *nervousness* but not to other novices who *appeared reasonably confident*. Some officers could not quite describe their recontextualisation criteria but were convinced of the effectiveness of what one called *instinct* (AO12) through impressions formed often *before interview* (AO15):

F   is it difficult to decide either how to vary it or who exactly needs how much [explanation]?
P   no you know straight away what the level is
F   any particular things that you'd use in making that decision?
P   no you're not aware of it

[AO44]

Others described how such impressions were formed through building *some sort of relationship*:

even within the first two minutes even when you're sitting there getting them to tell you their name their date of birth and their address ... even in the charge room before you actually go into the interview ... you know there's an instant- and not rapport in the way "great we're going to be buddies for the rest of our lives" but if you

can get on with that person or relate to them or find some common
ground then it's usually easy [to explain the caution]

[AO20]

Officers' use of criteria was not immutable. AO09 noted for example
that age influenced him in deciding whether to recontextualise, but not
age alone:

like anything else you get some children that are sort of 15 going on
21 you get some 21 year olds going on 15 so its all relevant and you
have to adapt to the individual

[AO09]

Furthermore particular factors assume different significance for different
officers and on different occasions. Whilst AO10 prioritised age, invariably explaining to juveniles *regardless of how many times they've been in
custody*, AO15, for example used both age and experience. AO33 illustrates the criteria which just one officer may invoke when planning a
recontextualisation (format mine):

AO33's recontextualisation (Words relating to her criteria are highlighted)	Criteria mentioned
I mean obviously an **adult** and a you know a **child**	Age
depending on their **level** of (.) of **understanding**	Perceived comprehension
or **how they come across** generally really	Disposition
what **their language** is like generally... often you can sort of get a rough idea of what um even even by their just their	Language abilities
occupation you know I mean sometimes we're dealing with people who are bank managers or solicitors... obviously	Occupation
with people like that they- they've got a good **education**...	Education
whereas some of your **juveniles** or I don't know maybe	Age
less fortunate people who whose sort of **English** and	Intelligence/deprivation? Language abilities
handwriting skills and things are not so good	Handwriting – Literacy?
you know I would take more time to make sure that they understood (.) before we started	

Although she does not claim to use all of these criteria when assessing every detainee she indicates the lengths to which officers will go when seeking to evaluate comprehension. Officers may additionally locate their decisions about whether or how to reformulate in a wide range of interactions.

What did officers accomplish through this scrutiny? Many officers claimed it led them to produce register shift; using *simpler terminology ...which everybody understood* (AO34) and *layman's terms...rather than...doing the official jargon* (AO40). Accomplishing this shift proved testing for some, requiring that officers' *language skills come into hand* (AO35). Some officers were articulate about how they identified the target register. They described drawing on notions of frequency incorporating *ordinary words* (AO48) or notions of appropriateness, either by invoking personal perceptions of difficulty (*you can use terms which you understand*, AO06) or by hypothesising their interlocutor (*I use terms which I think that the person will understand*, AO48).

If an official reformulation was to be introduced in Force A, where autonomous reformulations are viewed so positively and used so creatively, it would need to be 'sold' to officers, widely distributed, easy to work with, modifiable, and perhaps compulsory if adopted. A standard paraphrase may be inappropriate to a force like this.

10.5.3 The official paraphrase versus free reformulation

It is quite plausible that the Force A officers cited above do accomplish something like audience design (Bell, 1997), accommodation (Giles, Coupland and Coupland, 1991) or crossing (Rampton, 2005), as they suggest. However it is one thing to attempt deliberate accommodation towards one's addressee but quite another to style shift in a way which might promote comprehension (Solomon, 1996:289), especially within institutional constraints. On the other hand a script which specifies "every word" (Cameron, 2000:330) has risks too. Section 8.7.2 discussed the problems generated by formulaicity and resulting repetition in the official wording but concluded that there, standardisation offers substantial advantages. However, as Cushing points out, "standardisation of terminology and protocol, though necessary up to a point, may well be counterproductive beyond that point" (1994:63). For many Force A officers an official paraphrase is that point. Use of a script had many potentially undesirable consequences. While a script may appear to ensure that officers act "merely as conveyers of legal information" achieving "non-partisan" delivery (Leo and White, 1999:433), in my data officers who used the script delivered it using intonation which made their aloud reading (Goffman, 1981:171) very obvious. This was an intoxicating way to trivialise rights information. Less predictably, officers referred directly to the script, telling detainees that they had a "crib sheet", bringing their animator role explicitly into the interaction. Finally, most reformulations from throughout Force B were much shorter and much less dialogic than those in forces which do not offer a script.

So there appear to be points against an official formulation yet also against officer autonomy. Several officers accordingly presented a compromise solution, the introduction of *guidelines* (AO25) or of a specimen wording issued *for guidance* (AO38, AO31) which, they suggested, might offer authorisation with flexibility. Cameron too illustrates alternatives to scripting in institutions. First, a "prompt sheet" which specifies interactional moves and their sequence without prescribing "a standard form of words"; secondly, and involving less prescription, guidance on the "staging of a transaction" which leaves the accomplishment of each stage to speakers' discretion (Cameron, 2000:330). Such measures are a more appropriate basis for monolingual caution explanations than either free reformulation or total scripting because they acknowledge that officers themselves will dictate how any procedural change is taken up and they permit creativity where appropriate. Officers in these data resisted scripting both in use (Force B) and in principle (Force A).

10.6   Disparate practices within one force

Having examined the 1-2-3 sequence with its connection to tripartite metalanguage in Force A and re-sequencing with its connection to an official script in Force B, we turn finally to the third most common reformulation characteristic revealed by Figure 10.1, incompleteness. This afflicted 18 per cent of reformulations examined here and was most common in Force D. The incidence of incomplete reformulations in Force D was higher than in any other force, indeed 23 per cent of reformulations in this Force only explicitly included the caution's first and second sentences compared with 8 per cent in Force B and only 4 per cent in Force A. Identifying omissions indicates that officers would benefit from some sort of guidance on giving explanations. Examining the causes of omissions uncovers very different ways of reformulating from those discussed above.

The caution's third sentence appears the most likely candidate for omission because if one explains the second sentence (courts can consider evidence from interviews) the third sentence (interviews can become evidence) follows. Sure enough, of the 18 per cent of incomplete reformulations, 11 per cent included only two of the caution's sentences, invariably the first and second. Seven per cent included only one sentence, most commonly the middle sentence, occasionally the final one. No officer explained only the right to silence. The officer below demonstrates incompleteness:

	1	P	[official wording] do you understand that?
	2	D	yep
→	3	P	so basically now (.) we're going to be asking you some questions: (.) OK?
	4	D	yeh
→	5	P	and if when asked you- yous don't say anything but you later say something in court (.) do you understand that? you do? you're nodding
	6	D	yeh
	7	P	and (.) your solicitor's here to give you any (.) specific legal advice
	8	D	OK

[S18]

This reformulation, which begins in turn 3, appears to be focusing on the caution's middle sentence by turn 5. It does not introduce the semantic content of any other sentence and, due to the unresolved *if*-clause of turn 5, even the middle sentence remains unexplained resulting in a reformulation which is fairly indisputably nonsensical. It uses *and* to introduce the right to legal advice, suggesting that that too is part of the caution reformulation.

This is desperately insufficient as an explanation of the caution. The officer appears preoccupied with the middle sentence at the expense of completeness. This reformulation was from the supplementary set, issued during 1996 and early 1997 when the current caution was relatively novel. This novelty perhaps explains the tendency to directly address the change from its predecessor, which contained nothing of the current medial sentence. Another officer, for example, who also presented only the medial sentence, preceded it by saying *the difference between that caution and the old caution is* ... (S23). However, incompleteness occurred in the more recent data too:

→	1	P	what it means is [3] whatever is said here in the interview room can be used (.) if it goes to trial //if it goes to court yeh?//
	2	D	// oh yes yeh right //
→	3	P	so what I'm saying is it's <u>important</u> that we say the truth at this stage
	4	D	//yes//
→	5	P	//you// know because [3] it could be brought up in court if it goes to court do you understand what I'm saying that's what that's what it //means//
	6	D	// right//
	7	P	alright

[D3]

The officer presents this as a complete reformulation by introducing it with the words *what it means is* and following them with *that's what it means* where *it* in both cases anaphorically ties to *the caution* or being *cautioned* which were referenced five times in the preceding dialogue. However, the reformulation only presents the propositional content of the third sentence. Moreover, it is strictly not a reformulation. The officer's *so* (turn 3) hints at a causal relationship between propositions in turns 1 and 3 which does not necessarily pertain. While the officer does not claim that he and the detainee are compelled to be truthful, he does identify truth-telling as *important*. Part of the caution's pragmatic message is that detainees make independent decisions; yet in turn 11 the officer aligns himself with the detainee through the pronoun *we* (presumably inclusive *we*) and suggests action. If this explanation was from a solicitor it could be seen as rather successful, but it is not a neutral re-presentation of the caution's propositional and pragmatic content.

Examples like this are problematic. Are they reformulations or even intended as such? If not, what are they and should they occur where reformulations are analytically, logically and discoursally predictable and institutionally required? The requirement to explain gives officers a particular power, but their exercise of this power may result in detainees being calmed, confused, distanced, even misinformed.

Although Force D showed this tendency towards incompleteness, it also saw, as Figure 10.2 shows, 16 per cent of officers reformulating so fully that they covered parts of the caution several times. Typically, this occurred when officers interspersed reformulations of the caution's

	D29	D9	D26
1	I'm going to be asking questions ur with regard to the offence which you've been arrested for i.e. which is...	I'm going to basically I'm going to be asking you questions (.) in relation to the offences that you've been arrested for	I'm going to be asking you questions now yeh? with regards to what happened on Tuesday night
2	now	OK now	OK?
3	[1] if you want to you don't have to answer me any of those questions	[1] you- (.) you can choose not to answer any of my questions if you don't want to that's up to you (.)	[1] if you don't want to yeh? you don't have to answer my questions (.) if you don't want to
4	OK however	however (.)	OK? but
5	[2] if you don't and if the matter then goes to court the court may decide then well or may decide for themselves why you haven't given that explanation	[2] if the matter goes to court (.) yeh? um they may make up their own minds as to why you haven't answered the questions when you've been given this opportunity	[2] if the matter goes to court yeah? ... (.) and you tell the court a story there to them they may not want to believe it because (.) today's the day that you tell tells us what happened on the tape
6	OK? and likewise	OK because obviously	you understand that? OK hhh also
7	[3] if you provide me with an explanation today it is being tape recorded and that tape can be used in evidence	[3] what you're telling me (.) is being tape recorded here (.)	[3] if you tell me something today (.) yeh it's being tape recorded on here well it's being recorded on these tapes (.) hhh
8	so	and likewise	and again
9	[2] if you give me an explanation today for example and the matter goes to court ... and you provide them with a different explanation ... then they may choose not to believe that explanation in court because [3] obviously you have what you've said has been tape recorded	[2] if you do answer any of my questions (.) erm and the matter goes to court and if you change your story or whatever by the time it gets to court then again we can use these tapes because (.) [3] as I say at the end of the day they are evidence	[2] if the matter goes to court (.) yeh and you tell them a different story then they again (.) may not want to believe it because [3] obviously this is being recorded (.) and we can play those tapes to the court

Figure 10.3 Repetitive reformulations in Force D

second and third sentences. Figure 10.3 provides examples of this repetition. Each example in Figure 10.3 is divided into units which reveal how repetition materialised. Numbers in square brackets indicate the caution's three parts.[7]

These three reformulations are remarkably similar between and within delineated portions. Odd-numbered portions convey propositional content. In the first, each officer prospects questions and their topic. In the third, each outlines the right to silence. Each fifth portion introduces inferencing. Having dealt in this way with a situated account of silence and its possible consequences each officer moves, in portions 7 and 9, to discuss speech. This macrostructure, which presents all details of silence followed by all of talk, is innovative in Anglo-Welsh cautioning although the Northern Irish caution uses a similar presentation "if you do not mention ... if you do say anything ... "(Appendix 11). The even-numbered portions, containing discourse markers and conjunctions, also exhibit great similarity across officers; each presents interactions between propositional portions informatively. Reference to changing one's story has subsequently been outlawed from caution explanations following a judgment which deemed this to be beyond the caution's meaning (R v. Shulka, 2006). It seems that Force D is characterised by extremes, showing both some very 'poor' reformulations which are incomplete and loaded, and others which are systematic, complete and innovative. In Chapter 11, we will see that it was also Force D officers who had evolved impressive ways of listening and responding to detainees' explanations in order to reformulate collaboratively.

Officers' reformulations are not all 'the same' as one another, or even their source, in structure and sequence. The examples in this chapter have illustrated the three most common recontextualisation patterns in these data as they are distributed across different police forces, suggesting a correlation between officer's views, resources available to them and the realisation of their reformulations.

11
Checking Comprehension

11.1 Introduction

Incomprehension may be observable through language manifest in puzzled hesitation and in requests for clarification, repetition, detail and contextualising information (Adelswärd and Sachs, 1998:194–6). In detention however detainees may conceal incomprehension for all sorts of reasons. Therefore officer-driven comprehension checking potentially improves rights administration. In the USA, comprehension checking is obligatory within *Miranda*'s syntax (Shuy, 1997:177). In England and Wales, it is optional. In these data, some officers give it great prominence, breaking the caution or its explanation into three punctuated with comprehension checks (cf. Fenner, Gudjonsson and Clare, 2002:90; Grainger, 2006b), whilst others do not check comprehension at all. Usually comprehension checking occurs after reciting the full caution and comprises (i) a *yes/no*-inviting question and (ii) a reformulation request (introduced in Section 8.8, cf. Cotterill, 2000:17). The excerpt below is typical:

1	P	[official wording] do you understand?
2	D	yes
3	P	could you explain to me what you understand <u>by</u> that please?
4	D	anything that I don't mention now ((and I don't say anything)) (1.0) can (1.0) I do (((//a bit))//
5	P	//oh OK// I'll go through it for you alright?

[S13]

After hearing the official wording the detainee claims comprehension. The officer's rejection of this claim (turn 3) seems wise, as it is followed by an apparent failure by the detainee to explain any aspect of the caution in an immediately recognisable way (turn 4). Indeed the officer apparently takes turn 4 to have demonstrated non-comprehension as he responds with further explanation. Yet within turn 4, having aborted his attempt to reformulate, the detainee does not simply disregard comprehension instead returning to but reducing his comprehension-claim, asserting that he really does understand *a bit*. This excerpt raises four sets of questions: (1) Why does the detainee repeatedly claim comprehension but the officer repeatedly ignores those claims? (2) Why does the officer prospect his explanation as being *for* the detainee and include *please* and *alright* in turns which are essentially institutionally mandated? (3) What is the officer attempting to check and test here? What do his checks and tests yield? What does the detainee demonstrate? (4) How might the officer best respond to the detainee's reformulation? What might inform his response? These specific questions about this excerpt translate into generic questions about comprehension checking which are addressed in this chapter.

11.2 The value of comprehension checking

Comprehension checking appears prudent following a difficult, important wording. Officers had mixed feelings however about the efficacy of the *yes/no* question as a comprehension check. At one extreme, a few officers saw it as invincible, enabling detainees to question the caution's meaning (*if they don't understand they usually tell you* (AO23)). These officers trusted detainees to appraise their own comprehension correctly, honestly (AO12) and in detail (AO05) or were unperturbed if they did not (*if they say "yeah I'm happy with that" then you just go on*, AO35). Nonetheless, "officers should be wary of accepting suspects' reports that they understand the caution" (Clare, Gudjonsson and Harari, 1998:328) because such reports are likely to be "precarious" (Shepherd, Mortimer and Mobasheri, 1995:66). Indeed, the overwhelming majority of officers in these data were very sceptical about comprehension checking. AO11, with over 4 years of experience, spoke for most, explaining that he had *never* interviewed a detainee who admitted incomprehension. Officers were convinced that *most people say that they understand it even if they don't* (AO06). This was not just officers' impression. In the interview-room data, immediately after cautioning,

even detainees who did not answer to *do you understand* in the affirmative typically responded somewhat positively, claiming to understand
half, most (A33) or *some* (A20) of the wording. Indeed, of the 119 interviewees who audibly responded to this check, 116 (97 per cent) evaluated their comprehension positively. Of the remainder, two admitted
understanding *not much* (D26, D29) and one sought a repetition of the
official wording. None explicitly admitted complete incomprehension.
Yet when 85 of these detainees were immediately asked to explain in
their own words, only one explained all three parts.[1] Of the others:

- **45%** recontextualised propositional content of only **one sentence**
  (38), of which:

o 6%		the first sentence (5)
o 26%	of the total attended only to	the second sentence (22)
o 13%		the third sentence (11)

- **7%** recontextualised propositional content of only **two sentences**
  (6).
- **28%** recontextualised **something different** from the caution, either
  something which might be seen as not part of it, or as only distantly
  following from it (24).
- **20%** were **unwilling or unable** to try to recontextualise (17).

These detainees might be expected to want to prove their claimed
comprehension, yet over half recontextualised 'incompletely' and over
a quarter 'incorrectly'.

Why do detainees claim to understand the caution yet fail to
demonstrate understanding? First, possibly detainees pretend to understand because that is *people's natural reaction* (AO09), they feel
"obliged to affect signs of comprehension" (Goffman, 1981:26). Various
branches of linguistics identify agreement as the unmarked form
by studying, for example, preferred seconds (Coulthard, 1977:70;
Heritage, 1984:268; Nofsinger, 1991:89) such as expected answers to
questions (Levinson, 1983:336). Beyond linguistics too, psychologists
record related phenomena: acquiescence or yea-saying (Knowles and
Nathan, 1997); suggestibility (Gudjonsson, 2002) and social desirability
responding (Forgas, 1985). From these perspectives *yes* means "I have
processed, or purport to have processed, the preceding clause" (Prince,

1990:284) or 'I want you to think I understand'. There are certainly pressures to confirm understanding falsely in detention. First, interactional pressures: people who admit incomprehension admit that they have inconsiderately not listened, are not capable of understanding or that the speaker explains poorly, all things which the uncomprehending person may be "disinclined to convey" (Goffman, 1981:26). As an officer explained, detainees *don't want to appear stupid* adding *that's certainly not the reason for the question* (AO05). Secondly, there are institutional pressures to claim comprehension. Detainees may be motivated by their disenfranchisement (Antaki, 1988:13) or powerlessness in interview and by attendant unequal distribution of interactional rights (Harris, 1984). They may feel that claiming comprehension is the only allowable institutional contribution (Drew and Sorjonen, 1997:104) and the only contribution which claims status (Russell, 2000:43).

On the other hand, detainees' affirmations may suggest that they have misunderstood the whole cautioning exchange. In that case they may not hear *do you understand?* as a genuine request for information, instead taking the question as somewhat phatic (Coupland, Coupland and Robinson, 1992). In this scenario *yes* means 'I understand to the extent that I think this matters' and positive replies are essentially backchannel cues (Goffman, 1967) or receipts (Heritage, 1985), indicating little more than having heard (Russell, 2000:43). Many officers themselves described having come to see detainees' insincere responses as evidence that they do not buy into the response turn as a genuine opportunity to evaluate and rectify incomprehension. Others state that detainees do not recognise this opportunity, perhaps having been provided with insufficient or indistinct contextualisation cues (Gumperz, 1982:130–52). This can lead to misunderstanding pragmatic aspects of the comprehension check, taking it as a non-negotiable test or reprimand rather like that which occurs when adults tell children *you're not to do that again, do you understand?* In that exchange, *do you understand?* means 'do you comply?' and *no* becomes pragmatically inappropriate.

Alternatively, detainees may be "simply misguidedly confident" about their abilities to understand (Fenner, Gudjonsson and Clare, 2002:90), lacking appreciation of "baseline comprehension" which prevents them from realising what is expected of people who understand (Cotterill, 2000:20–1). In this case, *yes* means 'I understand as far as I know'. From this perspective, *do you understand?* becomes a rather silly question. As White and Gunstone observe, "language traps us here because we say 'I understand' ... when we really mean the level of understanding is above or below some arbitrarily set degree". So understanding is a continuum not a dichotomy (1992:6) and has no fixed meaning (Shuy, 1997:182). Detainees who 'understand' must presumably:

1. recognise the caution's words;
2. know their potential meanings;
3. identify the correct intended meanings, discarding others;
4. know the words' meanings in combination and collocation;
5. relate meanings to current and future contexts;
6. select a course of action.

The officer who asks *do you understand?* might intend 'have you reached stage 6, can you now make decisions so that we can proceed?'. Detainees may believe that they are being asked about one of the earlier stages.

Detainees' responses to comprehension checking may stem from the nature of interview preamble. McDermott distinguishes interactions whose organisation encourages or facilitates talk, such as greeting exchanges, from those which do not, such as court appearances. Inarticulateness prevails when "although one is invited to say something, the words are not available" (1988:37). Police interviews potentially "organise inarticulateness" (1988:38). McDermott recommends that, in examining articulate versus inarticulate talk, we should replace questions of ability with sociocultural questions about situations in which such talk arises (1988:41) and concludes that as analytic terms, "fluency and inarticulateness" distinguish "kinds of situations" not "kinds of persons" (1988:61). From this perspective, responses to the comprehension check routine do not index 'understanding'; instead they are artefactual instantiations of contextualised talk which evidence detainees' responses to the routine. Thus detainees who claim comprehension but then apparently invalidate that claim through 'inadequate' reformulations may have evaluated their comprehension successfully but produced explanations which do not demonstrate comprehension in an institutionally ratifiable way.

Institutionality is the final arbiter of comprehension checking. As well as its ostensible communicative function considered so far, the *yes/no* comprehension check question has an archival function which addresses both felicity: 'will you confirm understanding (whatever that may be) and thus enable this interview to proceed legitimately?' and authority: 'will you confirm understanding in a way which will convince any ratified overhearers of your confirmation's validity?' (cf. Goffman, 1981:9–10). Detainees may be unaware of, or at least unconcerned about, the need for their responses to unambiguously address these two questions.

In contrast, officers described being preoccupied with ensuring that cautioning has "fully performed" its institutional, archival function (Gibbons, 1999:160) and has successfully recorded "expert information for scrutiny by another expert" (Cooke and Philip, 1998:25). Officers described this preoccupation leading them to explain *to be on the safe side* (AO45), guarding against problems in court when detainees may suddenly assert *I just wanted to get out and I said "yes" [I understand] but I didn't really know what he was talking about* (AO40).

11.3 Mitigating comprehension checking

Despite officers' institutional motivation for comprehension checking, they oriented moment-by-moment to interpersonal concerns too. By asking a detainee whether they understand, responding to the detainee's answer with a request to explain and then delivering an explanation of their own, officers may appear to doubt detainees' honesty somewhat confrontationally. Indeed in the excerpt at the beginning of this chapter the detainee who found himself unable to authenticate his comprehension claim reasserted it, claiming to understand *a bit* (turn 4). This suggests that, to him, the cohesive ties between his comprehension claim and the officer's request for proof of that claim were direct. He can only respond to the challenging request for proof by rising to that challenge or reasserting his initial claim; when the first fails he resorts to the second. Many detainees similarly resort to restating comprehension after attempting recontextualisation (restatements highlighted in bold):

D	um I have the right to remain silent	
P	yep	
D	and erm phhh	
P	what it is =	
D	=**I do- I do know me rights**	[D19]

D	If I don't give you no evidence well if I don't say something now I say it later on (.) uhr (.) **well I understand it anyhow**	
		[A14]

Others, apparently similarly bemused by the recontextualisation request, reasserted comprehension claims by indicating awareness of the caution's source:

P what do you understand from that caution then?
D **what you just said**

[S28]

D if I don't mention anything now ((clears throat)) that I
   later rely on I in court then it can (.) I-**what it says on
   that sheet what you just said**

[S1]

These excerpts suggest that detainees do not take the comprehension
check routine as simply checking comprehension, appearing somewhat
flustered by being put on the spot.[2]

Any request to prove comprehension is rather unusual. In
private communication "participants tolerate a high degree of non-
acknowledged, unresolved potential misunderstanding" (Blum-Kulka
and Weizman, 2003:110), tending to presume "working agreement" on
meaning despite its implausibility (Goffman, 1981:10). This is normally
quite acceptable because language use tacitly assumes "that most of
the message can be left unsaid" with shared knowledge and, perhaps,
impatience maintaining communication (Slobin, 1982:131–2, in Lee,
1992:9). Ambiguity is indeed common and only becomes "significant"
when "interpretative uncertainties and discrepancies exceed certain
limits" (Goffman, 1981:10). In legal settings, limits of acceptable ambiguity are narrow. Yet labouring comprehension checking is as potentially
face-threatening in legal settings as elsewhere (House, 2003:110). The
comprehension check routine contains powerful Face-Threatening Acts
(FTAs) which can, if unmitigated, coerce detainees into claiming comprehension (Russell, 2000:43). These FTAs threaten detainees' negative
face through imposition and their positive face through challenge
and implications of failure (after Brown and Levinson, 1987:66). Bald
on-record recontextualisation requests are, however, legitimate within
cautioning procedure and accordingly some officers produce them:

1 P [states caution] what does that mean then?
2 D that it- jus- exactly as you said ((there))
3 P which means what?

[S11]

This detainee, perhaps in response to the lack of mitigation in turn
1, resists reformulating. Officers who recognised face threat described
attempting to caution without being *patronising* (AO20) or *insulting*
(AO24). During interview preamble, officers attended to face threat

through redressive action (Brown and Levinson, 1987:69), mitigation (Fraser, 1980), disclaimers or self-reports which shift frame (Goffman, 1981:284–92):

P   I'm going to explain it to you not because I think you're daft or anything like that but it's so that I know that you understand what I'm talking about OK?

D   yep

[A2]

This officer uses metadiscourse to mitigate face threat, combining positive and negative strategies (after Brown and Levinson, 1987:101–230):

• Positive strategies	Linguistic realisations
o warranting his recontextualisation	*because, so*
o attending to the detainee	having assessed whether he is *daft*
o using slang	*daft*
o hedging opinions	*anything like that*
o asserting concern	*I [want to] know that you understand*
o being optimistic (of mutual interest)	*I'm going to explain*
• Negative strategies	
o showing reluctance to impinge	Implicitly apologising throughout
o giving overwhelming reasons	*because* and *so*

Some officers positioned their recontextualisation-requests or their imposed recontextualisations as something other than challenges to detainees' professed comprehension, instead as:

1. Mutually beneficial:

so I can know that you understand it properly   [D19]
so that I'm satisfied you understand what that means   [A49]

2. For officers:

just for our peace of mind   [A8]
just for- for my benefit   [D11]

3. Circumstantially motivated:

it's the first time that I've met you	[D18]
because of your age and because you've never been ...	
interviewed on tape before	[A25]
because obviously you haven't been to a police station ((before))	[A43]
because you haven't got a legal rep with you	[A31]

4. Routine or procedural:

everybody says "yes" but I always like to go	
through it with them anyway	[A10]
for the benefit of the tape	[A37]

5. Non-malevolent:

| I don't wish to be awkward | [A9] |
| I don't want to insult your intelligence | [A11] |

6. Strictly unnecessary:

you've been educated and I don't really want	
to go over that too much with you	[D30]
I'm sure that you fully understand it	[S1]

7. Motivated by the difficulty of the wording:

it keeps ... lawyers fully employed sorting	
out words like that	[A9]
it's quite a mouthful	[C1]
it's quite a difficult- difficultly worded piece of legislation	[B10]
it's a bit of a long winded caution that isn't it?	[B33]

8. Motivated by the caution's importance:

I think it's important that you understand the	
implications of the caution	[D18]
it's quite important that you understand that	[C5]

9. Motivated by the need to go beyond the official wording:

I like to know that whoever I'm speaking to fully	
understands the implications of the caution	[D11]
it's a lot of words and uhm unless you actually break	
it down you don't necessarily get the full sort of	
meaning of it	[A19]

10. Motivated by features of comprehension:

you may have heard it being said (.) lots of times	
but do you understand	[B6]
I appreciate some people may understand that	
some people may not	[D11]

Strategies 1–4 seek to reposition face-threatening parts of the cautioning exchange as not driven by the detainee, 5 and 6 discount potentially face-threatening readings and 7–10 problematise the wording, thereby allowing officers to align with detainees. Theoretically, we might expect more uniformity as Brown and Levinson claim that "any rational agent will tend to choose the same genus of [politeness] strategy under the same conditions" (1987:71). The diversity above suggests that officers assess the seriousness of these FTAs variably, invoking social distance, relative power and ranking of imposition, perhaps case-by-case. One overriding concern does however underpin many of the ten strategies – dissatisfaction with the comprehension check apparatus itself:

1	P	can you just explain it to me
2		so that I know you've got an understanding of it huh
3	D	[silence] (3.4)
4	P	do you want me to explain it?
5		you understand it but you can't explain it? OK that's alright (.)
6		I've just got to explain it for the benefit of the tapes OK?

[C3]

This officer seeks (line 1) and legitimises (line 2) a recontextualisation. When the detainee appears unable to oblige (line 3) the officer does not problematise the resulting silence but resolves it, offering to recontextualise herself (line 4). Indeed she legitimises the detainee's silence (line 5), positioning it not as obstructive or indicating stupidity but simply as a consequence of the difficulty of reformulation. She similarly introduces her own recontextualisation not as correcting a poor performance but as obligatory within cautioning procedure. Alongside this attention to face however her account of the comprehension check routine is conflictual. In the lines highlighted with arrows, she first commodifies comprehension as demonstrable through talk (line 2) but then suggests that talk may not index comprehension (line 5) and may not even improve comprehension (line 6). This self-referential mitigation neatly identifies the tension between feeling discomfort with the comprehension check apparatus and having to use it. This discomfort does not, in itself, illustrate that officers found the apparatus unhelpful only that they were conscious of it, whilst using it.

11.4 Using comprehension checking

11.4.1 Co-construction

It seems self-evident that, having asked detainees to reformulate, officers should attend carefully to resulting talk. However, this is rarely straightforward. At the lexical level, detainees who recontextualised the medial sentence tended to include parts of the official wording, particularly *harm your defence, rely, mention* and *something* (see Chapter 9 and Rock, forthcoming). Some officers took this to indicate comprehension:

> they will actually use the words *harm my defence* because ... they've spoken to a legal representative on the telephone or ... they've read their rights ... and they're starting to get familiar with ... the words that are being used
>
> [AO05]

Conversely, even other officers admitted resorting to the official wording in their own talk when they did *not* understand, the more usual signification attached to regurgitation in the research literature (Grisso, 1998; Russell, 2000:44). Officers may not recognise indicators of comprehension or incomprehension at any level of language. How might officers respond to detainee-recontextualisations like the following?

	1	P	[recites caution] do you understand that caution?
	2	D	(.) yeh =
	3	P	=yes?=
	4	D	= yes
	5	P	what does it mean to you? (.) I have to be sh- p- like sure that you understand it before we start
→	6	D	that anything you ask me (.) erm (.) hhh ((and you get off me that I answer it)) and if I don't answer it of my own choice it can harm erm defence (.) I think [laughs] I can harm my erm-
	7	P	wha- probably best if I (.) break it down into three parts =
	8	D	= I do understand it I do understand it
	9	P	[recontextualises]

[S21]

This detainee's incomplete explanation, which implies that the caution permits coercion (turn 6), sits uncomfortably with his repeated comprehension claims (turns 2, 4 and 8) – possibly he is fabricating comprehension (Section 11.2). However, examples like this illustrate how difficult it is to demonstrate comprehension through explanation. Does this detainee think he understands, only to discover, through talk, that he does not? Does he 'understand' but find himself unable to articulate that? Do his words indicate greater understanding than they superficially suggest? It is unlikely that even he believes that his words demonstrate comprehension as he marks uncertainty and a possible call for clarification and assistance through *I think* and laughter. The officer apparently shares this view: implicitly negatively evaluating, by stating that it is *probably best* to disregard the detainee's recontextualisation move and 'replace' it with his own. An initiation-response-feedback sequence mapped onto turns 5–7 would place the disregarding turn (7) as decidedly negative feedback (Sinclair and Coulthard, 1975). Despite the detainee's protests of comprehension, the officer ultimately recontextualised all three sentences, making no further reference to the detainee's words, although referring twice to a recontextualisation which he, himself, gave before interview. Such minimal attention to specifics of detainees' reformulations was not unusual in these data:

> D it means if (.) I don't erm give the information (1.6) now and I were- (.) later rely on something in court maybe it (.) could be held against me.… [intervening side-sequence] …
>
> P right I'm quite happy that you understand that I presume also Mr. [solicitor name]'s also mentioned the caution to you
>
> [A42]

This detainee's reformulation is also incomplete. It mentions only the middle sentence without explaining even its implications fully. As in the previous excerpt, this officer disregards the detainee's turn. Here, however, disregard is realised through positive evaluation of the detainee's words. This officer too refers extratextually to an earlier exchange, in this case one which is assumed, thereby trivialising the extended cautioning-exchange by contextualising it within a macro-legal-interaction in which explanation has already been accomplished. This excerpt shows similar inattention:

D   well I do not have to say anything unless I wish to do so
P   [laughs deeply] you're quite happy you fully understand it?
D   yeah

                                                                  [A47]

Here, evaluation of the detainee's comprehension is not even explicit. Contrast these with the exchange below:

1	D	that if (.) I do not say anything it'll (.) it'll rely on in court (.) or
→ 2	P	that's right that- if it does go to court
3	D	it can be brought up
4	P	the magistrates might have an inf- an inferrance [pronunciation] infearance about the fact that you haven't said anything
5	D	right
6	P	OK?
7	D	yes

                                                                  [D1]

The initial detainee-recontextualisation here shows considerably less fluency than those in the previous excerpts. If it were taken to indicate a level of comprehension, that level would be low. The turn suggests particular difficulty with the metaphorical verb *rely*. However, after explicitly acknowledging and positively evaluating the detainee's recontextualisation (*that's right*), this officer does not dismiss that recontextualisation but extends it by qualifying the detainee's reference to *court*. Then something even more unexpected happens. The detainee re-joins the recontextualisation, having apparently incorporated the officer's contribution. Through turn 2, the officer accomplishes a transition from a monologic recontextualisation turn to a co-constructed recontextualisation exchange. He augments the detainee's contribution and the two then build a joint recontextualisation, over four turns, 'joint' in that no turn is 'discarded' and 'replaced' through talk but instead each turn augments and implicitly ratifies the emergent text (Coates, 2003:58–9; Trinch and Berk-Seligson, 2002:412). The detainee dictates the extent of the recontextualisation, introducing the propositional content of the medial sentence (turn 1) and the final sentence (turn 3) and the officer confines himself to those sentences. The excerpt below too shows speakers adding depth through co-construction:

```
         1   D   well if I say anything now and don't (.) if I say
                 something (.) like not now and it comes up later on
                 in court it can go against me [sniffs] ((inaud.))
  →      2   P   it could go against you doesn't doesn't mean that it
                 will go against you
  →      3   D   could go against me [sniffs]
         4   P   if you've got a good reason why you haven't said
                 something in here then the court may well
                 understand that OK?
```

[D20]

In turn 1, the detainee attempts a jumbled recontextualisation. It is cluttered with temporal reference. Additionally the position of the negator *not*, following a grammaticalised *like* after the direct object rather than with an auxiliary *do* within the verb group, suggests the meaning 'if I speak at another time' rather than 'if I am silent now'. Yet the officer does not disregard or unpick this recontextualisation instead building on it by highlighting an area where, as he understands it, the detainee has oversimplified. The detainee has presented inference-drawing ambiguously (using *can*). The officer apparently takes this to indicate that the detainee sees inference-drawing as being concerned with permission rather than possibility. He therefore realises reintroduction of unambiguous possibility by repeating the relevant section of the detainee's recontextualisation but changing the auxiliary verb to *could* and adding *doesn't mean that it will* which emphasises possibility. The detainee then adopts this change, through echoing. This addition and echoing co-construct a mutually acceptable formulation.

These officers, then, seek to ensure that detainees have understood the caution's lack of certainty, yet neither attends to the incompleteness of the resulting recontextualisations. These officers thus avoid imposing "the single voice of a transcendental order which does not allow for conversation or challenge", which acknowledges "the multiplicity of voices" here. However, they do not avoid producing "distorted" texts (Silverman and Torode, 1980:64) as 'full' reformulations are not accomplished.

In interviews with me, officers explored why layered, multi-party recontextualisations like these develop. AO33, for example, perceived a need to *get them to try and say it in their own words and just work round [explaining] that way*. Some officers did this only when necessary:

if they're way off the mark I might come in and say "yeah that's part of it but should it go to court and you change your mind" *et cetera* ... "do you understand that?" "yep?" "OK then and anything you do say may be given in evidence what do you think that means?"

[AO01]

This practice fits well with findings that the caution is understood better when administered piecemeal than in full (Fenner, Gudjonsson and Clare, 2002:90). Police training in some forces now recommends checking comprehension by asking detainees a question about each of the caution's sentences. For example, in relation to the first sentence detainees are asked *Do you have to answer my questions?* and in relation to the medial sentence: *If this matter goes to court and you tell the court something in your defence that they think you could have reasonably told me today, what might they think about that?* (Grainger, 2006b; Knight, 2006:pc). This final question does not ask detainees directly about the notion of inferences instead rather persuasively asking them to exemplify possible inferences. Other officers described encouraging their interlocutors to drive recontextualisations through their own questions:

"what don't you understand about it?" and they'll come out "well what does this bit mean?" and then you can elaborate on that ... "what else aren't you happy with?" and you go to that bit ... let them tell you what the problem is first and you can deal with it from there saves you time and they know exactly what they want

[AO35]

This officer suggests an interactive method, but one which requires from detainees both metalinguistic awareness and a willingness to disclose perceived difficulties. It also requires careful attention from cautioning officers to avoid 'incomplete' recontextualisations like those above. On the other hand, these expert cautioners raise the intriguing possibility that completeness might best be measured from the detainee's perspective ('I've had as much explanation as I need') rather than the institutional one ('the explanation must be complete to be successful'). The exchange below shows how officers' careful listening can bring completeness:

1	P	do you understand what that means?
2	D	yes
3	P	can you tell me in your own words what that means to you?

→　4　D　(2.1) it means (.) by opting to [1] the- my right to
silence at a later date [2] if th- any other th-
information I give to my solicitors comes to court
(.) the court could deemed it to be that it I had the
opportunity to give it today and that it is therefore
irrelevant and they would not believe me in the
courtroom

　　5　P　hhh. pretty pretty much spot on I'd say yeah I've
never heard that way of doing it before but I think
you've got the gist of it

　　6　P2　it's a good way =

　　7　S　　　　　　　　= I did explain it to my client before
we came in

→　8　P　[3] right not a problem just as uh- on top of that
obviously a record of this is being made and it can
be produced in court if necessary (.) yeah?

　　　　　　　　　　　　　　　　　　　　　　　[D20]

Here, the detainee recontextualises sentences 1 and 2 but neglects
sentence 3. The officer spots this omission from the detainee's turn
and, implicitly, from his 'understanding' and adds it (turn 8). This
impressive recontextualisation presents comprehension checking as for
the detainee by attending to the detainee's contribution and only
supplying content which the detainee has not. Ten per cent of officers
recontextualised jointly with detainees or oriented to their interlocutor's previous contribution. In Force D 16 per cent of recontextualisations were produced this way. Such active explanation positions
misunderstanding not as "an accident ... but ... a resource, a 'rich
point'" (Hinnenkamp, 2003:61), providing "occasions for learning"
(House, Kasper and Ross, 2003:2). These data suggest that attempts to
remove misunderstanding are best replaced with acknowledging and
using misunderstanding.

11.4.2　Is there a future for active comprehension checking?

Detainees' recontextualisations are typically syntactically incomplete,
which is problematic to the extent that it places fluency "well below
the surface" where institutional representatives may "not have time to
look" (McDermott, 1988:51):

　　it could be (.) used against me at a later date (.) by refusing

　　　　　　　　　　　　　　　　　　　　　　　[S5]

This detainee provides no clear referent for *it*, no qualifier linking to talk in interview (*now*) and an incomplete verb group (missing infinitival *to talk*). Yet, this does not necessarily indicate incomprehension. If we approach this recontextualisation not with the question 'does this adequately paraphrase the caution (as if for a naïve listener)?' but instead by asking 'what aspects of the caution are included (potentially recognisable to someone familiar with the wording)?' we find that the detainee takes in the ideas of:

- possibility (*could*);
- evidence-giving in court (*used*);
- negative inference (*against me*);
- temporality (*later date*);
- deliberate silence (*refusing*).

He does not demonstrate that he has fully worked out these ideas in isolation or combination but to say that he has not understood the caution grossly oversimplifies. Nonetheless, it is one thing to take such superficially incoherent ramblings as indicating some degree of comprehension but it would be quite another for all officers to use such formulations as the basis of co-constructions in police interviews amidst other demands. We have seen that some officers do just this very successfully and deliberately. Some had evolved ways of evaluating detainees' propositions speedily by integrating them into a tripartite structure (see Section 10.4), a practice also recommended implicitly by Grisso's experimental method which paraphrases for inclusiveness (1998; see also Shuy and Staton, 2000:131–6). With help from distilled research findings and dissemination of good practice officers might be helped to attend to detainees' reformulations when appropriate.

Increased use of collaborative recontextualisations would make it possible to embrace the comprehension check as more than an institutionalised performance of procedural adherence, an (un)official script in which the detainees' turns are incidental. It would re-cast detainee recontextualisations as catalysts to almost pedagogic exchanges and would widen the boundaries of what rights communication might involve by potentially encouraging attention to detainees' contributions. Officers themselves suggested this. Comprehension is not necessarily best achieved for all through interactivity and collaboration may be impossible for some officers or in some situations. Nonetheless, raising awareness of alternatives to officers' usual cautioning routines might be valuable.

12
Beyond Explanation: Using Cautioning

12.1 Introduction

Research on the caution has predominantly been concerned with its form, meaning and referential functionality. But what does the caution do? It is widely recognised that speakers do things through language, that they do multiple things simultaneously through language and that they do things through language whilst ostensibly doing other things. Clark, for example, disputes the dogma that "understanding what a speaker is doing consists of representing a single layer of actions" and motivations (1996:592–4). Gee denies that language primarily conveys information proposing instead that it functions mainly as scaffolding for two forms of social action: First, it structures and supports "the performance of *social activities*" and secondly it allows "*human affiliations*" within social groups to develop (1999:1). This chapter shows that the caution provides a form of linguistic scaffolding for interactants to accomplish interview as a *social activity* by creating boundaries and by providing opportunities to negotiate aspects of the upcoming interaction. The chapter then shows that the caution provides interactional scaffolding for *human affiliations* by allowing participants to locate themselves, constructing identities as cautioners, as procedurally adept police officers or as compliant or defiant detainees. The chapter is not a taxonomy of speech acts accomplished in cautioning but an exploration of what goes on, beyond the referential, in apparently tightly regulated, goal-oriented talk.

One of cautioning's most mundane but pervasive non-referential functions is to shape police officers' identities. Whilst officers see the caution as *a basic tool of the trade* (AO45) through which to pursue institutional objectives (AO44), it also takes on much greater significance. First, knowing the wording (AO42) and being able to recite it from memory (AO45) are central to being a police officer. Familiarity with official formulations is "a symbol of police professionalism" (Leo, 1998b:217). Secondly, the ability to explain the caution is definitive of officers, such that those who cannot explain *shouldn't be giving it in the first place* (AO42), explanation being an identity-constructing *police ceremonial* (AO45). This capacity for the caution to define also underpins interviews. Officers pointed out that some detainees exploit the caution to *play the system*, yet it more importantly offers *protection* (AO01). The many officers who noted this ethico-legal functionality saw the caution and cautioning exchange as *safeguards* for detainees and officers alike, describing cautioning as *important to me as a police officer who wants to keep his job and try and do as good a job as I can* (AO04) and *most certainly for the benefit of the people we're dealing with* (AO34). This chapter examines how far the caution moves beyond these key functions.

12.2 Scaffolding the performance of social activities

12.2.1 Framing and footing

Framing (Goffman, 1974) involves "using the linguistic features of a register [to bring] the situation associated with the register into interactional play" cueing, for example, "beginnings, endings and internal parts" (Johnstone, 2002:149) and denoting transitions between topics and activities. When cautioning, officers might usefully signal whether cautioning is in the frame of informing or testing, for example; if they do not, detainees must figure this out for themselves. Moreover, the caution itself acts as a frame, marking the change of state from 'not under arrest' to 'under arrest' and from 'not in interview' to 'in interview'.

Footing concerns "the alignment we take up to ourselves and the others present as expressed in the way we manage the production or reception of an utterance" (Goffman, 1981:128); each utterance signifies varying degrees of awareness and detachment, otherness or "our-own-ness" (Bakhtin, 1986:89). As Section 8.6.1 indicated, officers may shift footing when cautioning in order to accomplish a somewhat pedagogic role successfully.

The concepts of framing and footing resonate in officers' talk. In relation to framing, officers discussed the caution's interactional function in marking, dividing and solemnifying arrest and interview, AO39 proposing that they emphasise those functions prosodically when cautioning (*our voice alters* by becoming *more officious*). Officers claimed that this marking, dividing and solemnifying is salient to detainees. They specified that at arrest detainees recognise that cautioning signals *that something official is happening* (AO24), it marks *an official starting point* (AO31) whilst in interview it serves as *a physical marker ... almost like putting a flag up and saying "right now the investigation starts and everything that's said between us now is the real thing"* (AO24). Officers only caution if they hope to elicit evidence so, they pointed out, it is crucial that detainees recognise this framing function (AO31). They felt that even novice detainees do recognise framing, through exposure to television programmes in which cautioning suggests, very successfully, *somebody's in trouble* (AO42), or *things are being taken fairly seriously* (AO05). One perceived benefit of this recognition was that even if detainees cannot understand the caution, for one reason or another, they may still recognise that it changes their situation. As one officer explained:

> [detainees say] "I remember you giving me [a caution] but I couldn't tell you what it said" so they actually understand that you're doing something as far as the officialdom stands
>
> [AO39]

The caution's power in marking the frame transition from 'not under arrest' to 'under arrest' and 'not serious' to 'serious' was felt to have drawbacks however, being particularly problematic during interactions with 'voluntary attenders' and detainees stopped for 'minor' traffic offences.[1] For such addressees the caution can be *a shock*, distracting from subsequent procedure (AO38) and even leading addressees to erroneously conclude that they have been arrested because, they believe, *everybody who gets cautioned gets arrested* (AO29).

For some officers, the framing function was too potent, creating formulaicity and formality which potentially interfere with investigations. Some officers reduced the caution's perceived severity by claiming a footing of "only passing on information from another person" as Wood and Kroger would put it (2000:102). This distanced them from the reported text and responsibility for it. One, for example, concluded his reformulation by saying *that's not my words that's the words of the previous Lord Chief Justice OK?* (S13). AO01 noted that, following PACE

(1984), officers can no longer *do things on an informal basis*, so investigations may seem *to get very heavy very quickly*. Officers suggested
that this aspect of cautioning led them to attempt to shift to less
formal footings through talk, supported by non-verbal signals, after
cautioning:

> I'll ... say to [novices] "that's the formal bit out of the way and now
> we'll just speak fine" because that makes people more relaxed ... I'm
> quite relaxed when I interview if required I'll sit back I'll ... fold my
> hands
>
> [AO31]

AO14 sought to defuse *a terrifying moment* which novices in particular
could find *quite intimidating* through recontextualisation itself, telling
detainees *"well don't worry all it means is this"*. Reassurance can be
observed in interviews:

> right I will caution you first before we begin OK don't worry about it
>
> [D2]

For AO31, such apparent compassion has an agenda enabling her to
get more out of people than being oppressive. Thus, cautioning potentially reduces the interviews' investigative potential and recontextualisation and cotext offer redress. Leo's USA data illustrate that this
phenomenon is not confined to the UK or to sections of interview where rights are explained. He found officers using a series
of "background manoeuvres" such as friendly small-talk "intended
to disarm the suspect" (1998b:215) while "minimising, downplaying,
or de-emphasizing the potential import or significance" of rights
(2001:1018).

Officers in my UK data were particularly critical of the institutional
requirement to reiterate the caution "after any break in questioning"
(PACE Code C, 2006:para10.8); for example, when beginning each new
audio-cassette during interviews,[2] given that breaks between cassettes
may only last for seconds (AO48). They suggested that repetitive re-
cautioning can have negative repercussions on:

- Rapport – disturbing *the way that you've ... started to interact* (AO48);
- Delivery – becoming *a bit of a barrier* (AO45) which triggers hurried
  cautioning;
- Affect – being *excessive* and *oppressive* (AO48);

- Semantico-pragmatic interpretation – being *trotted out ... to be on the safe side ... which trivialises* (AO45).

The caution's framing function and the associated change in footing are so salient that overlooking them is institutionally noteworthy. In the excerpt below, the officer reads from his pocket-book[3] during interview. Such reading in interview is common, enabling officers to move their unsanctioned pre-interview recollections into the interview record.[4] Here, the officer opens the interview by referring to the detainee's arrest:

> [reads aloud (transforming third-person to second-person whilst reading)] I cautioned you and asked you "do you understand?" and you replied "no not really" and then you then laughed you giggled OK?
>
> [B2]

The officer's decision to put this exchange on record illustrates just one way in which the legal system itself recognises cautioning exchanges as doing more than just cautioning. Greeting the caution with laughter is likely to be seen as inappropriate due to the caution's function in changing the detainee's state. This inappropriate response is sufficiently marked that it may become evidentially or at least procedurally significant. Of course the laughter potentially indicates one of at least three things. First, that the detainee has recognised her state-change but not respected its seriousness – laughing indicates indifference. This is presumably the reading that the officer is proposing. Secondly, that she has recognised the state-change but responded inappropriately through nervousness, for example. Thirdly, that she has not recognised the state-change and therefore responds in a way which indicates only puzzled acknowledgement. In any case the caution's framing function appears deeply significant and detainees who do not fully recognise it and the significance of the framed state (under arrest), or the framed activity (interview), provoke comment.

Detainees who present the caution as only framing, only marking state change, also attract attention because this suggests that they may not attach full significance to interview as evidence-creation:

P   do you have any idea (.) what it means?
D   what the caution?
P   yeh when I cautioned you then wha- er what's your
    understanding of what those words mean?
D   I've c- I've been cautioned

                                                        [D3]

P   you may have heard it being said (.) lots of times but do
    you understand what it- what does it mean?
D   that I'm arrested?
P   you're arrested (.) OK it means a little bit more

                                                        [B6]

These detainees explain the broad function of the caution, the first flags only cautioning's performativity, whilst the second notes only state-change. The caution's functionality in framing apparently has different significance for different participants in legal processes and has different significance in different circumstances. Officers may seek to exploit this variability.

12.2.2   Prospecting interview

Utterance meaning "is not a straightforward matter of external reference but depends on the local and broader discursive systems in which the utterance is embedded" (Wetherell and Potter, 1988:169). The discursive systems which operate in interview may be unfamiliar to detainees, so officers use interview preamble including cautioning turns to provide orientation:

> as we go along I'll probably be taking notes you know depending on what you tell me right so I'm not being rude if I'm not looking at you writing notes it's OK so just bear with me and we'll just get on with it
>
> [B4]

This officer prospects his own language practices, explaining how they might break with more familiar norms of talk. Alternatively, such intervention around discursive systems might prospect the detainees' talk:

      D   [recontextualises]
→   P   (.) just in ke- sorry just didn't quite catch what you
          <u>said</u> then

→   P2   you've got quite a broad accent Fred if you can just
        eh- talk a bit slower for us <u>please</u> hhh uhm::
    D   ((what I'm say- what I say)) said (.) [repeats]

                                                              [S9]

The officers note the detainee's regional accent, through a side-sequence, ultimately suggesting that the detainee adjusts his pace before returning the detainee to explanation using prosodic cues. Frequently officers and indeed detainees use interview preamble to monitor form like this. Whilst one might criticise these officers for expecting the detainee to accommodate when he has more important things to attend to, all speakers' turns must be audible for interviews to proceed. The preamble can be seen as a good time to monitor volume, pace and accent, whether through metalanguage or less explicitly because such early intervention potentially minimises attention to form during the interview itself. These interventions may be risky, however:

    1 D   [recontextualises incompletely]
    2 P   right that's-
→   3 P2   could you just speak up a little //because//
→   4 D   // yeh //(.)//sorry//
→   5 P2   //it's er// it's obviously
           (.) on tape OK (.) thank you
    6 P   right I'm quite happy that you understand that

                                                              [A42]

Although turns 3–5 appear to be a side-sequence like the example above, they disrupt the ongoing talk, aborting rather than temporarily halting the main ostensible work of assuring comprehension. Attention to form here takes precedence over comprehension checking, delaying evaluation and allowing an extremely incomplete reformulation to be forgotten.

Officers negotiate terms of address (Ervin-Tripp, 1969) during cautioning too:

    P   [official wording] do you understand that so far Jason?
    D   yep
    P   yeh wha- what do you like to be called?

D   ((mumbles approx 4 syllables)) Jay Jay
P   Jay Jay?
D   mmm
P   OK erm do you understand th- the caution Jay Jay?
D   yeh

[S15]

This prospects the coming interaction by attending to identity issues for both the detainee, whose negative face has been threatened by the request for personal information but whose positive face will ultimately be attended to through an appropriate address term, and for the officer who has represented himself as interested in the detainee's comfort.

Leo and White suggest that in the USA officers dash from rights administration to interview to deny detainees time for rights decisions or to present rights waivers as *fait accompli* (1999:437–8). The officers cited above may similarly intend to distract by monitoring volume, pace, accent and address preferences. On the other hand, they may be well-motivated. In other examples from my data, attention to discursive systems did not seem designed to distract from rights, indeed it explicitly oriented detainees towards rights invocation. Officers became animated when explaining potentially alien discursive systems around silence. They indicated how to achieve silence by illustrating possible interview scenarios (Shuy, 1997:187–91). One said, for example, you *could if you wanted just stare* out the window (D30), again prospecting detainees' practices:

1   P   let's take- break it down three bits you do not have to say
2   anything what do you think that means?
3   D   don't ((say anything))
4   P   that's right
5   you can sit here and you if I ask you any questions or something
6   you can say to me "I don't want to answer that question"
7   or you can say "no comment"
8   or you can just not say anything
9   it's your right to remain silent
10   do you understand that bit?
11   D   yeh

[D7]

This officer exemplifies three ways that the detainee might perform and achieve silence, two verbal (lines 6 and 7) and one non-verbal (line 8). Other officers pointed out that silence would not be negatively evaluated or received. One explained for example *you can...say nothing...won't offend me alright* (A38). These speakers, then, go well beyond the caution's meaning, prospecting its realisation in interview. Their rather neutral reformulations all represent detainees' silences as passive but autonomous (cf. Section 9.5). Whilst these manoeuvres apparently empower detainees to assert their rights, a less charitable reading would note that, in some interviews, obtaining silence might be more likely to assure a conviction than obtaining talk by permitting detainees' silence in interview to be a basis for negative inferences to be drawn about the detainee in court.

12.3   Scaffolding human affiliation

12.3.1   Learning to caution

As well as using cautioning to prospect immediately upcoming activities, officers also used it to work on more distant general interactions: They learned through cautioning. Whilst officer reformulations are inescapably spoken, they would inhabit the writing-like end of any speech-writing continuum (Stubbs, 1980) being prepared and rehearsed, produced relatively slowly and comprising specified content within a predetermined message-producer-receiver relationship (Clark and Ivanič, 1997:94). This production context influences, and is influenced by, both institutionality and human affiliations: in learning, planning and executing cautioning, officers orient to the copious writing and speech which surrounds their work. The resulting explanations are:

- constituted by and constitutive of the institutional order;
- deeply intertextual with one another;
- adaptive, appropriating and disseminating discourses from outside the predictably influential institutional apparatus.

How are officers' cautioning practices influenced by both institutionally sanctioned guidance and informal learning?

Two forms of institutionally sanctioned guidance are potentially available: *training* and *monitoring*. Commonly, officers in my sample could not recall having received any cautioning *training*. Those who could, typically felt that training focussed on legal rather than interpersonal or linguistic matters.[5] Only AO02 remembered receiving formal instruction in explaining. Formal *monitoring* too officially focusses primarily on ethical or evidentiary matters. Force A monitors officers by requiring sergeants to check interview tapes periodically (AO16). AO45, a supervising officer, informally used such monitoring to check recontextualisations, particularly when evaluating new officers, but monitoring was predominantly concerned with legislative compliance and was not routine.

Thus, feedback on officers' explanations is predominantly informal. Many, who were already officers when the current wording was introduced, greeted the formulation with unease and incomprehension (AO20),[6] perhaps because of the lack of orientation they received. They described personal, rather than institutional, responses to this. For example, some sought explanation from colleagues (AO15), one worked on learning to apply the new legislation by *breaking it down and formulating an interpretation* (AO17) as she would when explaining. AO15 spoke for many, describing initially delivering the wording but avoiding reformulating *because I'd learnt it and not really understood it myself.* For such officers memorising and reciting did "not involve taking meaning from the text" (Barton, 1994:65–6). Officers described training as somewhat incidental to their own comprehension of the caution or their recontextualisation technique and, in any case, inferior to direct experience because *out there* things are *never the same* (AO03). Thus, cautioning exchanges themselves were not only significant to detainee–officer contact, but also in building relationships and practices between officers – officers did not stop "learning to caution" upon delivering their first explanation, rather contact with colleagues underpinned initial, and as it turned out, ongoing learning.

Officers described continually sharing practice, presenting their recontextualisations as an intertextual patchwork which they constantly looked to improve (AO19) through observing, learning and reflecting. These officers, as stylistic agents, appropriated resources "from a broad sociolinguistic landscape, recombining them to make a distinctive style" (Eckert, 1996:3, in Cameron, 2000:325). Some officers saw themselves as principally borrowing (*I interview along with a lot of different people ... somebody will explain the caution and I'll think "that bit's good I like that bit I'm going to use that"*, AO09), others as the source of good practice (*since they've been in some of my interviews everybody's doing it now*, AO12). For others, sharing was truly reciprocal. AO16, for example, described convergence within an interview team *because people tend to work with each other and figure out "oh I'll do it like that"*. Similarly, AO19, who had recently returned from a placement, described more widespread dissemination and convergence:

> eventually we all pick up similar explanations to some degree ... because I've picked some up from a colleague when I came back and some have maybe picked things up from me
>
> [AO19]

Such intra- and inter-team dissemination might eventually lead to homogenisation of recontextualisations until a normed explanation emerges, particularly in forces without a prominent standard paraphrase. Combining insights from data from different sources suggests that this process may be underway already. In research interviews officers describe using reformulation features which the interview-room data suggest typify their Force. AO09, interviewed in Force A, for example, described using delimiting metadiscourse (identifying tripartite structure) and evaluative metadiscourse (characterising parts of the caution as *straightforward and simple*), practices which are common in Force A officers' work (see Section 10.4). However, he presented these features as idiosyncratic, his *own way of explaining*, not force-wide practice. AO19, in contrast, presents tripartite metadiscourse as a collective norm:

> perhaps every police officer's probably said the same we always explain the caution in interview now and we break it down into the three parts
>
> [AO19]

Convergence is more obvious to some than others.

Formal and informal reciprocity seemed so important to reformulating, that officers who were unaware of such support described discomfort with explaining:

> you go for it but there's nobody dragging you back saying "oh you did that wrong" sometimes I've no doubt I've pitched things at certain levels and its been totally inappropriate but it's the best level that I've got
>
> [AO24]

This officer's disquiet seems to stem from both perceived lack of "styling" (Cameron, 2000:236) of his recontextualisations and from his concern to deliver individual recontextualisations appropriately. He shares Shuy's

belief in the need for some notion of the "range of permissible vari-
ations" between different formulations (1997:193). Officer practice and
comment suggest that observing and responding to what comes out of
cautioning exchanges may be more important than controlling what
goes in.

Use of multiple resources in designing talk is common in expert–
lay interaction. Adelswärd and Sachs note that doctors, in communicating risk, draw on three sets of information: specific families' genetic
analyses; epidemiological studies and official statistics (1998:203). In
custody, some officers combined resources while others relied predominantly on only one resource in reformulating. Some used detainees'
reformulations, listening carefully to their attempts to explain in order
to respond (see Section 11.4); others used their more general observations and knowledge of the detainee (Section 10.5.2). Others simply
trotted out the same words every time they explained (Section 10.5.2).
This section has shown that officers also inform their talk with observation of colleagues' cautioning.

12.3.2   The caution as performance

Because of the caution's archival function (Cooke and Philip, 1998:25;
Gibbons, 1999:160), being seen to have cautioned felicitously by
an overhearing audience is a priority (see Figure 8.5). Ratified overhearers (Fairclough, 1992: 79–80) or auditors (Bell, 1997:246–7) potentially include detainees' legal representatives, supervisory officers and
courtroom participants. Cameron describes the dilemma facing callcentre workers who, encountering a dual audience consisting of callers
and overhearing managers, "prioritised the 'in-house' audience whose
judgements on their performance had more direct and immediate
consequences" (2000:326). In the case of officers explaining rights,
meeting the requirements of the auditing audience (being seen to have
attended to comprehension) is altogether more straightforward than
meeting the needs of the immediate audience (ensuring comprehension). Achieving comprehension may indeed be impossible. The institutional salience of performing cautioning occupied officers who described
reformulating in response to a perceived need to be *more accountable all the time* (AO40) and because their recontextualisations could
be *brought up in court* (AO16). Although officers who presented such
perspectives usually offered alternative conceptualisations too, these
motives for explaining are not philanthropic but driven by anticipated
audit. Officers described cautioning thoroughly, having *been caught out*

[previously] (AO12) or because detainees claimed non-comprehension when *trying to get out of things* (AO14), not, for example, because they found such cautioning to most successfully ensure comprehension. Officers who took these positions assigned cautioning the capacity to demonstrate three things:

- **Comprehension**
  Officers strive towards observably performing, rather than genuinely achieving, comprehension. As AO25 observed, colleagues should *just make it very clear that [detainees] understand* in order to avoid courtroom challenges.

- **Compassion in officers and the legal system**
  Officers proposed that careful cautioning casts them as responsible individuals, pursuing justice and equity:

  > if [detainees] turn round in court and say "well I didn't understand what he was on about" it's going to make ... everybody else aware you've read something that's long winded
  >
  > [AO35]

  AO35 attends to the potential for overhearers to evaluate his treatment of detainees.

- **Fairness**
  Cautioning was integral to being seen to have collected evidence fairly; as AO31 explained, *the interview would be worthless if [detainees] didn't really understand.* This led officers to recap its meaning mid-interview;[7] for example at points when detainees might later claim to have forgotten its significance or around confessions (AO39). However, AO39 noted that revisiting the caution rarely influenced detainees, suggesting the recap is not simply humanitarian. AO44 was quite precise about its signification:

  > we never interrupt anybody ... but if it was a particularly important question or something that you particularly wanted ... to have introduced as evidence ... it's just wise to make it as watertight as possible
  >
  > [AO44]

Officers do not revisit the caution at key points (only) for detainees, rather to demonstrate that those key points are safe, buttressing evidence as valid, reliable and just. AO41 presented the entire interview preamble as *an endeavour on our part to show that we're being ultra fair*, rather than an endeavour to **be** ultra fair. So, for officers, cautioning can function to demonstrate, even perform, good practice.

12.3.3   The caution as diversion

Some officers appropriated cautioning very differently. They described re-cautioning during interview not for detainees' benefit or to fulfil institutional obligations but predominantly as a discoursal move – to prod detainees towards honesty, silence or talk. This had two useful side-effects: first, *throwing* detainees; secondly, *buying a bit of time for yourself ... if you need to gather your train of thought ... if you're losing your way* (AO15). In this representation, the caution helps to assert and maintain power:

> it's so easy to give a "no comment" interview and they gain confidence from it and the confidence should be on my side ... I [re-caution] to draw back in and "I'm in charge and it's you that's in trouble and I want you to think about what you're saying"
>
> [AO24]

AO24 explained that this worked occasionally, putting him *back in control*. Other officers similarly exploit cautioning during interview preamble:

> now and again ... you try and catch them out ... you say "can you explain that to me?" and they've got the story prepared but then they're thrown ... and they think "uh-oh hang on a minute what's that then?"
>
> [AO15]

This officer's comprehension check is a deliberate challenge, a deflection from the anticipated interaction. AO18 uses the same question to wrong-foot solicitors. He gleefully described how, having established that a solicitor had explained the caution to the detainee in front of him, he would then seek a detainee-recontextualisation:

> [the solicitor] may have gone over it a couple of times explained it but to actually repeat the knowledge is very difficult for [detainees] and they stumble and mumble and the solicitor gets embarrassed and it's all on tape
>
> [AO18]

This officer clearly recognises the difficulty of demonstrating understanding through talk but uses this recognition purposefully.

12.3.4 Orienting through cautioning

As well as officers, detainees were also finely tuned to the potential for cautioning exchanges to work hard. Although detainees who claim comprehension may be keen to prove that claim (see Section 11.2) there are many reasons to resist obsequiousness during police interviews. Resistance exhibits an "active responsive attitude" towards meaning (Bakhtin, 1986:68). The cautioning exchange offers opportunities to signal non-compliance, on-record, before the interview proper has even begun, or to try out the interview setting (cf. Section 7.3.2). Consider how this detainee explains the caution:

1 D well it thinks if I withhold information
2 P yep?
3 D uhr if there's something I do know that I don't really want to tell
 you (.) **but there is nothing**   [A12]

Her brief recontextualisation suggests that she believes that the caution concerns choices but she adds adverbial stance (bold), using her recontextualisation turn to display orientation. Detainees may recontextualise the caution incompletely because they simply do not understand, cannot remember it all or cannot explain, and this may be the case here. However, if this is selectivity rather than incompleteness, this excerpt evidences an attempt to contextualise subsequent contributions as being from someone intending to be exhaustively honest. The formulation below is also incomplete:

1 D if I say anything it could be used against me or for me
 it depends doesn't it what I say
2 P alright d'you understand what happens if you don't
 say anything?
→ 3 D (.) er (.) well I- **I want to talk** ((laughs)) yeh
  the- //   they yeh yeh   //
4 P   //I know you want to talk// alright well that's
  I- just in case it crops up through the interview
                                                              [S16]

Here, the officer spots turn 1's overly tight focus on prospecting talk not silence, yet the detainee resists his focus-expanding move, instead maintaining his original focus, talk. Seemingly, by turn 3, the detainee has already heard and 'understood' the caution. By 'understood', here, I mean that he has planned his own course of action on the basis of whatever he takes the caution to mean or had previously selected a course of action and has related the caution to that. This detainee has thus potentially proceeded to stage 6 of the simple schema of comprehension presented in Section 11.2. Therefore, his partial recontextualisation may be complete in that it contains everything that he feels is relevant. Even when the officer reminds him that there is more to the caution (and implicitly that he might consider additional options) he remains within the limits he had articulated, accordingly transforming the officer's question. This excerpt therefore restates the enticing possibility that detainees who only explain part of the caution do so not because they do not understand but because they see only, or particularly, that part as relevant to them. Nonetheless, their evaluation of relevance may itself rest on misunderstanding, making for circularity around this optimistic possibility.

The different orientations of this officer and detainee offer further insight. Throughout the cautioning exchange the detainee prospects the upcoming interaction whilst the officer orients to felicitous explanation. The detainee's assertion, *I want to talk* – coupled with the officer's overlapping acknowledgement – suggests that they have, not unusually, discussed the interview's likely progress already. The detainee invokes that shared knowledge to reject the officer's attempt to explain in more detail. His interpersonal focus on the interaction makes the officer's institutionally driven expansion nonsensical. Once the shared knowledge that the detainee wants to talk has been introduced, continuing with the cautioning exchange becomes somewhat superfluous. The officer must nonetheless legitimise continuing, with or without the detainee. He does so by presenting his words as being delivered *just in case*. For officers, the challenge of explanation can involve difficulty in even obtaining the floor to explain.

Some detainees, asked to recontextualise, bypassed recontextualisation altogether, moving straight to stating intentions in the recontextualisation turn:

I'll tell you the truth and nothing but the truth

[A18]

This detainee has appropriated another "frozen register" formulation (Joos, 1967), the oath used to preface courtroom evidence. The three detainees just cited all prospected talk and compliance through the turn-at-talk they were given in the cautioning exchange. Other detainees prospected silence and non-compliance:

> just means I don't have to say anything you know what I mean I've got my rights I'm not saying shit you know what I mean?
>
> [B19]

He is willing to play along with the ostensible aim of his turn-at-talk, recontextualisation, initially repeating the caution's first sentence but he ultimately uses his turn to state his intentions for the rest of the interaction. The detainee below could be said to hijack the recontextualisation turn-at-talk even more dramatically:

> D   er (.) I'm not guilty but I'll get sewn up with it (.) that's:
>   (.) // it's all //
> P   //basically//
> D   sealed isn't it and (.) all the evidence is a mess and it's
>   going to go to court-
>
> [S4]

His caution explanation is shot through with what we might call a discourse of wrongful arrest. Stating innocence and using words and phrases like *sewn up, sealed* and *evidence is a mess*, he uses the request for a recontextualisation to signal dissatisfaction with the legal process. These recontextualisations highlight the difficulty of assuming that own-words-explanations in any way relate to a flat, unproblematic concept of 'understanding', particularly in situations where individuals who provide recontextualisations might intend them to do more, or other, than simply signal understanding.

Some detainees similarly evaluated cautioning procedure and prospected their interview conduct by opting out of the cautioning exchange altogether. Fairclough proposes that, for those with limited power, silence is a "mode of intervention" (1992:206) which offers "a way of being non-committal about what more powerful participants say" (2001:113). McDermott similarly describes the potential for inarticulateness manifest in inappropriate, superficial and incoherent talk to enable expression outside institutional frameworks, to subvert and critique institutional norms (1988:50–2). Several detainees refused to recontextualise when asked to do so, instead using their recontextualisation turn to mark non-participation in comprehension checking:

P   do you understand the caution?
D   yeh
P   yes could you just explain the caution what it means
      to you?
→ D   no comment
P   no comment OK (.) what the caution generally means
                                                                    [B7]

In interview, answering questions with *no comment* is powerful as it
reduces the pressure of incompleteness which accompanies silence.
Answering *no comment* during comprehension checking is perhaps
even more powerful; it strictly prevents interviewing officers from
cautioning felicitously and being seen to have done so. This strategy also
affords the interviewee the opportunity to rehearse using *no comment*
responses. Some detainees appeared familiar with answering *no comment*
throughout cautioning exchanges. Others, however, seemed confused
about this tactic:

P   do you understand the caution?
D   yes
P   you do? (.) can you in your own words just explain to me
      what you believe it to mean?
→ D   [to solicitor] no comment yeah?
                                                                    [B18]

P   anything you do say may be given in evidence do you
      understand?
→ S   you may say "yes" to that ((5 syllables))
D   yes (.) yes yes
                                                                    [B10]

These detainees planned to give 'no comment interviews' on their
solicitors' advice. However, both appear unsure about when 'silent
speaking' should begin; therefore, when asked to explain the caution,
each looks to their solicitor for guidance. In the first instance, the
detainee nominates the solicitor to help in this decision; in the second,
the solicitor intervenes.[8] For these detainees, the boundary between pre-
interview and interview is unclear. By analogy detainees who participate
in cautioning exchanges may be similarly unsure of the status of rights
talk – they may even believe that they have revoked their right to silence
by participating (Cotterill, 2000:19; Shuy, 1997:189). This is a serious

shortcoming of explaining and exploring the caution during interviews rather than during a clearly delineated speech event.

Detainees' abstinence from cautioning was, on occasions, derailed by officers who were able to "force participants out of silence and into a response by asking *do you understand?*" (Fairclough, 2001:113) as powerful participants can ultimately "sideline ... subversion and critique as institutional practices rain down" (McDermott, 1988:50–2).

In some instances, institutional norms come into direct conflict with lay people's talk. In the following example, it is the detainee's 'helper', his appropriate adult, who resists the officer's attempt to caution, exploiting the cautioning exchange to insert his own perspective which should, in the normal course of events, not be explicit in the interview. The excerpt below is indicative of a cautioning exchange which extended over 40 turns and more than six agonising minutes:

1	P	for example if you wanted to say well it was so and so that did it it wou- do you understand (.) and they might (.) it's a //matter for the court//
2	AA	// what he's trying to // say is he's trying to put the blame on you saying you nicked // it (.) but you don't ((know who's)) nicked it //
3	P	// they might they might blame you for // something or draw an inference (.) // do you understand that //
4	AA	// ((can we get on with the)) // interview
5	P	sorry?
6	AA	can we get on with this urm questions
7	P	yeh it's important though I need to //((please))//
8	AA	// yeh he // understands all this because
9	P	well no that's- I need to hear that from him
10	AA	say it Fred
11	P	I need to know that you understand this
12	D	yeh
13	P	OK and anything you do say as I say (.) may be given in evidence that means // the tapes //
14	AA	//I'm starting// in a minute

[D23]

Here, the officer's and appropriate adult's discourses are incompatible: the officer seeks to pursue and be seen to pursue procedure, whereas the appropriate adult recasts the officer's turns as hostile provocation. Usually, in such confrontations between an institutional official speaking "with a technical vocabulary grounded in professional expertise" and an "ordinary" person speaking "in a common vernacular grounded in personal expertise", "the technical prevails over the vernacular" (Mehan, 1993:264). Here the commitment of each participant to their communicative practices to some extent decontextualises the other's words, rendering those words defunct (cf. Iedema and Wodak, 1999). The appropriate adult's discourse of resistance to authority cannot, in the interview setting, be recontextualised to be meaningful (Scheuer, 2001:234). The clash of worlds becomes most pronounced when the police officer invokes institutionality, seeking to legitimise cautioning as important (turn 7) while the appropriate adult calls on his lifeworld practices of speaking for his ward (turn 8) and demanding cooperation from the teenager (turn 10). The officer's power lies in "the continuous reassertion of the status of [his] discourse as 'true', objective, neutral or normal and [the displacement of] other emergent discourses" (Wright, 1994:25, in Iedema and Wodak, 1999:12), simultaneously the appropriate adult's power lies in dominating the floor, ultimately preventing a felicitous cautioning exchange from occurring. Here cautioning is hijacked by the appropriate adult yet recycled by the officer to demonstrate institutionality.

Sarangi proposes that relatively expert medical clients can advantageously "embed their lifeworld narratives in an institutionally recognisable fashion in order to bring about a desirable outcome" (1998a:303). In my data, relatively expert detainees occasionally exploit the very requirement that the caution has been fully understood. AO22 anecdotally described a detainee who repeatedly claimed incomprehension of the caution during interview preamble. Eventually the interview had to be suspended, until a passing officer revealed that he had interviewed the detainee many times before, concluding *"he does understand the caution he's messing you about"*. This detainee used his knowledge of police procedure to reclaim power, challenging officers to recontextualise in a way which would solve his claimed comprehension difficulties. Such uncooperative behaviour (House, 2003:21) or "parasitic misunderstandings" in which a speaker uses the expression of misunderstanding "in order to gain points at the cost of his fellow conversationalist" (Hinnenkamp, 2003:74) or where ambiguity is intentionally exploited (Goffman,

1981:10–11) is particularly potent in interactions which may eventually reach an overhearing audience.

Research which pretends that cautioning is only about conveying information offers insight into only one potentially rather incidental aspect of cautioning. By overlooking some important aspects of cautioning, such research cannot successfully comment even on transmission.

Part IV
Righting Rights

13
Description, Action and Uptake

13.1 Introduction

This book has presented a detailed study of (socio)linguistic aspects of rights communication in one contemporary, Western, adversarial law setting. In this book, explanation has been treated not as a skill but a technology; a way of making and re-making meaning, performing and addressing identity, and shaping and facilitating social participation. By explaining institutional texts, speakers and writers not only represent texts' institutionally sanctioned content but also accomplish a wide range of social, interpersonal and interactional goals. Indeed institutional texts' deliverers and addressees both use them to do a great deal beyond the transactional.

This chapter provides first a descriptive conclusion. This summarises the study's findings about the lived reality of transformation in police work. The chapter then explores tensions around transforming descriptive findings into artefacts such as recommendations. Taking action through description has been problematised within sociolinguistics yet it has been recommended and even accomplished by some. I pursue the ideals of those who seek to turn research into practice by providing, in this chapter, a cautious, research-based conclusion.

This work was conceived as a descriptive study of rights communication in police custody. However, when one researches such task-focussed settings one's questions are quickly recontextualised by academic colleagues and by people within the site of study who expect such work to be prescriptive rather than descriptive. Both groups assume that research in the police station must be aiming to fix problems. The problem which is usually assumed to exist in communicating rights is that people do not understand their rights or do not feel able to invoke them. My research suggests that any problem in communicating rights in custody is broader than this because it stems from the multifunctionality of human interaction.

13.2   Description

13.2.1   The *Notice to detained persons*

Part II of this book, the first analytic part, examined the written text which had been used to communicate rights in England and Wales relatively unchanged since 1986 (the Parent text). It compared that text to a revision by a police Sergeant and five individual revisions by commercial information designers. It also reported observations of, and interviews about, the police Sergeant's revision in use in a working custody suite. The Parent text featured grammatical forms like passives and lexical forms like formal vocabulary which would be condemned by plain language prescriptions. The rewriters addressed many of these potential lexico-syntactic shortcomings innovatively. Whilst their changes would improve the text according to 'objective' plain language criteria, the subjective question of whether their revisions would improve the lot of detainees or indeed police officers was impossible to answer through a focus only on the texts (Chapters 3 and 4).

The Parent text's discoursal arrangements, such as nonsensical sequence, were disorientating. They potentially led detainees to disregard their rights. Rewriters attended to all levels of document organisation by making sets of interdependent changes at different levels of language. This interdependence highlighted the difficulty of meaningfully evaluating the effect of any individual change. The rewriters made changes which attentively considered readers' likely activities and questions. Some specific reader-focussed changes were noticed and valued by readers. However, readers described feeling isolation and distance from these institutional texts illustrating that many difficulties with the texts were beyond the scope of simple textual revision and required a different response (Chapter 5).

Presumably, a legal system which distributes written rights notices intends those notices to be read. The Sergeant reviser whose text was evaluated in use had deliberately produced notices which would be accessible, short and detainee-centred. However, many people in detention did not read those notices completely or at all. This highlights the theoretical imperative to look beyond the text and the practical imperative to understand more about whether and how people in detention learn of their rights (Chapter 6).

Some detainees do not read in detention because they cannot read. Even those who may only find reading difficult in other situations may find it impossible in detention. However, being unable to read was not the only reason for not reading rights notices. Some, particularly novice detainees, rejected rights texts because they were overwhelmed by detention. Others, predominantly regular detainees, exploited rejection of the texts, showing antipathy for detention through antipathy for interest in the *Notices*. A final group did not read the text because they could not conceive of its purpose or relevance to them. The many detainees who cannot or do not read written rights information draw on other sources of information in their place. Non-reading detainees described using information gathered from prescribed talk at the custody desk but also during informal in-detention conversations. Detainees also described drawing rights information from sources beyond detention such as television, wider reading and social contacts. Yet, this did not suggest that the written texts were useless. Even for non-readers entextualisation drew attention to the texts' content and encouraged participation in other rights-giving activities. The notices were read in part by readers who either sought answers to particular questions or only had enough time or concentration for minimal reading.

Some detainees did read fully; if necessary, slowly and carefully. They did not necessarily respond predictably to what they had read, however. Some did not believe the information they encountered or assigned it a significance which it did not have. Others seized upon the information for purposes other than finding out about rights, particularly appropriating opportunities designated for talk about rights to self-present (Chapter 7). Rights texts and their formulation have limited influence on detention and influence detention in unexpected ways.

13.2.2 The caution

The current police caution attracts criticism. Many police officers expressed doubt about its effectiveness in conveying information or administering justice. Difficulties surround the caution from the outset – even its name is problematic, inadequately conveying pragmatic intent and lacking denotation for some detainees. Many officers saw the wording as simply token. Nonetheless, they recite and explain it repeatedly. They had evolved a sophisticated exchange structure for explaining the wording and most took explanation seriously (Chapter 8).

Chapter 9 mirrors the attention paid in Chapter 4 to rewriters' lexico-syntactic changes by examining attention to lexis in spoken explanations. Officers who explain in speech echoed their writing counterparts. They filled the caution's wording with meaning, illustrating, elaborating, specifying and personalising in order to translate the formulation's generality to fit their interlocutor. More obviously than the writers they were sometimes persuasive in the process.

The caution's sentence-sequence is confusing and somewhat misleading, appearing to encourage talk rather than silence. Officers changed this sequence when explaining the caution and the alternative sequences they chose, not to mention the ways in which they presented them, varied rather systematically between police forces. Officers in one force tended to maintain and metalinguistically mark the original sequence; officers in another preferred to re-sequence, seemingly under the influence of an official paraphrase; and officers in a third were rather idiosyncratic, omitting or repeating semantic components. Identifying use of a standard paraphrase of the caution in one of the forces was a catalyst to examining influence of scripting. Officers did not necessarily recite a standard paraphrase even if it was taped to a desk in front of them in interview rooms. They did use it to some extent, commonly as source or prop for explanations in their own words. Qualitative interviews revealed that a standard paraphrase would disrupt the many officers who explain differently each time they caution. These officers innovatively assess characteristics like detainees' age, occupation and education in deciding both whether and how to explain the wording. Such officers were resistant to prescribed explanations which would prevent them from attending to their interlocutor in styling their talk (Chapter 10).

The cautioning exchange appears to incorporate opportunities to check comprehension by asking detainees to confirm or demonstrate comprehension. However, confirmation and demonstration function poorly as measures of comprehension. Furthermore, checking comprehension potentially threatens face and officers used wideranging politeness strategies to mitigate this. Some officers used comprehension-checking turns to attend to detainees and co-construct understanding with them, going beyond monologic explanation. This required careful attention and significant metalinguistic ability; however, the strength of such collaboratively produced reformulations is compelling (Chapter 11).

Finally, the whole cautioning exchange can take on an existence which is neither institutionally sanctioned nor recognised. The functionality of the caution in framing upcoming interviews as serious was recognised by officers and, in some cases, they shifted footing, temporarily aligning with detainees in order to overcome its constraining formulaicity. Some detainees were so struck by this framing function that they overlooked every other aspect of the wording including its meaning. Officers appropriated cautioning to establish communicative norms for prospected interviews even if that involved facilitating silence in interview. As well as scaffolding interactions like this, the caution also scaffolds affiliations. Through cautioning, officers learn to caution, informally disseminate practice and show that they are 'good cops'. For detainees too, cautioning exchanges offer opportunities to show how they plan to proceed in interview, prospecting cooperation or resistance. In the final excerpt in Part III, a clash of discourses resulted in cautioning falling apart completely illustrating how far, and how dramatically, rights exchanges can move away from rights.

13.3 Application?

For many with a professional interest in communicating rights through speech and writing, a descriptive study is justified by subsequently drawing recommendations. In contrast, within the broadly defined field of sociolinguistics, intervention in the agencies or forms of life which one investigates is actively discouraged by some (Fairclough, 1992) while others recommend extreme caution (Labov, 1988:160) or "ethnomethodological indifference" (Garfinkel and Sacks, 1970), stemming "not from a position of moral cowardice, but from a deep uncertainty" about the safety of judgements about right and wrong (Komter, 2001). Intervention might be unsuccessful and fail to find anything generalisable (Barton 1994:24). Also, intervention might be misappropriated. Eades has demonstrated how her work became part of political and institutional contest and conflict, not her intention (2003:213–17). If our research recommends radical changes these might be impossible to implement (for example, Kurzon, 2000:248). Furthermore, our "findings" might not be "usable by the law" due to different discourse systems and communities in legal and non-legal disciplines (White, 1990:13). In the settings examined here, rapidly changing legal frameworks around detention and the high number of stakeholders render research difficult to incorporate. Nonetheless, some language researchers take an active stance in similar settings, disseminating their findings by translating them for use by practitioners (Gibbons, 2001a, 2003; Roberts, 2003). Several scholars indicate that there is indeed an obligation to genuinely apply language research and that "researchers should pay considerably more attention to the practical use of their work over and above the amassing of research findings" (Potter and Wetherell, 1987:174). This is particularly important in settings like those examined here, which "are closely connected to the exercise of power and to the construction of social difference" (Heller, 1999:260; see also Gunnarsson, 1997:285). Linguists, especially those who venture into other people's worlds, are likely to be asked for an opinion on language issues in those worlds, so we should "have some critical distance on what we do, and on whose interests are served by our actions and the knowledge we produce" (Heller, 1999:261). Indeed, if we think that we can quietly produce applied research projects without influencing social domains, we are wrong. Research may change the outlook of the researched, potentially dramatically and not necessarily to their benefit (Coupland and Coupland, 1998:185). Officers who simply took part in my study or have read even small parts of the work reported its influence in making them reflect on their talk in custody.

If one moves towards action, that action will be grounded in one's disciplinary, ideological framework. Psychologists' ideological framework, for example, centres on cognition; psychologists typically read data about rights communication as indexing cognitive competence. For example, in the various studies by Clare, Gudjonsson and colleagues cited throughout this book, incomplete explanations from detainees are taken to reveal incomprehension – cognitive deficit. This is not to say that particular disciplines have hidden agendas or do not seek authentic analyses, but simply that their disciplinary orientation gives particular foci primacy. Sociolinguists, working in a relatively young discipline, find that their disciplinary focus or ideological framework is not (yet) so fixed. This is another reason that sociolinguists may stop once they have accomplished description, even critical description. If they move beyond description their focus is not constrained. They may draw conclusions about competence but they may also draw many other themes from their data. This encourages a focus on data. An example will illustrate this point.

Section 11.3 presented comprehension-checking procedure as potentially face-threatening and illustrated officers' attempts to minimise that threat. Thus, an established focus within linguistics on facework provided a useful way into the data. The naturally occurring data themselves did not offer any 'reading' of officers' motivations; politeness was investigated as a linguistic phenomenon, not an example of people being 'nice', the lay meaning of *polite*. Officers' comments during research interviews suggested that some are uncomfortable with putting detainees on the spot during comprehension checking. Section 11.3 therefore frames officers' facework as being motivated by expressed desires to minimise imposition. However, it is entirely possible that officers attend to face during cautioning exchanges for very different reasons, staging benevolence. Leo, a legal scholar, examines very similar talk from USA police officers. Driven by his disciplinary focus and procedural adherence, he takes this talk to evidence attempts to deflect attention from *Miranda*'s sense and importance (1998b:216; 2001:1018). Leo's work consistently sees officers' rights talk as evidencing them having "learned to 'work *Miranda*'" (2001:1016), "transformed *Miranda* into a tool of law enforcement", "taken the advantage in *Miranda*" (2001:1021), used *Miranda* to "appear more professional" (2001:1024), and "learned how to sidestep the necessity of *Miranda*" (2001:1028). The language focus in turn uncovers similar motives. In Section 12.2.1, we encountered officers who recognised the caution's potential to frame interviews as serious and consequently to discourage talk. These officers reported shifting to a less formal footing and re-framing cautioning as harmless procedure. So in this study naturally occurring data revealed phenomena realised in talk: facework and shifts of footing. Describing these can be an end in itself for the linguist. Interviews with officers then provided a reading of those forms indicating that for officers they index both genuine attempts to reassure terrified detainees and, Leo's reading, manipulative attempts to woo potentially vulnerable people. In turn, interviews with detainees suggest that some view such forms as indexing supportive empathy while others view them as indexing manipulation. The upshot of this is that any recommendations which follow from research on humans and their social arrangements and activities should be both made and implemented with considerable care but that socio-linguistic methods make it possible to separate phenomena in the data from readings of those phenomena in order to show the bases of recommendations very clearly.

This study begins with language and juxtaposes this with the various phenomena uncovered and with interactants' comments in order to pull conclusions from the data themselves, rather than departing from disciplinary sense-making processes. This method uncovers very conscientious officers constantly striving to act fairly *and* officers who will appropriate procedures for investigative ends. The difficulty is then to decide how to respond to the revealed diversity of human behaviours and their manifestations in language. One good way to constrain anyone who is eager to abuse their power by exploiting procedure is to provide them with strict, unambiguous rules which they must follow exactly in order to discharge their duty whilst simultaneously implementing procedures to ensure that this happens. However, if all creativity, individuality and potential for response are removed from rights communication then officers cannot improve on the standard issue, detainees cannot ask for more and checks and balances can, at best, only ensure compliance. Without the latitude to be creative, the officer who revised the written rights notice discussed in Part II would not have put pen to paper and his ideas would certainly not have reached the Home Office. Similarly, if all individuality is squashed out of cautioning exchanges it will seep into other parts of detention procedure taking explanation with it. To have had access to the parts of people's lives lived-out in custody and then to trivialise and oversimplify what has been observed by converting it reductively to meek recommendations and banal generalisations potentially misses the point of the qualitative endeavour. Yet, to have had such access and simply to file it under 'interesting examples of language in context' may be unforgivable. Ultimately, any intervention should attend to "the social contexts of culture and power and to the assumptions and expectations which individuals project into language use" (Roberts, Davies and Jupp, 1992:6). This drives my recommendations below.

13.4   Uptake

13.4.1   General comments

I have suggested both substantial and subtle changes to rights administration throughout this book. It would be helpful, for example, to change the caution's wording on arrest to remove reference to distant *questioning* (see Section 9.3). I also recommend broader social measures to ensure that people who find themselves in contact with any aspects of the legal system already have a fair understanding of that system. Citizenship classes in schools are beginning to address this. Television programmes, print media and increasingly Internet-based resources also have a huge responsibility here (see Section 7.2.3.1).

Written rights notices are usefully complemented by speech and spoken rights exchanges by writing. Indeed, the data reviewed here contain little to recommend reducing diversity of modes. Some detainees were puzzled by repeated administration of rights but most found it beneficial (see Section 7.2.4.1). It was helpful to position repetition as reinforcement not as redundancy (see Section 7.2.4.2). Written rights information provides a fixed, constant reference point. It gives the institution something which measurably performs rights communication and gives readers a safety net beneath poor verbal explanations.

However, only or mainly providing a written text to communicate rights is clearly completely inadequate. Increased diversity in fixed modes using videos or even some degree of interactivity through computer mediation would offer the benefits of fixity without the drawbacks of written text, especially important for the many people who cannot or do not read in detention. Increasing spoken rights communication would also help here. All rights communication should emphasise, as far as possible, the specific applicability of rights information to addressees and the implications and practical consequences of both waiving and invoking rights.

13.4.2   Revising cautioning

The caution is dense, vague and prone to quick, inexpressive delivery. However, the wording has massive symbolic currency and a flexibility which allows it to adapt to administration in diverse situations and in response to case law. Replacing the wording with a new formulation would be risky for these reasons and particularly because the wording has become familiar to detention participants. The wording could usefully be administered on paper much more imaginatively, however, possibly re-named, and explained before detainees reach the interview room.

Providing a standardised, scripted explanation is enticing but requires that all detainees will, upon hearing that explanation, understand the whole caution without specific clarification. This book demonstrates that making meaning is not one-size-fits-all; it is impossible to imagine a universally successful explanation. Furthermore, if officers are de-skilled through reliance on a standard formulation, deviation from the script may become impossible. Officers might also come to pay little attention to the caution's meaning with no routine reason to consider it.

Officers should be encouraged to continue to disseminate cautioning practice as they currently do. They should also be regularly updated on relevant case law because case law ultimately determines what they can say in explanation. This would both reassure officers and promote legally compliant explanation. Officers should receive training or at least guidance on explaining. There are some promising models already in circulation although typically relying on scripting to a great extent (for example, Knight, 2006:pc). These data recommend explanation through interaction, where possible. There are many ways for officers to explain interactively without doing anything very different from what many already do. Officers are currently expected to explain this way by PACE Code C (2006:Note10D). However, they clearly need much more support in this. Below, I recommend a procedure for cautioning on the basis of the research described in Part III of this book. It is annotated with comments about its uptake:

(1) Recite the official wording. Do **not** ask *do you understand?*
(2) Tell the detainee that you will talk through the caution with them. Stress that you are doing this because the detainee needs to understand in order to use the information to make decisions about interview.
(3) Explore each part of the wording beginning with the right to silence (sentence 1), then moving to sentence 3 and finally sentence 2. This sequence explains that interviews will be recorded before mentioning using recordings in court. Use the following scheme:

    a. **Detainee explanation: Say which sentence you're delivering. Re-read the relevant part of the official wording and ask the detainee what they think it means.** [Asking about one sentence at a time places less pressure on both detainees' and officers' memories in explaining and evaluating respectively.] **Listen carefully to what the detainee says.** [Officers would receive brief, simple guidance on listening in this very particular situation. Officers cited in this book show that careful, responsive listening is quite possible. Guidance would be particularly important to explanations of the medial sentence which appears most difficult to explain and evaluate.]

    b. **Officer explanation: Using what the detainee has said, respond.** If they seem to have explained fully, clearly tell them that what they said was correct and remind them that it applies throughout interview. If you doubt their explanation then identify and explain the things that you doubt. Work with what the detainee gives you. Do not just recite your 'normal explanation' unless you have absolutely no alternative. [Again, officers would receive brief, simple guidance, devised using authentic explanations. This would specify, for example, that concepts like *opportunity* are best avoided. It would also specify ways of involving detainees.]

    c. **Double-check: Following your explanation do not ask** *do you understand that now?* **which leads people to just agree, instead ask something like** *is there anything in that part that you don't understand?* Again work with what detainees tell you repeating listening and explaining as above, if necessary. [In problem cases, officers might use radical approaches to checking and improving comprehension. For example, Grisso's experimental methods can be intriguingly adopted for this (1998). Officers could:

- provide bogus and genuine caution readings either to demonstrate their difference or check comprehension;
- request definitions of important words, such as *rely*, which might identify or fill conceptual gaps;
- present scenarios to test and illustrate rights application.

Whilst these devices would be too cumbersome for routine use they would broaden the range of resources at officers' disposal for tricky cases in cautioning and, indeed, in other explanation tasks.]

    d. **Once you have finished this procedure for each sentence in turn remind the detainee that what you have just discussed applies to the whole interview.**

(4) **Official check: Finally, you need ratifiable confirmation from the detainee that they understand the whole wording.** You should not have asked *do you understand?* at all until now. Ask that now and, if they confirm, stress that they can ask you to revisit any of that, at any time, if necessary. If they say that they do not understand do not just start explaining – you do not know what is causing the problem. Ask, and address that. [This procedure creates a genuine attempt to achieve comprehension before checking comprehension. This avoids using the question *do you understand?* to ask about both a psycholinguistic and legal state simultaneously. The procedure should be modified when explaining to detainees arrested recently or repeatedly.]

The present procedure pretends that officers can always explain, will invariably know whether and how to do so and will always make it through a long, difficult explanation. The procedure described above would benefit from operating alongside a fall-back procedure which would perhaps move cautioning out of interview if that became necessary.

It is difficult to identify an optimal cautioning situation. Clearly, explanations of the caution might be very different if not recorded and, while overhearers might be distracting, their influence is probably positive and their presence necessary. Cautioning away from interview and from the public, potentially busy custody desk, where interaction buzzes with additional significances, would allow detainees to consider their options well before interview and in relative privacy. However, that would break connections between caution and interview. Cautioning activities should be very clearly distinguished from other talk whenever they occur.

As for the ideal cautioner, practicality dictates this is likely to be a police officer although a neutral cautioner would be an interesting development. Custody sergeants might be well placed to explain the caution because their role is not investigative and they already explain rights to detainees. However, their availability is constrained by the duties they already have and, without a cautioning exchange, the dynamic between detainees and interviewing officers is stymied. Officer practice and comment suggests that observing and responding to what comes out of cautioning exchanges through, for example, training in which officers review their own cautioning may be more important than controlling what goes in through prescribed wordings. Few examinations of cautioning consider changes on these levels. The detailed data examined in this study, of which a relatively small part has been presented in this book, raise questions about even the basics of cautioning.

If you have never heard a caution explanation, you would be stunned by the reality of cautioning: by the effect of an officer laughing heartily in response to a detainee's explanation or by the power of a detainee claiming again and again not to understand in order to delay interview, by the scope for cautioning to be filled with light-hearted banter or with sharp hostility, by the potential for a repetitive explanation from an officer, winding in circles for many minutes to make detainees twitch. These are not neutral, manageable conversations, but are visceral, fraught, asymmetrical and uncertain. Anything can happen during cautioning, including one or more participants opting out of the whole enterprise. Those who have heard, or given, a caution explanation will recognise that the suggestions above are 'ideal world' recommendations. Reality would prune them. Indeed it might seem ridiculous to go to such lengths to work on comprehension. That is a moral decision for society. Society should not kid itself that the caution alone will inform detainees of their right to silence.

13.4.3 Revising the rights *Notice*

The legal institution of England and Wales has shown itself willing to listen to one of its own employees through the introduction of the revised *Notice*, written by a working custody sergeant. It has also been willing to attend to some aspects of research findings in incorporating recommendations from my research during the process of finalising that text. Whilst the communication of rights and indeed procedures in custody are too complex to be 'fixed' by simple textual revisions, willingness to make alterations to rights texts is an encouraging start. The Home Office have recently reviewed current detention procedures by inviting comments from practitioners, stakeholders and the public (Home Office, 2007). Perhaps this consultation will offer an opportunity for rights communication to become more informative, interactive and imaginative. This would involve using writing and speech more effectively through officer training and the dissemination of good practice as well as moving beyond relying only on speech and writing in detention to communicate rights information.

The combination of insights and ideas from a practitioner with empirical research on language, on linguistic contexts and on people involved in those contexts has proved useful in examining and altering processes of communicating rights, could be further developed in detention and is applicable to other settings.

14
Epilogue

The rights text now used around England and Wales (Appendix 12) is based on the Sergeant revision. However, the text underwent significant, sadly detrimental alterations since the Sergeant and I were involved. The alterations compromise the Sergeant's aims, throughout. He designed an uncluttered first page providing a short, distinctive rights summary. The version now used inserted the following words at the very beginning of the text:

> The following rights and entitlements are guaranteed to you under the law in England and Wales and comply with the European Convention on Human Rights.

The redundancy of this formulation is almost too obvious to point out and the placement of this highly bureaucratic wording, formal in both form and content, at the very beginning of the *Notice* has great potential to deter further reading. This formulation is like the instructions to custody officers which had been used at the beginning of the Parent *Notice* (Appendix 1) in that it does not seem to address detainees and is incidental to the text's main message (see Section 6.6.2).

More seriously, the version of the Sergeant's text which was circulated has introduced three errors which simply prevent the text from making sense. At various points throughout the explanation of the right to a solicitor the Sergeant's text stated:

> The police will help you get in touch with a solicitor.
> The police will help you contact him or her.
> The police will then help you contact a solicitor.

In the circulated version these have been changed:

> The police will help you get in touch with a solicitor for you.
> The police will help you contact him or her for you.
> The police will then help you contact a solicitor for you.

It would appear that someone intended to revise the Sergeant's wording. Perhaps, they were sceptical about the comprehensibility of the rather idiomatic *get in touch*. Yet, that featured in only one of the original formulations and the phrasal verbs *hold up* ('cause delay') and *turn up* ('arrive') which occur elsewhere in the Sergeant's text are untouched, suggesting that somewhat idiomatic grammar was not the focus. More likely then, the reviser intended to replace the notion that officers would help detainees to contact a solicitor, which implied detainees' autonomy perhaps too strongly, with the statement that the police would make contact *for you*. Whilst there are arguments for and against the changes, leaving them half-made is a serious blunder. It is shocking that a text containing such basic proofing errors is in national circulation, even more so as the document in question has such a crucial impact on citizens' lives.

Additionally, the circulated text alters the Sergeant's formulation of the idea that legal advice can be obtained in private:

> The Sergeant's text → You can talk to a solicitor on the telephone without the police knowing what you are telling him or her. A solicitor can also decide to come to see you at the police station.

> Altered text, now in circulation → **You are entitled to a private consultation with your Solicitor** on the telephone **or they may** decide to come **and** see you at the Police Station.

The clumsy, nominalised noun phrase *private consultation* and the condensing of two sentences into one would conflict with any writing guidelines. Indeed, the statement of the basic right is arguably less 'plain' even than the Parent formulation *You can talk to the solicitor in private*. Furthermore, *private consultation* may be construed as indicating that one must pay for this 'private', as opposed to public, service as one would in England and Wales if seeing a private doctor. Use of *your solicitor* potentially deters detainees who do not know a solicitor. Additionally, the verb *entitled* contributes to a very specific confusion. Detention observes an important technical difference between rights and entitlements. Access to a solicitor is, according to this distinction, a right not an entitlement. Furthermore, in my data, several detainees expressed uncertainty about the meaning of *entitlements* proposing that they are, for example:

- possessions:
  if they arrest you and they take your possessions off you and stuff like that these are what your entitlements are

  [Novice 09]

- things one cannot have:
  F do you know the difference between rights and entitlements?
  D what you are allowed and what you're not allowed

  [Regular 12]

It is worrying that such words, which the Sergeant deliberately excluded from his text, have been re-introduced particularly without consultation which could have highlighted them as problematic.

One remarkable difference between the version submitted to the Home Office and the version now in circulation is in pagination. The circulated version removes space which was deliberately introduced into the Sergeant's text using findings from this research. The space separated explanation of the three rights which can be invoked during custody from explanation of the right to a record of custody which cannot (see Section 3.7). A knock-on effect of removing the space is that the heading for the subsequent page appears in the wrong place entirely – not at the head of its page, indeed not on the correct page. All subsequent pagination is also scrambled with some disastrous consequences. The Home Office have been reluctant to rectify these matters to date.

The texts were also issued without any assembly instructions to police forces. The Sergeant had demonstrated the texts' format when we visited the Home Office and explained the rationale for that unconventional but effective format (see Section 6.2). The Sergeant reviser had rather idealistically envisaged his text being assembled during quiet periods in custody suites. He required officers to fold one page, insert other pages into the fold and then secure each individual copy using a staple-less stapler.[1] It was surprising that a writer who paid such attention to the needs of those who would both read and issue his text had overlooked the demand that this painstaking assembly would place on people who fulfilled the same institutional role as him. This perhaps reflects his level of conscientiousness and his desire for his text to draw prospective readers' attention by looking unusual. Without instructions on assembly or information about the reasons for the arrangement of pages (such as the main sheets visible inside the summary intending to draw readers in) and layout (such as the simple front page) (see Section 6.2), it is not surprising that forces have been puzzled about how to use the text. Preliminary observation of the uptake of the final text suggests that it is being appropriated by police forces with as much variability as its predecessor. Individual forces have altered both layout and structure. For example, converting it into a small three-way folded leaflet, cramming all of the text onto one page and removing the initial rights summary.

This is not intended as criticism of the Home Office. Their endeavours to introduce the new text at all are admirable and their willingness to consider wider procedural changes in rights communication bode well. Rather, this reinforces one of my concluding points. The sociolinguist can observe and even participate in language debates in institutions but ultimately those institutions and their parts mediate those efforts. The Sergeant's text will no doubt attract its own criticism yet it is evidence of an institution willing to listen to one of its own practitioners and to interested researchers. The changes that the Sergeant's text has already undergone is also evidence of the unending cycle of textual transformation in detention.

Appendix 1
The Parent *Notice to Detained Persons*

NOTICE TO DETAINED PERSON

The section in capital letters is to be read to the detained person by the Custody Officer before giving the notice to the detained person.

YOU HAVE THE RIGHT TO:

1. SPEAK TO AN INDEPENDENT SOLICITOR FREE OF CHARGE

2. HAVE SOMEONE TOLD THAT YOU HAVE BEEN ARRESTED

3. CONSULT THE CODES OF PRACTICE COVERING POLICE POWERS AND PROCEDURES

YOU MAY DO ANY OF THESE THINGS NOW, BUT IF YOU DO NOT, YOU MAY STILL DO SO AT ANY OTHER TIME WHILST DETAINED AT THE POLICE STATION.

If you are asked questions about a suspected offence, you do not have to say anything. But it may harm your defence if you do not mention when questioned something which you later rely on in court. Anything you do say may be given in evidence.

More information is given below:

FREE LEGAL ADVICE

You can speak to a solicitor at the police station at any time, day or night. It will cost you nothing.

Access to legal advice can only be delayed in certain exceptional circumstances (see Annex B of Code of Practice C).

If you do not know a solicitor, or you cannot contact your own solicitor, ask for the duty solicitor. He or she is nothing to do with the police. Or you can ask to see a list of local solicitors.

You can talk to the solicitor in private on the telephone, and the solicitor may come to see you at the police station.

If the police want to question you, you can ask for the solicitor to be there. If there is a delay, ask the police to contact the solicitor again. Normally the police must not question you until you have spoken to the solicitor. However, there are certain circumstances in which the police may question you without a solicitor being present (see paragraph 6.6 of Code of Practice C).

If you want to see a solicitor, tell the Custody Officer at once. You can ask for legal advice at any time during your detention. Even if you tell the police you do not want a solicitor at first, you can change your mind at any time.

Your right to legal advice does not entitle you to delay procedures under the Road Traffic Act 1988 which require the provisions of breath, blood or urine specimens.

THE LAW SOCIETY

The right to have someone informed of your detention

You may on request have one person known to you, or who is likely to take an interest in your welfare, informed at public expense as soon as practicable of your whereabouts. If the person you name cannot be contacted you may choose up to two alternatives. If they too cannot be contacted the Custody Officer has discretion to allow further attempts until the information has been conveyed. The right can only be delayed in exceptional circumstances (see Annex B of Code of Practice C).

The right to consult the Codes of Practice

The Codes of Practice will be made available to you on request. These Codes govern police procedures. The right to consult the Codes of Practice does not entitle you to delay unreasonably any necessary investigative and administrative action, neither does it allow procedures under the Road Traffic Act 1988 requiring provisions of breath, blood or urine specimens to be delayed.

The right to a copy of the Custody Record

A record of your detention will be kept by the Custody Officer. When you leave police detention or are taken before a court, you or your legal representative or the appropriate adult shall be supplied on request with a copy of the Custody record as soon as practicable. This entitlement lasts for 12 months after your release from police detention.

Appendix 2
The Parent *Notice of Entitlements*

NOTICE OF ENTITLEMENTS

This notice summarises provisions contained in Codes C and D of the Codes of Practice regarding your entitlements whilst in custody. The letters and numbers in brackets relate to appropriate Code and paragraph references. If you require more detailed information please ask to consult the Codes.

All persons should read Parts A and B of this notice. Part C explains provisions which apply to juveniles and persons suffering from mental disorder or mental handicap and Part D explains additional provisions which apply to citizens of independent commonwealth countries and nationals of foreign countries.

PART A – GENERAL ENTITLEMENTS
Whilst in custody you are entitled to the following:-
1. Visits and contact with outside persons.
   In addition to your rights to have someone informed of your arrest, and to legal advice, you may receive visits, at the custody officer's discretion. Unless certain conditions apply you may also make one telephone call, and be supplied with writing materials ('C' 5.4 and 5.6).
2. Reasonable Standards of Physical Comfort.
   Where practicable you should have your own cell ('C' 8.1), which is clean, heated, ventilated and lit ('C' 8.2). Bedding should be clean and serviceable ('C' 8.3).
3. Adequate Food and Drink.
   Three meals per day. Drinks with, and upon reasonable request, between meals ('C' 8.6).
4. Access to Toilets and Washing Facilities. ('C' 8.4).
5. Replacement clothing.
   If your own clothes are taken from you, you must be given replacements that are clean and comfortable ('C' 8.5).
6. Medical Attention.
   You may ask to see the Police Surgeon (or other doctor at your own expense) for a medical examination, or if you require medication. You may also be allowed to take or apply your own medication at appropriate times but in the case of controlled drugs the Police Surgeon will normally supervise you when doing so ('C' 9.4 – 'C' 9.6).
7. Exercise.
   Where practicable, brief outdoor exercise every day ('C' 8.7).
8. If in 'Police Detention' to make representations when your detention is reviewed.
   When the grounds for your detention are periodically reviewed, you have a statutory right to say why you think you should be released, unless you are unfit to do so because of your condition or behaviour ('C' 15.1).

PART B – CONDUCT OF INTERVIEWS
1. Interview rooms should be adequately heated, lit and ventilated ('C' 12.4).
2. Persons being interviewed should not be required to stand ('C' 12.5).
3. Unless certain conditions apply, in any 24 hour period you must be allowed at least eight hours rest, normally at night ('C' 12.2).
4. Breaks should be made at recognised meal times, and short breaks for refreshments should normally be made at intervals of approximately two hours ('C' 12.7).
5. Interviewing officers should identify themselves by name and rank (or by warrant or other identification number in terrorism cases) ('C' 12.6).

PART C – APPROPRIATE ADULTS
If you are under 17 years of age or suffering from a mental disorder or mental handicap, you should be assisted by an "appropriate adult" as explained in Code C, paragraph 1.7. A solicitor or lay visitor present at the station in that capacity may not act as an appropriate adult ('C' Note 1F). The appropriate adult will be present when you are:-
1. informed of and served with notices explaining the rights of detained persons, and when informed of the grounds for detention ('C' 3.11);
2. interviewed (except in urgent cases), or provide or sign a written statement ('C' 11.14);
3. intimately or strip searched ('C' Annex A, paragraph 5 and 11(c));
4. cautioned ('C' 10.6);
5. given information, asked to sign documentation, or asked to give consent regarding any identification procedure ('D' 1.11, 1.12, 1.13);
6. charged ('C' 16.1); or
7. when the grounds for detention are periodically reviewed ('C' 15.1).
   You should always be given the opportunity, when an appropriate adult is called to the police station, to speak privately to a solicitor in the absence of the appropriate adult should you wish to do so.

PART D – FOREIGN NATIONALS/COMMONWEALTH CITIZENS
If you are a citizen of a foreign or commonwealth country, you are entitled to the following:-
1. To communicate at any time with your High Commission, Embassy or Consulate, and have them told of your whereabouts and the grounds for your detention ('C' 7.1).
2. To private visits from a consular officer to talk, or to arrange for legal advice ('C' 7.3).

Appendix 3
Examples of Different Versions of the Parent
Notice to Detained Persons

This appendix contains the versions of the *Notice* used or considered by the police forces listed below.

(a) Leicestershire Constabulary, Durham Constabulary, Essex Police
(b) West Midlands Police
(c) Greater Manchester Police
(d) West Yorkshire Police
(e) Derbyshire Police.

LEICESTERSHIRE CONSTABULARY

NOTICE TO DETAINED PERSON

> *The section in capital letters is to be read to the detained person by the Custody Officer before giving the notice to the detained person.*

YOU HAVE THE RIGHT TO:

1. SPEAK TO AN INDEPENDENT SOLICITOR FREE OF CHARGE.

2. HAVE SOMEONE TOLD THAT YOU HAVE BEEN ARRESTED.

3. CONSULT THE CODES OF PRACTICE COVERING POLICE POWERS AND PROCEDURES.

YOU MAY DO ANY OF THESE THINGS NOW, BUT IF YOU DO NOT, YOU MAY STILL DO SO AT ANY OTHER TIME WHILST DETAINED AT THE POLICE STATION.

If you are asked questions about a suspected offence, you do not have to say anything. But it may harm your defence if you do not mention when questioned something which you later rely on in court. Anything you do say may be given in evidence.

More information is given below:

Free Legal Advice

You can speak to a solicitor at the police station at any time, day or night. It will cost you nothing.

Access to legal advice can only be delayed in certain exceptional circumstances (see Annex B of Code of Practice C).

If you do not know a solicitor, or you cannot contact your own solicitor, ask for the duty solicitor. He or she is nothing to do with the police. Or you can ask to see a list of local solicitors.

You can talk to the solicitor in private on the telephone, and the solicitor may come to see you at the police station.

If the police want to question you, you can ask for the solicitor to be there. If there is a delay, ask the police to contact the solicitor again. Normally the police must not question you until you have spoken to the solicitor. However, there are certain circumstances in which the police may question you without a solicitor being present (see paragraph 6.6 of Code of Practice C).

If you want to see a solicitor, tell the Custody Officer at once. You can ask for legal advice at any time during your detention. Even if you tell the police you do not want a solicitor at first, you can change your mind at any time.

Your right to legal advice does not entitle you to delay procedures under the Road Traffic Act 1988 which require the provisions of breath, blood or urine specimens.

THE LAW SOCIETY

The right to have someone informed of your detention

You may on request have one person known to you, or who is likely to take an interest in your welfare, informed at public expense as soon as practicable of your whereabouts. If the person you name cannot be contacted you may choose up to two alternatives. If they too cannot be contacted the Custody Officer has discretion to allow further attempts until the information has been conveyed. The right can only be delayed in exceptional circumstances (see Annex B of Code of Practice C).

The right to consult the Codes of Practice

The Codes of Practice will be made available to you on request. These Codes govern police procedures. The right to consult the Codes of Practice does not entitle you to delay unreasonably any necessary investigative and administrative action, neither does it allow procedures under the Road Traffic Act 1988 requiring provisions of breath, blood or urine specimens to be delayed.

The right to a copy of the Custody Record

A record of your detention will be kept by the Custody Officer. When you leave police detention or are taken before a court, you or your legal representative or the appropriate adult shall be supplied on request with a copy of the Custody Record as soon as practicable. This entitlement lasts for 12 months after your release from police detention.

DNA Profiling

In accordance with Sections 62, 63 and 63A Police and Criminal Evidence Act 1984 you may be required to give a sample of saliva or body hair for a speculative search and subsequent recording onto the DNA Database. The sample and record will be destroyed if you are:-

a) prosecuted for the offence and cleared; or

b) not prosecuted (unless you admit the offence and are cautioned).

Fingerprints/Photograph

In accordance with Section 61(2) Police and Criminal Evidence Act 1984 it is proposed to take your *fingerprints/photograph for identification purposes and also for the purpose of determining whether you have previously engaged in crime.

Your *fingerprints/photograph and all copies thereof will be destroyed if you are subsequently:-

a) prosecuted for the offence and cleared; or

b) not prosecuted (unless you admit the offence and are cautioned).

*   Delete where not applicable

* * You will be given the opportunity of seeing the destruction if within FIVE days of being cleared or informed that you will not be prosecuted, you make an application to LEICESTERSHIRE CONSTABULARY.

PERSON ATTENDING VOLUNTARILY AT POLICE STATION AND NOT UNDER ARREST

You can speak to a solicitor at the police station at any time, day or night. It will cost you nothing.

If you do not know a solicitor, or you cannot contact your own solicitor, ask for the duty solicitor. He or she is nothing to do with the police. Or you can ask to see a list of local solicitors.

You can talk to the solicitor in private on the telephone, and the solicitor may come to see you at the police station.

If the police want to question you, you can ask for the solicitor to be there. If there is a delay ask the police to contact the solicitor again. You can ask the police to wait for the solicitor to be at the interview.

THE LAW SOCIETY

Legal Aid

DURHAM CONSTABULARY

NOTICE TO DETAINED PERSON

The section in capital letters is to be read to the detained person by the Custody Officer before giving the notice to the detained person.

YOU HAVE THE RIGHT TO:

1. SPEAK TO AN INDEPENDENT SOLICITOR FREE OF CHARGE.

2. HAVE SOMEONE TOLD THAT YOU HAVE BEEN ARRESTED.

3. CONSULT A COPY OF THE CODES OF PRACTICE COVERING POLICE POWERS AND PROCEDURES.

   YOU MAY DO ANY OF THESE THINGS NOW, BUT IF YOU DO NOT, YOU MAY STILL DO SO AT ANY OTHER TIME WHILST DETAINED AT THE POLICE STATION.

4. A DRUG ARREST REFERRAL SCHEME OPERATES AT THIS POLICE STATION. IF YOU ARE INTERESTED I CAN ARRANGE FOR YOU TO SEE AN INDEPENDANT DRUGS WORKER IN DUE COURSE. ARE YOU INTERESTED? (If the answer is Affirmative pass the detainees details to the scheme).

If you are asked any questions about a suspected offence, you do not have to say anything. But it may harm your defence if you do not mention when questioned something which you later rely on in court. Anything you do say may be given in evidence.

More information is given below:

Free Legal Advice

You can speak to a solicitor at the police station at any time, day or night. It will cost you nothing.

Access to legal advice can only be delayed in certain exceptional circumstances (see Annex B of Code of Practice C).

If you do not know a solicitor, or you can not contact your own solicitor, ask for the duty solicitor. He or she is nothing to do with the Police. Or you can ask to see a list of local solicitors.

You can talk to the solicitor in private on the telephone, and the solicitor may come to see you at the police station.

If the police want to question you, you can ask for the solicitor to be there.

If there is a delay, ask the police to contact the solicitor again. Normally the Police must not question you until you have spoken to the solicitor. However, there are certain circumstances in which the Police may question you without a solicitor being present. (See paragraph 6.6 of Code of Practice C).

If you want to see a solicitor, tell the Custody Officer at once. You can ask for legal advice at any time during your detention. Even if you tell the Police you do not want a solicitor at first, you can change your mind at any time.

Your right to legal advice does not entitle you to delay procedures under the Road Traffic Act 1988, which require the provision of breath, blood or urine specimens.

THE LAW SOCIETY

The right to have someone informed of your detention.

You may on request have one person known to you, or who is likely to take an interest in your welfare, informed at public expense as soon as practicable of your whereabouts. If the person you name cannot be contacted you may choose up to two alternatives. If they to cannot be contacted the Custody officer has discretion to allow further attempts until the information has been conveyed. This right can only be delayed in exceptional circumstances (see Annex B of Code of Practice C).

The right to consult the Codes of Practice

The Codes of Practice will be made available to you on request. These codes govern police procedures. The right to consult the Codes of Practice does not entitle you to delay unreasonably any necessary investigative and administrative action, neither does it allow procedures under the Road Traffic Act, 1988, requiring the provision of breath, blood or urine specimens to be delayed.

The right to a copy of the Custody Record

A record of your detention will be kept by the Custody Officer. When you leave police detention or are taken before a Court, you or your legal representative or the appropriate adult shall be supplied on request with a copy of the Custody Record as soon as practicable. This entitlement lasts for 12 months after your release from police detention.

IMPORTANT

IF YOU HAVE A DRUGS PROBLEM YOU CAN ASK TO SEE A
DRUGS WORKER AT ANY TIME WHILST YOU ARE IN CUSTODY,
JUST INFORM THE CUSTODY SERGEANT.

IT MAY NOT ALWAYS BE POSSIBLE FOR A DRUGS WORKER TO COME
TO THE POLICE STATION AS THEY WORK 9am - 5pm WEEKDAYS ONLY.

IF YOU ARE WILLING THE CUSTODY SERGEANT CAN PROVIDE YOUR
CONTACT DETAILS TO THE DRUGS WORKERS AND THEY WILL CONTACT
YOU TO ARRANGE A MEETING AT A TIME AND PLACE TO SUIT YOU.

ALTERNATIVELY YOU CAN CONTACT THEM UPON YOUR
RELEASE ON THE FOLLOWING NUMBERS.

0191 - 3839420

OR

0781 - 8048902

NECA ACCESS

ARE AN AGENCY INDEPENDENT OF THE POLICE

THEY HAVE A TEAM OF WORKERS OPERATING THROUGHOUT
COUNTY DURHAM AND DARLINGTON

ON A ONE TO ONE BASIS THEY WILL GIVE YOU ADVICE
INFORMATION AND SUPPORT AND HELP YOU TO GET THE
RIGHT TYPE OF TREATMENT FOR YOUR PROBLEM.

NOTICE TO DETAINED PERSON

The section in capital letters is to be read to the detained person by the Custody Officer before giving the notice to the detained person.

YOU HAVE THE RIGHT TO:

1. SPEAK TO AN INDEPENDENT SOLICITOR FREE OF CHARGE.

2. HAVE SOMEONE TOLD THAT YOU HAVE BEEN ARRESTED.

3. CONSULT THE CODES OF PRACTICE COVERING POLICE POWERS AND PROCEDURES

YOU MAY DO ANY OF THESE THINGS NOW, BUT IF YOU DO NOT, YOU MAY STILL DO SO AT ANY OTHER TIME WHILST DETAINED AT THE POLICE STATION.

If you are asked questions about a suspected offence, you do not have to say anything. But it may harm your defence if you do not mention when questioned something which you later rely on in Court. Anything you do say may be given in evidence.

More information is given below:

Free Legal Advice

You can speak to a solicitor at the police station at any time, day or night. It will cost you nothing.

Access to legal advice can only be delayed in certain exceptional circumstances (see Annex B of Code of Practice C).

If you do not know a solicitor, or you cannot contact your own solicitor, ask for the duty Solicitor. He or she is nothing to do with the police. Or you can ask to see a list of local solicitors.

You can talk to the solicitor in private on the telephone, and the solicitor may come and see you at the police station.

If the police want to question you, you can ask for the solicitor to be there. If there is a delay, ask the police to contact the solicitor again. Normally the police must not question you until you have spoken to a solicitor. However, there may be certain circumstances in which the police may question you without a solicitor being present (see paragraph 6.6 of Code of Practice C).

If you want to see a solicitor, tell the Custody Officer at once. You can ask for legal advice at any time during your detention. Even if you tell the police you do not want a solicitor at first, you can change your mind at any time.

Your right to legal advice does not entitle you to delay procedures under the Road Traffic Act 1988 which require the provisions of breath, blood or urine specimens.

THE LAW SOCIETY

Legal Aid

The right to have someone informed of your detention

You may on request have one person known to you, or who is likely to take an interest in your welfare, informed at public expense as soon as practicable of your whereabouts. If the person you name cannot be contacted you may choose up to two alternatives. If they too cannot be contacted the Custody Officer has discretion to allow further attempts until the information has been conveyed. The right can only be delayed in exceptional circumstances (see Annex B of Code of Practice C).

The right to consult the Codes of Practice

The Codes of Practice will be made available to you on request. These codes govern police procedures. The right to consult the Codes of Practice does not entitle you to delay unreasonably any necessary investigative and administrative action, neither does it allow procedures under the Road Traffic Act 1988 requiring provisions of breath, blood or urine specimens to be delayed.

The right to a copy of the Custody Record

A record of your detention will be kept by the Custody Officer. When you leave police detention or are taken before a Court, you or your legal representative or the appropriate adult shall be supplied on request with a copy of the Custody Record as soon as practicable. This entitlement lasts for 12 months after your release from police detention.

PERSON ATTENDING VOLUNTARILY AT POLICE STATION AND NOT UNDER ARREST

You can speak to a solicitor at the police station at any time, day or night. It will cost you nothing.

If you do not know a solicitor, or you cannot contact your own solicitor, ask for the duty solicitor. He or she is nothing to do with the police. Or you can ask to see a list of local solicitors.

You can talk to the solicitor in private on the telephone, and the solicitor may come to see you at the police station.

If the police want to question you, you can ask for the solicitor to be there. If there is a delay ask the police to contact the solicitor again. You can ask the police to wait for the solicitor to be at the interview.

THE LAW SOCIETY

Legal Aid

We ask people about their ethnicity so that the fair treatment of different ethnic groups can be internally and independently monitored and to improve the service we provide.
Please look at this chart and tell me how you describe your ethnicity.

	White	(W)
W1	British	
W2	Irish	
W9	Any other White Background	
	Mixed	(M)
M1	White and Black Caribbean	
M2	White and Black African	
M3	White and Asian	
M9	Any other mixed background	
	Asian or Asian British	(A)
A1	Indian	
A2	Pakistani	
A3	Bangladeshi	
A9	Any other Asian background	
	Black or Black British	(B)
B1	Caribbean	
B2	African	
B9	Any other Black background	
	Chinese or Other Ethnic Group	(O)
O1	Chinese	
O9	Any other ethnic group	

taking a lead in making Essex safer

PEOPLE IN CUSTODY - YOUR RIGHTS AND ENTITLEMENTS

WC 338
(amended 7.99)

YOUR RIGHTS IF YOU ARE HELD IN CUSTODY

If you are held in custody you can:

1   *Speak to a solicitor free of charge*
2   *Have someone told that you have been arrested*
3   *Consult the Codes of Practice covering police powers and procedures*

You may do any of these things now OR AT ANY OTHER TIME while you are in custody.

If you are asked questions about a suspected offence, you do not have to say anything. But it may harm your defence if you do not mention something which you later rely on in court. Anything you do say may be given in evidence.

Your right to speak to a solicitor free of charge

While you are at the station you can speak to a solicitor at ANY time, day or night. It will cost you nothing.

If you don't know a solicitor or cannot contact your own, you can ask to see the duty solicitor or look at a list of local solicitors.

You can talk to your solicitor on the phone, and he or she may come to see you at the police station.

If police officers want to question you, you can ask for your solicitor to be there. If there is a delay, ask the police to contact your solicitor again. You can ask the police to wait for your solicitor to be at the interview.*

You can ask for legal advice AT ANY TIME while you are in custody. Even if you tell the police you do not want a solicitor, you can change your mind at any time.

Your right to legal advice does not mean you can delay the taking of specimens such as breath, blood or urine.

* NOTE: There are certain circumstances in which the police may question you without a solicitor being present - see paragraph 6.6. of Code of Practice C.

Your right to tell someone that you have been arrested

If you are arrested ONE person can be contacted to tell them where you are. If that person cannot be contacted you can suggest up to two other names. If they cannot be contacted, it is up to the custody officer to decide whether or not you can name further people to contact.

In *exceptional circumstances,* your right to let people know that you have been detained may be delayed *(see Annex B of Code of Practice C).*

Your right to look at the Codes of Practice

The Codes of Practice set out police procedures in full detail and you can ask for a copy at *any time* while you are in custody. The codes fully explain all of your rights and your entitlements.

However, your right to consult the Codes of Practice does not mean you can use it as an excuse to delay any investigation, for example the taking of specimens of breath, blood or urine.

Your custody record

A record of your time in custody will be kept by the custody officer. If you ask for a copy of this record you, your solicitor or an appropriate adult will be given one as soon as possible - when you leave the police station or are taken to court. You can ask for a copy of this document up to 12 months after your release from the police station.

If you attend a police station - and are not under arrest

You are not under arrest and you can leave the station at any time, unless you are placed under arrest. You have exactly the same rights to see a solicitor as if you were under arrest.

WHAT YOU ARE ENTITLED TO

This section gives a summary of the Codes of Practice and explains what you are entitled to while in custody.

EVERYONE should read **Parts A and B.**

Part C applies to people under the age of 17 or people suffering from mental disorder or mental handicap.

Part D applies to people from other countries.

PART A - GENERAL ENTITLEMENTS

● **Visits and contact with outside people**

As well as your right to legal advice and to have someone told of your arrest, you can receive visits if the custody officer agrees. Except in certain circumstances, you can ask to make one telephone call and be given something to write with.

● **Your physical comfort**

If possible you should have your own cell which is clean, heated, ventilated and lit. Bedding should be clean.

● **Adequate food and drink**

You should be given three meals a day with drinks. Other drinks will be available throughout the day.

● **Access to toilets and washing facilities**

● **Clothing**

If your clothes are taken away from you, you should be given replacements that are clean and comfortable.

● **Medical help**

You may ask to see the police doctor *(or other doctor at your own expense)* for a medical examination or if you need medication. You may be allowed to take your own medication if this is agreed by the police surgeon. In the case of controlled drugs, this will normally be supervised by the police doctor.

● **Exercise**

Where possible, you will be allowed to take brief outdoor exercise every day.

● **When your detention is reviewed**

If you are in police detention the grounds for keeping you in custody will be reviewed at certain times. At these times you have the right to say why you think you should be released or to raise other issues - unless you are unfit to do so because of your condition or behaviour.

PART B - INTERVIEWS

● Interview rooms should be heated, lit and ventilated.

● People being interviewed should not be required to stand up.

● Except in certain circumstances, in any 24 hour period you will be allowed at least eight hours rest *(normally at night).*

● Breaks should be taken at meal times and short breaks for refreshments should normally be taken every two hours.

● Officers carrying out the interview should give you their name and rank *(or other identification in cases involving terrorism).*

PART C - APPROPRIATE ADULTS

If you are under 17 years of age or are suffering from a mental disorder or mental handicap, you should be helped by an 'appropriate adult' - as explained in the Codes of Practice. A solicitor or lay visitor *(see separate entry)* may not act as an 'appropriate adult'.

The 'appropriate adult' will be present when:

● You are told about your rights and served with a notice explaining them in more detail

● You are told the grounds for your detention

● You are searched - intimately or strip-searched

● You are cautioned

● You are given information or asked to sign any documents or to agree to any identification procedure

● You are charged

● The grounds for holding you in detention are being considered

If you want to, you will be given the opportunity to speak to a solicitor privately, without the appropriate adult being there.

PART D - PEOPLE FROM OTHER COUNTRIES

If you are from another country, you are entitled to:

● Speak to your High Commission, Embassy or Consulate and have them told where you are and why you are being detained

● Have private visits from a consular officer to talk or to arrange legal advice

WHILE YOU ARE IN CUSTODY

Taking your fingerprints

● In certain circumstances *(see Codes of Practice)* you may be asked to have your fingerprints taken. You will be told the reason why your fingerprints are being taken. If you refuse, in certain circumstances reasonable force may be used to take them.

Taking your photograph

● In certain situations *(see Codes of Practice)* your photograph will be taken.

● If you alter your appearance between the taking of the photograph and any identity parade, the court may be told about this if the case comes to trial.

Taking of body samples

● In certain circumstances *(see Codes of Practice)* an intimate or non-intimate sample may be taken from you. This may be used to prove or disprove your involvement, or for recording and searching purposes.

● In these circumstances, the custody officer will fully explain what will happen and your rights.

Lay visitors

Lay visitors are members of the public who visit people held in police stations to check on their welfare. These visitors can call at police stations at any time and will listen to anything you want to say. They then write reports about the way you have been treated while you are in custody. You do not have to see lay visitors if you do not want to.

Form 602
Greater Manchester Police

Notice of your rights in police detention

You have been arrested and are being held in police detention. You are entitled to four rights which you can choose to take now or later.

1 The right to have someone told where you are.

2 The right to seek legal advice.

3 The right to read the Codes of Practice made under the Police and Criminal Evidence Act, 1984.

4 The right to receive, on request, a copy of your custody record on release. This right lasts for 12 months after release.

The police advise you that if you are questioned about any offence you do not have to say anything unless you wish to do so but what you say may be given in evidence.

For more details of your rights, please see over ▶

Your four rights

1 The right to have someone told where you are.

2 The right to seek legal advice.

3 The right to read the Codes of Practice made under the Police and Criminal Evidence Act, 1984.

4 The right to receive, on request, a copy of your custody record on release. This right lasts for 12 months after release.

Can the police delay my rights?

It is lawful for an officer of at least the rank of superintendent to delay Rights 1 and 2 for up to 36 hours if:

- you are suspected of a serious arrestable offence*, *and*
- you have not been charged.

But the officer must *also* have good reason to believe that to allow Rights 1 and 2 would:
- interfere with evidence or interfere with or harm another person, *or*
- lead to the alerting of other people suspected of an offence, *or*
- hinder the recovery of property obtained by crime.

If you are a citizen of an independent Commonwealth country or you are a national of a foreign country you always have the right to communicate with your High Commission, Embassy or Consulate. This right cannot be delayed or stopped.

What must the police allow me to do?

(This section only applies if Rights 1 and 2 have not been delayed.)

- Right 1 says you may ask for someone to be told where you are. If this person cannot be contacted, you may choose up to two other people to be told.
- You may receive visits from friends or relatives if the custody officer agrees.
- If you ask for writing materials you will be given them. Your letters will be sent and you will be allowed to make one phone call. The custody officer will decide whether you will have to pay for postage and phone calls.

How can I get legal advice?

The custody officer will give you a leaflet which explains:
- how to get legal advice,
- whether it will be free or not.

When may the police take my fingerprints?

Normally the police may not take your fingerprints without your agreement. And if you are at a police station your agreement must be in writing. However, the police may take your fingerprints without your agreement if you are in police detention and *either:*
- an officer of at least the rank of superintendent says they may be taken. Such an officer must have good reason for suspecting you are involved in a criminal offence and that he believes the fingerprints may confirm or disprove it, *or*
- you have been charged with a recordable offence* and have not had your fingerprints taken during the investigation of the offence.

The police may also take your fingerprints without your agreement if you have been convicted of a recordable offence.

Please ask the custody officer if you are not sure what these terms mean.

The information on this side of the form is only a summary of the law to help you understand your rights. It is not a full statement of the law.

WEST YORKSHIRE POLICE

NOTICE TO DETAINED PERSONS

The section in capital letters is to be read to the detained person by the Custody Officer before giving the notice to the detained person.

If you are asked questions about a suspected offence, you do not have to say anything. But it may harm your defence if you do not mention when questioned something which you later rely on in court. Anything you do say may be given in evidence.

YOU HAVE THE RIGHT TO:-

1. SPEAK TO AN INDEPENDENT SOLICITOR FREE OF CHARGE.

2. HAVE SOMEONE TOLD THAT YOU HAVE BEEN ARRESTED.

3. CONSULT A COPY OF THE CODES OF PRACTICE COVERING POLICE POWERS AND PROCEDURES.

YOU MAY DO ANY OF THESE THINGS NOW, BUT IF YOU DO NOT, YOU MAY STILL DO SO AT ANY OTHER TIME WHILST DETAINED AT THE POLICE STATION.

More information is given below.

Free Legal Advice

You can speak to a solicitor at the police station at any time, day or night. It will cost you nothing.

Access to legal advice can only be delayed in certain exceptional circumstances (see Annex B of Code of Practice C).

If you do not know a solicitor, or you can not contact your own solicitor, ask for the duty solicitor. He or she is nothing to do with the police. Or you can ask to seek a list of local solicitors.

You can talk to the solicitor in private on the telephone, and the solicitor may come to see you at the police station.

If the police want to question you, you can ask for the solicitor to be there. If there is a delay, ask the police to contact the solicitor again. Normally the police must not question you until you have spoken to the solicitor. However, there are certain circumstances in which the police may question you without a solicitor being present. (See paragraph 6.6 of the Code of Practice C).

If you want to see a solicitor, tell the Custody Officer at once. You can ask for legal advice at any time during your detention. Even if you tell the police you do not want a solicitor at first, you can change your mind at any time.

Your right to legal advice does not entitle you do delay procedures under the Road Traffic Act 1988 which require the provision of breath, blood or urine specimens.

THE LAW SOCIETY

Legal Aid

The right to have someone informed of your detention

You may on request have one person known to you, or who is likely to take an interest in your welfare, informed at public expense as soon as practicable of your whereabouts. If the person you name cannot be contacted you may choose up to two alternatives. If they too cannot be contacted, the Custody Officer has discretion to allow further attempts until the information has been conveyed. This right can only be delayed in exceptional circumstances (see Annex B of Code of Practice C).

The right to consult the Codes of Practice

The Codes of Practice will be made available to you on request. These codes govern police procedures. The right to consult the Codes of Practice does not entitle you to delay unreasonably any necessary investigative and administrative action, neither does it allow procedures under the Road Traffic Act 1988 requiring the provision of breath, blood or urine specimens to be delayed.

The right to a copy of the Custody Record

A record of your detention will be kept by the Custody Officer.

When you leave police detention or are taken before a Court, you or your legal representative or the appropriate adult shall be supplied on request with a copy of the Custody Record as soon as practicable. This entitlement lasts for 12 months after your release from police detention.

PERSON ATTENDING VOLUNTARILY AT POLICE STATION AND NOT UNDER ARREST

You can speak to a solicitor at the Police Station at any time, day or night. It will cost you nothing.

If you do not know a solicitor, or you cannot contact your own solicitor, ask for the duty solicitor. He or she is nothing to do with the police. Or you can ask to see a list of local solicitors.

You can talk to the solicitor in private on the telephone, and the solicitor may come to see you at the Police Station.

If the police want to question you, you can ask for the solicitor to be there. If there is a delay ask the police to contact the solicitor again. You can ask the police to wait for the solicitor to be at the interview.

DERBYSHIRE CONSTABULARY

Notice to Detained Person

The section in capital letters is to be read to the detained person by the Custody Officer before giving the notice to the detained person.

If you are asked questions about a suspected offence, you do not have to say anything, but it may harm your defence if you do not mention when questioned something which you later rely on in court. Anything you do say may be given in evidence.

YOU HAVE THE RIGHT TO:-

1.   SPEAK TO AN INDEPENDENT SOLICITOR FREE OF CHARGE.

2.   HAVE SOMEONE TOLD THAT YOU HAVE BEEN ARRESTED.

3.   CONSULT A COPY OF THE CODES OF PRACTICE COVERING POLICE POWERS AND PROCEDURES.

YOU MAY DO ANY OF THESE THINGS NOW, BUT IF YOU DO NOT, YOU MAY STILL DO SO AT ANY OTHER TIME WHILST DETAINED AT THE POLICE STATION.

More information is given below.

Free Legal Advice

You can speak to a solicitor at the police station at any time, day or night. It will cost you nothing.

Access to legal advice can only be delayed in certain exceptional circumstances (see Annex B of Code of Practice C).

If you do not know a solicitor, or you cannot contact your own solicitor, ask for the duty solicitor. He or she is nothing to do with the police. Or you can ask to see a list of local solicitors.

You can talk to the solicitor in private on the telephone, and the solicitor may come to see you at the police station.

If the police want to question you, you can ask for the solicitor to be there. If there is a delay, ask the police to contact the solicitor again. Normally the police must not question you until you have spoken to the solicitor.

However, there are certain circumstances in which the police may question you without a solicitor being present (see Paragraph 6.6 of the Code of Practice C).

If you want to see a solicitor, tell the Custody Officer at once. You can ask for legal advice at any time during your detention. Even if you tell the police you don't want a solicitor at first, you can change your mind at any time.

Your right to legal advice does not entitle you to delay procedures under the Road Traffic Act 1988 which require the provision of breath, blood or urine specimens.

THE LAW SOCIETY

Legal Aid

The right to have someone informed of your decision.

You may on request have one person known to you, or who is likely to take an interest in your welfare, informed at public expense as soon as practicable of your whereabouts. If the person you name cannot be contacted you may choose up to two alternatives. If they too cannot be contacted the Custody Officer has discretion to allow further attempts until the information has been conveyed. This right can only be delayed in exceptional circumstances (see Annex B of Code of Practice C).

The right to consult the Codes of Practice.

The Codes of Practice will be made available to you on request. These codes govern police procedures. The right to consult the Codes of Practice does not entitle you to delay unreasonably any necessary investigative and administrative action, neither does it allow procedures under the Road Traffic Act 1988 requiring the provision of breath, blood or urine specimens to be delayed.

The right to a copy of the Custody Record.

A record of your detention will be kept by the Custody Officer. When you leave police detention or are taken before a Court, you or your legal representative or the appropriate adult shall be supplied on request with a copy of the Custody Record as soon as practicable. This entitlement lasts for 12 months after your release from police detention.

Appendix 4
The Sergeant Revision

THE LAW SOCIETY

Legal Aid

Remember your rights:

1. Tell the police if you want a solicitor to help you while you are at the police station. It is free.

2. Tell the police if you want someone to be told that you are at the police station. It is free.

3. Tell the police if you want to look at the book called the Codes of Practice. It tells you what the police can and cannot do while you are at the police station.

Further information for people arrested by the police

> If you are asked questions about a suspected offence, you do not have to say anything. But it may harm your defence if you do not mention when questioned something which you later rely on in court. Anything you do say may be given in evidence.

1. Getting a solicitor to help you

- If you want a solicitor, tell the Police Custody Officer. The police will help you get in touch with a solicitor.

- If you do not know of a solicitor in the area or you cannot get in touch with your own solicitor, there is a person called the duty solicitor. The police will help you contact him or her. He or she is nothing to do with the police.

- You must be allowed to talk to a solicitor at any time, day or night, when you are at a police station. It is free.

- You can talk to a solicitor on the telephone without the police knowing what you are telling him or her. A solicitor may come to see you at the police station.

- Usually the police are not allowed to ask you questions until you have had the chance to talk to a solicitor. When the police ask you questions, you can ask for a solicitor to be in the room with you.

- If a solicitor does not come, or you need to speak to the solicitor again, ask the police to contact him or her again.

There are some special times when the police can ask you questions before you have talked to a solicitor. Information about these special times is given in the Codes of Practice. This is the book that sets out what the police can and cannot do while you are at the police station. If you want to look up the details, they are in paragraph 6.6 of Code C of the Codes of Practice.

There is also one special time when the police can stop you having a solicitor. Information about this is given in the Codes of Practice. If you want to look it up, see Annex B of Code C of the Codes of Practice.

2. Telling someone that you are at the police station

- You can ask the police to contact someone who needs to know that you are at the police station. It is free. They will contact someone for you as soon as they can.

- If the police cannot contact the first person you want to know that you are at the police station, they will try at least two more until someone knows.

There are special times when the police will not allow you to contact anyone. Information about these special times is given in the Codes of Practice. If you want to look up the details, see Annex B of Code C of the Codes of Practice.

3. Looking at the Codes of Practice

- The Codes of Practice is a book that tells you what the police can and cannot do while you are at the police station.

- The police will let you read the Codes of Practice but you may not read it for such a long time that it holds up the police finding out if you have broken the law.

4. Having the Custody Record

- Everything that happens to you when you are at the police station is put on paper and is called the Custody Record.

- When you leave the police station, you, your solicitor or your appropriate adult can ask for a copy of the Custody Record. The police have to give you a copy of the Custody Record as soon as they can. "Appropriate adult" is explained under "People who need help".

- You can ask the police for a copy of the Custody Record up to 12 months after you leave the police station.

Notice of entitlements

These are short notes about what you can expect while you are kept at the police station. To find out more, ask to see the book called the Codes of Practice. Inside its back cover you will find a list of where to find all these things.

Keeping in touch
As well as talking to a solicitor and having a person told about your arrest, you will usually be allowed to make one phone call. You can also ask for a pen and paper. You may be able to have visits but the custody officer can refuse to allow them.

Your room
If possible you should be kept in a room on your own. It should be clean, warm, and lit. Your bedding should be clean and in good order. You should be able to use a toilet and have a wash.

Clothes
If your own clothes are taken from you, then you must be given others that are clean and comfortable.

Food and drink
You must be offered 3 meals a day with drinks. You can also have drinks between meals.

Exercise
If possible you should be allowed outside each day for fresh air.

If you are not well
You can see the police doctor if you feel ill or need medicine. It is free. You can ask to see another doctor but you may have to pay for this. You may be allowed to take your own medicine but the police will have to check with the police doctor first.

How long can you be detained?
You can be detained for up to 24 hours without being charged. This can be longer but only if a police superintendent allows it to happen. After 36 hours, only a court can allow more time without you being charged. Every so often a senior police officer has to look into your case to see if you should still be in custody. This is called a review. You have the right to have your say about this decision, unless you are not in a fit state.

When the police question you

The room should be clean, warm and lit.

You should not have to stand up.

The police officers should tell you their name and their rank.

You should have a break at normal meal times and a break for a drink after about two hours.

You should be allowed at least eight hours rest in any 24 hours you are in custody.

People who need help

If you are under 17, or you have learning problems or a mental problem, then you should have an adult with you when the police do certain things. This person is called the "appropriate adult" and should be present when the police:

- Give you your rights and tell you why you are being kept at the police station.

- Interview you or ask you to sign a written statement or police notes.

- Caution you.

- Carry out a review.

- Have to remove more than your outer clothes.

- Carry out anything about an identification parade.

- Charge you with an offence.

You can speak to your solicitor with the appropriate adult out of the room if you want to.

People who are not British

If you are a citizen of a country other than Britain, then you can tell the police that you want to get in touch with your High Commission, Embassy or Consulate to tell them where you are and why you are in the police station. They can also visit you in private or arrange for a solicitor to see you.

Appendix 5
The Enterprise ID Revisions

This appendix contains the versions of the *Notice* produced by the following authors, all commercial information designers, in the order below:

(a) EnterpriseA
(b) EnterpriseB
(c) EnterpriseC
(d) EnterpriseD
(e) EnterpriseE.

EnterpriseA

NEWPORT PAGNELL CONSTABULARY
serving and protecting the community

Notice to Detained Persons

The Custody Officer will have read out the following statement to you before they gave you this notice:

"You have the right to:
- speak to an independent solicitor free of charge
- have someone told that you have been arrested
- consult the codes of practice stored in this station cover police powers and procedures.

You can exercise these rights at any time whilst you are being detained in this police station." *For further details of your rights, see below.*

You should also remember that if you are asked questions about a suspected offence, you do not have to say anything, but it may harm your defence if you do not mention when questioned something you later rely on in court. Anything you do say may be given in evidence.

If you do not understand this caution, or anything on this Notice, you can ask any police officer to explain it to you.

The right to speak to a solicitor

You can speak to a solicitor at the police station at any time, day or night. It will not cost you any money. Even if you say you don't want a solicitor or legal advice at first, you can change your mind at any time.

If you don't know a solicitor or you cannot contact your solicitor, you can ask for the duty solicitor or ask to see a list of local solicitors. The duty solicitor is nothing to do with the police. They are there to help detained persons who don't have access to legal representation. You can talk to the solicitor in private on the telephone, and they may come to see you at the police station.

You can ask for a solicitor to be with you if the police question you. Normally, the police cannot question you until you have spoken to a solicitor. However, under certain circumstances, your access to legal advice or representation can be delayed. These circumstances include arrests on suspicion of terrorism, drug trafficking, or if any delay in questioning might lead to physical injury to other people. The full list of circumstances are in section 6.6 and Annex B of Code of Practice C.

The right to have someone told that you have been arrested

You can have someone told that you have been arrested as soon as it is possible after you have been taken into custody. If the person you choose cannot be contacted, you can choose up to 2 other people to be contacted. If they cannot be contacted, it is up to the Custody Officer to decide whether you can try to contact anybody else.

The right to consult the Codes of Practice

You can ask to see the Codes of Practice, which set out police procedures, at any time.

The right to a copy of the Custody Record

You or your representative can ask for a copy of the custody record when you are released from custody or are taken before a court. Your custody record is only available for 12 months following your release.

EnterpriseB

Being in custody

While you are in custody, you have rights which affect what you can do, and entitlements which affect what you can expect the police to do. These rights and entitlements are explained in these Notices.

The police officer responsible for making sure that you understand your rights, and have the opportunity to use them, and that you receive your entitlements, is called the Custody Officer. They are also responsible for recording everything that happens while you are in custody in a Custody Record. You will be asked to sign parts of the Record to confirm that it is accurate. When you leave custody, or go to court, the police will give you a copy of this Custody Record if you ask for it.

Notice of   Your rights while you are in custody

You have 3 rights which you can use now, or at any time while you are held at a police station. If you decide not to use any of these rights, you can change your mind at any time.

Right 1   The right to speak to a solicitor in private, free of charge

Right 2   The right for someone to be told that you have been arrested

Right 3   The right to read the rules about how the police deal with people who have been arrested.

There is more information about each of the 3 rights below.

Right 1   The right to speak to a solicitor in private, free of charge

Solicitors help to protect the legal rights of people in custody, and also give them legal advice.

You have the right to speak to a solicitor privately – on the phone or face-to-face. This will not cost you anything. The police must ask you if you want to phone a solicitor.

If you choose to consult a solicitor, the police cannot normally interview you until you have spoken to your solicitor. And they must normally allow your solicitor to be there when they interview you. But the police can take specimens for possible road traffic offences without waiting for a solicitor.

If you choose not to consult a solicitor, the police will ask you to explain why, and will record your reasons.

Finding a solicitor

If you already have a solicitor, you may want to use them.

If you do not have a solicitor, you can use the duty solicitor or choose one from a list the police will give you. The duty solicitor is

.... The solicitors on the list are

.... Both the duty solicitor, and the solicitors on the list are completely independent of the police.

Right 2   The right for someone to be told that you have been arrested

If you give the police the name of someone you want to know about your arrest, the police will contact them and tell them where you are. You will not have to pay for this.

If the police cannot get in touch with the person you have told them about, you can give them the names of two more people to try to contact. If the police cannot get in touch with them, you may be allowed to give more names.

If you are not a British citizen, you have the right for your High Commission, Embassy or Consulate to be told where you are and why you are in custody.

Right 3   The right to read the rules about how the police deal with people who have been arrested

The rules about way that the police deal with people who have been arrested are set out in a legal document – 'The Code of Practice for the Detention, Treatment and Questioning of Persons by Police Officers', also called the PACE code.

You have the right to read this Code, but you cannot use this right to delay the police unreasonably. And you cannot use it to delay the police taking specimens for possible road traffic offences.

EnterpriseC

Sheet 1: About your arrest and your rights

Notice to detained person

> **Please read this panel before the rest of the sheet**
>
> This document tells you more about your rights while you are in police custody.
>
> You should also receive a sheet called 'About how you will be treated while in custody'. If you don't receive this sheet, please ask for it.
>
> If you have any questions about your rights, please ask a police officer for help. Your solicitor may also be able to help you.
>
> **Now please read the rest of the document through carefully.**

Your main rights

Your Custody Officer must read these rights to you before giving you this sheet. They are your main rights while in custody.

You have the right to:

1. speak to an independent solicitor free of charge
   (see the section called 'Getting free legal advice')

2. have someone told that you have been arrested
   (see the section called 'Letting someone know that you have been arrested')

3. look at the Codes of Practice covering how the police should treat you while you are in custody.
   (see the section called 'Looking at the Codes of Practice')

You can do any of these three things now or at any time while you are in custody. Please ask a police officer if you need any help.

You also have the right to have a copy of the Custody Record, which the Custody Officer keeps.
(see the section called 'Your copy of the Custody Record')

Caution – replying to questions

You may have been read this caution when you were arrested.

If you are being asked about a suspected offence, you do not have to say anything. But it may harm your defence if you d not mention when questioned something that you later rely on in court. Anything you do say may be given in evidence.

If this caution is not clear, or you would like more explanation, please let a police officer know straight away.

Getting free legal advice

Speaking to a solicitor: you can normally speak to a solicitor at any time, day or night. It will not cost you anything. If you tell the police that you don't want to see a solicitor, but change your mind later, you will still be able to see the solicitor.

There a few circumstances where the police can delay your seeing a solicitor or interview you without your solicitor's being there. Please ask to see the relevant part of the Codes of Practice if you want to know more about these circumstances.

You can either see the solicitor in person at the police station, or speak to them on the phone in private.

If you want to see a solicitor, tell the Custody Officer straight away.

If you do not know a solicitor, or cannot get in touch with your own solicitor, you can either ask for the duty solicitor, or see a list of other local solicitors. The duty solicitor is totally independent, and nothing to do with the police.

When you are interviewed, you can ask for your solicitor to be there. Your solicitor cannot be asked to leave your interview unless they are causing a nuisance. Normally the police will not interview you until you have spoken to a solicitor. If your solicitor has not been in touch by the time you are interviewed, you can ask the police to contact them again.

You cannot use your right to see a solicitor to delay any tests that you need to take under the Road Traffic Act 1988, such as providing a sample of your breath, blood or urine.

Letting someone know that you have been arrested

You can let one person know where you are. This will not cost you anything.

If the police cannot contact your first choice of person, they will ask you for up to two alternatives. If they cannot contact these people, it will be up to Custody Officer to decide how many more people can be tried. In a few circumstances, the police can delay this right.

Please also see the section called 'Contacting other people' on the sheet called 'About how you will be treated while in custody' [Would like to clarify the relation between these two section]

Looking at the Codes of Practice

The Codes of Practice tell the police how you should be treated while in custody. If you would like to see the Codes, please ask a police officer. You cannot use your right to see the codes to delay anything that the police need to do.

Your copy of the Custody Record

When you leave policy custody, or are taken to a court, you are allowed to take a copy of the Custody Record that the Custody Officer keeps. The police will provide this as soon as possible. You, your legal representative or the 'appropriate adult' will need to ask for the code. You can ask for a copy of the record up to 12 months after your release.

Now please read the sheet called 'About how you will be treated while in custody'

EnterpriseD

The Home Office

You are under Police arrest

If you are asked questions about a suspected offence, you do not have to say anything. But it may harm your defence of you do not mention when questioned something which you later rely on in court. Anything you do say may be given in evidence.

Your rights

You can exercise your rights now or at any time while you are under arrest. Tell the custody officer if you want to exercise these rights.

You cannot use any of your rights to delay Police work.

	Reference in Code of Paractice

- You have the right to have someone told that you have been arrested. This is free.   `ccc`

  You can choose someone who knows you or who will take an interest in your arrest. If the Police cannot contact the person, you may choose two others. The Custody Officer can allow further attempts to make contact if these two people cannot be contact either.

  The Police may only delay telling the person you choose in exceptional circumstances.

- You have the right to speak to your solicitor, in private on the phone or at the Police station. This is free.   `ccc`

  If you do not have a solicitor or you cannot contact them, ask to speak to the duty solicitor. They are totally independent of the Police.

  Even if you tell the Custody officer that you do not want to speak to a solicitor at first, you can change your mind and ask for free legal advice at any time.

- You have the right to have your solicitor present when you are interviewed.   `ccc`

  If you ask for your solicitor to be present, the Police must not normally interview you until your solicitor is there. If there is a delay, ask the Police to contact your solicitor again.

  If you do not have a solicitor or you cannot contact them, ask for the duty solicitor to be present. They are totally independent of the Police.

  Even if you tell the Custody officer that you do not want to speak to a solicitor at first, you can change your mind and ask for free legal advice at any time.

- You have the right to read the codes of practice that cover your treatment while you are under arrest.   `ccc`

  The Police must follow the Police and Criminal Evidence Act (PACE) codes of practice during the time you are held under arrest. The numbers in the boxes tell you where each right is mentioned in the code.

  You cannot use this right to delay Police work.

Your right to a copy of the Police record of your time in Custody

- You can ask for this for up to 12 months from the date you are released from arrest or taken before a court.   `ccc`

  Your legal representative or appropriate adult can ask for this for you.

  The Police will provide the record as soon they can.

EnterpriseE

Information for detained people

Please read this sheet carefully - it gives you important information about your rights while you are in custody.

The custody officer must read you the information in the grey boxes before giving you this notice.

The caution

If you are asked questions about a suspected offence you do not have to say anything. But it may harm your defence if you mention something which you later use in court when questioned. Anything you do say may be given in evidence.

You have the right to	What these rights mean for you
speak to an independent solicitor free of charge	It won't cost you anything to speak to a solicitor at the police station at any time of the day or night.
	If you would like to see a solicitor, tell the custody officer at once. Even if you say you do not want a solicitor, you can change your mind at any time and ask to see one.
[law society and legal aid logos in righthand margin]	The police can only delay access to legal advice under exceptional circumstances. *There are more details about this in Annex B of the Code of Practice*
	If you do not know a solicitor, or you cannot contact your own solicitor, ask for the duty solicitor or ask to see a list of local solicitors. The duty solicitor is completely independent from the police.
	You can talk to your solicitor in private on the telephone and the solicitor may come to the police station to see you.
	If the police want to question you, you can ask for the solicitor to be there. If there is a delay in getting a solicitor, ask the police to contact the solicitor again. Normally, the police must not question you until you have spoken to a solicitor. However, there are some circumstances when the police can question you without a solicitor there. *There are more details about this in paragraph 6.6 of the Code of Practice*
	This right does not allow you to delay procedures under the Road Traffic Act 1988 which mean you must give breath, blood or urine samples.
have someone told you have been arrested	You can have one person you know, or who is likely to take an interest in your welfare, told where you are.
	If the person you name cannot be contacted, you can choose up to two alternatives. If they cannot be contacted, it is up to the custody officer to decide if you can try other alternatives until someone has been told.
	This right can only be delayed in exceptional circumstances.
consult the Codes of Practice covering police powers and procedures	You can obtain a copy of the Codes of Practice if you ask for one.
	This right does not mean you can delay unreasonably any necessary investigative and administrative action, or delay procedures under the Road Traffic Act 1988 which mean you must give breath, blood or urine samples.

Your right to have a copy of the Custody Record

The custody officer will keep a record of your detention. When you leave police detention, or go to court, you or legal representative can be given a copy of the Custody Record as soon as it's available if you ask for it. This entitlement lasts for 12 months after you are released from police detention.

Appendix 6
The Government Revision

Remember your rights:

1. Tell the police if you want a solicitor to help you while you are at the police station. It is free.

2. Tell the police if you want someone to be told that you are at the police station. It is free.

3. Tell the police if you want to look at their rule-book called the Codes of Practice.

You will find more details about these rights inside

THE LAW SOCIETY

More information for people arrested by the police

Please keep this information and read it as soon as possible. It will help you to make decisions while you are at the police station.

> If you are asked questions about a suspected offence, you do not have to say anything. However, it may harm your defence if you do not mention when questioned something which you later rely on in court. Anything you do say may be given in evidence.

1. Getting a solicitor to help you

- A solicitor can help and advise you about the law.

- If you want a solicitor, tell the Police Custody Officer. The police will help you get in touch with a solicitor.

- The police must let you talk to a solicitor at any time, day or night, when you are at a police station. It is free.

- If you do not know of a solicitor in the area or you cannot get in touch with your own solicitor, you can speak to the duty solicitor. It is free. The police will help you contact him or her. The duty solicitor is nothing to do with the police.

- You can talk to a solicitor on the telephone without the police knowing what you are telling him or her. A solicitor can also decide to come to see you at the police station.

- Usually the police are not allowed to ask you questions until you have had the chance to talk to a solicitor. When the police ask you questions you can ask for a solicitor to be in the room with you.

- If you ask to speak to a solicitor it does not make it look like you have done anything wrong.

- If a solicitor does not turn up, or you need to speak to the solicitor again, ask the police to contact him or her again.

- If you tell the police that you don't want to speak to a solicitor but then you change your mind, tell the Police Custody Officer. The police will then help you contact a solicitor.

2. Telling someone that you are at the police station

- You can ask the police to contact someone who needs to know that you are at the police station. It is free. They will contact someone for you as soon as they can.

- If the police cannot contact the first person you ask for, they will try at least two more until someone knows.

3. Looking at the Codes of Practice

- The Codes of Practice is a book that tells you what the police can and cannot do while you are at the police station.

- The police will let you read the Codes of Practice but you cannot read it for so long that it holds up the police finding out if you have broken the law.

- If you want to read the Codes of Practice, tell the Police Custody Officer.

Getting details of your time at the police station

- Everything that happens to you when you are at the police station is put down on paper and is called the Custody Record.

- When you leave the police station, you, your solicitor or your appropriate adult can ask for a copy of the Custody Record. The police have to give you a copy of the Custody Record as soon as they can.

- You can ask the police for a copy of the Custody Record up to 12 months after you leave the police station

How you should be cared for

These are short notes about what you can expect while you are kept at the police station. To find out more, ask to see the book called the Codes of Practice. Inside its back cover you will find a list of where to find more information about each of these things. Ask the Police Custody Officer if you have any questions.

Keeping in touch
As well as talking to a solicitor and having a person told about your arrest you will usually be allowed to make one phone call. Ask the police if you would like to make a phone call. You can also ask for a pen and paper. You may be able to have visitors but the Police Custody Officer can refuse to allow that.

Your room
If possible you should be kept in a room on your own. It should be clean, warm, and lit. Your bedding should be clean and in good order. You must be allowed to use a toilet and have a wash.

Clothes
If your own clothes are taken from you, then the police must give you other ones that are clean and comfortable.

Food and drink
You must be offered 3 meals a day with drinks. You can also have drinks between meals.

Exercise
If possible you should be allowed outside each day for fresh air.

If you are not well
Ask to see the Police Doctor if you feel ill or need medicine. It is free. You can ask to see another doctor but you may have to pay for this. You may be allowed to take your own medicine but the police will have to check with the Police Doctor first.

How long can you be detained?
You can normally be detained for up to 24 hours without being charged. This can be longer but only if a Police Superintendent allows it to happen. After 36 hours only a court can allow more time without you being charged. Every so often a Senior Police Officer has to look into your case to see if you should still be kept here. This is called a review. You have the right to have your say about this decision. unless you are not in a fit state.

When the police question you

The room should be clean, warm and lit.

You should not have to stand up.

The police officers should tell you their name and their rank.

You should have a break at normal meal times and a break for a drink after about two hours.

You should be allowed at least 8 hours rest in any 24 hours you are in custody.

People who need help

If you are under 17, or you have learning problems or a mental problem then you should have someone with you when the police do certain things. This person is called your "appropriate adult".

Your appropriate adult must be with you when the police tell you about your rights and tell you why you are being kept at the police station. He or she must also be with you when the police read the caution to you.

The police might also need to do one of the things listed below while you are at the police station. Your appropriate adult should be with you for the whole time if the police do any of these things:

- Interview you or ask you to sign a written statement or police notes.

- Review your case.

- Remove more than your outer clothes.

- Carry out anything about an identification parade.

- Charge you with an offence.

You can speak to your solicitor without your appropriate adult in the room if you want to.

People who are not British

If you are not British, you can tell the police that you want to contact your High Commission. Embassy or Consulate to tell them where you are and why you are in the police station. They can also visit you in private or arrange for a solicitor to see you.

Special Times

Getting a solicitor to help you

There are some special times when the police might ask you
questions before you have talked to a solicitor. Information
about these special times is given in the Codes of Practice.
This is the book that that sets out what the police can and
cannot do while you are at the police station. If you want to
look up the details, they are in paragraph 6.6 of Code C of
the Codes of Practice.

There is one special time when the police will not let you
speak to the solicitor that you have chosen. When this
happens the police must let you talk to another solicitor. If
you want to look it up, it is in Annex B of Code C of the
Codes of Practice.

Telling someone that you are at the police station

There are some special times when the police will not allow
you to contact anyone. Information about these special times
is given in the Codes of Practice. If you want to look it up, it
is in Annex B of Code C of the Codes of Practice

Breath tests

If you are under arrest because of a drink drive offence, you
have the right to speak to a solicitor. That right does not
mean you can refuse to give the police samples of breath,
blood or urine even if you have not yet spoken to a solicitor.

Appendix 7
Demographic information about the detainees Interviewed

Sex

Of the 52 detainees interviewed:

    87% were male (45)   13% were female (7)

This is comparable with a national average for the years 2000–2001 (the equivalent time-span to that of this data collection) and to subsequent studies:

2001–2002	84% male	16% female
2002–2003	84% male	16% female
2003–2004	83% male	17% female
2004–2005	83% male	17% female

Age

Of the 52 detainees interviewed:

    64% were aged 21 and over (33)
        Of which:
        31% were aged 21–30 years (16)
        25% were aged 31–40 years (13)
        8% were aged over 40 years (4)
    13% were aged 18–20 years (7)
    23% were aged under 18 (12)
        (i.e. they would certainly need an appropriate adult)

This is comparable with a national average for the years 2000–2001 (the equivalent time-span to that of this study) and all subsequent years to date:

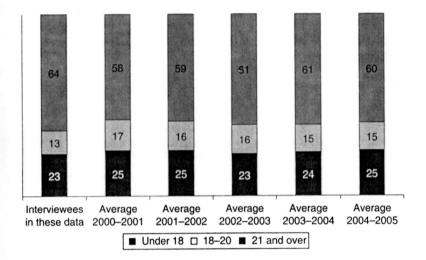

Interviewees in these data	Average 2000–2001	Average 2001–2002	Average 2002–2003	Average 2003–2004	Average 2004–2005

■ Under 18   □ 18–20   ■ 21 and over

The national arrest statistics used here are from:

Ayres, M. *et al.* (2001) *Statistical bulletin 19/01*, Home Office: London.

Ayres, M., Perry, D. and Hayward, P. (2002) *Statistical bulletin 12/02*, Home Office: London.

Ayres, M., Murray, L. and Fiti, R. (2003) *Statistical bulletin 17/03*, Home Office: London.

Ayres, M. and Murray, L. (2005) *Statistical bulletin 21/05*, Home Office: London.

Appendix 8

Sample of the *Notice to Detained Persons* Annotated to Indicate Difficult Features (Sample Section, for Illustration)

NOTICE TO DETAINED PERSONS [Introduces the document by prospecting readership rather than content] [Uses regular plural inflection, rather than the irregular "people"] [*Notice* does not indicate illocution]

The section in capital lettersis to be read [passivisation] to the detained person [odd noun phrase – why not 1st person pronominal reference *you*?] by the Custody Officer [jargon] before [rankshifted subordinate clause] giving the notice to the detained person.

YOU HAVE THE RIGHT TO [This must be read by being attached to the *to* + infinitive clauses below – each clause below looks more like a directive at first glance]:

1. SPEAK TO AN INDEPENDENT SOLICITOR [jargon] FREE OF CHARGE
2. HAVE SOMEONE TOLD [passivisation] THAT [Subordination] YOU HAVE BEEN ARRESTED [passivisation] [Open to garden-path interpretations from readers who believe that they *have the right to have* something rather than *to have* something happen – by analogy with the surrounding points]
3. CONSULT THE CODES OF PRACTICE [Jargon] COVERING [defining or restrictive relative clause which is not introduced with the relative pronoun *which*] POLICE POWERS AND PROCEDURES [Long noun phrase].

[What does the numbering suggest? Sequence? Dependency? Importance?]

YOU MAY[Ambiguous modal verb – may of permission or possibility?] DO ANY OF THESE THINGS NOW, BUT IF YOU DO NOT, YOU MAY STILL DO SO [Ellipses] AT ANY OTHER TIME WHILST [(you are) = whiz deletion] DETAINED[passivisation] [agent deletion] AT THE POLICE STATION.

If [adverbial conditional *if* clause – misleading as the detainee does not have to say anything irrespective of whether they are asked questions] You are asked questions about a suspected offence [Grammatical metaphor the verb *suspect* has become an adjective. Suspected offence = a specific offence which we (the investigative team, but not the custody staff) suspect you have committed] ... [Caution].

More ['poor' cohesive tie – as this immediately follows the caution, it suggests that more information about the caution will be given – yet the anaphora actually refers back to the capitalised section] information is given [passivisation] [agent deletion] below:

You can speak to a solicitor at the police station at any time, day or night. It [extraposition – using *It* to move the following section to the front of the sentence – *It* denotes *speaking to a solicitor*] will cost you nothing [Negation – why not 'It is free'?].

Access [nominalisation] to legal advice [Jargon – term used interchangeably with *solicitor*] [nominalisation] [long noun phrase *access to legal advice*] can only be delayed [passivisation and agent deletion – delayed by us] in certain exceptional [grammatical metaphor – except – preposition, exception = noun, exceptional = adjective] circumstances [vague – requires insider knowledge] (see Annex B of Code of Practice C) [confusing cross-reference which demands a particular literacy].

If [subordination] you do not know a solicitor, or you cannot contact your own solicitor [Coordination], ask for the duty solicitor. He or she has nothing to do with the police. Or you can ask to see a list of local solicitors [Coordination – where does this begin?].

You can talk tothe solicitor [change of article – previous paragraph used *a solicitor* – could be an elliptical form of *the solicitor you choose*] in private on the telephone and[coordination] the solicitor may come to see you at the police station.

If [subordinate clause – present conditional (i.e. *if* + clause (present simple), main clause (present simple) (Leech, Cruickshank and Ivanič, 2001:206)] the police want to question you, you can ask for the solicitor to be there. If [subordinate clause] there is a delay[to ...?], ask the police to contact the solicitor again [here *delay* relates to the solicitor's arrival – delay is something outside the control of anyone in the custody suit]. Normally the police must not question you until [subordination] you have spoken to the solicitor [complex negation here – normally ... not ... until]. However, there are certain circumstances in which the police may question you without a solicitor being present (see paragraph 6.6 of Code of Practice C) [Cross-reference].

If [subordinate clause – If +clause (present simple), main clause present simple imperative (Leech, Cruickshank and Ivanič, 2001:208)] you want to see a solicitor, tell the Custody Officer at once. You can ask for legal advice [nominalisation] at any time during your detention [nominalisation]. Even if [subordinate clause] you tell the police you do not want a solicitor at first, you can change your mind at any time.

Your right to legal advice [nominalisation] does not entitle you to delay [here detainees are potentially delaying] procedures under the Road Traffic Act 1988 [jargon] which require the provision [nominalisation] of breath, blood or urine specimens [jargon].

Appendix 9

PR1 – The Sergeant's Prescribed Custody Desk Procedure

For the Custody Officer to read out:

The police can get special help for people who have reading problems, people with learning difficulties or people who have been to a special school. Do you need this help?   YES/NO
Details: ....

The police can also get special help for people who have a mental illness. Do you need this help?   YES/NO
Details: ....

Do you have any injuries?   YES/NO   Details: ....
....
Any illness, including depression?   YES/NO   Details: ....
....
(If yes to either of the above) Have you seen a doctor or been to hospital for this injury/illness?   YES/NO
Details: ....

Are you, or should you be, taking any medicine or tablets?   YES/NO
Details: ....

Have you ever tried to harm yourself?   YES/NO
Details: ....

I will now tell you about your rights in the police station:

1.   Do you want a solicitor to help you while you are here? It is free. A solicitor has nothing to do with the police. The police will help you find a solicitor if you do not know one.   YES/NO
If yes, name: ....
If no, Ask: Is there any reason why you do not want a solicitor?
Note reply: ....

2.   Is there anyone you want to be told that you are at the police station? The police will do this for you, it is free.   YES/NO
If yes, details: ....

3.   There is a book called the Codes of Practice that sets out what the police can and cannot do while you are at the police station. You can ask to read this book.
If you do not want to do any of these 3 things now, you can change your mind later. Tell the police if you change your mind.
Here is a sheet that tells you the main things I have said. There is some more information attached to it.

This sheet is to be attached to the custody record.   Custody officers signature:

Appendix 10
Sample of Significant Judgments Relevant to s34

- **R v. Cowan, R v. Gayle, R v. Ricciardi (1996).** The defendants claimed that s34 only applies in exceptional circumstances. Whilst the appeal court did not accept that, they allowed the appeal on the basis that the judge's instructions to the jury did not convey that guilt is not the only reason for refusing to testify.

- **Murray v. UK (1996)** (under Northern Irish law, the Prevention of Terrorism (Temporary Provisions) Act (1989), in some senses, the precursor to the CJPOA (1994)). The defendant was questioned for 20 hours without legal advice and ultimately appealed to the European Commission for Human Rights proposing that this, in combination with inference-drawing, contravened Article 6(1) of the European Convention on Human Rights (ECHR). The court did not uphold his appeal, but hinted that a jury might have found differently.

- **Saunders v. UK (1997).** The defendant was tried under the Companies Act (1985) which made it an offence to refuse to answer questions and then allowed answers to be read out in court. This was found to breach Article 6 of the ECHR.

- **R v. McGarry (1998).** The defendant gave a no comment interview on legal advice. Five weeks later he was re-interviewed again; he gave no comment but submitted a written statement. At trial the Crown accepted that no adverse inferences could be drawn from the defendants failure to answer questions. It was held that the judge not only used a direction which did not make this clear but also that the direction he gave suggested that inferences could be drawn.

- **Condron v. UK (2000).** A couple accused of supplying heroin were under the influence of heroin when questioned. Their solicitor advised silence because of their intoxication and the trial judge advised jurors that they could draw negative inferences from this silence. The appeal court held that domestic courts should give weight to legal advice. As in Cowan *et al.*, the judge's directions were criticised.

- **R v. Betts and Hall (2001).** The court noted the importance of the accused's reliance on legal advice, as opposed to the quality of legal advice. It also sought to define "facts" which might be relied on in defence as not being those which the accused has agreed to as part of a prosecution case

- **Beckles v. UK (2002).** Here, the court held that the right to silence is not absolute, yet is essential to fair procedure as conceived under Article 6 of the ECHR. The court criticised the judge's directions in this case for failing to note the accused's explanation for his silence sufficiently.

- **R v. Rose (2003).** The defendant gave no evidence at interview or trial although a written statement was read on his behalf at trial. He argued that the jury should have been directed not to draw adverse inferences from his silence in interview and statement in court especially as he was tried with other defendants, so jurors would have heard the caution through their cases. As he had refused to answer questions throughout, not just at interview, it was ruled that the directions were adequate.

- **R v. Turner (2003).** The defendant handed a prepared statement to the police which is permissible and increasingly used as an alternative to answering questions in interview (although it does provide exemption from answering questions). The judge's directions implied that simply failing to answer questions could justify inferences. In fact, the jury should have been directed to consider whether Turner had relied on facts at trial that he had not mentioned in the statement or interview but could reasonably have been expected to have mentioned.

- **R v. Hoare and Pierce (2004).** Both defendants were silent in interview on legal advice but gave an account at trial. The case hinged on whether their silence in interview was because they had "reasonably" or "genuinely" relied on their solicitors' advice and whether questions had been put to them in interview which allowed adequate opportunity to them to mention facts.

- **R v. Armas-Rodriguez (2005).** The defendant was interviewed without having been cautioned and later interviewed again under caution. Evidence from the first interview was then admitted at trial. It was held that that interview was in breach of PACE Code C but that the judge correctly exercised his discretion to have the evidence admitted at trial.

- **R v. Shulka (2006).** Here the defendant gave one account in interview and a different account in court. The judge drew the jury's attention to this difference but did not relate this to s34. The defendant appealed claiming that the judge should have permitted s34 inferences. The appeal was dismissed because he had not failed to mention something in interview – he had mentioned something and then changed that something – so s34 did not apply.

- **R v. Shillibier (2006).** The defendant was interviewed under a partial caution and later interviewed again under full caution. Evidence from the first interview was then admitted at trial. The question of whether the defendant was a suspect at the time of the first interview was crucial. The judge's ruling, that he was not and therefore that no caution was necessary, was upheld.

Police forces offer detailed training in key cases and their implications (for example, Grainger, 2006a).

References

Beckles v. UK (2002) ECHR 44652/98.
Condron v. UK (2001) 31 EHRR 1 (2000) Crim LR 679.
Murray v. UK (1996) 22 EHRR 29.
R v. Armas-Rodriguez (2005) EWCA Crim 1081.
R v. Hoare and Pierce (2004) EWCA Crim 784.
R v. McGarry (1998) LTL 17/7/98.
R v. Rose (2003) EWCA Crim 1471.
R v. Shillibier (2006) EWCA Crim 793.
R v. Shulka (2006).
R v. Turner (2003) EWCA Crim 3108.
R v. Betts and Hall (2001) 2 Cr App R 257.
R v. Cowan, R v. Gayle, R v. Ricciardi (1996) QB 373 1 Cr App R 1, 7 D–G.
Saunders v. UK (1997) 23 EHRR 313 Cr App R 474–8.

Appendix 11
Caution wording in Northern Ireland

You do not have to say anything, but I must caution you that if you do not mention when questioned something which you later rely on in court, it may harm your defence. If you do say anything it may be given in evidence.

This caution is specified in Code C of the PACE Codes for Northern Ireland (Article 60 and 65). It is subject to Criminal Evidence (Northern Ireland) Order 1988, Article 3.

Appendix 12
The Version of the Sergeant's Rights Notice Which was Circulated

The following rights and entitlements are guaranteed to you under the law in England and Wales and comply with the European Convention on Human Rights.

Remember your rights:

1. Tell the police if you want a solicitor to help you while you are at the police station. It is free.

2. Tell the police if you want someone to be told that you are at the police station. It is free.

3. Tell the police if you want to look at their rule-book called the Codes of Practice.

You will find more details about these rights inside

The Law Society

More information for people arrested by the police

Please keep this information and read it as soon as possible. It will help you to make decisions while you are at the police station.

> If you are asked questions about a suspected offence, you do not have to say anything. However, it may harm your defence if you do not mention when questioned something which you later rely on in court. Anything you do say may be given in evidence.

1. Getting a solicitor to help you

- A solicitor can help and advise you about the law.

- If you want a solicitor, tell the police custody officer. The police will help you get in touch with a solicitor for you.

- The police must let you talk to a solicitor at any time, day or night, when you are at a police station. It is free.

- If you do not know of a solicitor in the area or you cannot get in touch with your own solicitor, you can speak to the duty solicitor. It is free. The police will help you contact him or her for you. The duty solicitor is nothing to do with the police.

- You are entitled to a private consultation with your Solicitor on the telephone or they may decide to come and see you at the Police Station.

- Usually, the police are not allowed to ask you questions until you have had the chance to talk to a solicitor. When the police ask you questions you can ask for a solicitor to be in the room with you.

- If you ask to speak to a solicitor it does not make it look like you have done anything wrong.

- If a solicitor does not turn up, or you need to talk to a solicitor again, ask the police to contact him or her again.

- If you tell the police that you don't want to speak to a solicitor but then you change your mind, tell the police custody officer. The police will then help you contact a solicitor for you.

2. Telling someone that you are at the police station

- You can ask the police to contact someone to inform them that you are at the police station. It is free. They will contact someone for you as soon as they can.

3. Looking at the Codes of Practice

- The Codes of Practice is a book that tells you what the police can and cannot do while you are at the police station.

- The police will let you read the Codes of Practice but you cannot read it for so long that it holds up the police finding out if you have broken the law.

- If you want to read the Codes of Practice, tell the police custody officer.

Getting details of your time at the police station

- Everything that happens to you when you are at the police station is put on paper and is called the custody record.

- When you leave the police station, you, your solicitor or your appropriate adult can ask for a copy of the custody record. The police have to give you a copy of the custody record as soon as they can.

- You can ask the police for a copy of the custody record up to 12 months after you leave the police station.

How you should be cared for

These are short notes about what you can expect while you are kept at the police station. To find out more, ask to see the book called the Codes of Practice. Inside its back cover you will find a list of where to find more information about each of these things. Ask the police custody officer if you have any questions.

Keeping in touch

As well as talking to a solicitor and having a person told about your arrest you will usually be allowed to make one phone call. Ask the police if you would like to make a phone call. You can also ask for a pen and paper. You may be able to have visitors but the custody officer can refuse to allow that.

Your Cell

If possible you should be kept in a cell on your own. It should be clean, warm and lit. Your bedding should be clean and in good order. You must be allowed to use a toilet and have a wash.

Clothes

If your own clothes are taken from you, then the police must provide you with an alternative form of clothing.

Food and drink

You must be offered 3 meals a day with drinks. You can also have drinks between meals.

Exercise

If possible you should be allowed outside each day for fresh air.

If you are unwell

Ask to see a doctor if you feel ill or need medicine. The police will call a doctor for you and it is free. You can ask to see another doctor but you may have to pay for this. You may be allowed to take your own medicine but the police will have to check with a doctor first. A nurse may see you first, but they will send for a doctor if you need one.

How long can you be detained?

You can normally be detained for up to 24 hours without being charged. This can be longer but only if a Police Superintendent allows it to happen. After 36 hours only a court can allow more time without you being charged. Every so often a senior police officer has to look into your case to see if you should still be kept here. This is called a review. You have the right to have your say about this decision, unless you are not in a fit state.

When the police question you

- The room should be clean, warm and lit.
- You should not have to stand up.
- The police officers should tell you their name and their rank.
- You should have a break at normal meal times and a break for a drink after about two hours.
- You should be allowed at least 8 hours rest in any 24 hours you are in custody.

People who need help

- If you are under 17, or you have learning problems or a mental problem then you should have someone with you when the police do certain things. This person is called your "appropriate adult".

- Your appropriate adult must be with you when the police tell you about your rights and tell you why you are being kept at the police station. He or she must also be with you when the police read the police caution to you. He or she must also be with you if you are interviewed.

- The police might also need to do one of the things listed below while you are at the police station. Your appropriate adult should be with you for the whole time if the police do any of these things:

  - Interview you or ask you to sign a written statement or police notes.

  - Review your case.

  - Remove more than your outer clothes.

  - Carry out anything about an identification parade.

  - Charge you with an offence.

You can speak to your solicitor without your appropriate adult in the room if you want to.

Getting an interpreter to help you

If you do not speak or understand English the police will arrange for someone who speaks your language to help you.

If you are deaf or have difficulty speaking the police will arrange for a British Sign Language / English interpreter to help you.

When the police ask you questions the interpreter will make a record of the questions and your answers in your own language. You will be able to check this before you sign it as an accurate record.

If you make a statement to the police, the interpreter will make a copy of that statement in your own language for you to check and sign as correct.

People who are not British
If you are not British, you can tell the police that you want to contact your High Commission, Embassy or Consulate to tell them where you are and why you are in the police station. They can also visit you in private or arrange for a solicitor to see you.

Special Times

Getting a solicitor to help you
There are some special times when the police can ask you questions before you have talked to a solicitor. Information about these special times is given in the Codes of Practice. This is the book that that sets out what the police can and cannot do while you are at the police station. If you want to look up the details, they are in paragraph 6.6 of Code C of the Codes of Practice.

There is one special time when the police will not let you speak to the solicitor that you have chosen. When this happens the police must let you talk to another solicitor. If you want to look up the details, it is in Annex B of Code C of the Codes of Practice.

Telling someone that you are at the police station
There are some special times when the police will not allow you to contact anyone. Information about these special times is given in the Codes of Practice. If you want to look up the details, it is in Annex B of Code C of the Codes of Practice.

Breath tests

If you are under arrest because of a drink drive offence, you have the right to speak to a solicitor. That right does not mean you can refuse to give the police samples of breath, blood or urine even if you have not yet spoken to the solicitor.

Independent Custody Visitors

There are members of the community who are allowed access to police stations unannounced. They are known as independent custody visitors and work on a voluntary basis to make sure that detained people are being treated properly and have access to rights. You do not have a right to see an independent custody Visitor and cannot request that an independent custody visitor visit you. If an independent custody visitor does visit you while you are in custody they will be acting independently of the police to check that your welfare and rights have been protected. However, you do not have to speak to them if you do not wish to.

Notes

3 Introducing written rights communication

1. Detainees will not receive rights information if they are too ill, violent or are otherwise "incapable of understanding". They should receive rights information "as soon as practicable" (PACE Code C, 2006: Para1.8).
2. The Plain Language Commission is a language consultancy akin to the PEC. They advise on and ultimately sanction texts, awarding the "Plain English Standard".

4 Working with syntax and lexis in writing

1. Solicitors usually decide whether they are needed in person, case-by-case.
2. These modalities would interpret the sentence respectively as "surely it is true that x", "someone is obliged to x" and "it follows that x".
3. Peculiarly, a lengthier gloss of the *Codes* appeared in the *Notice*'s initial summary section than appears in this ostensibly more detailed section.
4. One of the revisers (EnterpriseC) proposed producing dedicated documents for detainees from overseas and for juveniles which she intended to be particularly reassuring.

5 Working with organisation in writing

1. Shuy notes *Miranda*'s failure to specify why a lawyer, rather than any other authority figure, will help (1997:186).

6 Working with context: Rights texts in custody

1. Detainees who cannot read might be provided with someone "to help check any documentation" (PACE Code C, 2006: para3.20).
2. Four per cent (2) did not say whether they had taken the papers.
3. These figures inevitably rely on detainees' self-reports of reading practices (Meyer, Marsiske and Willis, 1993:235). It is quite possible that detainees who:

   - ignored the papers might claim to have read them or
   - having read them might claim to have ignored them.

   To attempt to uncover misreporting I asked not only whether detainees had read but also which parts they read, where they read and so on.
4. Detainees may be unable to read – this will be discussed in Section 7.2.
5. The source text for this revision was an earlier version of the *Notice* than the one investigated here.

7 Off the page: Detainees' reading practices

1. Detainees who identified themselves as finding reading difficult or impossible seemed comfortable in doing so. All others in the study demonstrated simple form-filling.
2. *Saftness* is a dialect word meaning roughly *harmless silliness*. You may have encountered *daftness* or *softness* used in the same sense.
3. This illustrates the limitations of terms like "understand" and the shortcomings of counting responses to structured interviews as unproblematic indicators of comprehension.

8 Introducing spoken rights communication

1. At charge the words *when questioned* are replaced with *now*, to indicate that the detainee's final routine opportunity to speak has arrived.
2. The caution was not introduced under PACE (1984), although its administration is governed by PACE and its wording revised with PACE (cf. Cotterill, 2000:5).
3. Adjacent sections of the CJPOA permit inference-drawing about responses to specific questions in some circumstances; for example, concerning "objects, substances or marks" on or near to accused persons when arrested (CJPOA, 1994:s36). Thus, the CJPOA intended to change the nature of interview evidence.
4. In some instances, for example within fraud investigations under s434(5) of the Companies Act (1985), it was already an offence to refuse to answer questions from investigators. In this respect, the right to silence could be seen as compromised even when the CJPOA was being debated.
5. An "on-record" confession.
6. This wording was never adopted as the standard caution wording (cf. Cotterill, 2000:21).
7. At the time of this study 16.8 per cent of police officers in Wales were female and 18 per cent in England (Office of National Statistics, 2006). In this sample, 18.8 per cent were female.
8. Significantly, lay representations of the caution, as here, frequently misquote the caution (cf. Section 9.5). Here, for example, *taken down* echoes the 1970s wording.
9. Russell describes a reduced version of this structure which occurs in interpreted interviews (2000:27).

9 Working with lexis in speech

1. Magistrates both decide verdicts and pass sentence.
2. When the caution is issued finally at charge *when questioned* is replaced by *now*. Officers doubted whether detainees even noticed this change.
3. Detainees may indicate such intentions themselves or through a solicitor.
4. This hypothesis is supported by the related observation that officers who used *fail* or *refuse* also all use a slight variant on the string *questions put to you* which also appears throughout various institutional texts.

10   Working with organisation in speech

1. This officer appears in the chart's 'miscellaneous' category.
2. As in other sections, Forces C and S have not been included in this quantitative overview as Section 8.5.1 explains.
3. Only a few officers who noted tripartite structure used the alternative of simply stating that the caution will be 'broken down' without specifying or numbering emergent parts.
4. This assumes that regulars do not benefit from such diversity. It also ignores the diversity which may confront detainees within a single detention through explanations from both an officer and a solicitor.
5. Some officers presented methods of explaining to juveniles as policy, others as personal choice. Several explored key concepts with children, particularly 'truth' and 'falsehood'. This is encouraged in response to high-profile difficulties in investigations involving children (see Haydon and Scratton, 2000).
6. Detainees who "may be mentally disordered or mentally vulnerable" should receive particular treatment (PACE Code C, 2006: Annex E).
7. Detainees' turns, consisting of minimal feedback, are omitted.

11   Checking comprehension

1. Fenner, Gudjonsson and Clare's experiments very similarly found that 96 per cent of subjects claimed to understand the caution, yet were unable to explain it correctly (2002:89).
2. The detainees hint at the futility of the cautioning routine and could be seen to be criticising the institutional agenda which they perceive as only pretending to address their needs. Detainees who I interviewed commented explicitly on such pretence.

12   Beyond explanation: Using cautioning

1. As well as being administered at arrest, interview and charge and when informing someone that they may be prosecuted (PACE Code C, 2006: para10.5b), the caution is also recited to people who agree to be questioned voluntarily. Thus cautioning may occur in various locations, including detainees' homes or the roadside.
2. Officers must record all interviews. Interview tapes typically last around 20–40 minutes so cautioning can be frequent.
3. A pocket-book is a small notebook carried by each officer.
4. To authenticate the transition, officers typically ask detainees to confirm the record by signing the pocket-book in interview; detainees often decline. This is an oblique practice; if detainees verbally recall mutual activities, their representations may compete with the semi-official, pocket-book record and will not be reciprocally ratified through signing.
5. These officers described training which explored relevant legislation, legal consequences of failing to caution, and the caution's impact on evidence-collection. Possibly, many more officers had received training in cautioning but had forgotten. Such training might nonetheless have been influential.

6. One non-operational officer who cautions infrequently admitted being resigned to understanding little of the caution, remaining *switched off* from its meaning (AO38).
7. Some officers had never considered using the caution when it is not prescribed. AO16 proclaimed that he *would never go through it again* after the preamble. However, for others, revisiting the caution during interview served many functions.
8. The solicitor in the second excerpt, B10, goes beyond his remit by implicitly assessing the detainee's comprehension.

14   Epilogue

1. A staple-less stapler is a small punch device which fastens sheets of paper together by tightly folding them rather than inserting a fastening device. Staples or paper-clips should not be distributed in custody because they could be used by detainees to harm themselves or others.

References

Cases

Miranda *v.* Arizona [1966] 384 U.S. 436.
R *v.* Argent [1996].
R *v.* Shulka [2006].

Legislation and Codes of practice

Constitutional Amendment V (1789) *Bill of rights* http://www.archives.gov/
national-archives-experience/charters/bill_of_rights_transcript.html
(Last accessed: 24/12/06).
Criminal Justice And Public Order Act (1994) HMSO: London.
Human Rights Act (1998) HMSO: London.
PACE Code C (2006) HMSO: London.
Police And Criminal Evidence Act (1984) HMSO: London.
Road Traffic Act (1988) HMSO: London.
Youth Justice and Criminal Evidence Act (1999) HMSO: London.

Books, journal articles and Internet sites

Adelswärd, V. and Sachs, L. (1998) "Risk discourse: Recontextualisation of numerical values in clinical practice", *Text* 18(2), 191–210.
Afflerbach, P. (2000) "Verbal reports and protocol analysis". In: Kamil, M. L., Mosenthal, P. B., Pearson, P. D. and Barr, R. (eds) 163–79.
Ainsworth, J. (1998) "In a different register: The pragmatics of powerlessness in police interrogation". In: Leo, R. and Thomas, G. (eds) 283–96.
Alexander, P. and Kulikowich, J. (1994) "Learning from physics text: A synthesis of recent research", *Journal of Research in Science Teaching* 31, 895–911.
Alexander, T. and Jetton, P. (2000) "Learning from text: A multidimensional and developmental perspective". In: Kamil, M. L., Mosenthal, P. B., Pearson, P. D., and Barr, R. (eds) 285–310.
Alschuler, A. (1996) "A peculiar privilege in historical perspective: The right to remain silent". In: Leo, R. and Thomas, G. (eds) 153–67.
Antaki, C. (1988) "Explanations, communication and social cognition". In: Antaki, C. (ed.) 1–14.
Antaki, C. (1994) *Explaining and Arguing: The Social Organization of Accounts*, Sage: London.
Antaki, C. (ed.) (1988) *Analysing Everyday Explanations: A Casebook of Methods*, Sage: London.
Aronsson, K. (1991) "Social interaction and the recycling of legal evidence". In: Coupland, N., Giles, H. and Wiemann, J. (eds) 215–43.
Atkinson, M. and Drew, P. (1979) *Order in Court: The Organisation of Verbal Interaction in Judicial Settings*, Macmillan: London.

Baker, M., Francis, G. and Tognini-Bonelli, E. (eds) (1993) *Text and Technology: In Honour of John Sinclair*, John Benjamins: Amsterdam.

Bakhtin, M. (1981) *The Dialogic Imagination: Four Essays*, University of Texas Press: Texas (ed. Holquist, M. and trans. Emerson, C. and Holquist, M.).

Bakhtin, M. (1986) *Speech Genres and Other Late Essays*, University of Texas Press: Texas (Trans. McGee, V.).

Barthes, R. (1977) *Image, Music, Text*, Hill: London (Trans. Heath, S.).

Barton, D. (1994) *Literacy: An Introduction to the Ecology of Written Language*, Routledge: London.

Barton, D. and Hamilton, M. (1998) *Local Literacies: Reading and Writing in One Community*, Routledge: London.

Barton, D. and Hamilton, M. (2000) "Literacy practices". In: Barton, D. Hamilton, M. and Ivanič, R. (eds) 7–15.

Barton, D., Hamilton, M. and Ivanič, R. (eds) (2000) *Situated Literacies: Reading and Writing in Context*, Routledge: London.

Baynham, M. (1995) *Literacy Practices: Investigating Literacy in Social Contexts*, Longman: Harlow.

Bazerman, C. (1997) "Performatives constituting value: The case of patents". In: Gunnarsson, B., Linell, P. and Nordberg, B. (eds) 42–53.

BBC News Online (2003) *Cell "Welcome Pack" for Suspects*, Monday 22 September http://www.news.bbc.co.uk/1/hi/england/beds/bucks/ herts/3129226.stm(Last accessed: 24/12/06).

BDA and BYOT (British Dyslexia Association and Bradford Youth Offender Team) (2004) *West Yorkshire Dyslexia Research Project*, BDA: Reading.

Bean, S. and Patthey-Chavez, G. (1994) "Repetition in instructional discourse: A means for joint cognition". In: Johnstone, B. (ed.) 207–20.

Beekman, J., Callow, J. and Kopesec, M. (1981) *The Semantic Structure of Written Communication*, Summer Institute of Linguistics: Texas.

Bell, A. (1997) "Language style as audience design". In: Coupland, N. and Jaworski, A. (eds) 240–50.

Bennetto, J. (1994) "New police caution alarms legal experts", *The Independent*, 20 August.

Berk-Seligson, S. (2000) "Interpreting for the police: Issues in pre-trial phases of the judicial process", *Forensic Linguistics* 7(2), 212–37.

Bernstein, B. (1990) *The Structuring of Pedagogic Discourse: Volume IV, Class, Codes and Control*, Routledge: London.

Bhatia, V. (1983) "Simplification v. easification: The case of legal texts", *Applied Linguistics* 4, 42–54.

Bhatia, V. (1993) *Analysing Genre: Language Use in Professional Settings*, Longman: London.

Biber, D. (1988) *Variation Across Speech and Writing*, CUP: Cambridge.

Bill, The (2006) *"Ask Julie" website* http://www.thebill.com/esther/esther_17_01_03.html (Last accessed: 24/09/06).

Birch, D. (1999) "Suffering in silence: A cost-benefit analysis of section 34 of the Criminal Justice and Public Order Act 1994", *Criminal Law Review*, 769–88.

Blatch, Baroness (1995) "Police and Criminal Evidence Act 1984 (Codes of practice) (No. 3) Order 1995", Hansard, 23 Feb 1995: Column 1276 (Vol. 561, part 46).

Blum-Kulka, S. and Weizman, E. (2003) "Misunderstandings in political interviews". In: House, J., Kasper, G. and Ross, S. (eds) 107–28.

Brandon, R. and Davies, C. (1972) *Mistaken Convictions and Their Consequences* George, Allen and Unwin: London.

Briggs, C. (1986) *Learning How to Ask: A Sociolinguistic Appraisal of the Role of the Interview in Social Science Research*, Cambridge University Press: Cambridge.

Brown, A., Armbruster, B. and Baker, L. (1986) "The role of metacognition in reading and studying". In: Orasanu, J. (ed.) 49–77.

Brown, D. (1997) "PACE ten years on: A review of the research", *Research Study 155*, Home Office: London.

Brown, G., Malmkjaer, K., Pollit, A. and Williams, J. (eds) (1994) *Language and Understanding*, OUP: Oxford.

Brown, P. and Levinson, S. (1987) *Politeness: Some Universals in Language Usage*, CUP: Cambridge.

Bucke, T. and Brown, D. (1997) "In police custody: Police powers and suspects' rights under the revised PACE Codes of practice", *Research Study 174*, Home Office: London.

Bucke, T., Street, R. and Brown, D. (2000) "The right of silence: The impact of the Criminal Justice and Public Order Act 1994", *Research Study 199*, Home Office: London.

Cameron, D. (1995) *Verbal Hygiene*, Routledge: London.

Cameron, D. (2000) "Styling the worker: Gender and the commodification of language in the globalised service economy", *Journal of Sociolinguistics* 4(3), 323–47.

Candlin, C. and Hyland, K. (eds) (1999) *Writing: Texts, Processes and Practices*, Longman: Harlow.

Candlin, C. and Maley, Y. (1997) "Intertextuality and interdiscursivity in the discourse of alternative dispute resolution". In: Gunnarsson, B., Linell, P. and Nordberg, B. (eds) 201–22.

Carlin, M. (2003) "Comments on testifying" (Personal communication, April).

Carol, A. (1994) *The Criminal Justice and Public Order Bill 1994 is Undemocratic, Unjustifiable and Dangerous*, Libertarian Alliance: London.

Carter, A. (2003) "Comments on *The Bill*, from a Story Editor" (Personal communication, April).

Chaiklin, S. and Lave, J. (eds) (1993) *Understanding Practice: Perspectives on Activity and Context*, CUP: Cambridge.

Chambers Dictionary, The (1994) Larousse: London.

Channell, J. (2000) "Working on the telephone – how telephone receptionists work with language". In: Coulthard, R. M., Cotterill, J. and Rock, F. (eds) 221–30.

Charrow, R. and Charrow, V. (1979) "Making legal language understandable: A psycholinguistic study of jury instructions", *Columbia Law Review* 79(5), 1306–74.

Clare, I. (2003) *Psychological Vulnerabilities' of Adults with Mild Learning Disabilities: Implications for Suspects During Police Detention and Interviewing*, Ph.D. thesis: Kings College, University of London.

Clare, I. and Gudjonsson, G. (1992) *Devising and Piloting an Experimental Version of the "Notice to Detained Persons"*, HMSO: London.

Clare, I., Gudjonsson, G. and Harari, P. (1998) "Understanding the current police caution (England and Wales)", *Journal of Community and Applied Psychology* 8(5), 323–9.

Clark, H. (1996) *Using Language*, CUP: Cambridge.

Clark, R. and Ivanič, R. (1997) *The Politics of Writing*, Routledge: London.

Clayman, S. (1990) "From talk to text: Newspaper accounts of reporter-source interaction", *Media, Culture and Society* 12, 79–103.

Coates, J. (1983) "Epistemic modality and spoken discourse", *Transactions of the Philological Society* 85, 110–31.

Coates, J. (2003) *Men Talk: Stories in the Making of Masculinities*, Blackwell: Oxford.

Cody, M. and McLaughlin, M. (1998) "Accounts on trial: Oral arguments in traffic court". In: Antaki, C. (ed.) 113–26.

Cole, P. and Morgan, J. (eds) (1975) *Syntax and Semantics: Volume 9, Pragmatics*, Academic Press: New York.

Conley, J. M. and O'Barr, W. M. (1998) *Just Words: Law, Language and Power*, University of Chicago Press: Chicago.

Cooke, D. and Philip, L. (1998) "Comprehending the Scottish caution: Do offenders understand their right to remain silent?", *Legal and Criminological Psychology* 3, 13–27.

Cotterill, J. (1999) "Comments on cartoon rights notices" (Personal communication, July).

Cotterill, J. (2000) "Reading the rights: A cautionary tale of comprehension and comprehensibility", *Forensic Linguistics* 7(1), 4–25.

Cotterill, J. (2003) "Comments on consulting on comprehension" (Personal communication, April).

Coulthard, R. M. (1977) *An Introduction to Discourse Analysis*, Longman: London.

Coulthard, R. M., Cotterill, J. and Rock, F. (eds) (2000) *Working with Dialogue*, Niemeyer: Tübingen.

Coupland, J., Coupland, N. and Robinson, J. (1992) " 'How are you?': Negotiating phatic communication", *Language in Society* 21, 207–30.

Coupland, N. and Coupland, J. (1998) "Reshaping lives: Constitutive identity work in geriatric medical consultations", *Text* 18(2), 159–89.

Coupland, N. and Jaworski, A. (eds) (1997) *Sociolinguistics: A Reader*, Palgrave: Basingstoke.

Craft, E. (2005) "Comments on rights in the curriculum from QCA Adviser" (Personal communication, March).

Crowther, J., Hamilton, M. and Tett, L. (2001) *Powerful Literacies*, NIACE: Leicester.

Crowther, J. and Tett, L. (2001) "Democracy as a way of life: Literacy for citizenship". In: Crowther, J. Hamilton, M. and Tett, L. (eds) 108–18.

Cushing, S. (1994) " 'Air cal three thirty six, go around three thirty six, go around': Linguistic repetition in air-ground communication". In: Johnstone, B. (ed.) 53–65.

Danet, B. (1984a) "Introduction", *Text* 4(1–3), 1–8.

Danet, B. (1984b) "The magic flute: A prosodic analysis of binomial expressions in legal Hebrew", *Text* 4(1–3), 143–72.

Danet, B. (1990) "Language and law: An overview of 15 years of research". In: Giles, H. and Robinson, W. (eds) 537–59.

Danet, B. (1997) "Speech, writing and performativity: An evolutionary view of the history of constitutive ritual". In: Gunnarsson, B., Linell, P. and Nordberg, B. (eds) 13–41.

Davies, H. (1997) "Ordinary people's philosophy: Comparing lay and professional metalinguistic knowledge", *Language Sciences* 19(1), 33–46.

Davis, K., Lewis, J., Byatt, J., Purvis, E. and Cole, B. (2004) *An Evaluation of the Literacy Demands of General Offending Behaviour Programmes: Home Office research study 233*, Home Office: London.

Davison, A. and Kantor, R. (1982) "On the failure of readability formulas to define readable texts: A case study from adaptations", *Reading Research Quarterly* 2(17), 187–209.

Dennis, I. (2002) "Silence in the police station: The marginalisation of S34", *Criminal Law Review*, January 25–38.

Denny, J. (1991) "Rational thought in oral culture and literate decontextualisation". In: Olson, D. and Torrance, N. (eds) 66–89.

Designer, The Bill (2003) "Comments on making *The Bill*" (Personal communication, March).

Diehl, W. and Mikulecky, L. (1981) "Making written information fit workers' purposes", *IEEE Transactions on Professional Communication* PC24, 1, 5–9.

Dixon, P. and Bortolussi, M. (2001) "Text is not communication: A challenge to a common assumption", *Discourse Processes* 31(1), 1–25.

Drew, P. and Sorjonen, M. (1997) "Institutional dialogue". In: van Dijk, T. (ed.) 92–118.

Duffy, T., Curran, T. and Sass, D. (1983) "Document design for technical job tasks: An evaluation", *Human Factors* 25(2), 143–60.

Dumas, B. (1990) "Adequacy of cigarette package warnings: An analysis of the adequacy of federally mandated cigarette package warnings". In: Levi, J. and Walker, A. (eds) 309–52.

Dumas, B. (2000) "US pattern jury instructions: Problems and proposals", *Forensic Linguistics* 7(1), 49–71.

Duranti, A. and Goodwin, C. (eds) (1992) *Rethinking Context: Language as an Interactive Phenomenon*, CUP: Cambridge.

Eades, D. (1996) "Verbatim courtroom transcripts and discourse analysis". In: Kniffka, H. (ed.) 241–54.

Eades, D. (2003) "The politics of misunderstanding in the legal system". In: House, J., Kasper, G. and Ross, S. (eds) 199–226.

Endicott, T. (2000) *Vagueness in Law*, OUP: Oxford.

Enkvist, N. (1990) "Discourse comprehension, text strategies and style", *Journal of the AULLA* 73, 166–80.

Ervin-Tripp, S. (1969) "Sociolinguistics", *Advances in Experimental Social Psychology* 4, 93–107.

Evans, R., Edwards, A., Elwyn, G., Watson, E., Grol, R., Brett, J. and Austoker, J. (2007) "It's a maybe test': Men's experiences of prostate specific antigen testing in primary care", *British Journal of General Practice* 57, 303–10.

Faigley, L. and Witte, S. (1981) "Analysing revision", *College Composition* 32(4), 400–15.

Fairclough, N. (1992) *Discourse and Social Change*, Polity: Oxford.

Fairclough, N. (2001) *Language and Power*, Longman: Harlow (2nd edition).

Fang, Y. (2001) "Reporting the same events? A critical analysis of Chinese print news media texts", *Discourse and Society* 12(5), 585–613.

Fawns, M. and Ivanič, R. (2001) "Form-filling as a social practice: Taking power into our own hands". In: Crowther, J., Hamilton, M. and Tett, L. (eds) 80–93.

Fenner, S., Gudjonsson, G. and Clare, I. (2002) "Understanding of the current police caution (England and Wales) among suspects in police detention", *Journal of Community and Applied Social Psychology* 12(2), 83–93.

Finn, S. (1995) "Measuring effective writing: Cloze procedure and anaphoric *this*", *Written Communication* 12(2), 240–66.

Flesch, R. (1948) "A new readability yardstick", *Journal of Applied Psychology* 32, 221–33.

Forgas, J. (1985) *Interpersonal Skills: The Psychology of Social Interaction*, Pergamon: Oxford.

Fowler, R. (1991) "Language in the news: Discourse and ideology in the press", Routledge: London.

Fox, G. (1993) "A comparison of "policespeak" and "normalspeak": A preliminary study". In: Sinclair, J. M., Hoey, M. and Fox, G. (eds) 183–95.

Fox Tree, J. (1999) "Listening in on monologues and dialogues", *Discourse Processes* 27(1), 35–53.

Fraser, B. (1980) "Conversational mitigation", *Journal of Pragmatics* 4(4), 341–50.

Frohlich, D. (1986) "On the organisation of form-filling behaviour", *Information Design Journal* 5, 43–59.

Fulero, S. and Everington, C. (1995) "Assessing competency to waive *Miranda* rights in defendants with mental retardation", *Law and Human Behaviour* 19(5), 533–43.

Garfinkel, H. and Sacks, H. (1970) "On formal structures of practical actions". In: McKinney, J. and Tiryakian, A. (eds) 337–66.

Garner, B. (2001) *Legal Writing in Plain English: A Text with Exercises*, University of Chicago Press: Chicago.

Gault, R. (1994) "Education by the use of ghosts: Strategies of repetition in *Effi Briest*". In: Johnstone, B. (ed.) 139–51.

Gee, J. (1999) *An Introduction to Discourse Analysis: Theory and Method*, Routledge: London.

Gee, J. (2000) "Discourse and sociocultural studies in reading". In: Kamil, M., Mosenthal, P., Pearson, P. and Barr, R. (eds) 195–207.

Gergen, K. (1985) "Social constructionist inquiry: Context and implications". In: Gergen, K. and Davis, K. (eds) 3–18.

Gergen, K. and Davis, K. (eds) (1985) *The Social Construction of the Person*, Springer-Verlag: New York.

Gibbons, J. (1990) "Applied linguistics in court", *Applied linguistics* 11(30), 229–37.

Gibbons, J. (ed.) (1994) *Language and the Law*, Longman: Essex.

Gibbons, J. (1999) "Language and the law", *Annual Review of Applied Linguistics* 19, 156–73.

Gibbons, J. (2001a) "Revising the language of New South Wales police procedures: Applied linguistics in action", *Applied Linguistics* 22(4), 439–69.

Gibbons, J. (2001b) "Legal transformations in Spanish: An 'audencia' in Chile", *Forensic Linguistics* 8(1), 24–43.

Gibbons, J. (2003) *Forensic Linguistics: An Introduction to Language in the Justice System*, Blackwell: Oxford.

Gibbs, R. (2001) "Authorial intentions in text understanding", *Discourse Processes* 32(1), 73–80.

Giles, H., Coupland, J. and Coupland, N. (1991) *Contexts of Accommodation: Developments in Applied Sociolinguistics*, CUP: Cambridge.

Giles, H. and Robinson, W. (eds) (1990) *Handbook of Language and Social Psychology*, Wiley: Chichester.

Gillon, B. (1990) "Ambiguity, generality and indeterminacy: Tests and definitions", *Synthese* 85, 391–416.

Gledhill, C. (1995) *Scientific Innovation and the Phraseology of Rhetoric: Posture, Reformulation and Collocation in Cancer Research Articles*, Ph.D. thesis: Aston University.

Goffman, E. (1959) *Presentation of Self in Everyday Life*, Anchor Books: New York.

Goffman, E. (1967) *Interactional Ritual: Essays on Face-to-Face Behaviour*, Pantheon: New York.

Goffman, E. (1974) *Frame Analysis: An Essay on the Organization of Experience*, Harper: New York.

Goffman, E. (1981) *Forms of Talk*, Blackwell: Oxford.

Goldman, S. and Rakestraw, J. (2000) "Structural aspects of constructing meaning from text". In: Kamil, M., Mosenthal, P., Pearson, P. and Barr, R. (eds) 311–35.

Goodwin, C. (1994) "Professional vision", *American Anthropologist* 96, 606–33.

Goody, J. (1986) *The Logic of Writing and the Organisation of Society*, CUP: Cambridge.

Graffam-Walker, A. (1985) "The two faces of silence: The effect of witness hesitancy on lawyers' impressions". In: Tannen, D. and Saville-Troike, M. (eds) 55–75.

Graham, E. (2003) "Comments on interpreting" (Personal communication, April).

Grainger, A. (2006a) *Drawing Inferences at Court – Legislation and Case Law* (Training materials, West Mercia Police, last updated: 29/08/06).

Grainger, A. (2006b) *The Caution and Significant Statements*, Presentation to police officers undertaking Level 2 Investigative Interview training.

Greenwood, J. (2002) "Comments on consulting on comprehension of the New Zealand caution" (Personal communication, July).

Grice, H. P. (1975) *Logic and Conversation*. In: Cole, P. and Morgan, J. (eds) 41–58.

Grisso, T. (1981) "Juveniles' waiver of rights: Legal and psychological competence", Plenum: New York.

Grisso, T. (1998) "Instruments for assessing understanding and appreciation of Miranda rights", Professional Resource Press: Florida.

Gudjonsson, G. (1990) "Understanding the 'Notice to detained persons'", *The Law Society's Gazette* 43, 28 November, 24–7.

Gudjonsson, G. (2002) "Unreliable confessions and miscarriages of justice in Britain", *International Journal of Police Science and Management* 4(4), 332–43.

Gumperz, J. (1982) *Discourse Strategies*, CUP: Cambridge.

Gumperz, J. (1992) "Contextualisation and understanding". In: Duranti, A. and Goodwin, C. (eds) 229–52.

Gunnarsson, B. (1997) "Applied discourse analysis". In: van Dijk, T. (ed.) 285–312.

Gunnarsson, B., Linell, P. and Nordberg, B. (eds) (1997) *The Construction of Professional Discourse*, Longman: London.

Gunning, R. (1968) *The Technique of Clear Writing*, McGraw Hill: London (2nd edition).

Guthrie, J. and Wigfield, A. (2000) "Engagement and motivation in reading". In: Kamil, M., Mosenthal, P., Pearson, P. and Barr, R. (eds) 403–22.

Hall, P. (2004) "Comments on Australian cautioning" (Personal communication, July).

Hall, S. (1997) "The work of representation". In: Hall, S. (ed.) 13–64.

Hall, S. (ed.) (1997) *Representation: Cultural representations and signifying practices*, Sage: London.

Halliday, M. (2004) *An Introduction to Functional Grammar*, Edward Arnold: London (3rd edition: Revised by Christian Matthiessen).

Halliday, M. and Hasan, R. (1976) *Cohesion in English*, Longman: London.

Harris, S. (1984) "Questions as a mode of control in a magistrate's court", *International Journal of the Sociology of Language* 49, 5–24.

Hartley, J. (1981) "Eighty ways of improving instructional text", *IEEE Transactions* PC24, 1, 17–27.

Hasan, R. and Williams, G. (eds) (1996) *Literacy in Society*, Longman: London.

Haydon, D. and Scratton, P. (2000) "Condemn a little more, understand a little less: the political context and rights implications of the Domestic and European rulings in the Venables-Thompson case", *Journal of Law and Society* 27(3) 416–48.

Hayes, J. (1996) "A new model of cognition and affect in writing". In: Levy, C. and Ransdell, S. (eds) 1–30.

Heath, S. (1983) *Ways with Words: Language, Life and Work in Communities and Classrooms*, CUP: Cambridge.

Heffer, C. (2005) *The Language of Jury Trial: A Corpus-Aided Analysis of Lay-Legal Discourse*, Palgrave: Basingstoke.

Heffer, C. and Sauntson, H. (eds) (2000) *Words in Context*, ELR Monograph 18.

Heller, M. (1999) "Ebonics, language revival, la qualité de la langue and more: What do we have to say about the language debates of our time?" *Journal of Sociolinguistics* 3(2), 260–66.

Heritage, J. (1984) *Garfinkel and Ethnomethodology*, Polity: Oxford.

Heritage, J. (1985) "Analysing news interviews: Aspects of the production of talk for an overhearing audience". In: van Dijk, T. (ed.) 95–117.

Heritage, J. and Watson, R. (1979) "Formulations as conversational objects". In: Psathas, G. (ed.) 123–62.

Heydon, G. (2002) *"Do You Agree that She Would Have Been Frightened?": An Investigation of Discursive Practices in Police-Suspect Interviews*, Ph.D. thesis: Monash University.

Hinnenkamp, V. (2003) "Misunderstandings: Interactional structure and strategic resources". In: House, J., Kasper, G. and Ross, S. (eds) 57–81.

Hodge, R. and Kress, G. (1993) *Language as Ideology*, Routledge: London.

Hoey, M. (1988) "Writing to meet the reader's needs: Text patterning and reading strategies", *Trondheim Papers in Applied Linguistics IV*, University of Trondheim: Trondheim, 51–73.

Holstein, J. and Gubrium, J. (1995) *The Active Interview*, Sage: London.

Home Office (1978) *Circular 89/1978*, Home Office: London.

Home Office (1985) *Circular 88/1985*, Home Office: London.

Home Office (1989) *Working Group on the Right of Silence: Report*, Home Office: London.

Home Office (1991) *Circular 15/1991*, Home Office: London.

Home Office (2004) *Circular 033/2004*, Home Office: London.

Home Office (2005) *Circular 030/2005*, Home Office: London.

Home Office (2006a) *Notice of Rights and Entitlements: Translations*, http://www.police.homeoffice.gov.uk/operational-policing/powers-pace-codes/rights-entitlements-foreign-lang (Last accessed: 24/12/06).

Home Office (2006b) *Circular017/2006*, Home Office: London.

Home Office (2006c) *Cautioning*, http://www.homeoffice.gov.uk/police/powers/cautioning/ (Last accessed: 24/12/06).

Home Office (2006d) *Police Homepage*, http://www.police.homeoffice.gov.uk/ (Last accessed: 24/12/06).

Home Office (2007) *Modernising Police Powers: Review of PACE 1984: Consultation Paper*, Home Office: London.

Horowitz, I. A., Forster Lee, L. and Brolly, I. (1996) "Effects of trial complexity on decision making", *Journal of Applied Psychology* 81, 757–68.

House, J. (2003) "Misunderstanding in intercultural university encounters". In: House, J., Kasper, G. and Ross, S. (eds) 22–56.

House, J., Kasper, G. and Ross, S. (2003) "Misunderstanding talk". In: House, J., Kasper, G. and Ross, S. (eds) 1–21.

House, J., Kasper, G. and Ross, S. (eds) (2003) *Misunderstanding in Social Life: Discourse Approaches to Problematic Talk*, Longman: London.

Howard, M. (1994) *Parliamentary Debates*, House of Commons, 11 January 1994: Column 26 (Vol. 235).

Hulst, J. and Lentz, L. (2001) "Public documents in a multilingual context". In: Janssen, D. and Neutlings, R. (eds) 85–103.

Hunston, S. and Thompson, G. (eds) (2000) *Evaluation in Text: Authorial Stance and the Construction of Discourse*, OUP: Oxford.

Hyland, K. (1999) "Talking to students: Metadiscourse in introductory course-books", *English for Specific Purposes* 18, 3–25.

Hymes, D. (1974) *Foundations of Sociolinguistics: An Ethnographic Approach*, University of Pennsylvania Press: Philadelphia.

Iedema, R. and Wodak, R. (1999) "Organisational discourses and practices", *Discourse and society* 10(1), 5–19.

International Institute for Information Design (2006) *Definitions*, http://www.iiid.net/FrameSet.htm (Last accessed: 24/12/06).

Jackson, B. (1995) *Making Sense in Law: Linguistic, Psychological and Semiotic Perspectives*, Deborah Charles: Liverpool.

Jansen, C. and Steehouder, M. (2001) "How research can lead to better government forms". In: Janssen, D. and Neutlings, R. (eds) 11–36.

Jansen, F. (2001) "The lack of clarity in a sentence: The style of official documents in Dutch". In: Janssen, D. and Neutlings, R. (eds) 125–45.

Janssen, D. and Maat, N. (2001) "Collaborative writing for the government". In: Janssen, D. and Neutlings, R. (eds) 171–210.

Janssen, D. and Neutelings, R. (eds) (2001) *Reading and Writing Public Documents: Problems, Solutions, and Characteristics*, John Benjamins: Amsterdam.

Jaworski, A. (1993) *The Power of Silence: Social and Pragmatic Perspectives*, Sage: London.

Jefferson, G. (1987) "Side sequences". In: Sudnow, D. (ed.) 294–338.

Johnstone, B. (ed.) (1994) *Repetition in Discourse: Interdisciplinary Perspectives: Volumes 1 and 2*, Ablex Publishing Corporation: Norwood, New Jersey.

Johnstone, B. (2002) *Discourse Analysis*, Blackwell: Oxford.

Johnstone, B. (an experimental form – composed with 37 others) (1994) "Repetition in discourse: A dialogue". In: Johnstone, B. (ed.) 1–20.

Johnstone, B. and Kirk, A. (1994) "Repetition in discourse: An annotated bibliography". In: Johnstone, B. (ed.) 176–98.

Jong, M, (1998) *Reader Feedback in Test Design: Validity of the Plus–Minus Method for the Pretesting of Public Information Brochures*, Rodopi: Amsterdam.

Jong, M. and Schellens, P. (2001) "Optimising public information brochures: Formative evaluation in document design processes". In: Janssen, D. and Neutlings, R. (eds) 59–83.

Joos, M. (1967) *The Five Clocks*, Harcourt Brace: New York.

JSB (2001) *Crown Court Bench Book: Specimen Directions*, Judicial Studies Board: London.

Kamil, M., Mosenthal, P., Pearson, P. and Barr, R. (eds) (2000) *Handbook of Reading Research: Volume 3*, Lawrence Erlbaum: London.

Kamisar, Y. (1990) "Remembering the 'old world' of criminal procedure: A reply to professor Grano". In: Leo, R. and Thomas, G. (eds) 264–70.

Kasper, G. and Ross, S. (2003) "Repetition as a source of miscommunication in oral proficiency interviews". In: House, J., Kasper, G. and Ross, S. (eds) 82–106.

Kempson, E. and Moore, N. (1994) *Designing Public Documents: A Review of Research*, Policy Studies Institute: London.

Kimble, J. (1995) "Answering the critics of plain language", *The Scribes' Journal of Legal Writing* (1994–5), 5, 1–23 http://www.plainlanguage.gov/whyPL/arguments_in_favor/criticisms.cfm (Last accessed: 24/12/06).

Kniffka, H. (ed.) (1996) *Recent Developments in Forensic Linguistics*, Peter Lang: Frankfurt.

Knight, A. (2006) "Comments on cautioning" (Personal communication, July).

Knowles, E. and Nathan, K. (1997) "Acquiescent responding in self reports: Cognitive style or social concern?" *Journal of Research in Personality* 31, 293–301.

Komter, M. (2001) "La construction de la preuve dans un interrogatoire de police" ["The construction of evidence in a police investigation"] *Droit et Société* 48, 367–93.

Komter, M. (2002) "Comments on detention in the Netherlands" (Personal communication, June).

Kress, G. and Van Leeuwen, T. (1996) *Reading Images: The Grammar of Visual Design*, Routledge: London.

Kurzon, D. (1995) "The right of silence: A socio-pragmatic model of interpretation", *Journal of Pragmatics* 23, 55–69.

Kurzon, D. (1996) "To speak or not to speak: The comprehensibility of the revised police caution (PACE)", *International Journal for the Semiotics of Law* 9(25), 3–16.

Kurzon, D. (2000) "The right to understand the right of silence: A few comments", *Forensic Linguistics* 7(2), 244–8.

Labov, W. (1988) "The judicial testing of linguistic theory". In: Tannen, D. (ed.) 159–82.

Labov, W. and Harris, W. (1994) "Addressing social issues through linguistic evidence". In: Gibbons, J. (ed.) 265–305.

Labov, W. and Waletzky, J. (1967) "Narrative analysis: Oral versions of Personal experience". In: Helms, J. (ed.) 12–45.

Law Society, The (2002) *Response to Home Office Consultation on the Revised PACE Codes of practice*, The Law Society: London.

Lee, D. (1992) *Competing Discourses: Perspectives and Ideology in Language*, Longman: Harlow.

Leech, G., Conrad, S., Cruickshank, B. and Ivanič, R. (2001) *An A–Z of English Grammar and Usage*, Longman: London.

Leo, R. (1998a) "From coercion to deception: The changing nature of police interrogation in America". In: Leo, R. and Thomas, G. (eds) (1998) 65–74.

Leo, R. (1998b) "The impact of *Miranda* revisited". In: Leo, R. and Thomas, G. (eds) (1998) 208–21.

Leo, R. (2001) "Questioning the relevance of Miranda in the twenty-first century", *Michigan Law Review* 99, 1000–29.

Leo, R. and Thomas, G. (eds) (1998) *The Miranda Debate: Law, Justice and Policing*, North-eastern University Press: Boston.

Leo, R. and White, W. (1999) "Adapting to *Miranda*: Modern interrogator's strategies for dealing with the obstacles posed by *Miranda*", *Minnesota Law Review* 84, 397–472.

Levi, J. (1994) "Language as evidence: The linguist as expert witness in North American courts", *Forensic Linguistic* 1(1), 1–26.

Levi, J. and Walker, A. (eds) (1990) *Language in the Judicial Process*, Plenum: New York.

Levenson, H. Fairweather, F. and Cape, E. (1996) *Police Powers*, Legal Action Group: London (3rd edition).

Levinson, S. (1983) *Pragmatics*, Cambridge University Press: Cambridge.

Levy, C. and Ransdell, S. (eds) (1996) *The Science of Writing*, Lawrence Erlbaum: Hillsdale.

Lindsay, J. (2006) "We caution you – but you might not understand it", *The Times* (25 April), 4.

Linell, P. (1998) "Discourse across boundaries: On recontextualisation and the blending of voices in professional discourse", *Text* 18(2), 143–57.

Lindsey, G. (2003) "Comments on *The Bill*: The scriptwriter" (Personal communication, April).

Louw, B. (1993) "Irony in the text or insincerity in the writer? The diagnostic potential of semantic prosodies". In: Baker, M., Francis, G. and Tognini-Bonelli, E. (eds) 157–76.

Lyon, J., Dennison, C. and Wilson, A. (2000) *"Tell Them so They Listen": Messages from Young People in Custody: Research Study 201*, Home Office: London.

Mace, J. (1992) *Talking about Literacy: Principles and Practice of Adult Literacy Education*, Routledge: London.

Malone, N. (2003) "Comments on detention" (Personal communication, January).

Martins, D. (1982) "Influence of affect on comprehension of a text", *Text* 2(1–3), 141–54.

Maschler, Y. (1994) "Metalanguaging and discourse markers in bilingual communication", *Language in Society* 23, 325–66.

Matoesian, G. (2001) *Law and the Language of Identity: Discourse in the William Kennedy Smith rape Trial*, OUP: Oxford.

McDermott, R. (1988) "Inarticulateness". In: Tannen, D. (ed.) 37–68.

Mehan, H. (1993) "Beneath the skin and between the ears: A case study in the politics of representation". In: Chaiklin, S. and Lave, J. (eds) 241–68.

Mellinkoff, D. (1963) *The Language of the Law*, Little, Brown and Company: Boston.

Merritt, M. (1994) "Repetition in situated discourse – exploring its forms and functions". In: Johnstone, B. (ed.) 23–36.

Merseyside Police (2006) *Glossary of Terms*, http://www.merseyside.police.uk/html/aboutus/glossary/index.htm (Last accessed: 24/12/06).

Mertz, E. (1996) "Recontextualization as socialization: Text and pragmatics in the law school classroom". In: Silverstein, M. and Urban, G. (eds) 229–49.

Meyer, B., Marsiske, M. and Willis, S. (1993) "Text processing variables predict the readability of everyday documents read by older adults", *Reading Research Quarterly* 28(3), 235–49.

Mishler, E. (1984) *The Discourse of Medicine: Dialectics of Medical Interviews*, Ablex: Norwood.

Morgan, D. and Stephenson, G. (1994) "The right to silence in criminal investigations". In: Morgan, D. and Stephenson, G. (eds) 1–17.

Morgan, D. and Stephenson, G. (eds) (1994) *Suspicion and Silence: The Right to Silence in Criminal Investigations*, Blackstone: London.

Morris, L., Lechter, K., Weintraub, M. and Bowen, D. (1998) "Comprehension testing for OTC drug labels: Goals, methods, target population, and testing environment", *Journal of Public Policy and Marketing* 17(1), 86–96.

Mumby, D. and Clair, R. (1997) "Organisational discourse". In: van Dijk, T. (ed.) 181–205.

Myers, G. (2004) *Matters of Opinion: Talking About Public Issues*, CUP: Cambridge.

National Crime Faculty (1998) *A Practical Guide to Investigative Interviewing*, NCF: Bramshill.

National Curriculum (2006) *National Curriculum Online: Citizenship*, http://www.nc.uk.net (Last accessed: 24/12/06).

Nevile, M. (1990) "Translating texts into plain English: The cost of increased readability", *Australian Journal for Adult Literacy Research and Practice* 1(2), 27–38.

Nofsinger, R. (1991) *Everyday Conversation*, Sage: London.

Norrick, N. (1987) "Functions of repetition in conversation", *Text* 7(3), 245–64.

OED (2006) Oxford English Dictionary Online http://www.dictionary.oed.com (Last accessed: 24/12/06).

Office of National Statistics, (2006) *Police Manpower: By Type, March 2002*, http://www.statistics.gov.uk/STATBASE/ssdataset.asp?vlnk=7786 (Last accessed: 24/12/06).

Olson, D. and Torrance, N. (eds) (1991) *Literacy and Orality*, CUP: Cambridge.

Orasanu, J. (ed.) (1986) *Reading Comprehension: From Research to Practice*, Lawrence Erlbaum: New Jersey.

Orasanu, J. and Penney, M. (1986) "Comprehension theory and how it grew". In: Orasanu, J. (ed.) 1–9.

Ormerond, F. and Ivanič, R. (2000) "Texts in practices: Interpreting the physical characteristics of texts". In: Barton, D., Hamilton M. and Ivanič, R. (eds) 91–107.

Owen, C. (1996) "Readability theory and the rights of detained persons". In: Kniffka, H. (ed.) 279–95.

Parker, I. (1988) "Deconstructing accounts". In: Antaki, C. (ed.) 184–98.

Penman, R. (1998) "Communication and the judicial process", *Communication News* 5, http://www.communication.org.au/cria_publications/publication_id_37_888040038.html (Last accessed: 24/12/06).

Perkins, M. (1983) *Modal Expressions in English*, Pinter: London.

Pettersson, R. (2002) *Information Design: An Introduction*, John Benjamins: Amsterdam.

Plain English Campaign (1993) *The Plain English Story*, PEC: Stockport (3rd edition).

Polanyi, L. (1981) "Telling the same story twice", *Text* 1(4), 315–36.

Police Mutual Assurance Society (1976) *Useful Definitions for Police Officers*, PMAS: Lichfield.

Police Review, (1997) Jane's Information Group: London.

Postman, N. (1995) *The End of Education: Redefining the Value of School*, Alfred Knopf: New York.

Potter, J. and Wetherell, M. (1987) *Discourse and Social Psychology: Beyond Attitudes and Behaviour*, Sage: London.

Prince, E. (1990) "On the use of social conversation as evidence in a court of law". In: Levi, J. and Walker, A. (eds) 279–89.

Prince, M. (2003) "Comments on investigations by the Police Complaints Authority" (Personal communication, June).

Psathas, G. (ed.) (1979) *Everyday Language: Studies in Ethnomethodology*, Irvington: New York.

Quirk, R., Greenbaum, S., Leech, G. and Svartvik, J. (1985) *A Comprehensive Grammar of the English Language*, Longman: London.

Rampton, B. (2005) *Crossing: Language and Ethnicity among Adolescents*, St. Jerome: Manchester.

Raney, G., Therriault, D. and Minkoff, S. (2000) "Repetition effects from paraphrased text: Evidence for an integrated representation model of text representation", *Discourse Processes* 29(1), 61–81.

Rapley, T. (2001) "The art(fulness) of open-ended interviewing: Some considerations on analysing interviews", *Qualitative Research* 1(3), 303–323.

Ravotas, D. and Berkenkotter, C. (1998) "Voices in the text: The use of reported speech in a psychotherapist's notes and initial assessment", *Text* 18(2), 211–39.

Rayner, K., Pacht, J. and Duffy, S. (1994) "Effects of prior encounter and global discourse bias on the processing of lexically ambiguous words: Evidence from eye fixations", *Journal of Memory and Language* 33, 527–44.

Reddy, M. (1979) "The conduit metaphor: A case of frame conflict in our language about language". In: Ortony, A. (ed.) 164–201.

Renkema, J. (2001) "Undercover research into text quality as a tool for communication management". In: Janssen, D. and Neutlings, R. (eds) 37–57.

Richardson, J. (2007) *Archbold's Criminal Pleading, evidence and practice*, Sweet and Maxwell: London.

Roberts, C. (2003) "Applied linguistics applied". In: Sarangi, S. and van Leeuwen, T. (eds) 132–49.

Roberts, C., Davies, E. and Jupp, T. (1992) *Language and Discrimination: A Study of Communication in Multi-Ethnic Workplaces*, Longman: London.

Rock, F. (2000) "Concern, discouragement, reprimand, threat". In: Heffer, C. and Sauntson, H. (eds) 143–55.

Rock, F. (forthcoming) "Silence, caveats and video-tape: Explaining the unexplainable in the police interview".

Roter, D. and Hall, J. (1992) *Doctors Talking to Patients/Patients Talking to Doctors: Improving Communication in Medical Visits*, Auburn House: Westport.

Royal Commission on Criminal Justice (1993) *Report*, HMSO: London.

Royal Commission on Criminal Procedure (1981) *Report*, HMSO: London.

Russell, S. (2000) " 'Let me put it simply': The case for a standard translation of the police caution and its explanation", *Forensic Linguistics* 7(1), 26–48.

Sanders, A., Bridges, L., Mulvaney, A. and Crozier, G. (1989) *Advice and Assistance at Police Stations and the 24-Hour Duty Solicitor Scheme*, Lord Chancellor's Department: London.

Sarangi, S. (1998a) "Rethinking recontextualisation in professional discourse studies", *Text* 18(2), 301–18.

Sarangi, S. (1998b) "Interprofessional case construction in social work: The evidential status of information and its reportability", *Text* 18(2), 241–70.

Sarangi, S. and Coulthard, R. M. (eds) (2000) *Discourse and Social Life*, Longman: Harlow.

Sarangi, S. and van Leeuwen, T. (eds) (2003) *Applied Linguistics and Communities of Practice*, Continuum: London.

Schank, R. and Abelson, R. (1977) *Scripts, Plans, Goals and Understanding: An Inquiry into Human Knowledge Structures*, Lawrence Erlbaum: Hillsdale.

Scheuer, J. (2001) "Recontextualisation and communicative styles in job interviews", *Discourse Studies* 3(2), 223–43.

Schriver, K. (1989) "Evaluating text quality: The continuum from text-focussed to reader-focussed methods", *IEEE Transactions* 32(4), 238–55.

Scollon, R. (1998) *Mediated Discourse as Social Interaction: A Study of News Discourse*, Longman: London.

Scollon, R. (2000) "Methodological interdiscursivity: An ethnographic understanding of unfinalisability". In: Sarangi, S. and Coulthard, R. M. (eds) 138–54.

Scollon, R. (2001) *Mediated Discourse: The Nexus of Practice*, Routledge: London.

Shannon, C. and Weaver, W. (1949) *The Mathematical Theory of Communication*, Illinois University Press: Illinois.

Shepherd, E., Mortimer, A. and Mobasheri, R. (1995) "The police caution: Comprehension and perceptions in the general population", *Expert Evidence* 4(2), 60–7.

Short, M. (1994) "Understanding texts: Point of view". In: Brown, G., Malmkjaer, K., Pollit, A. and Williams, J. (eds) 169–90.

Shuy, R. (1990) "Warning labels: Language, law and comprehensibility", *American Speech* 65(4), 291–303.

Shuy, R. (1993) *Language Crimes: The Use and Abuse of Language Evidence in the Courtroom*, Blackwell: Oxford.

Shuy, R. (1997) "Ten unanswered language questions about Miranda", *Forensic Linguistics* 4(2), 175–95.

Shuy, R. and Staton, J. (2000) "Review of Grisso, 1998", *Forensic Linguistics* 7(1), 131–6.

Silverman, D. (1987) *Communication and Medical Practice*, Sage: London.

Silverman, D. and Torode, B. (1980) *The Material Word: Some Theories of Language and its Limits*, Routledge: London.

Silverstein, M. and Urban, G. (1996) "The natural history of discourse". In: Silverstein, M. and Urban, G. (eds) 1–17.

Silverstein, M. and Urban, G. (eds) (1996) *Natural Histories of Discourse*, Chicago University Press: Chicago.

Sinclair, J. and Coulthard, R. M. (1975) *Towards an Analysis of Discourse: The English Used by Teachers and Pupils*, OUP: Oxford.

Sinclair, J. M., Hoey, M. and Fox, G. (eds) (1993) *Techniques in Description: Spoken and Written Discourse*, Routledge: London.

Solin, A. (2001) *Tracing Texts: Intertextuality in Environmental Discourse*, Ph.D. thesis: University of Helsinki.

Solomon, N. (1996) "Plain English: From a perspective of language in society". In: Hasan, R. and Williams, G. (eds) 279–307.

Spolsky, B. (1994). "Comprehension testing, or can understanding be measured?" In: Brown, G., Malmkjaer, K., Pollit, A. and Williams, J. (eds) 141–52.

Steinberg, E. (1986) "Promoting plain English", *Visible Language* 20(2), 153–4.

Steiner, G. (1975) *After Babel: Aspects of Language and Translation*, OUP: Oxford.

Steiner, G. (1978) *On Difficulty and Other Essays*, OUP: Oxford.

Sticht, T. (1972) "Learning by listening". In: Carroll, J. and Freedle, R. (eds) 285–314.

Stone, C. (2002) "Comments on interpreting" (Personal communication, September).

Street, B. (1984) *Literacy in Theory and Practice*, CUP: Cambridge.

Stubbs, M. (1980) *Language and Literacy: The Sociolinguistics of Reading and Writing*, Routledge: London.

Sudnow, D. (ed.) (1987) *Studies in Social Interaction*, Free Press: New York.

Swales, J. (1990) *Genre Analysis: English in Academic and Research Settings*, CUP: Cambridge.

Tannen, D. (ed.) (1988) *Linguistics in Context: Connecting Observation and Understanding*, Ablex: Norwood.

Tannen, D. (1989) *Talking Voices: Repetition, Dialogue and Imagery in Conversational Discourse*, CUP: Cambridge.

Tannen, D. and Saville-Troike, M. (eds) (1985) *Perspectives on Silence*, Ablex: New Jersey.

Taylor, W. (1953) "Cloze procedure: A new tool for measuring readability", *Journalism Quarterly* 30, 415–33.

Teers, R. and Menin, S. (2006) *Deaths During or Following Police Contact: Statistics for England and Wales 2005/06*, http://www.ipcc.gov.uk/death_report_0506_v7.pdf (Last accessed: 24/12/06).

Thompson, G. and Hunston, S. (2000) "Evaluation: An introduction". In: Hunston, S. and Thompson, G. (eds) 1–27.

Tiersma, P. (1999a) *Legal Language*, University of Chicago Press: Chicago.

Tiersma, P. (1999b) "The language of silence", *Rutgers Law Review* 48(1), 1–99.

Tiersma, P. (2001) "A message in a bottle: Text, autonomy and statutory interpretation", *Tulane Law Review* 76(2), 431–82.

Trinch, S. and Berk-Seligson, S. (2002) "Narrating in protective order interviews: A source of interactional trouble", *Language in Society* 31, 383–418.

Urban, G. (1996) "Entextualisation, replication and power". In: Silverstein, M. and Urban, G. (eds) 21–44.

van Dijk, T. (ed.) (1985) *Handbook of Discourse Analysis: Volume 3, Discourse and Dialogue*, Academic Press: London.

van Dijk, T. (ed.) (1997) *Discourse as Social Interaction, Discourse Studies a Multidisciplinary Introduction: Volume 2*, Sage: London.

Walker, A. G. (1990) "Language at work in the law: The customs, conventions, and appellate consequences of court". In: Levi, J. and Walker, A. (eds) 203–44.

Walton, D. (1996) *Fallacies Arising from Ambiguity*, Kluwer Academic: Dordrecht.

Wetherell, M. and Potter, J. (1988) "Discourse analysis and the identification of interpretative repertoires". In: Antaki, C. (ed.) 168–83.

White, J. (1990) *Justice as Translation: An Essay in Cultural and Legal Criticism*, University of Chicago Press: Chicago.

White, R. and Gunstone, R. (1992) *Probing Understanding*, Falmer: London.

Williams, J. (1986) "Plain English: The remaining problems", *Visible language* 20(2), 166–173.

Wilson, A. (2000) "There is no escape from third space theory: Borderland discourse and the 'in-between' literacies of prisons". In: Barton, D., Hamilton, M. and Ivanič, R. (eds) 54–69.

Wilson, P. and Anderson, R. (1986) "What they don't know will hurt them: The role of prior knowledge in comprehension". In: Orasanu, J. (ed.) 31–50.

Winston, B. (1986) *Misunderstanding Media*, Routledge: London.

Wolverhampton City Council (2004) *Streetwise: The Law Relating to Young People*, http://www.wolverhampton.gov.uk/streetwise/str_law.html (Last accessed: 01/09/04).

Wood, L. and Kroger, R. (2000) *Doing Discourse Analysis: Methods for Studying Action in Talk and Text*, Sage: London.

Wright, P. (1979) "The quality control of document design", *Information Design Journal* 1, 33–42.

Wright, P. (1981) "Five skills technical writers need", *IEEE Transactions* PC24, 1, 10–16.

Wright, P. (1999) "Writing and information design of healthcare materials". In: Candlin, C. and Hyland, K. (eds) 85–98.

Index

about, 171
abstract, 104
accent 228, 229
acco ..no tion, 29, 121, 94–9, 228
acce ntable, . 132, 233
acce unting, 22, 2. 27, 4?, 158, 173,
    174, 178, 204, 21
  see also recontextualisation;
    reformulation; transformation
accuracy, 93, 117, 143, 145, 172
acknowledging, 21, 25, 93, 132,
    175–6, 191, 211, 217, 220, 226,
    237
ACPO, see Association of Chief Police
    Officers
ac iescenc. 207
ac dress, see terms of address
administration of rights
  uninterested, 119, :??–4, 125
adolescents, 53–4
adversarial law systems, 139, 245
adversative relationships, 181
adverse inference, see ir erences
advertising, 27, 121
advising, 76, 104, 127, 41, 151–2,
    164
affect, 68–70, 8?, ı'0, 1 9, 123–4,
    164, 165, 167, 1/ 25
  detainees on, 70
  officers on, 225
  see also experiential meaning
age, 20, 43, 104, 108–9, 118, 168, 196,
    198–9, 213, 248
agency, 51, 65, 105, 1?? 214
agent, 51, 53, 64–5 104–5
  deletion, 54
agentless passives, see passivisation
agreeing, 25
agreement, 207
alibi, 175
aligning, 76, 15? 181, 202, 214
    223, 248

aloud reading, see reading, aloud
ambiguity, 4, 9, 26, 51, 55, 56, 65, 73,
    79, 81, 83–4, 93–4, 127–8, 151,
    169–70, 176, 179, 218
  acceptable, 211
  exploiting, 241
  modality and, 57–9
analogy for comprehension, 28, 46,
    67, 86, 116
anaphora, 45, 60, 61–2, 63, 94–5, 181,
    202
animator, 15, 22, 42, 122, 144, 152,
    200
antecedent, 60, 61, 63
anything, 175–7
appeals, 139–40, 144
appellate opinion, see appeals
appropriate adult, 64–5, 91, 103–4,
    109–10, 159, 240–1
appropriation, 10, 12, 131, 133, 138,
    193, 230–2, 239, 247, 261
  of cautioning, 165, 173, 235, 249
  of lifeworld voice, 27
  of official discourses, 67, 178, 191,
    230, 237–8
  of resources, 231, 251, 261
  see also misappropriation
Archbold, 113
army personnel, 119
arrest, 33, 36, 117, 118, 129, 137
  cautioning at, 137, 147, 154,
    169–70, 252
  experiences of, 33–4, 138
  talk at, 169–72, 174
  wrongful, 238
article, 36, 65, 173–4
Association of Chief Police Officers,
    36–7
assumptions, 66, 85, 115–16, 126,
    161–3, 216, 252
at any time, 81–2, 96–7
at public expense, 96

attending the police station
  voluntarily, 37, 176, 224
audience design, 199–200
audiences
  auditing, 160–1, 233
  captive, 100
  immediate, 196–8, 233
  involving in revision, 41, 215–21
  limited, 82–3
  multiple, 9–10, 65, 197, 233
  needs of, 134, 166, 194, 197
  overhearing, 122, 160, 182, 194,
    209, 233–4, 242, 255
  reinterpreting, 24
  restricted, 73, 78
  small, 78
  specialist, 87, 168–9
audio-recording investigative
  interviews, 142, 161, 225
audio-recording research interviews,
  148–9
audio-recordings as rights
  communication, 39, 122
Australia, 146
author, 15, 144, 152
authority, 56, 69, 156, 209
  calling on, 41
  figure, 75, 129
  resistance to, 241
  text as, 79–80
autonomous texts, 11, 200
autonomy, 11, 110, 178, 194–5
  detainees', 110, 259
  officers', 193–4, 199, 200
  readers', 90
  silence as, 230
  solicitors', 59

backchannel cues, 208
bald-on-record, 211
Barton, D., 7, 10, 11, 20, 76, 87, 109,
  112, 118, 133, 144, 151, 231, 249
beat officers, 148–9
Bernstein, B., 22, 24, 25, 28
bias, 165, 173–4
The Bill, 117–18, 143
boredom, 100
brief to rewriters, 43
British Sign Language, 145–6

bullets, 96
bureaucratic forms, 100, 123
bureaucratic triviality, 34, 156, 200
  see also triviality
business, 119
busybodies, 34
but, 181–2
by, 171–2

call for help, 109, 129, 193, 239
callcentre, 233
Cameron, D., 15, 155, 165, 192, 193,
  194, 197, 199, 200, 231, 232, 233
can, 57–8, 59, 218
cartoon presentation, 69
case law, 139, 140, 143, 253
cataphora, 62–3, 94, 150
categorisation, 92–3, 131–2
  as analysis, 43–4, 101, 159
causal relationship, 202
caution, the
  as bureaucratic triviality, 156, 200,
    216, 226
  conspicuous through repetition, 156
  contamination through poetisation,
    156
  criticism of, 139, 143
  difficulty of, 157–8
  formulation of, 137
  as immaterial waste of time, 138
  impotence of, 156
  as ineffectual, 141, 152
  influence of, 138
  introduction of, 5–6
  medial sentence of, 139, 151, 175,
    177, 181, 188–9, 193, 201, 215,
    217, 219, 254
  necessarily vague, 171, 179, 218
  problematising, 214
  as protection, 223
  reception of, 137
  significance to detainees of, 157–8,
    166–7
  (strategic) use of, 138, 164, 169–74,
    176–7, 178
  as symbol of professionalism, 223
  as three sentences, 181–5, 219–20

see also checking caution
comprehension; three-part
structure
caution (as label), 150, 150–4, 247
referent of, 152–4
caution explanation, 6, 137–8, 143–5
ability for, 194
assumptions underlying, 163
collaborative, 189–91, 216–21, 248
corrective, 160
criteria for delivery of, 195–9
data on, 147–50
deciding how to provide, 195–7
deciding whether to provide, 194–7
from detainees, 160, 190–1, 205–21
diversity of practices in, 182–5,
200–4, 231–2
incomplete, 160, 183–4, 191, 200–4,
207, 216–21, 228, 236–7, 239,
250
integral to cautioning, 144–5
learning to give, 144, 161, 230–3,
254–6
length of, 167
not neutral, 175–7, 201–2
in officers' own words, introducing,
180
official paraphrase, 180, 191–200,
248
processing, 189–91
reasons for giving, 144
repetitive, 180, 183–4, 200–2
requesting, 160
resequencing, 182–91
tailored to a particular individual,
165, 193–9, 254–6
see also standard paraphrase,
standardisation
caution official wording, the, 137,
150, 154–5
assumptions underlying, 162
audibility of, 155
changing, 142
as conduit, 162
criticism of, 154
delivery of, 143, 154–5, 158, 225,
253
drafting, 143
field testing of, 143

flexibility of, 255
forgetting, 158
formulaicity of, 156–8, 199,
224, 249
learning, 143, 230–3
length of, 142–3, 154
praise of, 154
symbolic currency of, 156, 253
cautioning
appropriation of, 165, 173, 235, 249
embarrassment during, 109,
155, 235
experience of, 148, 197–9, 231
felicity and, 156, 209, 233, 237,
239, 241
function of, 151, 154, 156, 165,
209–10, 222–42, 248–9
interpersonal aspects of, 149, 152,
161, 165, 173, 185, 195–9, 210,
230, 237
at interview, 158
length of, 151
optimal situation for, 255–6
performativity of, 162, 227, 233–5
reality of, 147–8
resources for, 149, 204, 233
strategic, 170–4
token, 146, 154, 247
training in, 140, 146, 149, 180, 188,
191, 219, 230–1, 253–7
see also checking caution
comprehension
cautioning exchange, the, 147,
158–63
opportunity to personalise, 7, 104,
170–2, 248
seeking comprehension through,
190–1, 216–21
see also exchange structure
cautioning guidelines, 171, 200, 254–5
cautioning practice, 148–50
disseminating, 146, 221, 231–2,
249, 253, 257
sharing, 231
caveats to rights, 91, 127
*certain exceptional circumstances, see
circumstances, certain exceptional*
challenge, 210–12, 218, 235
chance, 173

charge, 7, 56, 67, 137, 139, 156
Charrow, R., 9, 16, 17, 18, 51, 53, 74, 122, 188
Charrow, V., 9, 16, 17, 18, 51, 53, 74, 122, 188
checking caution comprehension, 248
  audio-recording, 255
  by requesting a reformulation, 215–21
  pragmatic aspects of, 210–14
  recommendations on, 253–6
  routine for, 158–61, 211, 254–5
  through a yes/no question, 206–10
child abuse, 178
chronology, 52, 74
CID officers, 149
circumlocutions, 59
circumstances, certain exceptional, 77–8, 83–5
circumstantial elements, 171, 172–3
citizenship, 118, 252
  see also National Curriculum
CJPOA, *see* Criminal Justice and Public Order Act (1994)
Clare, I., 17, 18, 21, 37, 42, 44, 66, 83, 89, 90, 98, 109, 115, 119, 137, 138, 139, 142–3, 149, 188, 205, 206, 208, 219, 250
clarification
  requesting, 94, 191, 205, 216
  offering, 121, 150, 171, 253
classification through language, 10–11, 28, 83, 104, 150, 172, 179
clause relations, 50–1, 62–5
clause structure, 193
cloze procedure, 17
co-construction, 215–21, 248
COBUILD Corpus, 153, 171–2
Codes of practice, *see* PACE Codes of practice
coercion, 131, 179, 182, 211, 215–16
cognition, 20, 23, 40, 109, 250
cognitive energy, 52
cognitive impact, 156
coherence, 25
  topical, 72–7
cohesion, 25, 45–7, 59, 63, 81, 104–5, 210

collaborating, 25, 42, 188–91, 204, 217–21, 248
collocation, 93, 171–2, 178, 209
colonisation, 27, 129
commodification, 27, 132–3, 162, 214
Common Law, 151
common sense, 127
communication, 4, 14–15, 18, 23, 29, 161–2, 211
  assumptions about underlying cautioning, 162
  linear, 162
  professional-lay, 33, 122
  see also transmission model of communication
compassion, 225
  performing, 234
complex language, 40–1
  see also difficult language
compliance, 128, 222, 231, 236, 238, 252, 253
comprehensibility, 16–17, 96–9
  critical view of measuring, 51, 55, 59, 62, 65, 162–3
  improving, 15–16
  measuring, 15–16, 20–1, 48, 49–71, 96–8, 145–6
  as polar category, 14
  as product, 16
  reality of, 45–8, 88
  in relation to comprehension, 68, 96–8
  as relative concept, 167
  sociolinguistics and, 19–22, 51
comprehension, 17–19
  achieving, 255–6
  analogy and, 26, 46, 67, 86, 116, 181
  articulation and, 163, 209, 216
  assessing likely, 195–8
  checking through speech, 120, 188–9, 205–21, 255
  claims of, 206–10
  commodification of, 162, 214
  complexity of, 45–8, 87–8
  confirming, 161
  as continuum, 208–9
  expectations about own, 128
  and familiarity, 122–3

improving, 15–16
indicators of, 215
measuring, 15–16, 160, 163, 197–9,
  207; *see also* testing
  comprehension
moment-by-moment, 182
monitoring, 186
optimal formulations for, 162
performing attention to, 234
perlocution and, 152, 174, 178–9
as polar or binary category, 14, 18,
  163, 208–9
as process, 16
pronouns and, *see* pronouns
proving, 210
in relation to comprehensibility, 68,
  96–8
restating, 210
as skill, 15
as social phenomenon, 22, 88
and sociocultural factors, 211
and sociolinguistics, 19–22, 197–9
style shifting and, 199
testing, *see* testing comprehension
as the reader's problem, 16
versus believing, 127–8, 247
see also understanding,
  misunderstanding
computers, 122, 253
conditional, 85, 106, 175–6
confession, 132, 153, 234
confidence, 16, 67, 71, 76, 112, 113,
  197, 208, 235
confrontation, 79–80, 210, 241
congruence, 51–2, 74
conjunctions, 62, 204
  readability and, 62
connotations, 23–4, 47–8, 58, 60,
  83–4, 87, 173, 178, 181
constitutional privilege, 146
constitutive, 29, 73, 84, 121, 129, 173,
  177, 184, 230
constructionist approach, 7, 17,
  130–1, 175, 250
content, 10, 24, 37, 43, 66, 77, 87,
  97–8, 101, 104, 105, 106, 114,
  122, 128–9, 134, 154, 191, 220,
  230, 258

context, 5, 18, 19, 23, 24, 48, 49, 53,
  65, 71, 89, 92, 115, 126, 134, 137,
  152, 162, 170, 211
  comprehension and, 195, 209
  explanation in, 149, 179
  influencing explanations, 63,
    176, 179
  primary, 28
  production and, 230
  recontextualising, 28
  reading in, 128
  secondary, 28
  see also social context
contextualisation cues, 124, 208
contextualising information, 205,
  214, 216
contradictory information, 81–2, 85,
  132
contrast, 181
control, 10–11, 24, 25, 29, 69, 116,
  122, 124, 192, 233, 235, 236
controlling, *see* control
convergence, 146, 196–8, 231–2
coordination, 61, 62, 63–5, 181
cotext, 47, 78, 81–2, 91–2, 94, 171–2,
  225
Cotterill, J., 37, 69, 128, 137, 143,
  147, 149, 151, 152, 166, 167, 180,
  192, 205, 208, 239
court, 167, 168–9, 175
  hypotheses about, 175
courtroom, 10–11, 158, 161, 172, 210,
  234, 237
  audience, 160, 174, 192, 194, 233
  examination, 10, 158, 237
  inferences and, 139, 164
  oath, 156, 237–8
  work of, 25
creativity, 29, 156, 200, 251
crest, *see* logo
Criminal Justice and Public Order Act
  (1994), 37, 139
  section 34, 139–41
criminal record, 67–8, 153
critical readers, 125–6, 149
  see also readers
cross-references, 46, 85–8
  using, 86
  see also intertextuality

crossing, 197, 199
Crown Court Bench Book, 140–1
cues, 114
  back-channel, 208
  contextualisation, 124, 208
  extra-linguistic, 196
  prosodic, 189, 228
  sequential, 77
  visual, 76–7
custody, 33
  accounts of, 33–4, 138
  experience in, 44, 97–101, 110,
    112–13, 126
  health and welfare in, 120–1
  oversights in procedure, 105
  stress in, 99, 110–11, 154–5, 195
  time pressures in, 120
  see also detention procedure
custody desk, 99, 105, 109, 112, 119,
    120, 121–5, 247, 255
  cautioning at, 137, 147
  talk at, 118–21, 125
custody officer, 35–6, 53–4, 61, 79,
    104–6, 109, 119–20, 123, 125, 256
  see also custody sergeant
custody record, 66–7, 71, 95, 98, 102,
    121
  defining, 67
  see also right to a copy of the
    custody record
custody sergeant, 6, 92, 105–6, 119,
    120, 124, 258
  see also custody officer

data protection, 37–8
day and night, 81–2, 96
day or night, 97, 126–7
deaf people, 53
deaths in or following custody, 33
declarative, 53, 85, 101–3, 106
decontextualisation, 22, 241
  see also recontextualisation;
    reformulation; transformation
decontextualised thought, 23
defence, 139–40, 164, 172, 175
  ambush, 139
  representations of, 175–7
defendants
  decisions of, 140–1, 166–7

deixis, 123, 150–1
delay, 79, 84, 93–4
delimit, 15, 82, 132, 188, 190–1, 232
demystifies, 179
depersonal, *see* depersonalisation
depersonalisation, 26–7
  see also personalisation
Derbyshire Police, 45–6
descriptive research, 245–6, 249
detail
  excessive, 167, 179
  increase in, 168, 172–4
  packaging differently, 171
  reduction in, 65
  requesting, 205
detainees
  on affect, 70
  on comprehensibility, 97
  comprehension claims of, 206, 208,
    210–11
  on difficulty, 19
  diversity of, 195, 251
  expectations about, 90–2, 197–200
  experience of, 99–100, 112–14, 126,
    196–8
  on formality, 70
  inattention to, 216–17
  on intertextuality, 92
  naïve, 43, 95, 125, 130, 142, 221
  needs of, 61, 70, 95, 101–3, 109–10,
    134, 160, 165, 194, 254, 260
  opinions of, 41
  orienting to, 92–6
  as pedagogy, 221
  practices of, 229
  reception of revised rights notice
    by, 88, 89–107
  research on, 44–5
  on revision, 77
  roles, 112, 144, 148
  self-presenting as reasonable and
    considerate, 131–3
  on stating the obvious, 98
  as strategic players, 174
  views of, 129, 134
  who cannot read, 108–10, 247
  who chose not to read, 110–11

see also novice detainees; occasional detainees; readers; regular detainees
detention procedure, 36, 105, 201
  adept in, 222, 243
  changing, 5, 261
  communicating changes in, 112–13
  officers learning, 144, 229–33
  repetitive, 156
  reviewing, 257
  see also custody
determiners
  inconsistent use of, 65
  possessive, 53
dialogicity, 74
  cautioning through, 200, 248, 253–6
dialogue
  recorded to communicate rights, 122
dictionary conventions, 86
difficult language, 9–10, 40, 49, 206
  affective force of, 69–70
  perceptions of, 16–17
  power and, 69, 204
difficulty
  critical view of measuring, 51
  frequency and, 199
  of long noun phrases, 59–60
  measuring texts', 15, 48, 49–71
  perceptions of, 199
direct, 168–9
directive, 53, 77, 82, 85, 86, 102
disadvantage, 10–11, 39, 70, 84, 110, 153
disagreeing, 25
disbelief about rights, 24, 114, 127–8, 144, 232–3, 247
disciplinary action, 35
disclaimers, 212
discomfort, 214
discoursal move, 235
discourse, 22–3, 24, 28–9, 34, 112, 115, 132–3, 139, 179, 238
  conflicting, 238, 241, 249
  official, 178, 226
  public, 118
discourse markers, 122, 204

discourse sequence, 65–6, 67–8, 79–82, 84, 133, 147, 182–4
discourse structure, 24, 45–8, 81–2, 92, 123, 150, 180–204
discourse technologies, 27, 245
discursive system, 227
  unfamiliar, 229
disempowerment, *see* language and empowerment
disenfranchisement, 208
disfluency, 145
dishonesty, 177
diversity
  of cautioning practices, 7, 185–6
  linguistic, 39, 251
  lived, 29
  of modes of rights administration, 121, 252–3
  of people and practices in detention, 10, 134, 196, 251
  of perspectives on understanding, 165
  of speech act functions of the caution, 151
do you understand?, 206–10, 255–6
doctors, 115, 233, 259
document design, *see* information design
Domino Effect, the, 55, 63, 81
downplaying rights information, 123, 225
drink driving, *see* Road Traffic Act
drugs referral schemes, 38, 134
duration, 95
Durham Constabulary, 37
Dutch, 39
duty solicitor, 62–3, 97, 101, 127
DVD players, 122
dyslexic, 108–9

easification, 9–10
echoing, 156, 187, 218
ecological approach, 7
education, 39, 109, 117, 118–19, 198, 248, 252
elaborating, 45, 90, 219, 248
electronic versions of rights texts, 121–2

elision, 60
embarrassment, 109, 155, 235
emphasis, 155, 184, 224
empirical
    evidence, 128, 151, 188, 257
    laws, 21
    research, 52
employment, 20
empowerment, *see* language and
    empowerment
engagement, 5, 20, 69, 86, 88, 91,
    102, 111, 114, 123, 129
English, 39, 145–7
Enterprise IG, 43
Enterprise texts, introduction of
    the, 43
entertainment, 117
entextualisation, 22, 247
    see also recontextualisation;
        reformulation; transformation
entitlements, 34–6, 259–60
    see also Notice of entitlements
equity, 16, 33, 234
errors, 258–9
Essex Police, 37
ethnicity, 20, 38, 146
ethnography, 5, 12, 35, 44, 100, 246
evaluation, 193, 197–9
evaluation of detainees' explanations,
    160, 190–1, 228
    positive, 216, 220
everyday, 7, 26–7, 89, 110, 142, 147,
    167, 169, 171
evidence, 139, 164
    exclusion of, 35
    modality and, 55–8
    representations of, 175–6
examination, 10
*exceptional, see circumstances, certain
    exceptional*
exchange structure, 158–61, 247
    obligatory slots, 160, 214
    see also cautioning exchange
exclusion of evidence, 36
exemplifying, 83
exophoric, 105
expectations, 252
    about content, 78, 80–1, 114–15
    about literacy, 85

about memory, 85
about sequence, 187
about text conventions, 86–7,
    114–15
background, 128
competing with, 127
decisions and, 110
generic, 86, 114–15
institutional, 5
intertextuality and, 29
expected answer, 207
experience
    of police officers, 148, 231
    see also caution explanation;
        caution official wording
experiential meaning, 55, 68–70
    see also affect
experimental studies, 21, 59, 83, 117,
    137–8, 143, 221, 255
expert, 26, 210
    cautioners, 219
    detainees, 10, 112–13, 241
    expert-lay interaction, 235, 241
    professionals, 76, 145
    readers, 87
    scrutiny of, 210
    writers, 43
explanation, 4–5, 14, 22, 147–9,
    158, 180
    ability to, 162–3
    co-constructed, 215–21
    collaborative, 189–92, 204, 221,
        248
    deciding whether to, 197–9, 255
    learning to, 162, 229–33
    length of, 168
    as pedagogy, 221
    representations of, 165
    as skill, 245
    as technology, 245
    unconvincing verbal, 120
    see also recontextualisation;
        reformulation; transformation
explicit reference, 186
extra-linguistic cues, 16, 196
extrapolation, 179
extratextual ties, 91–2, 134, 216
    see also intertextuality

face, 10, 211–14, 250–1
 negative, 211, 229
 positive, 211, 229
 see also politeness
Face Threatening Acts, 213–16
facilitating, 5, 132, 209, 245, 249
facts, *see* social facts
fail, 139, 177–8
fairness, 234
feedback, 15, 159, 216, 231
 positive, 4
 negative, 216
felicity conditions, 156, 209, 237,
 239, 241
film, 117
filming, 143
Flesch index, 40
Flesch readings, 41
floor
 dominating the, 241
 obtaining the, 237
 using the, 131
fluency, 145, 209, 217, 220
 as indicator of comprehension, 217
focus groups, 17
footing, 152, 223–6, 248, 251
Force A, 147–8, 184, 191, 192–9,
 231–2
Force B, 147–8, 191–3, 200
Force D, 147–8, 184, 191, 200–4, 220
foregrounding, 26, 66, 78, 85, 91, 105,
 141, 156, 179, 181, 186
forgetting the caution wording, 158
form, 15, 23, 104, 154, 220, 236, 256
formal, 26–7, 70, 224, 246, 258
forms, 100, 123
formulaicity, 10, 156–8, 199, 224,
 249
formulation, 22, 23, 137
 see also recontextualisation;
  reformulation; transformation
framing, 130–1, 223–7, 248, 249, 251
France, 146
free, 96, 127, 150
frozen register, 156, 237
FTAs, *see* Face Threatening Acts
function, 15, 22–3, 25–6, 104–5,
 114–15, 222–3

affective *or* experiential, 12, 25,
 69–70, 110, 123
archival, 209–10, 233
communicative, 123, 209
ideational, 105
interactional, 25, 137, 166
interpersonal, 106
referential, 165, 214, 222
and voices, 28
functional texts, 100, 101

gaze, 155
 durations, 153
gender, 20
 see also sex
generalisability, 249, 252
generic expectations, *see* expectations
genre, 10
 familiarity, 114, 123
 plain English and, 17
Gibbons, J., 9, 15, 22, 24, 51, 52, 54,
 69, 114, 120, 146, 151, 160, 167,
 187, 210, 233, 249
gist, 101, 103–4
givens, 91, 106
gloss, 65–6, 67, 85, 87, 102, 168
glossaries of police language, 9
Goffman, E., 15, 112, 120, 144, 152,
 156, 160, 200, 207, 208, 209, 211,
 212, 223, 241
Government, *see* Home Office
Government text, introduction of the,
 42–3
grammatical metaphor, 50–3, 84
grammaticalised *like*, 218
graphological, 67
Greater Manchester Police, 37, 101–2
greeting exchanges, 209, 226
guardian, 104
Gudjonsson, G., 17, 18, 21, 37, 41, 45,
 66, 83, 89, 90, 98, 109, 115, 119,
 137, 138, 143, 149, 188, 205, 206,
 208, 219, 250
guessing, 115
guessing, educated, 115
guidelines for writing, 16, 27, 40, 51,
 55, 65, 70–1, 93, 115, 117, 171,
 200, 259
 recommendations, 17, 27

guilt, 130, 139, 168, 176–7, 238
  admitting, 129, 131–2
  deciding, 168
  mitigates, 176
  proving, 139

handing, 123–4, 125
harm your defence, 215
headings, 91, 101–2, 104–5, 187, 260
  see also titles
hesitation, 150, 205
Home Office, 41, 118, 144, 260–1
Home Office research grants, 40
homogenisation, 232
homograph, 153
homonym, 152–3
  biased, 153
honesty, 130–2, 177, 210, 235, 236
hostile, 241
House of Lords, 143
humour, 156
hyperfluency, 156, 157
hypertext, 121–2

ideal reader, the, 20
ideational sections, 180
identities, *see* social identity
ideology, 22, 250
idioms, 127, 261
illocution, 152
illocutionary complexity, 144
illustrating, 248–9
impatience, 211
imperative, 106
impersonal texts, 27, 82
implicature, 63, 81, 87, 130–1, 169,
    177–8, 181–2
imposition, 93, 96, 214, 250–1
inaccuracy, 145, 171
inarticulateness, 219, 238
inattention to detainees, 215–17
inclusiveness, 175, 221
incommunicado, *see* right to have
    someone informed of your arrest
incompleteness, 74, 100, 103, 107,
    117, 160, 183–4, 190–1, 200–2,
    204, 207, 216, 218–19, 228, 236,
    239, 250
  from detainee's perspective, 219

incomprehension, 4, 21, 73, 98, 161,
    163, 205–8, 215, 221, 231, 241,
    250
  observable through language, 205
  see also misunderstanding
incongruity, 46
incongruence, 52
independent solicitor, *see* solicitor
index, 86–7
indifference, 87–8, 99, 110–11, 112,
    226
indirect object, 218
indirectness, 89
inequality, 10–11, 79
  socio-economic, 22
inferences, 17, 47, 54, 66, 97, 126,
    139–41, 164
  adverse, 139, 140–2, 146–7, 164,
    193, 204, 218, 219, 221, 230
infinitival clauses, 102, 106, 221
inflective ambiguity, *see*
    nominalisation
informal talk constituting written
    rights texts, 28–9, 121, 155, 230,
    231, 232, 247, 249
informal, 26–7, 70, 129, 227, 232
information design, 5, 43
information designers, 43, 49–50, 60,
    246
information load, 85
information overload, 99–100
informing, 104, 151–2, 223
initiation, 159, 216
innocence, 129–31
  proving, 139
innocence, 176–
  claims, 129–33, 238
  deciding, 168–9
  proving, 139
insiders, 58, 104
institutional
  actors, 129, 134
  agenda, 131, 161
  allowable contributions, 208
  categories, 104
  concerns, 210, 223
  constraints, 199
  formulations, 192–3
  needs, 110, 134, 170, 194

order, 230
orientation, 105, 236–42
perspective, 96
policy, 184
pressures, 208
ratification, 209, 233
requirements, 225
salience, 233, 237
setting, 48
institutionality, 161, 178, 237, 241
institutions, 27, 109–10, 149
constituted by person reference, 129
lay people and, 240
stigmatisation of information from, 119
instruction, 26, 105–6, 123, 258
assembly, 260
insurance claims, 49
intelligence, 134, 197, 198, 213
intentions, 15, 43, 133, 152, 176, 237, 238
revisers', 89
inter-ethnic communication, 146
see also ethnicity
interactional, 144, 159
aims, 26, 165, 245
complexity, 28
functions, 25, 137, 223–4
literacy as, 20
moves, 208
play, 223
pressure, 208, 228
rights, 208
scaffolding, 222
work, 197
interactionally producing, 133
interactive implications, 181
interdiscursivity, 22
see also recontextualisation; reformulation; transformation
interference, 15, 80, 167
internalisation, 157, 195
International Institute for Information Design, 43
internet, 118, 252
interpersonal, 149, 173
concerns, 161, 165, 194, 210, 230–1, 237
context, 152

function, 106
goals, 245
needs, 194
networks, 184
observation, 197
power asymmetry, 120
interpretable, 126, 129
interpretation, 20, 92–3, 131, 175
pragmatic, 226
interpreter, 145–6
competent, 145
police officers and, 146
professional, 145
interrogatives, *see* questions
interruption, 234
intertextual chains, 8, 28–9, 36, 85, 134
intertextuality, 28, 50, 72, 85–8, 90–2, 121–3, 134, 186, 230, 231
detainees' comments on, 92
influencing explanation, 177–8
see also exophoric; extratextual ties; intratextuality; syntagmatic relations
intervention, 227–8, 249, 252
interview preamble, 130–1, 145, 150–1, 155, 158–61, 191, 209, 211, 227–8, 234–5, 241
simulating, 149
interview room, 160–1
interview tapes, 231
interviews (investigative), 75–6, 130–1, 137, 138, 158, 169
audio-recording of, 142, 160
cautioning at, 158–61, 169
end of, 173
as evidence-creation, 226–7
influenced by the caution, 141
procedure in, 241
research on, 147–8
video-recording of, 160
see also questioning (investigative)
interviews (research), 12, 17, 20–1, 100, 149, 245, 251
audio-recording, 149
benefits of, 149
limitations of, 98
semi-structured, 5, 21, 43, 148–9

intonation, 4, 155, 200
intratextuality, 91–2
    see also intertextuality
introduction, 104, 108
investigative interviews, *see* interviews
    (investigative)
investigator, 152
invoking rights, 35, 46–7, 79, 82–3,
    91, 98, 102, 106, 121, 147, 176,
    245, 260
    results of, 147–8
Israel, 146–7

Jackson, B., 10, 22, 47, 53, 69, 85, 87,
    117, 118, 121, 129, 156, 167
jargon, 50–1, 65–8, 199
    used accidentally, 65
    used maliciously, 65
jobseekers, 133
journey to the police station, 36, 121,
    169–70
judges, 140–1, 167–8, 174, 185
Judges' Rules, 35, 142
juries, 140–1, 167–8, 194
jurors' decisions, 49, 140–1
jury directions, 140–1
jury instructions, 49, 139–40
justice, 34, 234, 247
    miscarriages of, 34
juveniles, 103–4, 154, 167, 196, 198

knowledge
    background, 115, 126, 153
    shared, 211
knowledge asymmetries, 69
knowledge informing revision, 63
known to you, 60

labelling, 84, 150–4, 247
language learners, 52
languages, 39–40, 145–7
    authorities on, 41–2
    complex, 40–1
    controlled, 184
    and empowerment, 10, 27, 87, 137
    of mediators, 28
    in organisations, 29–30
    in pedagogic settings, 28
    of police, 4–5

in psychotherapists' work, 28
    simple, 40–1, 89–90, 167, 199
    skills, 199
    as transfer, 19
    at work, 4–5, 7
latching, 185
laughter, 155, 215–16, 217, 226, 256
law, 154
    authorities on, 41–2
Law Society, The, 41, 169
lay people, 43–4
    a continuum of, 44
    expert lay people, 87, 112–14, 241
    institutions and, 239–40
    professionals and, 115, 122, 233
layout, 37, 46, 81–5, 90, 96, 99, 261
    see also presentation
learning, 26, 109, 230–3, 249
    from colleagues, 231
    through misunderstanding, 220
learning difficulties, 40, 41, 53–4, 69
legal advice
    access to, 35
    free, 127–8
    independence of, 63
    unease about invoking, 75–6
    see also solicitor
legal language, 41, 89–90
    affective force of, 69–70, 173–4
    assessing the difficulty of, 18,
        61–2
    characterisation of, 8–12
    critique of, 49
    officers on, 168
    power and, 69
    revision of, 49
legislation, 140–1
legitimising, 42, 132, 151, 176, 178,
    214, 237, 241
Leicestershire Constabulary, 37
length of service of officers, 148
    see also gender
levels of language, 49, 81, 109, 246
lexical replacement, 68
lexis, 12, 49, 50, 65–70, 78, 81–2,
    83–4, 89–90, 91, 92, 166–79,
    246–7, 247–9
    echoing through, 187

everyday, 167, 169
as evidence of comprehension,
    215, 255
high frequency, 93, 199
legal *vs.* non-legal senses, 167
short, 93
specialised, 167, 169
technical, 167, 241
vague, 83–4
lifeworld, 26–8, 133, 166–7,
    196, 241
voice of, 26
linguistic awareness, 16, 18, 219
listening, 175, 188, 204, 208, 219,
    231, 254
lists, 62–3, 105–6
literacies, 9, 11, 20, 112
literacy, 20, 85, 198
identity and, 112
literacy events, 11, 109–10
familiarity and, 85–6, 123
literacy practices, 11–12, 87, 90–1,
    109, 118–19, 124
as currency, 110
of custody officers, 79–80
of detainees, 96–7, 98–100, 113
diversity of, 100–1
expectations and, 85–7
incomplete reading, 100–7, 114
of rewriters, 40, 51, 74, 85–6
social networks and, 109–10
in using cross references, 85–6, 87
in using indexes, 86–7
location, 171–2
logical structure, 187
see also discourse, structure;
    structure
logo, 38

macro-sequence, 45–8, 76, 183
macro-structure, 150, 204
magistrates, 140–1, 167–8, 174,
    185, 217
marked, 47, 216, 226
marking, 185
uncertainty, 216
maxim of relation, 169
may, 56–8, 59
mealtimes, 127

meaning, 163–5, 222, 249
constructed, 22, 174
intended, 151, 209
making through explanation, 245
obliviousness to, 157
potential, 209
situated, 25, 96
underlying, 96
universal, 19–20
unpacking, 166, 179
using, 209
variable, 169, 227
working agreement on, 211
media, the, 115–18
representations, 156
mediation, 21, 253, 261
mediational means, 29–30
mediators, 28
memory, 85, 106, 122, 158, 162, 223
residual, 158
mental health, 197
mental lexicon, shared, 20
mentally disordered or vulnerable,
    103–4
mention, 56, 140–2, 175, 186, 215
facts, 140
metadiscourse, *see* metalanguage
metalanguage, 35, 37, 49–50, 92, 137,
    149, 160–1, 185–91, 228, 232, 248
completeness and, 191, 219
evaluative, 187
in Force A, 191
mitigating face-threat through, 212
orientation through, 186–7, 193,
    236–42
tripartite, 188–90, 200
metaphorical transfer, 172
metonymy, 167–9
migration, 39
minimising
crime, 132
face threat, 250
imposition, 96, 251
rights, 225
see also face; Face Threatening Acts
Miranda warning, 75, 117, 128, 147,
    151, 156–7, 173, 205, 251
misappropriation, 67–8, 153
of research findings, 251

miscarriages of justice, 33–5
miscommunication, 120
misconduct, 144
misunderstanding, 15, 16, 42, 66, 68,
    77, 82–3, 89, 128, 130–1, 141–2,
    143–4, 146, 150–1, 153, 160–1,
    167, 208, 211, 221, 237
  negotiated, 160
  as occasion for learning, 220
  parasitic, 241
  recognising, 144
  as rich point, 220
  as rights waiver, 72–3
  see also incomprehension
mitigation, 176, 211–14
modal auxiliary verbs, 55, 61
  see also particular modal verbs
modality, 50–1, 55–9, 70–1
  alethic, 58–9
  ambiguity and, 56, 218
  deontic *or* intrinsic, 55–6, 58
  epistemic *or* extrinsic, 55–6
  scheme of, 58
modes of rights communication
  diversity in, 121–2, 124, 143, 252–3
  see also multimodal rights
      administration
monologic explanation, 122, 217, 248
moral, 33, 132, 249, 256
morality, 34, 256
more information is given below, 45–6
motivation to read, 87, 114
motivations of discourse sequence, 74
motivations of explanation, 162–3,
    177, 185, 196, 210, 222, 229
motivations of police officers, 250
motivations of revision decisions, 43,
    65, 68, 90
motivations of rights waivers, 4
motivations to claim comprehension,
    208
multifunctionality of legal language,
    9, 10
multilingualism, 39–40, 121, 145–7
  training in, 146
multimodal rights administration, 122
  see also modes of rights
      communication
multiparty talk, 218

multiple choice tasks, 17
multivoicing, 22
  see also recontextualisation;
      reformulation; transformation
must, 55, 59

narrative
  recontextualisation and, 23, 241
  as rights communication, 121–2
narrativisation, 158, 173
National Curriculum, 118
  see also citizenship
National form, 7, 36
nationality, 20
naturally occurring data, 6, 7, 12,
    138, 147–8, 171, 180, 250, 251,
    256
navigation through text, 21, 86, 96,
    102, 113, 128
necessary, 84
need, 60–1
negation, 74, 177–8, 218
  see also negative sentence
negative
  effects, 109
  evaluation, 50, 157, 168, 178, 216,
      230
  feedback, 216
  hidden, 177
  polarity, 175
  pronoun, 177
  significance of silence, 137
  see also negation; negative face; Face
      Threatening Acts
negative face, *see* face; Face
    Threatening Acts
negative inference, *see* inferences
negative sentence, 47
negotiate, 120, 160, 222, 228
nervousness, 87, 197, 226
Netherlands, the, 39, 124, 146
newspapers, 153, 171
no comment, 235, 239–40
noise, 15, 184
nominalisation, 50–5, 59, 61, 70–1,
    104–5, 133, 259
non-compliance, 128, 236, 238, 252
nonsense, 201, 246
normally, 82

norms, 31, 146, 227, 232, 240, 249
  subvert, 238
Northern Ireland, 146, 147
not, 167, 177–8, 218
Notice of entitlements, 35, 86–7, 97,
  102, 259–61
  concerns about, 35
Notice to detained persons, 5–6, 33–40
  caution in, 145
  comprehensibility of, 37
  concerns about, 35
  criticism of, 37
  decisions about, 98–100, 101–2
  legal origins of, 35–6
  reading, 98–100
  revising, 5, 74
  revisions of, 37
noun phrases, long, 50–1, 55, 59–62,
  64, 93, 103, 259
novelty, 114, 201
novice detainees, 44, 110–12, 154,
  197, 247
  see also detainees
novice readers, 52
numbering, 47–8, 106, 187–8
  ordinal, 189
  removing, 48

oath, courtroom, 156, 237
obligations of officers, 34, 64, 73, 106,
  130, 144, 235
observation, *see* ethnography
occasional detainees, 44
  see also detainees
on-record, 130, 132, 172, 211, 226,
  236
opportunity, 172–3
optimal formulations for all, 162
opting out, 238, 256
or, 62
ordering, 26, 151, 180
organisation of talk, 189
organisation, of text, 72, 75–7, 81–2,
  246
  between sections of the rights
    notice, 77–85
  within sections of the rights notice,
    72–7
organisational talk, 29–30

orientation, 21, 68, 104, 105, 106,
  125, 132, 163–4, 189–90, 193,
  227, 231, 236–42, 250
  of rewriters, 65
  through Multilanguage, 46, 50, 187
  to overhearing audience, 160, 170,
    233–4, 242
  to writing through talk, 122–3
otherness, 223
outsiders, 104
overhearers, 122, 160, 182, 194, 209,
  233–4, 242, 255
overlapping, 237
overlay, 22
  see also recontextualisation;
    reformulation; transformation
overview, *see* summaries
Owen, C., 18, 48, 64, 65, 84, 89, 93,
  110, 128

PACE, *see* Police and Criminal
  Evidence Act 1986
pace, 155, 228, 229
PACE Codes of practice, 35–6, 66–7,
  85–8, 92, 113
  defining, 67
pagination, 47, 260
panic, 111–12
paradigmatic relations, 8, 11
  see also polyvocality
paragraphing, 75
paraphrase, 14, 18, 19, 20, 22, 25,
  192–4, 221
  characterising, 183–4
  as a test of comprehension, 17, 20
  see also recontextualisation;
    reformulation; transformation
paraphrase task, the, 17–18, 20
Parent text, introduction of the, 38–9
  opening sections of, 105–6
  title of, 104–5
parenthesis relation, 62
parents, 104–5, 121
parrot fashion, 157
part, 185–8
partial readers, 100–7, 247
participants, 24, 227
participation, 24, 238, 245, 247

passivisation, 50–1, 53–5, 59, 61, 70–1, 246
  agentless, 54
  benefits of, 54–5
  strategic, 55
patient decision-making, 69, 122
patient information, 127
pausing, 155
pedagogic talk, 23, 25, 221, 223
pedagogic text, 105
pedagogy
  plain language and, 16
  television and, 118
pedants, 34
pensioners, 167
people, 104, 168–9
performance-based document testing, 17
performativity, 9, 10, 11, 162, 210, 221, 222, 227, 230, 233
performing, 147, 221
  archiving, 210
  expertise, 113
  procedural adherence, 221
periodic sentence, 63–4
perlocution, 152, 174, 178, 179
personal reference, 60, 64, 104, 226
personalisation, 7, 27, 104–5, 172–4, 231, 248
  see also depersonalisation
persons, 104
persuading, 25, 123, 124, 248
persuasion, 25, 96, 173, 248
  influencing explanations, 177
  subtle, 179
phatic, 208
phonological, 16, 67
plain English, 16–17, 27, 50–1, 52, 71, 133
  genre and, 17
  objective prescriptions, 246
  subjective prescriptions, 246
  see also plain language movement, the
Plain English Campaign, the, 16, 17, 37, 53, 65, 101, 104, 156
  see also Plain Language Commission
plain language, *see* plain English
Plain Language Commission, 41–2

plain language movement, the, 16–17, 43, 50–1, 246
  aims of, 16
  methods of, 16
  and public debate, 16
  responses to, 17
  see also plain English
planning
  actions, 109
  contents of a message, 43, 198, 230
  strategically, 179
  time, 187
plural, 83
  irregular, 104
plus-minus method, the, 17
pocket book, 226
poetisation, 156
Polanyi, L., 24–5, 166
polarity, 175
Police and Criminal Evidence Act 1986, 35–6, 56, 85, 119, 139
  see also PACE Codes of practice; right to consult the Codes of practice
police caution, *see caution* (as label)
police forces, *see under individual names*
police language
  glossaries of, 9
police officers
  comprehension of the caution by, 154–5
  on difficulty, 18–19, 167–8, 196–200
  on explanation, 193–200
  inattention to detainees, 215–18
  interpreters and, 146
  learning from colleagues, 231
  length of service, 18
  metalinguistic awareness, 149
  monitoring, 230–1
  obliviousness to the caution's difficulty, meaning and significance, 157–8
  pedagogic role of, 223
  policy, 28, 256
  processing by, 189–91
  ranks, 148
  roles, 148

sex, 148
supervisory, 233
training of, 28, 40, 149, 180, 188,
   230–1, 253–6, 257
working lives, 7
Police Review, The, 142, 155
police trainers, 148–9
politeness, 214, 248, 250
   negative, 212
   positive, 212
   see also face; Face Threatening Acts
politics, 9, 10–11, 22, 119, 144, 249
polysemy, 167–9
polyvocality, 22
   see also recontextualisation;
      reformulation; transformation
polyvocality, 8, 22, 26–8
   as difference, 9, 113, 168
positive face, *see* face; Face
   Threatening Acts
possessive, 53, 65, 173
posters, 121
power asymmetry, 120, 179, 214
power, 27, 29–30, 69, 137, 152, 179,
   202, 235, 241, 250, 256
   of incomprehension claims, 256
   relative, 214
   silence and, 238
powerlessness, 208
pragmatic
   features, 16, 173, 185, 208
   force, 179, 182, 202–3
   intent, 104, 150–2, 226, 247
pre-patterning, 156
preamble, *see* interview preamble
predicates, 174, 193
preferred second, 207
prepositional phrases, 45, 81, 102–3,
   193
prescribed talk, 7, 140, 149, 150, 247,
   248, 256
prescriptivism, 16–17, 245–6
presentation, 37, 97–8, 113
   see also layout
pressure, 110, 154–5, 208, 239, 254
   time, 120
presupposition, 23, 47, 129
principal, 15, 144, 152
prison, 108–9

privacy, 93, 256
private sphere, 129
processing
   deep, 110
   passives, 54–5
   time, 52, 118
production format, 144
professional
   criminals, 139
   expertise, 241
   experts, 76
   interpreters, 145–6
   knowledge, 44, 178–9, 223, 233
   meaning, 65
   rewriters, 5, 6, 249
   voice, 26–8
professionalism of police, 223, 251
professionals, 44
   deference to, 76
   lay people and, 44, 118, 122, 233
   other experts and, 210
   see also voices
promising, 151
prompt sheet, 200
pronouns, 60, 61, 82, 84, 103, 129,
   168, 175–6, 193, 202, 226
   possessive, 173–4
propositional content, 105, 183, 204,
   217
   presenting repeatedly in the
      caution, 182–3, 189
   removing from the caution, 182–3,
      201, 207
prosodic sentence, 102–3
prosody, 49, 224, 228
prospection, 45, 84, 95, 104, 106,
   131, 153, 160, 169–70, 204,
   206, 227, 229–30, 236, 237,
   238, 249
protocol analysis, 17
psychologists, 17–18, 20–1, 22, 138,
   143, 207, 250
psychotherapists' notes, 28
public expense, see at public expense
purism, 16–17
purpose, 12, 20, 101, 108, 114,
   236, 247
   see also readers

qualifiers, 59–62, 112, 217, 221
questioning (investigative), 140–1,
    147, 171, 173, 174–5, 252
  breaks in, 225
  see also interviews (investigative)
questions
  cautioning and, 163
  comprehension and, 101–2
  detainees', 101–2
  yes-no, 20, 159, 160, 163, 205, 206

R *v*. Argent (1996), 139–40
R *v*. Shulka, 164, 204
radical approaches to rights
    communication, 122, 249
radio, 117
rank-shifting, 60–1, 102–3
rapport, 197, 225
re- prefix, 23
readability
  conjunctions and, 62
  scores, 40–1
  tests *or* formulas, 40, 41, 68
readers
  as active, 20, 87, 125–6
  expectations about, 90–2
  experiences of, 96
  likely activities of, 246
  needs of, 20, 96, 260
  orientation to, 92–6
  partial, 100–7
  prior knowledge of, 89, 96
  problems of, 101–2
  purposes and goals of, 101–2, 108
  questions of, 75, 101–2, 246
  reception of revised rights notice
    by, 89–107
  role of, 89
  see also detainees
reading, 20
  ability, 90, 109
  activities, 100–1
  alone, 109
  aloud, 21, 109, 180, 192, 200
  assessing, 109
  decisions about, 98–100, 101–2
  decisions, 99–100, 101–2, 114,
    123–5
  difficulties, 108, 247

  during police interviews, 74–5
  and embarrassment, 109
  incompletely, 100–7
  intentions, 90
  in part, *see* partial readers
  social networks and, 109–10
  speedy, 122
  to-assess, 108
  to do, 108
  to learn, 108
  to make decisions, 74–5, 108–9
  to plan, 109
  see also literacy; literacies
reading practices, *see* literacy practices
reading times, long, 77
reanimation, 22
  see also recontextualisation;
    reformulation; transformation
reasonable, 84
reasoning, 115
reassuring, 25, 151, 225
recast, 170, 241
receipts, 208
receivers, 15
reciprocity, 24
reciting, 21
recommendations, 13, 48, 101, 151,
    169, 188, 192, 209, 219, 221, 245,
    249, 251–3, 256–7
  on cautioning, 253–6
  officers' interest in, 150
  on rights notices, 256–7
  unfinalisability and, 21
recontextualisation, 11, 12, 14, 22–3,
    25, 26, 28, 29, 144, 158, 163, 167,
    196–8, 204, 210, 211, 212, 214,
    215, 216–21, 225, 231–3, 235–8
  criteria for, 196–8
  as a discursive resource, 144
  functions of, 25–6
  pervasive, 23
  tensions of, 25
  see also reformulation;
    transformation
recurrence, 22
  see also recontextualisation;
    reformulation; transformation
redressive action, 211–12

redundancy, 85, 104, 105, 112–13, 122, 124, 252, 258
reformulation, 14, 22–3, 153, 160, 163, 167
as artefact, 149
biased, 165, 204
obligatory, 143–4
practices, 192, 195–6, 227, 231, 241
research interviews about, 148–9
risks of, 144–5
spontaneous, 143–4
see also recontextualisation; transformation
refuse, 80, 139, 178–9, 186
regional accent, *see accent*
register, 24, 50–1, 68–70, 132, 145–6, 225
legal, 133, 225
shift, 68–9, 70, 168, 200
target, 200
regular detainees, 41, 112–13, 249
see also detainees
regularly, 83
regulation, 116
reinspection, 77
relation, 169
relevance, 47, 65–6, 94, 108, 237
across all situations, 172
institutional, 66, 161, 239
personal, 168
situated, 25
to detainees, 47, 66, 86, 124, 161, 167–8, 239, 249
relexicalisation, 169–70
reliability, 71, 128, 234
of content, 127–8
religion, 20
rely, 215
rely on, 137, 217
reminding, 25, 36, 106, 157, 173, 254, 255
repair, 120
reperspectivisation, 92–6
repetition, 22–3, 24–5, 80–1, 141, 156, 161, 193
change and, 14, 24, 113, 162, 183–4
characterising, 183–4
control and, 29
as creativity, 29, 156, 201, 251

diachronic, 156
exact, 24–5
global, 156
impotence and, 156
increased attention through, 122
requesting, 207
speedier reading through, 122
synchronic, 156, 202–3
understanding through, 122
value of exact, 189
see also recontextualisation; reformulation; transformation
replay, 22
see also recontextualisation; reformulation; transformation
representation, 22, 87, 129, 156, 163, 172, 178, 229
see also recontextualisation; reformulation; transformation
reprimand, 152–3, 208
reprimand caution, 152–3
research, 256–7
critical distance on, 250
stakeholders in, 249
research into practice, 245
researcher influence, 147
resequencing, 46, 62–3, 66, 74–5, 78–80, 81–2
the caution's sentences, 181–4, 248
extent of, 183–4
officers on, 183
see also three-part structure; sequence
resistance, 69, 110, 200, 211, 236, 241, 248–9
residence, place of, 20
response, 160, 216
responsibility, 118, 124, 145, 152, 164, 224, 252
retrieval, 102
revision, *see rewriting*
rewording, 60, 173, 193
rewriters, 5, 6, 40, 43, 46, 55, 59, 62, 65–6, 68–9, 72, 75–6, 78, 81, 82, 83, 94, 106, 246, 247–8
literacy practices of, 40, 51, 74
orientation of, 50, 65
resources available to, 41–2

rewriting, 17
  benefits of, 49–50
  complexity of, 48
  costs of, 50
  decisions about, 43, 65
  definitive, 101
  expert-judgement-focused methods,
    40–1
  help with, 40–1
  patronising, 69
  practices, 43
  presentation of, 45
  reader-focussed methods, 40–1
  text-focussed methods, 40–1, 89
right to a copy of the custody record,
    36, 46–8, 63–5, 95, 98, 115
  see also custody record
right to a solicitor, *see* legal advice;
    right to legal advice
right to consult the Codes of practice,
    36, 65–6, 79, 86–7
  see also Codes of practice
right to have someone informed of
    your arrest, 36, 60–1, 80, 96–7
right to legal advice, 58–9, 62–3, 73–7,
    81–3, 93–4
  invoking, 74, 253
  statement of, 36
  timing of offer, 147
  waiving, 3–4, 72–3, 253
right to legal advice, the, 3, 8–9, 79,
    121, 126–7
right to silence, 137
  decisions about, 138, 202
  history of, 139
  implications of invoking, 137, 147
  initial position of, 181
  performing, 147
  removal of, 139
  resilience of, 146–7
  timing of offer, 147, 169
rights in custody
  caveats to, 127
  communicating changes in, 113
  modifying, 80–1
  prohibitions of *or* denial of, 77–85
  restrictions on, 77–85, 115–16
  statement of, 36
  time and, 81–3

withholding, 79–81
  see also individual rights; rights
    invocation; rights waiver
rights information
  alternative sources, 115–22
  anomalous, 79
  audio-recorded delivery of, 122,
    255–6
  as authority, 79–80
  counterpoint to, 118
  delivery through dialogue, 122
  delivery through narrative, 122
  disregarding, 19
  downplaying, 123, 225
  electronic delivery of, 121–2, 225
  outside detention, 116–18, 145
  radical approaches to delivery, 122
  removing, 78
  resequencing, 78–80, 181–4
  sources of, 115–16
  unbelievable, 127–8
  unexpected, 78
  uninterested delivery, 124–5
  using, 79–80, 109
  verbal delivery of, 120–1
  video-recorded delivery of, 122
  see also verbal rights delivery
rights invocation, 35, 46, 47, 74, 76,
    82, 91, 98, 107, 121, 147, 245, 260
  through writing, 121
rights waivers, 3–4, 8–9, 72–3, 122,
    128, 130, 253
  ambiguous, 3–4, 72–3
  benevolent, 131
  motivated, 128–33
  through writing, 121
risk, 196, 233
ritual, 156
Road Traffic Act 1988, 38, 78–9, 93
roles, 22, 25, 29, 41, 64, 73, 76, 89,
    104, 112, 117, 130, 144, 146, 148,
    149, 151, 171, 194, 208, 223, 256,
    260
  allocation of, 168
Roman Law systems, 146
Royal Commission on Criminal
    Justice 1993, 139
Royal Commission on Criminal
    Procedure 1981, 35, 139

Russell, S., 111, 138, 145, 146, 150, 180, 181, 182, 184, 185, 186, 192, 208, 211, 215

salience, 10, 37, 93, 104, 224, 226, 233
scaffolding social action, 222, 249
  affiliations, human, 222
  social activities, 222, 247
scenarios, using to explain, 229, 255
schema, 24, 126, 237
schools, delivering rights information in, 118, 252
Scotland, 39, 146
script, 105, 117, 120, 122, 123, 125, 144, 146, 156, 195–6, 199–200, 219, 248, 253
  arguments against, 194–9
  arguments for, 194–5
  television, 117
second person, *see* pronouns; personal reference
section 34, *see* Criminal Justice and Public Order Act (1994)
seldom, 83
selection, 11, 92–3, 176–7
selectivity, 25
self, 131–3
  presenting, 113, 131–2
  reference, 214
  reports, 212
self-incrimination, 146
self-presentation, 131–2, 247
semantic, 24, 48, 51, 60, 61, 65, 74, 144, 163, 172, 179, 185, 201, 226, 248
  bleaching, 104
  complexity, 144
  prosody, 76, 173
semi-structured interviews, *see* interviews (research), semi-structured
senders, 15, 43, 71, 128
sentences, of the caution, 180, 181–4, 248–9
  criticism of division into, 180
  see also three-part structure
sequence, 45–6, 63, 64–5, 66, 72, 75–6, 77, 81, 165, 180–206, 216, 246, 248, 254

see also discourse, sequence; macro-sequence; resequencing
sequential cues, 77, 80–1
sergeant reviser, the, 40–2, 61, 246
  expectations about detainees, 90–2
  experience of, 94
  intentions of, 89–92
  orientation to detainees, 92–6
Sergeant text
  brevity and, 90
  decisions about, 98–100, 101–2
  discarding, 99
  introduction of the, 40–2
  opening sections of, 104–6
  physical aspects of, 91, 104–5, 260–1
  reading, 98–100
  reception of, 89
  structure of, 90–2, 259–60
  title of, 104–5
  uptake of, 259–61
sex, 43, 148
shall, 55, 64
Shuy, R., 20, 73, 75, 77, 126, 146, 147, 180, 182, 205, 209, 221, 229, 232, 239
side-sequence, 228
signature, 46, 98, 109, 121, 123
  as authorisation, 121
signification, 129, 137, 179, 215, 234
signposting, 49–50, 187–8, 190
silence, 23, 137, 146–7, 164
  autonomous, 232
  calculated, 178
  discouraged by officers, 172, 173, 178, 235
  encouraged by caution wording, 181–2
  encouraged by officers, 170–1, 177, 235
  partial, 164, 248
  passive, 230
  power and, 238
  prospecting, 238–40
  representation of, 177
  significance of to jurors, 140–1
  total, 164
simple language, 40–1, 69, 70, 89–90, 167, 187, 199, 232, 261

simplification, 20, 70, 71, 82, 199, 218
  affect and, 69
  text length and, 90, 167, 246
situated meaning, 19, 20, 25, 96, 169, 227
situation of use, 12, 58
skim reading, 101, 102, 103, 108
small-talk, 225
social conscience, 34
social context, 12, 16–17, 24, 112, 132, 142, 164, 252
  comprehension and, 196–200, 209
social desirability responding, 207
social distance, 104, 129, 214, 224, 246, 250
social facts, production of, 26, 130–1
social identity, 132, 222–3, 229
  shaping through explanation, 245
social networks, 109–10, 114–15
  private, informal and everyday, 110
  public, formal and official, 110
social participation through explanation, 245
social worker, 103–4
socialisation, 26
socio-economic class, 197
sociocultural factors, 30, 209
sociolinguistic awareness, 18, 251
  exhibited by detainees, 19
  exhibited by police officers, 18–19, 149, 167–8, 196–200
sociolinguistic perspective, *see* sociolinguistics
sociolinguistics, 12–13, 14, 17, 19–22, 35, 51, 71, 231, 245, 249, 250–1, 261
  comprehension and, 19–22
  repetition and, 24–5
solicitor, 40
  as authority figure, 75–6
  behaviour of, 141, 235, 239
  independent, 93
  see also duty solicitor; legal advice; right to legal advice
solicitor's likely activities, 75, 115
solicitors' independence, 63
solicitors' list, 62–3

Solomon, N., 16–17, 39, 52, 55, 70, 199
something, 167, 175–7, 215
speaker
  as respondent, 23
SPEAKING mnemonic, the, 17
special times, 80, 83–4
specialist, 10, 26–7, 87, 169
  audience, 9
  legal, 4, 9
specificity, 93, 94, 167, 171–2, 175, 248
specimen directions, 140–1
speech, 26–7, 118–21
  at arrest, 169–70
  as a check on comprehension, 120, 205–21, 248, 255
  evaluation of, 160
  explicitly linked to written rights texts, 124
  ineffective, 120
  in preference to writing, 111, 118–19
  prospecting, 236–7
  reinforcing writing, 252–3
  as source of rights information, 115–16, 120
  writing in relation to, 187–8, 230, 252–3
  see also style; verbal rights delivery
speech acts, 104, 151–2, 222
speech event, 124–5, 153, 240
  delimiting, 232
staging, 200, 251
stance, 16, 133
  adverbial, 236
standard paraphrase, 192–200, 232, 248, 253
  appropriation of, 193–4
  attitudes to, 193–200
  de-skilling, 253
  innovation on, 192
  institutionally advocating, 193
  making compulsory, 199
  officers against, 194–9
  officers in favour of, 193–4
  practice and, 192

standardisation of cautioning
  explanation, 192
  see also caution explanation, official
    paraphrase; standard
    paraphrase
status, 10, 11, 112, 124, 131, 141, 208
  of discourse, 241
  evidential, 178–9
  of rights talk, 239
stress (emotional), 99, 110–11, 154–5,
  195
structure, 12, 14, 40, 45–8, 49–50, 71,
  95–6, 106, 114, 123, 181, 185,
  187–8, 261
  of cautioning, 150
  of cautioning exchange, 150, 160
  congruence of, 74
  detainees on, 92
  instruction on unfamiliar, 123
  lexis and, 90
  network, 110
  of power and equality, 10
  question-based, 101
  sergeant rewriter on, 95
  of Sergeant text, 90–2, 102
  social, 7, 222
  surface structure, 40, 62
  three-part, 185–91, 223, 232, 254–6
  three-tiered, 90–2
  see also discourse, structure;
    exchange structure
style, 69, 191, 231
  communicative, 27
  speech, 27
style shift, 199
styling, 155, 232–3, 248
stylistic agents, 15, 231
subject position, 105–6
  vacant, 129
subordination, 63–5
subversion, 131, 133, 240
suggestibility, 207
summaries, 25, 45–6, 56, 74, 76, 81,
  86–7, 90–2, 101, 103–6, 119, 150,
  165, 168, 194, 195, 258, 261
synonyms, 68
syntactically flat, 52
syntagmatic relations, 8, 11
  see also intertextuality

syntax, 12, 49, 50, 51–65, 89–90, 133,
  177, 205, 246–7
  *see also individual syntactic
    phenomena*

talk, *see* speech
teacher, 152
teaching, 26, 118
technical
  knowledge, 44
  talk, 27, 241
  terms, 68, 102, 167, 241
  texts, 100
technologies, 16, 27, 122, 245
technologisation, 11, 27, 245
television, 116–18, 224, 247, 252
  accuracy in rights portrayal, 117
  as pedagogy, 118
temporal referents, 36, 38, 64, 95,
  171–2, 218, 221
  see also time
terminology, 22–3, 66, 199
terms of address, 228–9
terrorist, 82, 87, 88, 139
testing comprehension, 17–19, 96–8,
  109
  see also comprehension
texts
  as authority, 79–80
  orientations to, 21
  as practice, 7, 74
  as process, 7
  written reinforcing spoken, 106, 252
texts in use, 12
thematising, 170
third-person reference, 59, 61, 105,
  226
  see also personal reference;
    pronouns
threatening, 151–2
  see also face; Face Threatening Acts
three-part structure, 232
  to check comprehension of the
    caution, 188–91, 221, 254–6
  to explain the caution, 185–91,
    254–6
  see also three-part structure;
    structure

Tiersma, P., 4, 10, 11, 47, 51, 53, 55, 59, 77, 129, 137, 152
time, 10, 37, 56–9, 67, 81–2, 95, 96–7, 120, 126–7
  adverb, 115, 172
  buying, 235
  changes in procedure over, 120
  limit, 67, 95
  passing the, 100
  planning, 187
  pressures, 120
  processing, 52, 118
  reading, 77
  to read, 104, 123
  see also temporal referents
titles, 38, 73, 75, 81, 83–4, 102, 104–5
  see also headings
topic, 53, 74, 75, 78–9, 170–2, 204, 223
traffic offences, 224
training, *see* cautioning; multilingualism; police officers
transfer, *see* language, as transfer; transmission
transformation, 4–5, 7–8, 14, 22–4, 138, 245, 261
  as constitutive process, 29–30
  functions of, 25–6, 30
  intertextual chains and, 28–9
  as lived reality, 245
  see also recontextualisation; reformulation
translation between languages, 39–40, 145–7
translation of 'difficult' language, 9–10, 56
translator, 152
  task of, 146
transmission model of communication, the, 15–22, 87, 162
transmission, 14–30
  as metaphor, 15
  as shorthand, 15
trial
  explaining, 175, 202
  mode, 168
  preparation for, 113
  procedure, 168

tripartite structure, *see* structure, three-part; three-part structure
triviality, 34, 156, 200, 216, 226, 252
truth, 117, 121, 174, 202, 237
two audience dilemma, the, 9, 10
typeface, 37, 90

understanding, 22, 163
  common notions of, 163
  difficulty of demonstrating, 207–9, 236
  pretending, 207, 215–16
  as problematic category, 71, 126, 238
  responsive, 20
unexpectedness, 42, 83, 131, 181, 217, 247
  of rights information, 78–9, 80–1
uniformed interviewing officers, 149
uniformed patrol officers, 148
United States of America, 18, 117, 145–7, 151, 156, 205, 225, 229, 251
unmarked, 207
usability studies, 17

vagueness, 9, 26, 51, 63, 83–4, 169, 179, 181, 253
validation, 46, 79, 133, 209
validity, 71, 234
variation
  across time, 36–7, 142–3
  between police forces, 37–8, 147–8, 184–5, 192, 201, 203, 204, 248
  permissible, 233
verbal rights delivery, 120–1
  from written source text, 143
  innovation in, 121
  see also speech, rights information
verbs, 24, 51, 52–3, 55–6, 58, 59, 79, 91, 171, 174, 177, 217–18, 221, 259
  active voice, 53, 64–5
  auxiliary *do*, 218
  -*ing* participle verbs, 91
  passive voice, *see* passivisation
  phrasal, 259
  see also modal auxiliary verbs
vernacular, 27, 241

versioning, 22
  see also reformulation,
    transformation,
    recontextualisation
video-recordings as rights
  communication, 122, 253
visual cues, 76, 77
visual images in rights
  communication, 43, 46–8, 76–7,
  81, 121
vocabulary, *see* lexis
voice, 55, 64–5
  complexity within verb groups, 59
voices, 25, 26, 2–28, 218, 241
  officers on, 224
  plurality of, 28
  professional, 27, 241
volume, 228, 229
voluntary attenders, *see* attending the
  police station, voluntarily

waiving rights, *see* rights waivers
want, 61
warning, 104, 151–2
  conspicuous through repetition, 156
  contamination through poetisation,
    156
warning caution, 152–4
website, 29, 118

welfare entitlement appeals, 49
Welsh, 39, 146–7
West Midlands Police, 37, 45–6
when questioned, 166, 179–4
whether, 171
will, 95
workplace language, *see* language
Wright, P., 17, 18, 40, 43, 51, 53, 59,
  62, 69, 83, 96, 101, 109, 127, 128,
  241
writing, 26–7
  formulations to be spoken, 143
  in preference to speech, 118–19
  proactive, 107
  reinforcing speech, 106, 252
  speech in relation to, 187–8, 230,
    252–3
writing practices, 40, 43, 51, 64–5, 74,
  110
writing processes, 41, 69, 89–90
  collaborative, 42
writing technologies, 16, 27, 70, 93
  see also guidelines for writing

yea-saying, 207
young offenders, 108–9
your, 65
Youth Justice and Criminal Evidence
  Act (1999), 140, 141

LaVergne, TN USA
26 August 2009
155768LV00001BC/7/P